THE DYNAMIC
IN CHRISTIAN THOUGHT

THE DYNAMIC IN CHRISTIAN THOUGHT

Edited by Joseph Papin

The Villanova University Press

McCORMICK THEOLOGICAL SEMINARY
McGAW MEMORIAL LIBRARY
800 WEST BELDEN AVENUE
CHICAGO, ILLINOIS 60614

Copyright © 1970
The Villanova University Press
Villanova, Pennsylvania 19085
All rights reserved

Library of Congress Catalog Number 70-107942

Complete Series—SBN 87723-007-2
This Volume—SBN 87723-008-0

Printed in the United States of America by
Abbey Press
Saint Meinrad, Indiana 47577

First printing: 1000 copies
1-100 are numbered

ADVISORY BOARD
TO THE INSTITUTE

Robert J. Welsh
Bernard Cardinal Alfrink
Krister Stendahl
Piet Schoonenberg
Abraham I. Katsh
Bernard Häring
Roland E. Murphy
Joseph Fichter
Eugene H. Maly
Eugene Fontinell
Joseph J. Gildea
Sister Mary George O'Reilly
Arthur J. Ennis
Charles E. Curran

John M. Driscoll
George Cardinal Flahiff
Bernard Lonergan
Eugene Carson Blake
Walter J. Burghardt
James Gustafson
Barnabas Ahern
Godfrey Diekmann
Eulalio R. Baltazar
Donald X. Burt
Robert P. Russell
Charles P. Bruderle
Bernard A. Lazor
Michael J. Scanlon

EDITOR and DIRECTOR of the INSTITUTE

Joseph Papin

ASSOCIATE EDITORS

James J. Cleary   Francis A. Eigo

ASSISTANT EDITORS

James J. McCartney   John F. O'Rourke

Joseph C. Reino

Dedicated to the faculty, students, and participants in the Symposium at Villanova University commemorating its one hundred twenty-fifth anniversary.

Editor

Contents

Post-Conciliar Perspectives	Joseph Papin	1
God: A Pragmatic Reconstruction	Eugene Fontinell	15
The Role of the Bible in the Theology of the Future	Krister Stendahl	44
The Meaning of Revelation	Avery Dulles	52
De-Judaization and Hellenization: The Ambiguities of Christian Identity	Jaroslav Pelikan	81
Morality: Underlying and Unchanging Principles?	Bernard Häring	125
Scriptural Basis for Secularity	Eugene H. Maly	152
Jewish-Christian Dialogue: Early Church versus Contemporary Christianity	Walter J. Burghardt	186
Developing Moral Teaching	John T. Noonan	208
Evolution of the Human Soul	Eulalio R. Baltazar	223
The Institutional Church	John L. McKenzie	254
Biographical Notes		279
Index of Names		281

> "Haec ergo coelestis civitas dum peregrinatur in terra, ex omnibus gentibus cives evocat, atque in omnibus linguis peregrinam colligit societatem; non curans quidquid in moribus, legibus, institutisque diversum est... nihil eorum rescindens...: quod licet diversum... ad unum tamen eundemque finem terrenae pacis intenditur, si religionem qua unus summus et verus Deus colendus docetur, non impedit."
> Augustinus, De Civ. Dei, PL 41, 646.

Post-Conciliar Perspectives

Joseph Papin

THE relevant affirmation of faith requires a new understanding and reinterpretation of dogma.

The post-Conciliar years left religious thinking in some kind of peculiar vacuum. However, when we compare this period with the decades that it took the Council of Trent to implement its doctrine, we realize that Vatican II is moving at contemporary speed.

Villanova University, commemorating its one hundred twenty-fifth anniversary with the intention of making a significant contribution to the work of theology and religious education, after long and serious deliberation has established a forum for nationally and internationally recognized scholars "to build a bridge toward the contemporary world," according to the express intent of Vatican II.

In his opening remarks to the participants in the Symposium, John M. Driscoll, speaking in the name of Robert J. Welsh, stated the purpose and the goal of such a forum at Villanova University with the following words: "In providing the forum for such inquiry, Villanova University fulfills in part its ideological commitment as a Catholic University: first, to acknowledge the primacy of God and His Revelation in human affairs, and, secondly, to contribute to the enrichment of our Catholic intellectual life by insisting on the essentiality of revealed truth and theological speculation."

The problems facing the Church of today and the entire humanity are not primarily of a practical nature. Sound practice presupposes sound theory. No one age can develop a theory with ready-made answers for every day, every age. The continuous progress of man in history compels contemporary thinking to evaluate the historical situation of man and his reflexive expression of God's eschatological and salvific work.

The world we live in demands greater dimensions in theology. The problems of God, of the world, and of life are really the problems of love for the pilgrim man. Has man a future he can call his own? "A theology which is no longer in tune with its time in a false theology" (H. Bouillard). Today's theology must be viable for the Christian of the future. We cannot speak in the categories of the previous eras.

Chalcedon (modern Kadiköy) formulations were intelligible to the fifth-century world in which Christians lived. So were the words of Christ. Sadducees, their contemporaries, the Pharisees, unruly and violent Zealots, and Herodians spoke most clearly to their own groups, but their ideology, even their concepts, eluded the 'am-ha-aretz, the rural man.

The irrelevancy and concaveness of their complicated and caustic dispute left the little man in expectancy of a rendez-vous with history in Christ.

Christ came and spoke the language which was understood by every group. The Sadokite, the Essene, and especially the 'am-ha-aretz, who was considered irreligious by the official groups, understood Christ's language. It was the 'am-ha-aretz (rural man) who finally manifested his intense interest in the Messiah and his revolutionary Sermon on the Mount.

The Dynamic in Christian Thought[1] of man confronting the contemporary changing world is expressed by The Dynamic in Christian Action.[2] I am speaking here of the first two Symposia held at Villanova University. Both themes, Christian thought and Christian action, from a viewpoint of retrospective theology, were probes to lay a groundwork for Openness to the World[3] of The Pilgrim People with a vision of hope.[4] We intend by our research to recapture the continuous renewal of the Church found in the Living Tradition of the Councils. There was a great silence between Trent and Vatican II. The unfinished Vatican I did not fill the gap of four hundred years. We have no intention of digressing into the particulars. But an important question does arise about the relation between collective and individual eschatology, a question between human progress in history and the supernatural event of the Parousia which is indispensable for the consummation of faith.

The Council teaches and declares the faith. The teaching of the Council constitutes major premises rather than conclusions. Hence there enters into the exercise of the magisterium a prophetic element. It is the theologian's task to discern this element and to work with it for a better understanding of faith.

A Council need not speak of everything. Theological schools are not tested for their coherence. A Council is not a particular school of theology. The fact that it is articulating in time a particular understanding of the world and its culture does not identify a definite national culture and language with the revealed truth of God. A Council is aware of the necessity to dejudaize, to dehellenize, and even to deamericanize the Church in modern world affairs.

Rumbles of the new theology of the "Requiem for God," (theologians of the death of God) proved to be a totally inadequate foundation for spanning a theological river with a bridge. The school of theology of the "Requiem for God," not even implementing a "Requiem for Satan," will constitute only a footnote to the history of theology. The peasant-like tenacity of conviction evidenced in various schools of religious thought with a bearing on man's self-understanding in history eluded the short-lived school of theology of the death of God. "The Grave of God" was the death rattle for the continuancy of the aforementioned school without any noticeable echo.

Erasmus of Rotterdam, a great humanist, probably a greater and a more influential scholar in Europe than Martin Luther, produced a religious humanistic thought but failed in producing action. Luther's thoughts, relevant to the self-understanding of men, evoked an action which is still alive after four hundred years.

The real accomplishment of Vatican II, and its significance, with its preparatory role for the development of the ever-changing world, will be a task of theological generations to come. But we can say now that the Council gave the Church courage and impetus to challenge the modern problems in a way unknown even in previous eras of the Church's openness to the world. The Council replaced a defensive attitude in history with the awareness of contemporary problems facing the contemporary situation. As a result a greater responsibility is imposed upon Christians for the development of the modern world and man's spiritual life. Ecclesiology, which was considered the central issue, has undergone in the last five years remarkable changes. Ecclesiological theology must become a theology of a world Church.[5]

Our subsequent Symposia will consider pluralistic theologies and their particular relations to the universal Church regarding the questions of common creed and the theology of the magisterium of the Church.

Only through studies of this crucial problem of the universality of the Church, in a spirit transcending a geographical universality, will we confront the central issue of today's theology, God in Jesus Christ in a hopefully relevant terminology, intelligible to modern man.

In regard to the processes, development, and evolution of man in the world, we should consider the thought of an architect of new cosmic dimensions.

The writings of Teilhard de Chardin helped to raise many issues in Christian thought which had been quietly smoldering due to the influence of "Process Philosophy" and "Historical Development" in theology. Suddenly there appears to be an enthusiastic acceptance of the notion of growth, change and development. Is this only an apparent acceptance? For some there is still wonder. For many there may be a lack of complete acceptance of what may be implied in and may result from the application of "evolution" to the areas of Christian thought commonly gathered under such phrases as "Dogma" and "Moral Principles."

Teilhard de Chardin was not a professional theologian, but he did definitely influence some of the tendencies of Vatican II. His insights were often diffused and not too certain.

Teilhard de Chardin is judged perhaps unjustly. Professional atheistic philosophers behind the Iron Curtain do not intend to accept Christianity, but if they were to accept it, they would accept Teilhardian Christianity.

Teilhard de Chardin[6] must be credited with making the problem of the end of the world an actual problem for us, which—if we are guided by faith—will culminate in an expectancy of the Parousia.

Human development was necessary but not sufficient for the Incarnation, and such must be the case with the Parousia, the Second Coming. And in all humility I venture to say that this Institute could contribute to the development of the Council's doctrinal and moral teaching and open new vistas of the new concept of Christian Eschatology for the fulfillment and consummation of the Christian faith.

In much of the writing and discussion today there is a hint that there must be "something within," which pushes the growth or evolution further and higher—something which might be called a "dynamic" which gives sense and direction to this movement. What is this "dynamic" within Christian Theology? More importantly, what is it doing to the areas which many presumed were (and some would like to maintain are) finally determined or permanently stable? And, possibly most important of all, will we allow ourselves to be opened to this movement or will we suppress the growth and development which may be trying to take place in our time?

A number of lectures and articles during the past several years have drawn attention to the values in what is known as "Process Philosophy." Process Thought and more recently the relationship of these processes with Teilhard de Chardin's thought[7] resulted in conflict instead of harmonious post-Conciliar perspective.

The demand for going beyond the historical research of theological questions to examining the matter of the relevancy of some fundamental questions for modern theology dramatized how such research highlights basic issues rather than debates traditional cliches.

In the area of biblical studies, some American professors are known for their excessive hardening of positions which could lock the more recent findings in static categories and thereby hold captive the living Word of God. Krister Stendahl warns Catholics not to enthrone the Bible as an object of worship, lest they repeat Lutheran mistakes.[8]

The work of synthesizing Christian Tradition into a viable position for the present while allowing for future development is a task for the theologian of tomorrow.

A Christian action presupposes a background of Christian thought. A theology which is either all thought or all action fails to meet both poles essential to Christianity and "shared fellowship," (koinonia).

Regarding the unrest, resistance and revolution, we dare propose to say that the Incarnation is the model for a healthy resistance and a conamen in changing the "status quo."

The sense of on-going movement, of pilgrimage, of an upward and forward direction on the part of mankind has been heightened by the apparent disturbances in the previously accepted "status quo." This "new" phenomenon is only an apparently new phenomenon, because there has always been unrest which could be more or less resisted by "the Establishment" until it was either recognized and adapted to, or was forced to the point of revolution, or was simply compromised.

The Christian person and the Christian community are in the world, and often tend to become absorbed into it. Christians have been involved in the revolution and/or evolution that has taken place in the last 2000 years of man's life on this planet. The dynamic within the Christian can be seen and expressed in Christian action, which, if resisted, can be brought to the point of revolution. There is a healthy unrest within the Christian life which, despite disinterested apathy and external resistance, will bring about the Kingdom of God.

Within the past two decades, the American Catholic community has been awakened to the vitality which might be found in biblical studies and in the liturgical experience. "Prophetic" writers and speakers in these areas of religious thought and action directed our attention to the potential for dynamic life contained in the Scriptures and in Eucharistic celebrations.

Most Christian communities are being awakened to the potential for a genuine renewal[9] of our understanding of the Christian faith by the encounter and dialogue that is taking place among members of the various Christian traditions. Both Protestant and Catholic Christians have been awakened to the values in the Eastern or "Orthodox" Christian Church. An analysis and critical evaluation of the experience of the difficult issue of cooperation in matters which engage both the Church and the State will reflect and will offer some judgments as to which direction this dialogue is presently taking and whether this pluralistic understanding of the Christian message should be resolved in an eventual synthesis in doctrine, not withstanding pluralities of theologies.[10]

While much of the initial "ecumenical" spirit was directed toward attempting to face and hopefully to resolve some of the differences among Christians who tend to identify with a specific Christian tradition, a more recent trend has been to widen the "dialogue" and see all

Christians within the broader human Community facing the possible "identity crisis"[11] which may develop in some Christians as they honestly try to meet and live with the so-called "secular" areas of thought and action. For this purpose we will consider the role of the theologian as being concerned with speaking to the Christian community in order to maintain traditional values and/or with speaking from the Christian community in an effort to reach the total community.

Within the Catholic community there is some tension due to what might be called "internal dialogue." There seems to be an effort to lead the Church[12] to a more meaningful understanding of the traditional Christian truths, and to encourage this spirit with the result of a real growth in love and understanding within the Church despite some attempts to check or stifle this area of vitality within the universal Church.

God told us what to do, but He did not tell us how to do it.

In our third Symposium on MAN, WORLD and SPIRIT, we came to a clearer realization, that the mountain is high and the climb is arduous. But we are willing to accept the challenge because the road to the House of a Friend (Tchelovekoljubec-Lover of man) from Nazareth is never long.

While much of the initial on-going movement was directed toward a meaningful dialogue between Christians, a more recent conception of Christians as a minority in the world community has compelled religious thinkers to widen their dialogue to re-integrate a world community of believers.

"The Heart Open to the World" (Le coeur ouvert sur le monde), a motto of a humble Dominican friar, Fr. Pire, Nobel Peace Prize winner, helped to bridge a gap between races and religious convictions on a social basis. The heart open to joy, peace and love, going beyond all forms in the service of the spiritual man, will bridge the gap reflected everywhere, especially in the temptation to a dual trend which (a) triumphs and (b) refuses to hear the appeals for renewal required by our times. The post-Conciliar era of openness is comparable to the Roman era, especially under Marcus Aurelius' reign. The confused Roman mind was frustrated with paganism but not yet ready for Christianity.

The Roman principle[13] which proved to be very helpful in the Christianization of the world was that ecclesiastical organization should follow the pattern of the political division of the Roman Empire, contributing thus to the solid foundations of the structure of early Christian communities.

In the process Christian society, once the Christianization was officially on its way from the fourth century, benefited from the Roman political pattern. This was especially true of the newly emerging nations, not only from the point of view of their acceptance of Christianity, but also in regard to stabilizing their socio-political units as well.

Once Christianity was established, the golden era of theology began.

At the center of any viable theology is a metaphysics of openness. So it was for Augustine, for Thomas Aquinas, and so it is for today's man as the mid-point between spirit and world. The American contribution of fresh and meaningful insight in Ecumenism with a youthful approach crossing the boundaries of the world helped to unite people in their doubts, divided by their convictions.

Loss of identity has accelerated the confusion of mind of today's generation. The unique blending of psychology and theology relating to the needs and aspirations of the perplexed Christian contributed to a message rich, yet unadorned, bespeaking a Christianly gentle manner of openness to the world.

Judaism paves a new way in the tradition of people with a great religious history in this traditionless age.

A biblical scholarship immersed in the Wisdom of the people who paved the way to a Christian era, integrates, not politically organized religion, but traditional theological concepts with present-day thought forms and at the same time interjects a new revealing insight in word and action.[14]

A confirmation and amplification of changes in the world in the light of modern sociological research provokes profound insight and deep awareness of the problems and questions that arise in an epoch in which institutions are no longer taken for granted, providing a first step of analysis of a "status quo" which for so long seemed proper to the institutions.

An effort to lead theology to a more meaningful understanding of the traditional Christian truths has encouraged a greater understanding of re-examining the essential truths of Christianity; e.g., progression from a two natures Christology to a Christology of Presence.

The *leitmotif* heralding each expression and its discussions is a trumpet call for the theologians to forge ahead, to examine and re-examine these vital truths and to express them in language understandable to today's man.

Modern culture, including modern sciences and technology, sheds a new light on the development of some theological topics which were untouched for centuries. The doctrine of original sin, for example, demanded for a long time a monogenic explanation of the origin of man, while a reverse process had to be employed in the speculative theology of original sin. Men of science can illuminate the shadow of night of the origin of man. The scientific, polygenic explanation of man's origin will not overshadow the revealed and theologically established supernatural destiny of man. In the domain of salvation history many forms of "being-in-situation" may occur. It should not be restricted only to the doctrine of man's entering a world of sin in general and original sin in particular, but extended also to the salvific entering into a world of God in Christ with the sacramental characters. A revealed message of salvation does not give man a doctrine replete with factual information but only a statement of the bond of love with God in Christ.[15]

This revealed bond of love with God in Christ urges Christians to be one in Christ.

Unity of Christians is not within reach, but the official pronouncements of the Pope are most encouraging because unity will not inflict dishonor on the countries.[16] The organizations[17] so highly revered in the past are now viewed from a different angle. Even the best organized institution will hinder rather than build the universal Church.

The Villanova Institute intends to add its voice to the other schools of religious thought, not for universal belief, but for a consideration of the theologian and of the magisterium of the Church.

With the intention of understanding "current trends" and the "theology in transition" through the perennial disparity between the thinking giver and the thought receiver, we have initiated our Villanova series with "The Dynamic in Thought." An understanding of the creative processes of today in the creative march of Christian thought in history mobilizes a Christian into dynamic action.

Although we will re-examine academically even basic truths, we will keep unity in the necessary things—for the rest, liberty and always charity. In matters which are not clear Revelation, we must allow full liberty of discussion.

Villanova University opens its forum to the representatives of different schools because its contribution is intended for the world Church. It is inconceivable to have a homogeneous theology for the entire Church. True, Thomistic, Scotistic, Suarezian-Molinist schools differed, but they kept the same process of mind common to scholastic re-interpretation of Christianity. Our new era with new problems makes neo-orthodox repristination obsolete. Today's theology calls for a more daring speculative theology.

Because of the news media, continental development of theological ideas penetrated American contemporary thought with a shocking speed. We can say that typical American theology was definitely more conservative before Vatican II than continental theology. Today, however, American willingness to change conservative thinking exceeds the continental speed. This speed without the preceding history of theological thought necessitates caution if the many risks and dangers are not to outweigh the great promise for the future development of theological thought in America.

Subsequent symposia will deal with fundamental questions of theology in crisis, treating contemporary ecclesiology and the Church's structure, the impact of revelation on human thought, Christian ethics in the secular age (especially revolutionary genetic engineering),[18] anthropological dimensions, contemporary theological methods, the transcendental turn of Rahner's and Lonergan's[19] school, religious life in religious orders, the layman's theology, the woman—shaper of the future, the emergence of charisma in the twentieth century, the Marxist ideology, despair and hope—socio-religious movements encompassing race, war, revolution and peace. "The Eschaton: A Community of Love"[20] will conclude the first of the Villanova series.

In a work like this, at Villanova University, marking its one hundred twenty-fifth anniversary, interest, felicitations and blessings of the Holy Father Paul VI through his Secretary of State are more appreciated than can be expressed in these pages. Augustine Trapé, Charles H. Pickar, James J. Sherman and Edward L. Daley, the preoccupations of their high positions in the Augustinian Order notwithstanding, were most generous in encouraging the present undertaking. John Cardinal Krol assisted us immensely by giving his gracious hospitality to our distinguished speakers. Robert J. Welsh and John M. Driscoll have supported us most beneficently by placing facilities at our disposal.

I wish to express my cordial thanks to Joseph J. Gildea, whose initial assistance, so kindly given, lightened the heavy burden of preparing the groundwork for the Institute and the subsequent Symposia.

Lastly, I would like the work to be considered a sign of affection for the late Edward V. Stanford, who was among the first to point out Villanova University to me as a receptive field for such an expanded scholarly activity.

In nomine Domini, with the Villanova motto Unitas, Veritas, Charitas, we started The Villanova University Series on its road forward. "... I shall bring my own work to an end here ... skill in presenting the incidents is what delights the understanding of those who read ... On that note I will close."[21]

In pointing out our direction in the two subsequent volumes on the dynamic in Christian action towards openness to the world, I have chosen the motto of the late Fr. Pire, Nobel Prize winner, "With an open heart to the world" (Le coeur ouvert sur le monde) to close these pages of our first volume.

NOTES

[1] *The Dynamic in Christian Thought,* The Villanova University Series, ed., Joseph Papin, Vol. 1.

[2] *The Dynamic in Christian Action,* The Villanova University Series, Vol. II.

[3] *Openness to the World,* The Villanova University Series, Vol. III.

[4] *The Pilgrim People—A Vision with Hope,* The Villanova University Series, Vol. IV.

[5] Karl Rahner, *The Dynamic Element in the Church* (New York: Herder and Herder, 1964), p. 83.

[6] Pierre Teilhard de Chardin, *The Future of Man,* trans. Norman Denny (New York: Harper & Row, Publishers, 1960), pp. 306 ff.;

The Divine Milieu (New York: Harper & Row, 1960), pp. 150 ff.

[7] Christopher Mooney, *Teilhard de Chardin and the Mystery of Christ* (New York: Harper & Row, 1964), p. 224; Eulalio R. Baltazar, *Teilhard de Chardin and the Supernatural* (Baltimore: Helicon, 1966), p. 24.

[8] Krister Stendahl, "The Role of the Bible in the Theology of the Future," *The Dynamic in Christian Thought*, The Villanova University Series, Vol. 1.

[9] Bernard Häring, *Road to Renewal* (Staten Island, N.Y.: Alba House, 1966), pp. 81, 89.

[10] Nicholas Berdyaev, *The Destiny of Man* (New York: Harper & Row, Publishers, Inc., 1960), p. 168, Sobornost - and - pure - conscience.

[11] Bernard Häring, "Morality: Underlying and Unchanging Principles?" *The Dynamic in Christian Thought*, The Villanova University Series, Vol. 1; Harvey Cox, "Secular Holiness: Loss or Gain of Christian Identity?" *The Dynamic in Christian Action*, The Villanova University Series, Vol. II.

[12] "True, genuine Christianity is not a dogma, or hierarchy, or liturgy, or morality, but the life-giving spirit of Christ really though invisibly, present in humanity and acting in it through complex processes of spiritual growth and development." S. L. Frank, ed., *A Solovyov Anthology*, trans. by Natalie Duddington (New York: Charles Scribner's Sons, 1950), p. 43.

[13] Joseph Papin, *Christian Inroots into the Territory of Present Slovakia Prior to the Cyrilo-Methodian Era*, Slovak Studies III (Rome: Slovak Institute, 1963), p. 10.

[14] Walter J. Burghardt, "Jewish-Christian Dialogue: Early Church versus Contemporary Christianity," *The Dynamic in Christian Thought*, The Villanova University Series, Vol. I; Abraham I. Katsh, "The Religious Tradition or Traditions in a Traditionless Age," *Openness to the World*, The Villanova University Series, Vol. III; Roland E. Murphy, "The Wisdom of Israelites and Their Attitude Toward the World," *Openness to the World*, The Villanova University Series, Vol. III.

[15] Piet Schoonenberg, *Man and Sin, A Theological View* (Notre Dame: University of Notre Dame Press, 1965), p. 198.

[16] Yves Congar, *A Gospel Priesthood* (New York: Herder and Herder, 1967), pp. 215 ff.

[17] Bernard Häring, *Toward a Christian Moral Theology* (Notre Dame: University of Notre Dame Press, 1966), p. 59.

Gustav A. Wetter, *Dialectical Materialism* (New York & London: Frederick A. Praeger, Publisher, 1963), pp. 214 ff.

Johannes B. Metz, *Theology of the World*, trans., William Glen-Doepel (New York: Herder and Herder, 1969), p. 149.

Jaroslav Pelikan, *The Christian Intellectual* (New York: Harper & Row, Publishers, Inc., 1965), p. 17.

[18] Paul Ramsey, "Genetic Engineering," *The Pilgrim People: A Vision With Hope*, The Villanova University Series, Vol. IV.

[19] Bernard J. Lonergan, *Verbum Word and Idea in Aquinas* (Notre Dame: University of Notre Dame Press, 1967), pp. 226, 235, 253, 266, 270; see also Karl Rahner's *The Trinity*, regarding Lonergan's School, p. 118, footnote 44.

[20] *Eschaton—A Community of Love*, The Villanova University Series, Vol. V.

[21] *The Jerusalem Bible*, 2 Maccabees 15:37 ff.

BIBLIOGRAPHY

Abbott, Walter M., ed. *The Documents of Vatican II.* New York: Guild Press, 1966.
Baltazar, Eulalio R. "*Teilhard de Chardin: A Philosophy of Procession.*" *Continuum*, II (Spring, 1964), pp. 87-97.
Barth, Karl. *Church Dogmatics.* Edited by G. W. Bromiley and T. F. Torrance. Edinburgh: T. & T. Clark, 1963.
Berdyaev, Nicholas. *The Destiny of Man.* New York: Harper & Row Publishers, Inc., 1960.
Berdyaev, Nicholas. *Dostoevsky.* Trans. by Donald Attwater. Cleveland & New York: The World Publishing Co., 1968.
Bonhoeffer, Dietrich. *Creation and Fall.* New York: The Macmillan Company, 1967.
Buber, Martin. *Eclipse of God.* New York and Evanston: Harper & Row Publishers, 1957.
Chenu, M.-D. *Is Theology a Science?* Trans. by A. H. N. Green-Armytage. New York: Hawthorne Books, 1959.
Congar, Yves M. J. *Tradition and Traditions.* New York: The Macmillan Company, 1967.
Danielou, Jean. "The Timeliness of Teilhard de Chardin." *Philosophy Today*, VI (Fall, 1962), pp. 212-222.
D'Arcy, M. C. *The Mind and Heart of Love.* Cleveland and New York: The World Publishing Co., 1967.
Dulles, Avery. "The Meaning of Revelation." *The Dynamic in Christian Thought.* The Villanova University Series. Vol. I.
Frank, S. L., ed. *A Solovyov Anthology.* Trans. by Natalie Duddington. New York: Charles Scribner's Sons, 1950.
Häring, Bernard. *Road to Renewal.* Staten Island, N.Y.: Alba House, 1968.
Häring, Bernard. *What Does Christ Want?* Notre Dame: Ave Maria Press, 1968.
Harnack, Adolph. *History of Dogma.* Trans. by Neil Buchanan. New York: Dover Publications, Inc., 1961, Vols. I-VII.
Hughes, Philip E. *Theology of the English Reformers.* Grand Rapids, Michigan: William B. Eerdmans Publishing Company, 1966.
Jaspers, Karl, and Bultmann, Rudolf. *Myth and Christianity.* New York: The Noonday Press, 1968.
Küng, Hans. *The Church.* New York: Sheed and Ward Co., 1967.
Latourelle, René. *Theology of Revelation.* Staten Island, N.Y.: Alba House, 1966.
Lonergan, Bernard J. *Verbum Word and Idea in Aquinas.* Notre Dame: University of Notre Dame Press, 1967.
Lubac, Henri de. *The Mystery of the Supernatural.* Trans. by Rosemary Sheed. New York: Herder & Herder, 1967.
———. *The Discovery of God.* Trans. by Alexander Dru. Chicago: Henry Regnery Company, 1967.
———. *The Religion of Teilhard de Chardin.* Trans. by René Hague. New York, Rome, Paris, Tournai: Desclee Company, 1967.
Metz, Johannes. *Theology of the World.* New York: Herder & Herder, 1969.
Murray, John Courtney. *The Problem of God.* New Haven: Yale University Press, 1964.
Niebuhr, H. R. *The Meaning of Revelation.* New York: Macmillan, 1967.

North, Robert. *Teilhard and the Creation of the Soul.* Milwaukee: The Bruce Company, 1967.
Papin, Joseph. *Doctrina De Bono Perfecto.* Leiden: E. J. Brill, 1946.
——. *Christus Bij Dostojevskij.* Nijmegen-Utrecht: Dekker & Van De Vegt N.V., 1946.
Rahner, Karl. *The Trinity.* Trans. by Joseph Donceel. New York: Herder & Herder, 1970.
Schillebeeckx, E. *Revelation and Theology.* Trans. by N. D. Smith. New York: Sheed and Ward, 1967, Vols. 1-2.
Schmaus, Michael. *Dogma.* New York: Sheed and Ward, 1968, Vols. I-II.
Solovyev, Vladimir. *Lectures on Godmanhood.* London: Dennis Dobson, Ltd. Publishers, 1948.
Tavard, George H. *The Church Tomorrow.* New York: Herder & Herder, 1965.
Tillich, Paul. *The Eternal Now.* New York: Charles Scribner's Sons, 1962.
Weigel, Gustave. *Where Do We Differ?* London: Burns & Oates, 1961.

Acknowledgments

Work like this presupposes the collaboration of many people. This collaboration was generously given by the Administration on all levels and particularly by the Faculty of all departments. The panel which constitutes an integral part of the Symposium relied mostly on the speakers: Dulles, Stendahl, Fontinell, Baltazar, Häring, Pelikan and Burghardt. With profound sadness it must be noted that Weigel, Courtney Murray, and Nogar promised to be with us at our first Symposium, but their untimely deaths prevented their participation.

However, our own faculty gave the Institute invaluable service. The faculty of Liberal Arts and Sciences conducted two sessions. One was on the topic: "The Dynamic in the Human Sciences," under the leadership of Raymond L. Cummings and Donald X. Burt. The other session, "The Dynamic in Natural Sciences," conducted under the direction of William J. Barnhurst, James J. Markham, and Lawrence Gallen, manifested a positive appreciation of modern sciences in recognizing that theology or the plurality of theologies, as well as sciences, can not remain an island and yet be aware of modern man's conamen to find responsible solutions by seeing both poles as a unity rather than as alternatives.

"It's Tearing Me Apart," based on Soloviev's* Anti-Christ and Dostoevsky's Grand Inquisitor, translated by the Editor, directed by Robert Hedley, and played by members of the Administration, the Theology Faculty and professional players of the Theatre Department, highlighted the Eschatology and the Parousia in a very dramatic way.

Besides the lively departmental contributions to the success of the Symposium on "The Dynamic in Christian Thought," individual members of Villanova departments and other institutions, such as Bernard A. Lazor, John M. Buckley, Arthur J. Ennis, Terrence Monihan, Bishop Walter Schoenherr, Donald X. Burt, Thomas W. Busch, Charles McFadden, Daniel T. Regan, Lawrence Gallen, John E. Hughes, Joseph Wimmer, Anthony Massimini, Joseph M. Bradley, Charles D. Tirrell, Arthur B. Crabtree, Robert C. Totaro and Thomas M. Casey made a substantial contribution to the discussions in different sessions.

The Symposium was greatly advanced by the support and advice of William E. Farrell and by the help given generously by Eugene J. Ruane and the University Office of Public Information.

A task like this cannot be accomplished without the help and assistance of the library. Louis A. Rongione and his staff contributed abundantly.

John F. O'Rourke, genuinely interested in the project, gave his office facilities for our use and spent many nights with us laboring on the detailed arrangements.

The Augustinian Fathers and their seminarians, especially those at St. Mary's Hall, by providing their traditional hospitality for the guest-speakers and participants, greatly contributed to the enduring effect of the Symposium, turning it into a joyous historical event, marking the great anniversary of the founding of Villanova University. Seminarians James H. Lomastro, James J. McCartney and Joseph J. Reynolds were always in the forefront ready to help.

Many Universities, Colleges, and Convents sent their best theologians to our Symposium. Among those representatives who became our most faithful participants are John A. Klekotka, Charles H. Pickar, Bishop Walter Schoenherr, Denis A. Boyle, Carmelita G. Thill, Elizabeth M. Brady, Grace Kennedy, Joanne M. Schmidt, and John P. Doyle. Among many students participating, mention must be made of Joseph Armenti, Linda Kerrigan, Anthony Morgan and Joseph Solus.

We wish to acknowledge at this time the inclusion by Doubleday Company, Inc., of our article: "God: A Pragmatic Reconstruction" in their book *Toward a Reconstruction of Religion* by Eugene Fontinell.

The final proofs were read and corrected with a vigilant eye by Francis A. Eigo. For his solicitous reading of this difficult manuscript I am deeply appreciative.

The Index in this volume covers only the names and does not include the concepts. The indices covering the concepts, names, and bibliography will be implemented in the fifth volume of the Villanova University series.

The present index of names has been prepared by James J. Cleary. It is impossible to thank him sufficiently for his work done with such care.   J. P.
                                          DIRECTOR of the INSTITUTE

NOTE

* For general information see *The New Catholic Encyclopedia*, 1967, Vol. 13, "Soloviev V. S." by J. Papin.

God: A Pragmatic Reconstruction

Eugene Fontinell

I. BACKGROUND REMARKS

THE title, "God: A Pragmatic Reconstruction," will offend many ears. It smacks of an arrogant humanism that would reduce God to an object or plaything of man. There is, to be sure, a certain "playfulness" in an undertaking such as this. Yet, I hope that it is possible to be playful without being frivolous. More important, I hope that such activity can play a constructive role in human life. Whether the particulars of my God-speculation are constructive is, needless to say, of no great moment. The question of whether any efforts along these lines are worthwhile is, however, a matter of some concern. It is also a matter of faith. No one can "prove" the worth of reflecting upon God; the reflection begins, is sustained, and is consummated as a continuing act of faith. I hope, however, to be able to indicate what some experiential fruits of such faith might be.

It must be immediately and repeatedly emphasized that pragmatic reconstruction is not an isolated and abstract theory about God. Theorizing and speculating will have their roles, but pragmatism insists that these activities take place within a more inclusive and diverse context. Personal and institutional transformations are every bit as essential to pragmatic reconstruction as new ideas or theories. Though such ideas often articulate the experience of the community and point the way for new experiences, they take their meaning from their function in the ongoing life of the community.

A pragmatic reconstruction, whether of God, of law, or of liturgy, takes place within a living context, which is personalistic, communitarian, existential, and historical. Ultimately a pragmatic reconstruction of God must endeavor to comprehend the full history of man, but proximately it must respond to the more pressing cultural context. Today, the cultural context is characterized by the collapse or near collapse of many of the key values, ideas, and institutions of Western civilization. Pragmatism minimizes neither the seriousness nor the loss that results from this collapse; but, since it presupposes a dynamic and developmental world, it maintains that collapse can occasion and stimulate a new human effort of reconstruction which can create new values, ideas and institutions that will better serve the human community than those which have been lost.

Since pragmatism denies that human activity can be impersonal, any reconstruction, particularly one of religion, will properly be influenced by the faith of the person or persons doing the reconstructing. If they consider themselves members of the Christian Church with a responsibility to continue and if possible develop the vision and life of this historical community, it would be foolish to deny that this faith will influence, both consciously and unconsciously, the resulting reflections.

Before mentioning a few of my own controlling assumptions, I would like to underline the inevitability, diversity, and unprovability of all assumptions. Morris Raphael Cohen expresses the point well:

> The way to make progress in any field of learning is not by resolving to free ourselves of dogmatic assumptions—such resolutions are vain—but by making clear to ourselves what are the various assumptions that are possible, and thus envisaging our position as one of a great number. This widens our sympathetic understanding and breaks the backbone of fanaticism. It makes us humble because it indicates to us that ultimately we cannot prove the truth of our fundamental assumptions, for our fundamental assumptions determine the kind of a world which we can perceive and the world of phenomena is wider than that of our knowledge.[1]

For the purposes of this paper, it is most important to stress that any symbols, concepts, categories, or doctrines concerning God—in short, any theology, natural or other—are grounded in a specific metaphysics and permeated by metaphysical assumptions. Without going into the many nuances and difficulties surrounding the meaning of the term metaphysics, I will simply assert that it combines a fundamental perspective or angle of vision or world-view with a set of principles and categories in terms of which all phenomena are to be explained.

Another and more specific assumption of mine is that the traditional doctrine of God in Western or Christian history is closely, though not exclusively, bound up with Greek metaphysics. I also assume that the Greek categories which served the Christian faith so well in the past have become increasingly more irrelevant to the developing structure of human life. Hence, our doctrine of God needs radical reconstruction, one which will not simply assimilate new data and insights to a central core of unchanging doctrine, but will even dare to challenge and attempt to supplant many of what heretofore have been considered indispensable elements or principles of that doctrine.

Such a reconstruction demands the greatest openness and involves a tremendous risk. John Dewey has noted the dire consequences of such an undertaking: "Let us admit the case of the conservative," he tells us. "If we once start thinking, no one can guarantee where we shall come out, except that many objects, ends and institutions are surely doomed. Every thinker puts some portion of an apparently stable world in peril and no one can wholly predict what will emerge in its place."[2]

Only the need and hope to bring forth a new world can make taking such a risk worthwhile. But again Dewey warns us, "No one discovers a new world without forsaking an old one; and no one discovers a new world who exacts guarantee in advance for what it shall be, or who puts the act of discovery under bonds with respect to what the new world shall do to him when it comes into vision."[3]

The discovery of a new world is beyond the scope of one or a hundred essays such as this. It demands a great community effort: a plurality of approaches which share some assumptions and principles but differ in others. Though every approach must acknowledge other approaches, each must avoid premature synthesis of diverse insights. Each approach will be made from its particular perspective, or point of view or metaphysics which will give it order, form, and direction. At the same time its perspective will limit it and cut it off from the insights gained through other approaches. Each will be self-consciously partial and, as William James has noted, "Any partial view whatever of the world tears the part out of its relations, leaves out some truth concerning it, is untrue of it, falsifies it."[4]

James presupposes "a pluralistic restless universe, in which no single point of view can ever take in the whole scene."[5] Even those who question the pluralism of the universe must concede the pluralism of contemporary philosophy; I shall only add that it is an asset, not a liability. I maintain that it is possible to commit oneself to reflection within a particular set of categories without presuming that only these are worthwhile. At the same time, I do not rule out, indeed I hope for, "convergence" of the many insights which emerge from a diversity of metaphysics. Perhaps the most significant long-run test of the important and enduring insights of human thought and experience are those which emerge from and remain central to a variety of metaphysics. Such convergences, however, can never be more than guidelines to further thought and experience. Any attempt to use them as "proofs" or to bring them together in a new synthesis is itself another metaphysics and hence subject to the limitations already noted.

My final assumption is really a set of assumptions: the principles and categories which compose the metaphysics or world-view of pragmatism. Any attempt to describe a metaphysics succinctly cannot help but be misleading. This is particularly true when one is attempting to describe a metaphysics that remained to a great extent inchoate and non-systematized in the writings of its founders. Indeed one might well dispute whether there is a "pragmatic metaphysics." Certainly the phrase denotes no formally articulated metaphysical system. Chauncey

Wright, Charles Sanders Pierce, William James, and John Dewey are the chief founders of pragmatism: it is quite apparent that there is sufficient similarity of approach to warrant use of the rather vague phrase, "the metaphysics of pragmatism." Different as these thinkers might be when compared with each other, they are strikingly similar when compared with other philosophical movements or periods in philosophy.[6] My concern here, however, is not with the thought of these thinkers as such, but with the service certain aspects of their thought render to the question under consideration. Put in its simplest terms, I am endeavoring to discover the possibilities for and the consequences of reflection upon God, which emerge from a world-view constructed in its basic dimensions by these men. I wish to acknowledge my debt to these thinkers without either saddling them with my conclusions and interpretations or, on the other hand, restricting my speculative conclusions, in form or content, to those arrived at by them. Allow me, then, to describe briefly what I believe to be the crucial features of the distinctive world-view which I term "pragmatism."

To say that we inhabit a processive world is to mouth a commonplace; but to affirm a world in which no reality or sphere of reality is unchanging, is something else. Further, the processive world as envisioned by pragmatism is characterized by the emergence of really novel events and realities. These are not simply the actualization of pre-existing potencies, whether ultimately located in something called Nature or in the reality of God. Though such a world insists upon the need for order and regularities, these are deemed relative, the result in great part of man's transactions within reality. The processive world of pragmatism is neither eternally ordered nor in chaotic flux.

Closely allied to the processive dimension of that world is its relational aspect. Pragmatism rejects any world composed of atomistic individuals or substances which are only *accidentally* related. "In actual experience," Dewey maintains, "there is never any such isolated singular object or event, *an* object or event is always a special part, phase or aspect, or an environing experienced world—a situation."[7] This point of a world of relations is most subtle and difficult to communicate. James, in order to describe this world of processive relations, employed the metaphor "field," a metaphor which has been increasingly used in such diverse disciplines as physics, psychology and sociology. It is interesting to note that Bishop John Robinson speaks of "the divine field" in an effort to overcome some of the traditional problems attached to any "God-talk."[8]

A central feature of this pragmatic world of relations and process is its distinctive interpretation of experience. Experience is neither passive nor subjective nor radically distinct from reason. Instead, in the language of Dewey, experience designates all transactions between the organism and environment. Yet neither the organism nor the environment is radically independent of the other: they are co-constitutive of one another. This metaphysics of experience makes it impossible to split reality into subjective and objective orders. Subjective and objective are derivative categories—distinct functions within ongoing experience.[9]

Such empiricism insisted that knowledge itself is but one of many modes of experience by which man can participate in reality. By acknowledging a variety of experiences with distinct and indispensable functions in human life, we are able to break the hold of destructive rationalism or intellectualism without falling prey to superficial anti-intellectualism. There is no need to prove that art and religion, for example, are modes of knowledge since knowledge is not the privileged or exclusive pathway to reality. Most important for my purposes, it is possible to defend a philosophy of faith which denies that faith is a form of knowledge. I shall return in a moment to the relation between faith and knowledge with reference to God but would first call attention to a few final assumptions.

To begin with, belief or faith is not an activity peculiar to some men and totally absent in others. All men are believers, since every moment of their lives involves, directly or indirectly, commitments and actions for which there is no conclusive rational evidence. The continuing task of men is to evaluate their beliefs or faith and here, as we shall see, reason or intelligence plays an indispensable role.

The pragmatic world-view also implies that all experiences are primarily participational rather than representational; that is, we do not simply discover or interpret the world through knowledge, art, and faith, but in a very real sense we change the world and thereby help create it.

One last introductory point: the choice is not between positing ontologically separate or at least radically distinct orders, such as the religious, the scientific, the artistic and the like, or collapsing all experiences into an indistinguishable and undifferentiated mass. There is a third alternative. This third alternative is a "functionalism" whereby we respect the distinctness of a variety of human experiences while acknowledging that they interpenetrate and shade into each other. This view permits us to speak of religion, art, science, and the like, since by a deliberate and temporary restriction of concern and consideration one enters, or better re-enters, more deeply into the on-going relational continuum called reality. The key, as James and Dewey never failed to stress, is that our theoretic meanderings, if they are successful, eventually return us to a deeper experience in our everyday life.

II. ON KNOWING GOD

THE permeating principle as well as the conclusion of a pragmatic reconstruction such as I am suggesting is that one can have "faith in God," but one cannot "know" God. Stated so starkly this is by no means a new idea. It will be necessary to indicate what this means within a pragmatic framework in order to differentiate it from similar assertions. At the outset, it must be stressed that my view avoids fideism; it is neither hostile to knowledge or reason nor does it maintain faith in isolation from whatever knowledge man has achieved. On the contrary, my intention is to render the relation between faith and knowledge more intimate and dynamic. My contention is that to characterize faith as knowledge leads to an isolation of faith inasmuch as it then must remain untouched by the ever-changing knowledge which characterizes man's intellectual endeavors. Hence, the alleged knowledge which results from faith has to be assigned to a distinct realm of being which is basically (if not totally) irrelevant to knowledge in other realms. Thus there develop knowledge-claims for faith which, in order to avoid such destructive conflicts with science and philosophy as have taken place in the past, form a protective isolationism whereby more and more our "faith-knowledge" is emptied of experiential content and relevance. In this way, regardless of what new facts or theories emerge in science, religious faith is safe, since supposedly it is concerned with a methodology and a sphere of reality which is only peripherally related to that with which science is concerned.

The relation which I am suggesting between faith and knowledge distinguishes them, but neither assigns them to separate realms of reality, nor puts them in competition with each other. Any living and reflective faith must express itself in concepts, metaphors and symbols, and in doing so it will be obliged to utilize the concepts, metaphors and symbols which the culture makes available to it. I believe that this has always been the situation but now we are conscious of it. Today no one can doubt some influence of the historical and cultural context upon one's faith, but the dominant Roman Catholic tradition has been to insist that its beliefs, at least in their fundamental or essential dimensions, are independent of historical and cultural conditioning and hence can be continually affirmed without need for nor the possibility of any fundamental and radical change. This is equivalent to absolutizing historical and cultural forms and freezes faith into relatively static doctrines. Paradoxically, by admitting the necessary and ever-present historical and cultural features of the faith expressions of any moment, we are able to liberate the faith from reduction to or identification with particular historical and cultural forms. Such an attitude should maximize the possibilities for creative and imaginative reflection upon the faith-mystery. At the same time, it must continually maintain a dynamic and relatively coherent and consistent relation both with its earlier expressions and the best knowledge and experience of its time. This, of course, is a very big order, and I do not suggest that in asserting it as a goal I have proved that it can be accomplished, much less that I have accomplished it. My aim is more modest—to indicate that by insisting on the uniqueness of faith and on its non-cognitive function and quality, I am not calling for fideism or pseudo-mysticism. Rather, I am calling for a new approach that will avoid both the rationalism of a religious objectivism and the emotionalism of a religious subjectivism.

Though I am urging an effort which breaks with the traditional approach, I am quite willing to characterize this effort as a form of rational or philosophical theology and express the belief that it is in the tradition of "faith seeking understanding," though, of course, *both* faith and understanding are continually undergoing transformation, since every generation of believers has the task of justifying or rationalizing its faith. I make no pretense of doing otherwise. Most would agree that there will be a difference in the form such justification takes; I insist that there is also a difference in the content. This, to some extent, is evident even in those approaches apparently closer to the dominant traditions of Roman Catholic thought, from theistic realism to what might be called transcendental theism. Different as each may be one from the other, however, they all have something in common that separates them from the pragmatic approach: they all maintain the possibility and even the necessity of establishing through rational argument the knowability of God. Such a "preamble of faith" may take the form of the classical proofs for God's existence or utilize some version of the "transcendental method"[10] which establishes through reason the reality of the Absolute as a necessary or transcendental condition for knowledge. While none of these thinkers would suggest that faith in any way is a rational deduction from their metaphysics, they all seem to affirm a rational world with God as the knowable first principle. Such a world then serves as the rational underpinning or framework for faith.

I am, of course, giving a grossly over-simplified description of the dominant trend of the Roman Catholic philosophical tradition. At the risk of an even greater over-simplification, I would suggest that in an effort to avoid reducing faith to some kind of arbitrary, subjectivistic, emotional and individualistic activity, Roman Catholic thinkers have tended to cut the mystery of faith to fit the bed of their particular version of a rational world.

In contrast, as I will develop in a bit more detail below, I would assert a kind of *agnosticism* concerning any absolutely ultimate principle of rationality. Hence, any faith in God will be radically irreducible and ultimate in relation to both the person and the community. In attempting to establish the necessity of proving God's existence, Henri Bouillard asks: "How can we know that our faith is the result of a miracle, that is to say of God's action, and that it is not simply an arbitrary human act?"[11] To which I would reply, "We cannot *know* that it is God's action and that is why we must have faith." In the final analysis, then, I would assert that there is no ground for faith except faith itself. I would further maintain that this holds whether the faith is Christian, Marxist, or humanist.

Having asserted the radically non-cognitive quality of faith, I would now affirm the other dimension of the dialectic by contending that every reflective faith must make an effort to show that it is, if not fully compatible, at least not incompatible with the thought and experience of the age. This is why all believers—I again include Marxist and humanistic as well as Christian—have felt compelled to do more than simply say, "This is what I believe, take it or leave it!" In every faith tradition, the more reflective believers endeavor to make manifest the concordance of faith with reason, whether in the form of proofs for the existence of God or demonstrations of the inevitability of the self-destruction of capitalism. Pragmatism does not oppose such efforts, indeed it insists upon them, but it avoids deceiving itself about the ultimate unprovability of the worth and truth of its basic acts of faith.

While a pragmatic approach to faith, as I will attempt to indicate, must present "reasons" or, better, justifications for believing in God, it is under no compunction to prove the irrationality of one who does not believe in God. Since the pragmatist affirms a world in which it is impossible to prove or disprove the existential reality of God, both rational theism and rational atheism are possible . The proponents of both must constantly act and hence believe beyond the available rational evidence; at the same time both will argue that their beliefs are more in accordance with the evidence now at hand. Neither can escape the possibility that he is wrong; both are willing to risk error because of the positive values of their faith. Needless to say, both the theist and the atheist must to some degree judge the other to be misguided; but we have moved beyond the nineteenth century form of disagreement that compelled each party to accuse the other of irrationality, or worse. Today, I suggest, a man whose faith is secure *only* if he has persuaded himself that all other faiths are irrational, is a man who in a significant way lacks faith.

III. A PRAGMATIC CRITERION

Now the fact that it is not possible to disprove the reality of God is no excuse for smugness or complacency on the part of the concerned believer in God. It is not sufficient that one can somehow manage to live *with* one's faith; perhaps we should only affirm that faith which we cannot live *without*. Any faith worth its salt must include positive values. Though such values cannot be advanced as "proofs" or absolute validations, a faith that lacked them completely would not long hold the allegiance of those who profess it, to say nothing of attracting those who do not. Before addressing myself to some of the values a belief in God might incorporate, let me pose in its most simple form the question confronting any contemporary God-believer. Given the history of man in all its dimensions—religious, social, philosophical, artistic and scientific—can one with some degree of rational consistency continue to have faith in God within the Judaeo-Christian tradition? I believe that one can, but this is faith. If it is to be a reflective faith, effort must be made to indicate the compatability of contemporary man with faith in the Judaeo-Christian God. One way to approach this question would be to affirm the traditional doctrine of God, at least in its basic principles, and then respond to the objections against it either by accidentally modifying this doctrine or by refutation of the objections. In my opinion this has been, and remains, the dominant approach on the part of Christian thinkers.

A better approach, I believe, is to consider the traditional doctrine of God as itself the product of history and culture and, having accepted this fact, attempt to create a suitable contemporary doctrine of God. Now anyone endeavoring to reflect within a tradition for which God is ultimately an ineffable mystery is always in the paradoxical position of thinking and talking about what is, strictly speaking, incapable of being thought and talked about. This can be a fruitful paradox as long as we avoid the ever-present temptation to reduce the mystery of faith by absolutizing the concepts or symbols which are employed in our reflections. Any God-believing community will to some extent have a doctrine of God, but this doctrine cannot be formulated, even in its most basic principles, in any once-and-for-all form. No particular doctrine of God can lay claim to being *the* Christian doctrine in the sense that all authentic reflection on the Christian faith must conform to it. On my hypothesis, there can be no absolutely non-debatable or non-developmental philosophical or theological principles, concepts or symbols concerning the faith which characterizes the Christian community. For this reason, I think that the way of describing faith in God which gives rise to the least distortion and allows for the maximum of speculation and reflection is to view this faith as a personal-communal-existential orientation and relationship; that is, a dynamic and developing relationship in virtue of which man is moved beyond himself, not toward some outward or external object or goal, but to a richer life which is at once a fuller realization of himself and a sharing in the life of that mysterious Other whom we have traditionally called God.

Minimal as this statement is, it allows for both the continuity and the development of faith. It is the living historical community, however, which continues and develops, and not any particular patterns of thought or action. Further, it places the emphasis where it belongs in reflecting upon the God-belief of the community. The life of the community is the primary locus and reality of faith, rather than the concepts, doctrines or symbols which are employed to express and develop this life. At the same time, there is no belittling or diminishing both the importance and the necessity of concepts, doctrines, and symbols and of any theology—rational or other—which is charged with the task of creating and giving order to the concepts, doctrines, and symbols utilized by the believing community. While insisting on the need for these functions and activities, viewing faith in God as an existential relationship allows for the widest range of creative and imaginative theologizing. Finally, such an hypothesis gives a criterion by which the various interpretations, concepts, doctrines and symbols can be evaluated. That criterion is the life of the community itself; in other words, does a particular doctrine contribute to the enrichment, illumination, development, in short, to the quality of life, of the community? This is the central pragmatic question.

I am aware that such a succinct description of pragmatism will raise more questions than it answers. What, for example, does one mean by "quality of life"? Which community is to be the determining one in any evaluation of an idea, belief or action? How is one to determine whether or not something really does contribute to the quality of life of a community? These and many other objections inevitably and properly have been and will be raised against any pragmatic approach.

Without presuming to handle all the levels and implications of the classical objections against pragmatism, allow me to give at least a preliminary response—positive, not polemical—to these questions. It should be acknowledged at the outset that to make the life of the community the central and ultimately decisive criterion in evaluating the truth or worth of any idea, belief or action, is itself an option or act of faith which is irreducible and unprovable. I am not concerned to argue here whether this is the best criterion available to man, though I obviously *believe* that it is. I would, however, recall the point I made earlier concerning the faith dimension at the base of any metaphysics.

Granted that the life of the community is to be our ultimate determinate—I am not saying that it is the ultimate reality—for thought and action, how are we to understand the phrase "quality of life"? Negatively, it does not refer to any external or transcendent norm according to which particular ideas and actions are judged. Every life, individual and collective, is permeated by a pervasive quality which is directly experienced. The judgment that the quality of life of a person or community is better or higher is always a comparative judgment. Just as it is possible to judge the quality of one painting as better than another, although there does not exist some absolute quality against which both are judged, so it is possible to judge the quality of life of one community as better than another, though there exists no absolutely perfect community. Because it is also possible and indeed necessary to project an ideal in terms of which actual communities are to be formed and developed, there has been the tendency since the time of Plato to conclude that we can judge one reality better than another only if we have some absolute norm as the ultimate basis for our judgment. Pragmatism, however, is able to assign a role to ideals which avoids either positing them as absolute antecedently existing entities or reducing them to useless subjectivistic fictions. "Ideals," James asserted, "ought to aim at the *transformation of reality*—no less."[12] Dewey links ideals to possibilities, novelties, and creative imagination. In contrast to the classical meaning, Dewey contends that in modern life "potentiality" means "the possibility of novelty, of invention, of radical deviation."[13] In another place, he insists that "all possibilities are ideal in character," but, he goes on to say, "the reality of ideal ends as ideals is vouched for by their undeniable power in action. An ideal is not an illusion because imagination is the organ through which it is apprehended. For *all* possibilities reach us through the imagination."[14] Here again is an instance of a running theme of this paper, namely, that pragmatism offers us a third alternative beyond both subjectivism and objectivism.

Up to this point I have been using the term "community" without further specification. Since, however, there are many communities, how are we to decide which is to be the criterion for judgment? It might appear that this question can be answered easily by simply stating that the human community is to be our touchstone. Now there is a sense in which I believe this to be true, but a few qualifications are in order. To begin with, as of this moment of history, there are really many human communities. *The* human community is still in a very real sense an ideal, a project, a task—it is what we believe should be created and that which, hopefully, we are creating. True, we have at this juncture of man's development a few clues as to what will further this development and what will obstruct or retard it. Most important, perhaps, is the awareness that in the life of communities, as in that of persons, whatever cuts them off from others, whatever isolates them or turns them toward themselves, tends to impede their growth and leads to such destructive forms as egoism, racism and religious and political nationalisms. Hence, any community, religious or other, must continually reflect upon its beliefs, doctrines and actions in order to determine whether they are contributing to or obstructing the movement toward the realization of the human community.

There remains the all-important question of just *how* we determine whether our beliefs, ideas, or actions do further the well-being of the human community. The pragmatic response is at once deceptively simple and highly controversial—only by observing the consequences which follow from an idea or an action, according to pragmatism, can we discover those which are worthwhile. The objection springs to mind, which consequences? Actually any idea or action might and does give rise to numerous consequences, sometimes conflicting ones. For example, a consequence may be, or at least appear, good for an individual person but bad for the community. Or, an early consequence might appear good and later issue in bad consequences. I need not multiply these objections nor will I claim to be able to refute them. Actually I do not believe they can be refuted. They describe the complexity of the human condition rather than difficulties peculiar to pragmatism. Again, of course, one of my crucial assumptions is showing. I am assuming that there are no absolute or definitive resolutions to significant human problems; further, that while we do advance in many different ways, each advance gives rise to new problems or difficulties. If one objects that pragmatism is deficient because it cannot give, *a priori*, absolute resolutions to human problems, pragmatism can only reply that it cannot give such resolutions because it does not believe that the human situation allows them. At the same time, pragmatism refuses to accept as an alternative to absolutism, a destructive individualism, subjectivism or nihilism. Whatever shortcomings or difficulties are to be found in such thinkers as Pierce, James and Dewey, it is simply a failure to read them on any but the most superficial level which would interpret them as saying that "anything goes" or that every individual can make up whatever values or truths he *feels* like. No, each of these men in his own way believed and endeavored to show that men can live and live more fully without the aid of absolutes and in the absence of absolute certainty even in those matters which bear most deeply and intimately upon human life.

Critics often overlook the fact that the pragmatist does not pretend to start from scratch—to think and act as if man had no past. "We can be aware of consequences," Dewey tells us, "only because of previous experiences."[15] Experience cumulates and it is this cumulative experience, funded with intelligence, which is the basis for projecting beyond the present. Ideas, beliefs, ideals, are all in a sense hypotheses; they are guides to further thought and action but the only way we have of winnowing out and developing those which are of worth is by continually attending to the consequences which ensue—by observing the quality of life to which they give rise. Hence, the human community is, in the broad sense, experimental and self-correcting. Though it does achieve consummatory moments, these are never absolute or final but simultaneously serve as instruments for further development.

I am contending that these are the general conditions for all beliefs and actions, and the belief in God or religious activities are not exempt from them. I am, of course, rejecting any claim to a privileged source of knowledge or experience which enables a religion or its beliefs or doctrines to escape the demanding test of service to the human community.

Given a framework such as I have all too briefly described, how does one go about handling the God-question? It should be immediately evident that the inability of man to prove God's existence or even to "know" him is not as disastrous within this framework or world-view as it is in a more rationalistic one. Since knowledge is but one of a number of important and indispensable human experiences, faith in God is not ruled out or relegated to an inferior role in human life simply because it is not a form of knowledge. Lest one imagine that this is offered as a facile defense of such faith, I would quickly add that justification for faith in God or pragmatic terms is a more, not a less, demanding task. As I have already indicated, the lived life of the community (in contrast to some idealization or conceptualization of it) is, in the long-run, the only compelling evidence for the worth and authenticity of its faith. But an important element in its life is what I shall simply call "the reflective." This is not manifest to the same degree in all the members of the community, but it is the function of some of the members to attempt to express and develop faith by means of creative and imaginative thought patterns. Of course, the enormity of this task will lead to a number of sub-divisions of this function. Though no group of thinkers can remain in complete isolation from any others, I might suggest as working-designations that those who try to relate the scientific or philosophical thought and experience of mankind to the faith of the community be called "philosophical theologians"; those who concentrate on the central texts of the community be known as "biblical theologians"; and those who center their attention upon the doctrines or the particularized expressions of the community's faith might be called "doctrinal theologians."

Regardless of how we label the reflective or intellectual effort of the community, "the experiments of history make clear," as Randall points out, "that the scheme of understanding employed must be a scheme which illuminates man and his experience."[16] Of course, in the initial stages of its presentation, no theology, philosophical or other, can be much more than a rather vague and imprecise hypothesis or string of hypotheses. These hypotheses suggest the fruits which possibly will follow from adhering to them, but only actual emergence of these fruits will lend depth and authenticity to such hypotheses. Even at best no such effort can do more than give a relative fulfillment or verification. Thus there can be no finished or complete theology, even in its basic principles, for the very dynamism and mystery of faith will always elude definitive expression.

Before venturing some speculations or hypotheses on God, I would like to touch upon the possibility of "experiencing God" and the meaning of the activity which I am referring to as "reconstructing God."

IV. ON EXPERIENCING GOD

SINCE I have made so much of the point that God is unknowable, it might be assumed that I am preparing the way for some kind of experience of God. This is so only in a highly qualified sense. In the first place, there is no direct experience of God such as there is of other persons or of things. Still, I have acknowledged a mode of experience which I have designated "faith," and I have allowed for the possibility of an experience called "faith in God." "Faith in God," however, is not the equivalent of "direct experience of God." This is not a question to be managed in a few words, but perhaps I can indicate something of what I mean by showing how Dewey explains the role of "mystical experience" and what he calls the "sense of the whole."

Dewey does not deny the existence, authenticity and importance of experiences called "mystical." He insists, however, that they cannot be employed as proofs of God's existence, either for the one who undergoes such experiences or for others who recognize them in their fellow-men. "In reality," Dewey states, "the only thing that can be said to be 'proved' is the existence of some complex of conditions that have operated to effect an adjustment in life, an orientation, that brings with it a sense of security and peace."[17]

Dewey is, in my opinion, quite correctly distinguishing between "mystical experience" as a phenomenon and "mystical experience" as conclusive evidence of God's existence. I would add that if a mystic says that he has experiences of God, or the Absolute or Being or whatever, he is here making an act of faith. Again, I am emphasizing the radical and inescapable dimension of faith in man's relationship to God, even in those men who appear to be favored with experiences of great depth and intensity.

The situation is similar, I believe, in the question of the possibility of knowing and experiencing the "whole" or the "totality." Various forms of rationalism claim the ability to know the whole, whether as the Absolute or Being-as-such or as an ultimate principle of rationality in relation to which everything has reality. On the other hand, various empiricisms deny the possibility of such knowledge and tend to restrict knowledge to a plurality of particulars. Needless to say, there are temptations to excess, though in opposite directions, in both traditions. The great rationalistic efforts have tended to transform the mystery of the "whole" into a metaphysical principle, thereby leading to a loss of the richness of concrete experience and, incidentally, to a disastrous split between the God of the philosophers and God of Abraham. Reacting against these efforts, the great empiricisms have tended to suppress or minimize the "sense of the whole" attested to by the long and varied mystical tradition. The result has been an impoverishment of that very experience which empiricism hails.

Without suggesting that pragmatism has succeeded, or that it is alone in its effort, I would maintain that pragmatism does endeavor to incorporate the best in both the rationalistic and the empirical traditions. With empiricism it denies the possibility of either experiencing or knowing the "ultimate" or the "whole" or the "totality." With rationalism, however, it does allow for a role for some such reality. This can be seen quite clearly not only in James but perhaps more significantly in Dewey. It is well known that James did not hesitate to describe himself as a "theist" and even as a "crass supernaturalist." In a number of places he affirmed that we are "part and parcel of a wider self"[18] —that we are "continuous with a more."[19] These, of course, are always faith-affirmations for James, but to those unsympathetic to any God-belief, such assertions are usually dismissed as an excess of emotion or superficiality of thought on the part of James. Hence, to discover somewhat the same phenomenon (not the same interpretation) or experiential claim in Dewey, who was profoundly critical of theism and supposedly much less "tender-minded" than James, suggests that we are dealing with a phenomenon which cannot be simply written off as a mere psychological and subjectivistic projection.

A number of texts might be cited to make my point, but nowhere does Dewey express more movingly and sensitively man's relation to the "whole" than in the following:

> A work of art elicits and accentuates this quality of being a whole and of belonging to the larger, all-inclusive, whole which is the universe in which we live. This fact, I think, is the explanation of that feeling of exquisite intelligibility and clarity we have in the presence of an object that is experienced with esthetic intensity. It explains also the religious feeling that accompanies intense esthetic perception. We are, as it were, introduced into a world beyond this world which is nevertheless the deeper reality of the world in which we live in our ordinary experiences. We are carried out beyond ourselves to find ourselves. I can see no psychological ground for such properties of an experience save that, somehow, the work of art operates to deepen and to raise to great clarity that sense of an enveloping undefined whole that accompanies every normal experience. This whole is then felt as an expansion of ourselves. For only one frustrated in a particular object of desire upon which he had staked himself, like Macbeth, finds that life is a tale told by an idiot, full of sound and fury, signifying nothing. Where egotism is not made the measure of reality and value, we are citizens of this vast world beyond ourselves, and any intense realization of its presence with and in us brings a peculiarly satisfying sense of unity in itself and with ourselves.[20]

A passage such as this presents a great temptation to the God-believer, since it is difficult to avoid appropriating it and seeing in it a variation on the traditional, "In Him we live and move and have our being." Easy appropriations are usually misleading especially in the case of Dewey. His hostility to all forms of theism never diminished, and I have no desire to show that "deep-down" he was a theist. But I do find his thought congenial to a radically reconstructed theism, particularly when that reconstruction employs to such a great extent Dewey's own principles and categories. My concern here, however, is to stress that for Dewey not only can we not claim to "prove" the existence of God from mystical or religious experiences, but we cannot even claim to have an experience of the whole-as-such, since the whole is never presented to us as a really existing object. We do have an experience of a certain "complex of conditions" which can be described as a "sense of the whole." Within such experiences we construct "particular interpretations" or "imaginative construings" and this is what, according to Dewey, is manifest in the various religious doctrines.

We are confronted, then, with a widely reported phenomenon which might be and has been interpreted in a variety of ways. Some call it

God, some, the universe, and some describe it as "nothingness," but in every instance there is an act of faith inasmuch as each interpretation is an affirmation beyond the evidence, whether that evidence is understood as experiential or rational. This faith-dimension is present even in the great rational or philosophical endeavors which are usually called speculative metaphysical systems. John Herman Randall's understanding of such systems is quite instructive.

"We never encounter *the* Universe," Randall says, "we never act toward, experience, or feel being or existence as 'a whole.' " Hence, there is "no discoverable 'ultimate context,' no 'ultimate substance' . . . . 'Ultimate' . . . is always relative, never 'absolute'; it is always 'ultimate for.' " Thus, Randall concludes that " 'the Universe,' or 'Nature,' is not 'a process'—a single process." Further, the "Universe" or "Nature" does not have any single meaning.[21]

The point which Randall is making is central to and distinctive of the kind of process philosophy which I have designated pragmatic. Randall's interpretation of process distinguishes pragmatism from other process philosophies such as Bergson's, Whitehead's, Hartshorne's or Teilhard's. The mark of distinction is that the empirical process philosophy of pragmatism does not admit the possibility of knowing or experiencing the process of reality as a single, unified whole. At the same time, pragmatism is distinct from more positivistic empiricisms in that it does not deny the legitimacy of thinking of or believing in reality as a single process. The propriety of such speculative constructivism is affirmed by Randall when, after denying that the universe can be known or experienced as "a whole" or a "single process," he maintains that nevertheless, "it is quite possible to take 'the universe' as a single process, with a single 'meaning.' Most of the great philosophies have done just this, to say nothing of a multitude of religious schemes." When this is done, however, it is necessary to "invent a further 'context' for 'the Universe' or Nature"—it is necessary to construct "metaphysical myths" such as the "Unmoved Mover" or the "Unconditioned Conditioner" or the "First Cause." These myths, Randall maintains, "are logical constructions or extrapolations, like physical theories, and they possess similar functions." Without going into the more complex aspects of these functions, suffice it to say that they serve to unify and give direction to a plurality of human and natural processes. Randall insists, then, not only that these "metaphysical myths" are not meaningless but that "they have a perfectly definite function which can be objectively inquired into. They may well be basic in the living of human life, which often gets *its* 'meaning' from their use—or rather, which uses them to find and express its 'meaning.' " In any event, Randall, citing Woodbridge, asserts that "it is faith, and not knowledge, that 'justifies.' "[22]

In summation, therefore, great mystical experiences and the great metaphysical systems are important, not because they are modes of knowledge which inform us about or in some way "represent" something called "God" or "Nature," but because they play an indispensable role in human life by contributing to its meaning, illumination, enrichment and development.

V. ON RECONSTRUCTING GOD

AT the outset of this essay, I acknowledged that many people will be offended by the suggestion that man "reconstructs God." Those whose ears are less sensitive and whose minds are less literal might quickly conclude that I have merely chosen a dramatic phrase or metaphor to express the activity which is more precisely and properly designated as reconstructing man's *concept* of God. Such an interpretation is quite tempting for it pacifies those who are outraged at the thought of any human influence on the reality of God and at the same time allows for some very radical revision and transformation of the traditional doctrine of God. Such a distinction, however, will not suffice. The conclusion that only man's concept of God can be reconstructed presupposes a particular concept of God, that of an absolutely immutable God. This, in my opinion, is the basic shortcoming of all theories of doctrinal development which try to restrict change to language, or concepts, or patterns of understanding. They are all variations on the assumption that the form of faith changes while the content remains the same. The world-view which I presuppose permits no such dualism. I cannot begin to treat the formidable question of the relation between thought, language and reality, but I hope that from what I have already said about pragmatism, it is evident that in a really processive world, thought and language are human means of participating in and contributing to this process. I readily acknowledge that the concept of a "process God" is a symbol, or, to use Randall's phrase, a "metaphysical myth." Hence, I am making no claim of knowing God "as he is in himself." The metaphysical absolute of "process" is not a substitute for the metaphysical absolute of "immutability." Since there is, on my terms, no possibility of our forming a concept or symbols of God which can then be proved, or even believed, as *representing* him, all such symbols must be evaluated on the pragmatic criterion which I have earlier described.

Pragmatism insists, as we have seen, that all activity, whether intellectual, artistic or religious, is ultimately justified in terms of its usefulness to the human community. Now the term "useful" is ambiguous at best and grossly misleading at worst. Critics of the pragmatic tradition accuse it of crass utilitarianism, of denying any value that goes beyond the practical. It is over forty years since Dewey lamented "the depreciated meaning that has come to be attached to the very meaning of the 'practical' and the useful." He goes on to say,

> Instead of being extended to cover all forms of action by means of which all the values of life are extended and rendered more secure,

including the diffusion of the fine arts and the cultivation of taste, the processes of education and all activities which are concerned with rendering human relationships more significant and worthy, the meaning of 'practical' is limited to matters of ease, comfort, riches, bodily security and police order, possibly health, etc., things which in their isolation from other goods can only lay claim to restricted and narrow value.[23]

This one text scarcely handles all the subtleties and aspects of a long-standing philosophical controversy. It does indicate, however, that the pragmatic criterion of "useful" is more complex than many critics think. If one understands "useful" at its deepest level to mean whatever contributes to the enrichment and development of the quality of life, one avoids the more restricted meaning of individual or short-range satisfaction. Paradoxically, even the value of an approach which claims to seek knowledge or art for their "own sakes" is due to the fruitful consequences which result from such an approach. By not seeking the immediate practical results or the use for a limited and restricted context, great scientists and artists have contributed immeasurably to the quality of life of the human community.

Again, I do not mean to imply that pragmatism supplies us with a precise and clear-cut standard of judgment. On the contrary, all our judgments are relative and in continual need of refinement and reconstruction. Even the judgment that the worth of ideas or activities depends on their usefulness must be constantly refined. The paradoxical dimension of this judgment is nowhere more in evidence than in the religious sphere.

Recent religious self-criticism would seem to be an explicit repudiation of any pragmatic defense of religion or faith in God. We have recently heard that the "god of gaps," the god who answers our questions or serves as an explanatory principle of the world, is dead. We have become acutely aware of how religion can be used to fulfill neurotic needs, to pacify men and protect them from the anguish and terrors of the human situation. These and other such "uses" of God or religion are, I am sure, repugnant to most reflective men. Yet, at the same time, from many of those advancing such criticisms, there is the demand that God or religion be relevant to the on-going questions of man; and there is also the insistence that the Church is justified only in terms of its service to the human community. What is happening is not that we are discarding a God and a religion which were "useful" in favor of a God and a religion which transcend use. Rather, we are attempting to transform our faith in God so as to render it *more* useful, that is, useful in a fuller, richer and wider context.

VI. SOME SPECULATIVE FORAYS

AGAINST this background, I would like to indicate a few of the speculations which arise by way of a pragmatic reconstruction of God.

At best such speculative forays can only be probes, tentative suggestions or hypotheses. These initial steps, if they are in any way successful, must bring forth criticism, qualifying refinements, and developments from other members of the community. Of course, such steps are not peculiar to speculation in the realm of religious thought—these are the operating conditions of all thought. It is now a commonplace to assert that the absolutely solitary thinker is a non-existent abstraction. It is only in and through community that man is able to be and to think. This does not deny a dimension of individuality but recognizes that the only adequate corrective for and stimulus of individual ideas or theories is the community, not, of course, the community as some abstract or absolute norm, but the community as a living and developing interrelationship of individual persons. Neither the members nor the community have any reality in themselves—they are literally co-constitutors of each other.[24] Such a view of the relationship between person and community enables us to avoid excesses of both individualism and collectivism. Though it does not present us with definitive and absolute resolutions to basic human problems, it does give us guidelines according to which we can make some progress in our struggle with these problems.

In general, the scientific community presents us with a model for speculation in that it sets no absolute limits on speculation nor does it allow even its most basic principles to escape creative critical scrutiny. Nevertheless, not every speculation is accorded equal weight. To receive serious consideration, a hypothesis must have an inner coherence, be reasonably consistent with what is already known, and explain the phenomena which it is formed to explain. Of course, only a further process of experimental verification can determine whether it does explain those phenomena. If the scientific community is able to function and flourish in the absence of absolutes and absolute certainty, I would suggest that a religious community supposedly characterized by a faith in what must ultimately be acknowledged as beyond conceiving, beyond naming and beyond experiencing directly—in short, a faith in the mystery of reality—such a community ought also to be able to live without any absolutely certain underpinning or conclusions. I would go further, such a community should itself be the model of openness, rich diversity of thought and experience, constant self-criticism and continual and radical reconstruction. When the Church has become such a community, there will no longer be need for long-winded apologies such as this to prepare the way for some rather modest speculations.

In an age characterized by the "death of God" and an encroaching despair and nihilism, the particular features of the various religions, including so-called secular religions, are secondary to the prior question as to whether there is any longer the possibility for some kind of meaning-affirmation concerning human existence. A character in one of the plays of Albert Camus says the following:

> To lose one's life is no great matter; when the time comes I'll have the courage to lose mine. But what's intolerable is to see one's life being drained of meaning, to be told there's no reason for existing. A man can't live without some reason for living.[25]

Camus concludes "that the meaning of life is the most urgent of questions."[26] Surely the current dissatisfaction and rebellion on the part of young people cannot be understood apart from a deep desire and longing for meaning. During the student upheaval at Berkeley several years ago, one of the students was quoted as saying, "We insist upon, we demand meaning." To recognize the desire and need for meaning, however, is much easier than being able to satisfy it.

I believe that "faith in God" is one mode of meaning-affirmation. To indicate how I understand this, let me briefly describe the various interpretations which might be attached to the general assertion that "man's life has meaning." This might be understood as maintaining either that meaning is rooted in the essential structures of reality or that reality allows for the creation of meaning on the part of man. Each of these can then be subdivided; thus, some of those who hold that meaning is rooted in the essential structures of reality interpret this to say that there is meaning because there are values in the structure of reality whether or not God exists, for example, certain Renaissance and Enlightenment philosophers. Others account for these values in terms of God as the giver of meaning as do most religions.

Similarly, the view that man is the creator of meaning or values is understood in two different ways. For some it means that man, acting alone, grafts meaning onto reality, as the various forms of atheistic and secular humanisms believe. I contend, however, that man the creator of meaning can also be understood as affirming that man, in response to a "call" from and in cooperation with the *Other*, whom we traditionally call God, grafts meaning onto reality. Thus, as I would interpret this, man recognizes and accepts responsibility for the creation of himself and the world, without falling prey to any self-deification. The "call," symbolically understood, is the awareness which man has of the need continually to move beyond himself in order to realize himself and the world. But the manner and form of this movement must be *created* by man, and it is not merely the imitation of some eternally ordained pattern rooted in the mind of God. Man is, nevertheless, spurred on and energized by the belief that he is responding to and cooperating with an *Other*. Man thereby believes that what he is doing is participating in a process that is more inclusive than himself. Further, he can trust this *Other* to support those human efforts and achievements which are worthy of support. He cannot, however, expect this *Other* to play the role of a *Deus ex machina* and thereby protect man from hurt or get him out of "jams" or even give absolute assurance that the entire human effort will not fail.

Before indicating some of the more crucial implications of this position, I wish to suggest that what I have just done is the initial phase of a pragmatic reconstruction of "faith in God." Such a reconstruction affirms continuity with the earlier faith of the community while at the same time introducing a radical transformation of that faith. Further, it is reasonably consistent with the processive and relational worldview which I am presupposing. Finally, I believe that it enables "faith in God" to meet the pragmatic criterion which I described earlier.

To continue with this pragmatic reconstruction, let me cite a few reasons advanced by James as justification for "faith in God." James states: "If the hypothesis of God works satisfactorily in the widest sense of the word, it is true. Now whatever its residual difficulties may be, experience shows that it certainly does work, and that the problem is to build it out and determine it so that it will combine satisfactorily with all the other working truths."[27] In a later work, James notes that "Christian and non-Christian critics alike accuse me of summoning people to say 'God exists,' *even when he doesn't exist,* because forsooth in my philosophy the 'truth' of the saying doesn't really mean that he exists in any shape whatever, but only that to say so feels good."[28] His critics, according to James, miss the point of what he was trying to do, which is to express the meaning of the concept of God in terms of a "positive experiential operation." Specifically, the concept of God means "the presence of 'promise' in the world. 'God or no God?' means 'promise or no promise?'"[29]

Elsewhere James asserts that theism "changes the dead blank *it* of the world into a living *thou,* with whom the whole man may have dealings."[30] Also, for James, "theism means the affirmation of an eternal moral order and the letting loose of hope."[31]

James does not intend that any of these assertions be understood as beyond argument or as supplying definitive evidence or proof for the reality of God. It is worth noting that Dewey gave a sharply different interpretation to "faith in God"—at least as expressed in the history of religion. More often than not, Dewey held, such faith tended to de-energize rather than energize men. According to Dewey,

> Men have never fully used the powers they possess to advance the good in life, because they have waited upon some power external to themselves and to nature to do the work they are responsible for doing.[32]

My concern here is not to argue for the interpretation of either James or Dewey but rather to underline what has been an underlying theme of this paper, namely, that in the matter of the meaning of human life, there is no avoiding an act of faith which can at best be reinforced by experience and evidence which will always remain ambiguous and inconclusive.

This point must be continually kept in mind by those desirous of extending the dialogue between theists and atheists. Both manifest a deep concern for the meaning of human life, the necessity for hope, and the crucial role of the future, but one believes that "faith in God" is a help while the other believes that it is a hindrance. Those on both sides of the question are now becoming aware that they must avoid any polemical approach which attempts to prove the superiority of their respective faiths. Nevertheless, a sentimentalized dialogue surely must also be avoided. To assert that we are all saying or believing the same thing, but that we are using different words to express it, is an affront to the seriousness of both positions.

Following James, I would hold that "faith in God" makes a difference in the life of both man and the universe. Did it not, the entire pragmatic justification which I have been advancing would be undermined. "The whole defense of religious faith hinges upon action," according to James. "If the action required or inspired by the religious hypothesis is in no way different from that dictated by the naturalistic hypothesis, then religious faith is purely superfluity, better pruned away, and controversy about its legitimacy is a piece of idle trifling, unworthy of serious minds."[33] Again I stress that the affirmation of difference is a *belief* and hence one should not imagine that there will be clear and definitive evidence to support it. This is especially important at the present moment when Christianity is undergoing a transformation whereby increasingly the characteristics which allegedly differentiated it from humanism are being dropped or radically modified. There is, consequently, a deep crisis of identity on the part of those Christians who now recognize that many who profess no faith in God live lives of deep meaning and commitment. Since such Christians are hesitant to claim that so-called secularists or humanists are Christians without knowing it, it becomes more and more difficult to isolate values or activities which can be designated Christian. Actually, I do not think that such an effort, particularly at this time, is very fruitful. We must have the courage to act as we claim to believe and trust that the life which ensues will be adequate testimony to the authenticity of our faith.

That faith in God does make a difference follows from James' understanding of faith as an indispensable creative principle in the development of the universe. If the universe were an essentially finished entity, or if man's destiny were already determined, then faith would be little more than a guess as to what the universe is and whether man will reach his pre-determined goal. Since, however, man and the universe are very much in the making, faith and hope play creative roles in what man and the universe shall be. As James puts it, "Work is still doing in the world-process,"[34] and, hence, faith "may be regarded as a formative factor in the universe."[35]

Much of what I have been saying up to this point will appear, even to those of a more traditional mind-set, acceptable or at least reconcilable, when properly qualified, with classical Christian doctrine. After all, it is very difficult today to be against man accepting his responsibility for the making of himself or man playing a more creative role in the universe. Now I am not prepared to *prove* that these new affirmations cannot be simply added onto the earlier doctrines without any basic modifications of those doctrines. Nevertheless, I am prepared to argue against this possibility, for I think that it betrays an inadequate philosophy of change. It tends to view change after the fashion of a mechanical building-block image whereby new ideas are simply laid upon old ones without any real change in the old ideas. Such a view is, in my opinion, manifest in certain Roman Catholic leaders who keep hailing the great and significant changes made since Vatican II but quickly add that nothing basic, essential or fundamental has changed.

A more organic view of change recognizes that there can be no significant addition to the organism which does not, to some extent, transform the organism in *all* its aspects. Such a view, of course, does not claim that all ideas or activities are equally transforming of the organism nor that some parts are not more immediately affected by certain actions than others. Nor does it overlook varying rates of change such that some aspects of the organism may change so slowly and imperceptively as to give the impression of being unchanging. For the purposes of this paper, I simply wish to keep open the possibility that the changes which are now being accepted, and indeed sought, by Christians in general and Roman Catholics in particular, will lead to transformations of doctrine more radical than anything we have yet encountered. While this will be threatening to many and appear to jeopardize, if not destroy, Christianity, I believe that such a challenge can be met and indeed welcomed by a view of "faith in God" which refuses to identify this faith with even its most ancient and cherished formulations.

In order to illustrate a bit more concretely what I am driving at, let me briefly consider the traditional attributes of divine immutability, omniscience and omnipotence. Again, I must emphasize that these, like all other concepts, symbols or images, whether they appear in theology, in conciliar or papal documents, in dogmatic formulations or in the Scriptures, are historically and culturally conditioned; all are human constructs. This does not mean that they are merely subjectivistic or psychological projections, since the Christian can *believe* that they are articulations of the community involving a continuing existential faith-encounter with God. Nevertheless, we must accept responsibility for the language, concepts and symbols. We cannot attribute them to God and then refuse to do the hard work of continually evaluating them in the light of new experience. A pragmatic reconstruction does not determine, *a priori,* that *any* much less *all* of these symbols or concepts must be discarded. It does, however, refuse to admit, *a priori,* that any of them has such a privileged status as to escape the continuing critical scrutiny of the community.

When we turn to "divine immutability," the first question is whether that notion still serves as a meaningful symbol in which to express our faith in God. It is understandable that in an age and culture in which *immutability* was the distinguishing mark of reality as against appearance, of knowledge as against opinion—that in such a culture reflection upon God would inevitably assign this characteristic to him in the highest degree. In a culture, however, in which growth, creative novelty, development and process are viewed as the most significant traits of reality, it would seem that the symbol of a "processive God" is more meaningful. As I have indicated above, this is not a claim of knowing God "as he is in himself"—such a possibility has been ruled out since the concept of "God existing in Himself" is unacceptable within a world-view for which there are no radically independent entities. This, of course, does not mean that God cannot possess a reality greater than that expressed in our symbols. On the contrary, it is the awareness that the symbols are *our* constructs which continually protects the "moreness" of the mystery which faith affirms. Nor does the "construct" aspect of our concepts or symbols render them subjectivistic or unreal. Since symbolization and conceptualization are means by which man participates in and contributes to the development of reality, the worth and truth of such symbols and concepts depends upon their serving this function.

The objection might be raised that while religious symbols can be shown to have served an illuminating and energizing function in the past, they were able to do this because they were not consciously recognized as symbols. The question now is, can we be conscious that we are the authors of our symbols and still have them serve the function which they have served in the past. Needless to say, the only convincing evidence that they can so function depends upon the life of the community which employs symbols in this manner. The best that a speculative effort such as this can do is to suggest what the positive fruits of a particular symbol might be. It can also call attention to the fact that works of art and literature play roles similar to that suggested for religious symbols, and no one seems compelled to suggest that they are not human constructs or creations. "Art," Dewey contends, "has been the means of keeping alive the sense of purposes that outrun evidence and of means that transcend indurated habit."[36]

What advantages, then, might there be in substituting the symbol of a "processive God" for that of a "immutable God"? First, it is a symbol more congenial to the best thought and experience of the present age. It also enhances the importance of man's activities, for in a very real sense we are involved in the creation of the world, ourselves and, perhaps, even God. If God is really related to man, and if man can really bring forth novel realities which are not simply pale imitations of ideas in God's mind, then what God will be is to some extent dependent upon us. This is not a simple restatement of Feuerbach's assertion that God is merely a creation of man. Instead, it is an attempt to forge a new alternative beyond both objectivism and subjectivism. This is made manifest by recognizing that a "processive God" can also be an everlastingly enduring God; that is, he can continue to be, without necessarily continuing *to be* in the same way. From a religious point of view, therefore, we retain the value of believing in a God whose life is greater and more extensive than man's, while simultaneously affirming an intimate involvment of man in this life. As James tells us, "God himself . . . may draw vital strength and increase of very being from our fidelity."[37] Surely such a belief would seem to have the possibility of enhancing man's life and spurring him on to greater efforts without placing him in competition with God.

The notion of divine omniscience also presents great difficulty within the world I am assuming. Any contention that there is a being who knows everything, past, present and future, must presuppose that there is no possibility for any radical novelty emerging in reality. Hence, from such a perspective, reality does not really change except in some surface fashion of particularizing what already pre-exists in some manner in God. Since the concept of divine omniscience would seem to reduce man to a mere imitator, thereby depriving him of creative autonomy, I suggest that it is no longer a serviceable symbol.

What about the doctrine of divine omnipotence? There is, of course, nothing new in affirming the reality of God and denying that he is all-powerful. It has always been assumed, however, that one could not believe as a Christian without believing that God is omnipotent. If it is man, as I am suggesting, rather than God, who has formed the concept of divine omnipotence, then, as a minimum, the matter is open for reconsideration even on the part of Christian thinkers.

I will make no attempt to present even in sketchy form the arguments for and against divine omnipotence. It will suffice to recall that the classical objections to this attribute have always centered around the reality of evil. If one is determined to continue believing that God is omnipotent then nothing will really count against this and, as the history of philosophy attests, there will never be lacking explanations for any data which appear to threaten this belief. The question I would pose is this: would we believe in divine omnipotence unless we believed that it is inseparably bound up with other aspects of the faith which we are unwilling to surrender? I do not believe that we would; "divine omnipotence" has been an albatross carried by the Christian faith long enough and it is high time we jettisoned it. We cannot disprove the reality of divine omnipotence; the question is whether this is a worthy symbol for man at his present level of consciousness. I submit that it is not, for in spite of all the distinctions, qualifications and rationalizations, does not divine omnipotence ultimately imply that God has the power to stop the misery and suffering which characterize the world but he chooses not to use it? Is it any wonder then, that a significant group of reflective men, when forced to choose between such a God or no God, have without hesitancy declared their atheism?

I do not wish to sentimentalize an immensely complex question, but I must insist that the anguished experience of contemporary man cannot be dismissed as simply the latest expression of the failure to grasp the distinction between God's *causing* evil and his *permitting* it.

The question has been raised, "After Auschwitz, can one continue to believe in God?" There is, in my opinion, a companion question, "After Auschwitz, can one continue to believe in man?" My response to both questions is really a response to a single question, namely, is human life meaningful? I have affirmed that it is, but only on the condition that both man and God are cooperatively involved in an unfinished work. While a God of power is no longer a fruitful symbol of man's faith, a God of love is, particularly when the processive incarnation of that love depends upon man's faith, hope and love.

NOTES

[1] Morris Raphael Cohen, *A Preface to Logic* (New York: Meridian Books, 1956), p. 200.

[2] John Dewey, *Experience and Nature* (New York: Dover Publications, 1958), p. 222.

[3] *Ibid.*, p. 246.

[4] William James, *The Writings of William James—A Comprehensive Edition*, edited with an "Introduction" and "Annotated Bibliography" by John J. McDermott (New York: Random House, 1967), p. 513. Hereafter referred to as *Writings*.

[5] James, *Writings*, p. 606.

[6] This is true, of course, of any group of thinkers who are gathered together under the same label or within the same period.

[7] John Dewey, *Logic: The Theory of Inquiry* (New York: Holt, 1939), p. 67.

[8] John A. T. Robinson, *Exploration in God* (Stanford: Stanford University Press, 1967), Chapter five. Also, on the all-pervasiveness of the relational, see Alfred North Whitehead, *Religion In The Making* (New York: Meridian, 1960), p. 104. "There is no entity, not even God, 'which requires nothing but itself in order to exist'. ... Every entity is in its essence social and requires the society in order to exist."

For a fine analysis of "the nature of existence as relatedness," see Eulalio R. Baltazar, *Teilhard and the Supernatural* (Baltimore: Helicon, 1966), pp. 121-129; *The Dynamic in Christian Thought*, ed. Joseph Papin, pp. 223-53.

[9] Of course the effort to overcome the destructive dualism implicit in subjective and objective as different realms of being or reality is not restricted to American philosophers. Contemporary Existentialists and Phenomenologists are also struggling with this question.

[10] For an exposition of the "transcendental method" as employed by such men as Karl Rahner, André Marc, Emerich Coreth and Bernard Lonergan, see Otto Muck, S.J., *The Transcendental Method* (New York: Herder and Herder, 1968).

[11] Henri Bouillard, "A Dialogue With Barth: The Problem of Natural Theology," *Cross Currents* (Spring, 1968), p. 218.

[12] William James, *The Letters of William James*, 2 vols., edited by Henry James (Boston: Atlantic Monthly Press, 1920), I, p. 270.

[13] John Dewey, *Reconstruction In Philosophy* (Boston: The Beacon Press, 1957), p. 58.
[14] John Dewey, *A Common Faith* (New Haven: Yale University Press, 1960), pp. 23, 43.
[15] John Dewey, *Experience and Education* (New York: The Macmillan Company, 1956), p. 79.
[16] John Herman Randall, Jr., *The Role of Knowledge in Western Religion* (Boston: Starr King Press, 1958), p. 37.
[17] Dewey, *A Common Faith*, p. 13.
[18] James, *Writings*, p. 297.
[19] William James, *Varieties of Religious Experience* (New York: Modern Library, c.r. 1902), p. 499.
[20] John Dewey, *Art As Experience* (New York: Capricorn Books, 1958), p. 195.
[21] John Herman Randall, Jr., *Nature and Historical Experience* (New York: Columbia University Press, 1958), pp. 198-199.
[22] *Ibid.*, pp. 199-201.
[23] John Dewey, *The Quest For Certainty* (New York: Minton, Balch & Co., 1929), p. 32.
[24] For a description of the way in which man and society have their reality only in an ongoing dialectical relationship, see Peter L. Berger and Thomas Luckman, *The Social Construction of Reality* (New York: Doubleday & Co., Inc. 1966).
[25] Albert Camus, *Caligula And Three Other Plays*, translated by Stuart Gilbert (New York: Alfred A. Knopf, 1958), p. 21.
[26] Albert Camus, *The Myth of Sisyphus*, translated from the French by Justin O'Brien (New York: Alfred A. Knopf, 1955), p. 4.
[27] James, *Writings*, pp. 471-472.
[28] *William James*, edited by Joseph L. Blau (New York: Washington Square Press, 1963), p. 137.
[29] *Ibid.*, p. 137.
[30] William James, "Reflex Action and Theism," in *The Will To Believe* (New York: Dover, 1956), p. 127.
[31] James, *Writings*, p. 354.
[32] Dewey, *A Common Faith*, p. 46.
[33] James, *Writings*, p. 734.
[34] *Ibid.*, p. 736.
[35] *Ibid.*, p. 737.
[36] Dewey, *Art As Experience*, p. 348.
[37] James, *The Will to Believe*, p. 61.

SELECTED BIBLIOGRAPHY

Altizer, Thomas J. J. and Hamilton, William, *Radical Theology and the Death of God* (New York: The Bobbs-Merrill Co., Inc., 1966).

Baltazar, Eulalio R., *Teilhard and the Supernatural* (Baltimore: Helicon, 1966).

Baum, Gregory, ed., *The Future of Belief Debate* (New York: Herder and Herder, 1967).

Berger, Peter L., *The Precarious Vision* (New York: Doubleday & Co., Inc., 1961).

——— and Luckman, Thomas, *The Social Construction of Reality* New York: Doubleday & Co., Inc., 1966).

Blau, Joseph L., ed., *William James* (New York: Washington Square Press, 1963).

Blewett, John, ed., *John Dewey: His Thought and Influence* (New York: Fordham University Press, 1960).

Camus, Albert, *Caligula and Three Other Plays*, tr. by Stuart Gilbert (New York: Alfred A. Knopf, 1958).
────── *The Myth of Sisyphus*, tr. from the French by Justin O'Brien (New York: Alfred A. Knopf, 1955).
Carey, John J. and Ice, Jackson Lee, editors, *The Death of God Debate* (Philadelphia: The Westminster Press, 1967).
Cohen, Morris Raphael, *A Preface to Logic* (New York: Meridian Books, 1956).
Dewart, Leslie, *The Future of Belief* (New York: Herder and Herder, 1966).
Dewey, John, *Art As Experience* (New York: Capricorn Books, 1958).
────── *A Common Faith* (New Haven: Yale Univ. Press, 1960).
────── *Experience and Education* (New York: The Macmillan Co., 1956).
────── *Experience and Nature* (New York: Dover Publications, 1958).
────── *Logic: The Theory of Inquiry* (New York: Holt, 1939).
────── *Reconstruction In Philosophy* (Boston: The Beacon Press, 1957).
────── *The Quest For Certainty* (New York: Minton, Balch & Co., 1929).
Flew, Antony and MacIntyre, Alasdair, *New Essays In Philosophical Theology* (New York: The Macmillan Co., 1955).
Fontinell, Eugene, "Reflections on Faith and Metaphysics," *Cross Currents* (Winter, 1966), pp. 15-40.
────── "Religious Truth in a Relational and Processive World," *Cross Currents* (Summer 1967), pp. 283-315.
Garaudy, Roger, *From Anathema to Dialogue*, tr. by Luke O'Neil (New York: Herder and Herder, 1966).
Hick, John, ed., *Faith and the Philosophers* (New York: St. Martin's Press, 1964).
James, William, *The Writings of William James—A Comprehensive Edition*, edited with an "Introduction" and "Annotated Bibliography" by John J. McDermott (New York: Random House, 1967).
────── *The Letters of William James*, 2 vols. edited by Henry James (Boston: Atlantic Monthly Press, 1920).
────── *Varieties of Religious Experience* (New York: Modern Library, c.r., 1902).
────── *The Will to Believe* (New York: Dover, 1956).
Johann, Robert, *The Pragmatic Meaning of God* (Milwaukee: Marquette University Press, 1966).
Michalson, Carl, *The Rationality of Faith* (New York: Charles Scribner's Sons, 1963).
Muck, Otto, *The Transcendental Method* (New York: Herder and Herder, 1968).
Novak, Michael, *Belief and Unbelief* (New York: The Macmillan Co., 1965).
Ogden, Schubert M., *The Reality of God* (New York: Harper & Row, 1963).
Randall, John Herman, Jr., *Nature and Historical Experience* (New York: Columbia University Press, 1958).
────── *The Role of Knowledge in Western Religion* (Boston: Starr King Press, 1958).
Robinson, John A. T., *Exploration In God* (Stanford: Stanford University Press, 1967).

Thayer, H. S., *Meaning and Action: A Critical History of Pragmatism* (New York: The Bobbs-Merrill Co., Inc., 1968).
Whitehead, Alfred North, *Religion In The Making* (New York: Meridian, 1960).

The Role of the Bible in the Theology of the Future

Krister Stendahl

THE role of the Bible in the theology of the future is an important question at this stage of theological development. My thesis is quite simply that those of us who have been riding high and beautifully on the wave of biblical theology during the last decades have perhaps had our best time. The imperialism of the biblical theologians in the theological enterprise has come to an end. And this might be difficult to face, especially in the Roman Catholic realm, where such a major role of the biblical theologian has just begun. To be sure, the last decades have been strong on biblical theology. The biblical theologians have caught the imagination, engendered the hopes for renewal, and given nurture to genuine *reformatio*. In most Protestant theology called neo-orthodox and post-liberal, there has been the tacit respect for the biblical starting point. This all has its more recent Roman Catholic equivalents with the Congars and the Schnackenburgs and the Benoits, and with David Stanley and John McKenzie and Raymond Brown in this country.

An indication of the strength of biblical theology in the theological discussion is that for quite some time the words which a theologically literate person should be able to pronounce and spell have been "kerygma" and "hermeneutics." Each age is marked by its catch-words. Two generations ago it was "eschatology" and then it was "kerygma," and now it is "hermeneutics," the principles of interpretation. In that mood much theology has been written in a way that suggests that the basic problem of theology is one of translation or of interpretation of the biblical material. This interest in hermeneutics is indicative of our present theological climate. It is striking that the first and the second editions of the famous German encyclopedia *Religion in Geschichte und Gegenwart* had no article on hermeneutics but the third edition which came in the 60's has 20 columns on hermeneutics. The great interest in hermeneutics is a monument to the fact that, for a long period, theology has worked on the presupposition that *im Anfang war der Text*—in the beginning was the text—and it is with the biblical material that all begins. When one starts to think about it, it is not surprising that the impact for this kind of hermeneutical theology came from Protestant Germany. Its tacit presuppositions are that of an evangelical biblicism.

This biblicism has joined forces with other tendencies in the academic theological enterprise. We are faced with what is best understood as a somewhat unholy alliance between secular historicism and Christian biblicism. This is a strange and bewildering mixture where the historian kept talking about how it was in the first century, but the biblically believing Christian felt that he was nurtured by the good book. Thus, traditional biblicism merged with the pure historian's great preoccupation with the origin of Christianity. There is the genetic fallacy, so natural to Protestant theology, i.e., the conviction that once you know the origin, the original, then you have the essence and the full truth. Later developments are seen in negative terms. The pure Gospel is polluted, diluted, etc., and this unbeatable combination has given a very strong impact to what I call biblical theology—an impact which has given to the theological enterprise many of the best things that are around today.

When I suggest that this era is about to come to an end, I want to make clear, nevertheless, that this has been an extremely productive and significant period; and although I hail its coming to an end for good reasons, I also hail and rejoice in the contribution of this period of biblical theology. Some of the more common results of this period of biblical thelogy are well known and commonplace today. The most famous ones I suppose are found in slogans like "the biblical God is the God of action, not the God of propositions"; G. Ernest Wright's book *God Who Acts* is representative of a whole stream of thought-habits, now deeply ingrained in the minds of theologians and preachers in our land. The value-laden distinction between the Greek and the Hebrew was one of the marks of this kind of theology: Hebrew thought was dynamic, psychosomatic, divine; Greek thought was inferior, static, marred by the dualism between soul and body and other terrible things. The breakdown of good Christian theology took place when the Greek mind polluted the biblical, Hebraic, Semitic understanding of man, God, history, etc. This was the era of word studies, and etymology became a delightful tool for theologizing. We learned with awe that the word for "word" in Hebrew, *dabar,* means not only word, but thing, and you have the thing and the word in one, and anyone with a fertile theological mind gets much stimulation out of such linguistic observations. So the word was not only the word but the action, even the saving act of God, and it was all wrapped up in Semitic beauty.

The lasting impact of biblical theology with its emphasis on the mythopoeic and Semitic nature of much biblical thought is perhaps well understood if we quote a phrase of Jesus from his discussion of divorce: "but from the beginning it was not so" (Mt. 19:8). Biblical theology gave to the theological enterprise a refreshing and powerful leverage against the orthodox tradition of development. There was a time—even *the* time of pristine origin—when the faith was expressed in other terms than those of the Western tradition of creedal orthodoxy.

Even the great mind of St. Paul did not understand substances, or *con-* and *trans*-substantiation. There was even a time, says the biblical theologian—and he is right—when it was quite proper to have an adoptionist Christology (Acts 2:36, Rom. 1:4). It is certainly very difficult if not impossible to find any explicit reference or even implicit reference to trinitarianism in the Bible. So "from the beginning it was not so," has been the refrain of the biblical theologian. And this has given to the theological enterprise a vision of rich alternatives, a liberating relativism, a critical leverage. I think this is and will remain the main contribution of the era of biblical theology.

Let me give another example. I have my serious doubts that according to the New Testament record the God and Father of Jesus Christ is half as almighty as the proper philosophical theologian likes to picture him. As far as I can learn from the Gospels, all the evil that happens is not referred to God, or even God's permission, but to Satan, the infamous doublecrosser. God's omnipotence is an *eschatological* omnipotence—he will ultimately be victorious, but for now it is touch and go at best. That is why we pray in the Lord's Prayer, "lead us not into temptation but deliver us from evil," because if we really got entrapped by evil, we would have no chance at all. That is why we do not ask for strength but plead that we be rescued and plead that the situation will not come where we are caught; cf. Mt. 24:22, "If those days were not shortened, no human being would be saved." Or remember how Paul says to the Corinthians that they have not been tested to the utmost, but if that situation comes God would supply an *ekbasis,* an emergency exit (1 Cor. 10:13). This kind of thinking about good and evil, God and Satan, is not quite the proper theological way of expressing the different attributes of God where there could be no word before which one could not add the *omni-*.

That is another world. Thus, what biblical theology has given us is that critical leverage "from the beginning it was not so." And that is good. But as this era is now coming to an end, it does so partly because this leverage has been abused in a dangerous way. We must guard ourselves against tendencies according to which we are informed that God wants "good Christians" to act like first century Semites. It does not follow that since it was different in these ancient times, it was also better in all respects. Such is the over-zealous claim implicit and explicit in much biblical theology, where one somehow confuses the fact that things were different with the claim that there should or could be no further development.

That claim has never had a natural home in the Roman Catholic Church, due to its well-known sensitivity to doctrinal development. But the impact of the biblical theologian in the Roman Catholic Church has started to raise this question. The contribution of biblical theology, then, was very substantial in all that was good in Vatican II, which depended on the voice "from the beginning it was not so." It strengthened the hand of the minimalists and gave leverage, the biblical, critical leverage against the maximalists. In the World Council of Churches on the other hand biblical theology has played a monumental role. There was a presupposition that since we all have the Bible together, the Bible is the great promise of unity. To a very large extent this is true, but that truth should not be achieved by trying to have us all have a biblical theology. It should rather be achieved by giving us that leverage toward new theological creativity.

One of the most significant contributions of biblical theology is, and may in the future also be, in the relation between Christianity and Judaism. When the biblical theologian cuts through the layers of interpretation, he at least opens up the possibility of the question whether something actually went against the will of God in the relations between Judaism and Christianity in the first and second generation of the Church. We would discern how even the New Testament material itself is shaped and darkened by the Christian disappointment over the Jewish non-acceptance of Jesus as the Messiah; and how this disappointment grew into bitterness and repulsion and hatred. I have seldom read a book where I have felt the clash between the heart and the mind as much as in the recent book by Cardinal Bea on the relation between the Church and the Jewish people.[1] It is written as an apologia for the fact that so little of his hopes were realized in the statement on Judaism from Vatican II. It is a book painful to read because somehow Bea is full of love and full of horror in the light of the history of Christian anti-Semitism. But he just can't rewrite the Bible, and he is aware of the fact that there are statements in the New Testament which are not only potentially but actually brim-full of the frustrated and hurt feelings of the early Christians. The good Cardinal tries his best to say that past difficulties must be completely overcome by Christian love. But he cannot deny that 1 Thess. 2:16 is as hateful as it is,[2] and it is hard to believe that admonitions to Christian love would help more now unless we acknowledge anti-Semitic sentiments in the good book itself. Unless we see and admit that, we cannot uproot the "cause" of anti-Semitism; and the biblical theologian, sensitive to the thinking of the first century, as far as the New Testament is concerned, may be able to lay new foundations for our relations to Judaism.[3]

Having expressed our gratitude to the era of biblical theology, let us now give some reasons for saying that that era has come to an end. Our own enthusiasm about "Athens—no; Jerusalem—yes," crumbles before a generation that asks what it has to do with either Athens or Jerusalem. In this new climate there are serious questions whether all our problems were solved at that time, and whether our problem is just one of proper application by proper hermeneutical theory. We become more and more aware of the fact that we may have new problems, not just a new twist of the old problems. This is quite a challenge to theology and to the Church. By habit and by trade the theologian is perhaps the most facile man in describing new problems as old problems. There is a habit of thinking that all the basic problems of man and theology have been faced and solved in the early period. That attitude is quite questionable. I have often taken great joy in the fact that Paul is our guide in this matter. In 1 Cor. 7, Paul discusses divorce. He starts with a word from the Lord but then points out special cases and says that for those he has no word from the Lord. I think that Paul was the last preacher in Christendom who was great enough to admit that. What is really interesting in what Paul does here is that he does not fall for the theological temptation to over-apply certain principles. Of course, he could just as well have said that from the word of the Lord it follows that in case A we do so, and in case B we do so, and in case C we do so; but he limits the word for case A, and he says of the other ones that he thinks we are facing new problems which Jesus has not spoken of. That is a very different attitude. And it is this awareness of new problems that is needed and that shakes the simplistic imperialism of biblical theology in the theological enterprise today.

When I came to the United States fifteen years ago, Professor Johannes Munck of Aarhus—of blessed memory—gave me sound advice. He warned me that as a professional New Testament scholar I would be bombarded by people and by letters asking what is the biblical view of this or that, or what does the Bible say to this or that. If you are honest and a good scholar and a good pastor, you should always start your answers by saying, "Dear sir or madame, actually the Bible says nothing directly about your problem. But in considering your problem you should perhaps keep the following biblical data in mind...." That advice is even more timely today although we get fewer requests of this kind from colleagues, students and the general public.

But the crisis in the relation between the Bible and theology has a deeper level. It goes to the very quest for truth. The biblical theologian can be felt to be a magician who can recreate the biblical world before the eyes of his audience. He is well steeped in the language of demons and Satan and all the rest. He can picture that world, and it is a fascinating and suggestive world. By various hermeneutical principles that world, and the biblical message contained and expressed within that world, can be translated and applied to the present situation. But the more faithful our understanding of the biblical world becomes, the wider becomes the gap between the biblical world and our own. And the more drastic becomes the hermeneutical surgery required. To many of us it appears doubtful whether biblical language with its mythopoeic character really is translatable into respectable dogmatic or philosophical prose. I would be inclined to think that it is not. It may well be that much biblical language is primary religious language, and as such it is "poetic" in a way that cannot be translated into propositional prose.

Under such circumstances it may well be asked whether the best or only approach to systematic and dogmatic theology is to begin with the Bible and its interpretation. It is my suspicion that we should rather begin with what traditionally has been called "natural theology," i.e., theological reflection concerning the world in which we find ourselves. We should begin with *homo religiosus*. We should set the contemporary theologian free from the imperialism of biblical theology.

It should be remembered that the imperialism of the Bible is of rather recent vintage. Throughout the history of Christianity until the 18th century there was no biblical theology. Although the Reformers stressed biblical authority in a special way, they did not think of themselves as doing biblical theology. They did theology; they reflected theologically on man, world, and God; they did not just interpret the Scriptures.

It is this more open and creative stance that theology is recapturing these days, and if I read the signs aright, we are embarking on a new era that calls for a more daring speculative theology. It follows from the recognition of new data that new problems make biblical or neo-orthodox repristination obsolete. Without commenting on its ultimate value, I would consider the speculative theology of Teilhard de Chardin symptomatic of this mood and this need. I would think that some of the work done by the "death of God" theologians or by Leslie Dewart is a preparatory work for such new approaches. In their case it is only preparatory since I consider them still too much caught in the apologetic task of interpreting the old tradition in new terms. What must follow is a more drastic departure. They sometimes strike me as thoughtful and disenchanted men who try to make the best of the tradition received—but with diminishing returns.

One area in which new horizons may open is that of a new theology of religions on the global scale. I am not thinking of a new united world religion created by theological reflection. That is not how religions grow or come into existence. Rather, I am thinking of a new and serious Christian reflection concerning the fact of religious pluralism in a shrinking world. By the year 2000 the Christians will constitute at most 15%

of the world's population, and that will be in a world with increased communication and culture interchange in the "global village." This does not change the truth, but it brings before us the urgent task of reflecting upon what may be the will and plan of God for the Church and for man's religious life. Together with technology and all the rest, there may well be new implications never considered in earlier times, including the biblical era itself.

If it be true that we need and must endure new and more speculative forms of theology, and if such theologies will take their departures by theological reflection directly on the experience of *homo religiosus* today, where indeed does the Bible fit into that situation?

It is clear that we need a larger framework than just "Bible and Theology." For the Christian, that larger framework ought to be the Church. Neither the Bible, nor theology, nor the faith is the primary datum, but the Church, i.e., "the people of God" in its total existence, living, praying, hoping, preaching, thinking, acting through all the past generations, and now in this living and breathing generation of ours. A vital Church does not "preserve" tradition, for tradition is just as much a vehicle for change as it is a vehicle of continuity. A living Church creates and recreates tradition as it responds to the will of God in its own time.

Within that living Church the Bible is read and interpreted toward the spiritual vitality of the community. It works moral sensitivity and gives the Church its vision and self-understanding. But it does not claim to be or to contain the treatises of perennial systematic theology. To the extent that it contains theological reflection, it is as "dated" as are any other ancient documents. Most of us are eager to stress how the Bible is a product of its own time as to geology and biology, etc. But it is equally obvious that as long as we speak of "-ologies" this "datedness" covers the whole list. One can therefore ask Bultmann why he thinks that anthropology alone is the valid inner core of the New Testament. One must recognize that the theology of the Bible also falls into the same category of datedness as all other "-ologies."

The decisive question is not how to relate Bible to theology. In the wider setting of the Church we should rather attend to the question: How does the Church live with its Bible? How does the Church practice openness, obedience, willingness to be judged and renewed by the Bible?

The "datedness" of the biblical material has another implication, and that one may well supply the key for the use of the Bible in the life of the Church. The biblical material speaks for specific situations and even its various "theologies" (Johannine, Pauline, Priestly, Isianic, etc.) grow out of and address themselves to specific issues and conditions. This *ad hoc* character of biblical texts is perhaps most obvious in the Pauline epistles, where there are striking differences even within the Pauline corpus due to the problems at hand and the churches addressed.

This suggests that the Scriptures must be interpreted with due attention to the problems at hand. A primary hermeneutical task is to establish the degree of analogy or similarity between the questions addressed by the biblical writer and the issue at hand in the present situation. Such similarities are never total but are analogous at best. When this is fully recognized then the biblical material functions as highly suggestive guidance in the decision making process of the Church and of its members. The Bible becomes not so much the safe proof for being right; it, rather, becomes a guiding and prompting force as the Church and its members seek the will of God and the guidance of the Spirit. The Bible is then not primarily the vehicle for theological or moral security. It becomes, rather, the source for vision, perspective, and inspiration. It blends into the religious experience of the contemporary Christian and becomes welded into that experience not as a closed system to be accepted but as a "word of God," a command or a promise to be acted upon. The Christian theologian of our time will do his creative and speculative work out of a community that has been so nurtured and prompted. The Bible reaches him through the filter of the total life of the Church of which he is a member with a very special and taxing task.

NOTES

[1] Augustin Cardinal Bea, S.J., *The Church and the Jewish People* (New York: Harper and Row, 1966).

[2] A significant argument for this passage being a later, non-Pauline addition has been made by Birger Pearson. His article appears in *Harvard Theological Review*, 64 (1971), 79-94.

[3] See further my article "Judaism and Christianity: A Plea for a New Relationship," *Cross Currents*, 17 (1967), 445-58.

The Meaning of Revelation

Avery Dulles

THE title of this lecture, *The Meaning of Revelation*, is a deliberate echo of that of a book of identical title published by H. Richard Niebuhr in 1941, and still widely read in a recent paperback edition.[1] This book is perhaps the most distinguished contribution thus far made by an American theologian on the subject of revelation. At the time, such a contribution could only have been made by a Protestant. Catholics did not as yet feel a serious need to analyze the meaning of revelation. Most of them would no doubt have been scandalized by the thought that a theologian might have difficulty in figuring out just what the term really did mean. But as Carl Braaten recently observed, "Roman Catholic theology today is catching up with Protestant theology; it is no longer sure of what it means by revelation."[2] This paper will undoubtedly give a certain measure of substantiation to Braaten's statement.

Niebuhr wrote at a time when it was unfashionable in Protestant circles to talk about revelation at all. Among Ritschl and his followers, as John Baillie reminds us, the concept of revelation "suffered virtual suppression."[3] As Niebuhr himself noted in his introduction, the very term aroused suspicion in many quarters that an obscurantist effort was being made to demolish the solid gains of the modern enlightenment in religious thought. "Whether it be reactionary or fancifully antiquarian, revelation theology seems irrelevant to many modern Christians."[4]

This charge of irrelevance has of course recurred in our own generation. But the twenty years immediately following the publication of Niebuhr's book witnessed a great resurgence of revelation theology in the Protestant world. The work of Barth and Bultmann, Brunner and Tillich, and many others during the 1940s and 1950s, made it once more possible to talk about revelation without embarrassment. In the confidence of that era, Richard Niebuhr's own essay seemed too modest and timid. More aware than some of his successors of the dangers of an uncritical dogmatic confessionalism, he grappled courageously with the problem how to combine the personal stance of faith with ruthless honesty in acknowledging the historically and culturally conditioned quality of all human knowledge.

Niebuhr attempted to meet the difficulty by introducing a sharp distinction between "external" history, as a strictly objective science, and "internal" history, as a highly personal evaluation. In the latter he saw the locus of revelation and faith. Insisting on the non-scientific character of faith, he refused to erect any kind of apologetic in its favor. But his abandonment of defensiveness gave a certain impression that Christian faith might be intellectually indefensible. His acceptance of revelation looked suspiciously arbitrary. Contemporary theologians such as Wolfhart Pannenberg have rightly protested against the excessive dualism which Niebuhr introduced between history, as a positivistic science, and interpretation, as a subjective stance.[5] When revelation is proposed in these terms, one has an unhappy feeling that the standpoint of universal reason has been unjustifiably relinquished to unbelievers. In the words of Carl Braaten, such preaching invites men to make the leap of faith on the basis of what reason regards as very dubious.[6]

Unsatisfying as Niebuhr's views on the relationship between faith and scientific history may have been, he did at least establish the intimate connection between the two. He rightly characterized revelation as an occurrence in our inner history which enables us to discern a meaningful pattern in the events of the past and present. For the Christian, as Niebuhr understood it, revelation fastens on the event of Jesus Christ, insofar as, grasped in faith, it lends intelligibility to the whole of history, including the varied occasions of our personal and communal life. In Jesus, as Niebuhr recognized, the Christian discerns the "righteousness of God, his power and wisdom."[7]

Niebuhr's basic concept of revelation has stood up well in Protestant and Anglican theology since his day. It bears clear analogies to that of Alan Richardson, who finds revelation in existential crises in the life of an individual or nation, giving rise to "disclosure situations" in which persons or groups find the meaning of their lives and discover their historical vocation.[8] Somewhat along the same lines, Van A. Harvey has described revelation as a paradigmatic event that is believed to "focus some insight into the nature of reality itself, or more precisely into the nature of reality so far as it bears on the human quest for liberation and fulfillment."[9]

This historical and existential view of revelation, which has been widespread in Protestant theology since the time of Niebuhr (though of course its roots go back much further), is far removed from any theory of revelation which would be likely to have appeared under Catholic auspices until very recent years. According to the standard seminary manuals, which formed the thinking of priests and, through them, of the faithful, revelation was essentially a message from God to man. More specifically, it was an extraordinary intervention by which God, speaking through the prophets and, finally, by his own Son, manifested in an obscure way certain truths of the supernatural order. These truths were committed to the Church to be taught infallibly until the end of time. On this view of revelation, which might be characterized as supernaturalistic, authoritarian, and extrinsic, revelation comes not from within history but from above it; its primary content is not the interpretation of our personal history but the saving truth about God and the way to him; its vehicle is not so much events as words, by which it is given to men to express the thoughts of God. Niebuhr's historical concept of revelation would strike most Catholics as naturalistic or at least anthropocentric. The divine dimension, they would complain, is scarcely more than an afterthought.

But what I have called the standard Catholic view of revelation, like other theological ideas, is culturally conditioned. In particular, it owes a heavy debt to St. Augustine and to medieval Scholasticism, which depicted revelation in terms of a master-pupil relationship. For St. Thomas Aquinas, revelation was a body of sacred doctrine resting primarily on the authority of God as teacher. St. Thomas contrasted two diametrically opposed modes of knowledge. First, there was the ascending action by which the mind advanced through rational inquiry; then there was the descending action by which God freely bestowed knowledge that was inaccessible, or scarcely accessible, to reason. Revelation in this view appeared almost as a divinely given supplement to philosophy. Where the philosopher's competence ended, the theologian's was supposed to begin. The philosopher, according to St. Thomas, has no way of telling whether God is one person or many; whether the world is of definite or indefinite temporal duration; whether or not there are created spiritual beings above man or not, etc. Revelation gave answers to philosophically unanswerable questions such as these, as well as to other religiously important questions which reason could not solve without great difficulty.

St. Thomas and the Scholastics did not neglect the crucial problem of ascertaining whether an allegedly revealed doctrine does actually come from God. The mysteries of faith, since they exceed the grasp of reason, obviously cannot be established by probative intrinsic evidence. The only possible proof must therefore take the form of extrinsic signs, such as miracles and fulfilled prophecies, which make it prudent to believe a messenger who claims to be speaking in the name of God.

Having received its basic form in high Scholasticism, the standard Catholic theology of revelation developed still further under the pressure of historical events during and since the Reformation. In this period the focus of attention shifted from the authority of God to that of the institution which was regarded as the custodian of revealed truth. While no Catholic would have doubted that faith was an assent to the teaching of God or of Jesus Christ, his first thought would have been the Church: faith is the virtue by which we accept with full confidence that which the Church teaches as divinely revealed.

So exaggerated was the insistence on docility to the teaching Church that in some presentations one gets the impression that Catholics had little interest in the content of revelation. Institutional loyalty took precedence over joyful acceptance of the saving message. Implicit faith was looked upon as the paragon. This new emphasis was occasioned, at least in part, by the polemical confrontation between Protestants and Catholics. The needs of the hour called for almost military discipline and solidarity. Any attempt to probe new aspects of revelation or to raise speculative questions on which the magisterium had not as yet pronounced was regarded as temerarious. A disinterested concern for theological truth was a luxury which the beleaguered Church of the Counter-Reformation could ill afford.

About the end of World War II it became apparent that the standard Catholic doctrine of revelation was not the only possible one. The more creative Catholic theologians were no longer content to work within the restrictive framework of pre-Tridentine or post-Tridentine Scholasticism. Some found new stimulation in a return to biblical theology, some tried to relate the theology of revelation to the needs of Christian preaching, some derived stimulus from the liturgy, some turned to the Church Fathers or to the monastic tradition of the early middle ages; still others sought to renew Catholic theology by contact with modern Protestant thought, or with the non-Christian religions, or with certain currents of modern secular thinking, such as existentialism, scientific evolutionism, or personalistic phenomenology.

These new currents in the theology of revelation were at first met with suspicion and hostility by the partisans of the Roman school, who warned grimly of a resurgence of the Modernist heresy. In 1950 the conservatives prevailed upon Pius XII to issue his famous encyclical on modern theological errors, *Humani generis*.

As it turned out, *Humani generis* was perhaps the last great effort to contain Catholic theology within the categories of classical Scholasticism. Eight years later John XXIII ascended the papal throne, and began the great *aggiornamento* which resulted in Vatican Council II. This council, dominated by the progressive theologians of Transalpine Europe (France, the German-speaking countries, and the Low Countries), many of whom had been under a cloud of suspicion since *Humani generis,* had little use for the objectivism and extrinsicism of the post-Reformation tradition. In *Dei Verbum*, the Constitution on Divine Revelation, the ecclesiocentric point of view was abandoned in favor of one that was biblical, personalistic, and theocentric. Getting away from the "blank check" approach, which would put all the dogmas on pretty much the same level, the Council stressed that there was a hierarchy of importance, since some doctrines were more closely connected than others with the central mystery of our salvation.[10]

In accordance with its personalistic approach, *Dei Verbum* looks upon revelation less as a communication of doctrine than as a communication of life. "Through this revelation," says the Council, "the invisible God out of the abundance of His love speaks to men as friends and lives among them, so that He may invite and take them into fellowship with Himself."[11] Propositional dogmatic teaching is certainly not rejected, but it is subordinated to man's interpersonal relationship with the God of love. Attention is centered on the Christ-event as the point where God reveals his saving mercy by an unsurpassable gift of himself to mankind.

With a more existential and less biblical concern, the same Christocentric view of revelation reappears in Vatican II's Constitution on the Church in the Modern World. Here we read: "Christ, the final Adam, by the revelation of the mystery of the Father and His love, fully reveals man to man himself and makes his supreme calling clear."[12] "Through Christ and in Christ, the riddles of sorrow and death grow meaningful."[13] And again, in the eloquent conclusion to Part I:

> For God's Word, by whom all things were made, was Himself made flesh so that as perfect man He might save all men and sum up all things in Himself. The Lord is the goal of human history, the focal point of the longings of history and of civilization, the center of the human race, the joy of every human heart, and the answer to all its yearnings.[14]

In passages such as these, revelation is no longer treated primarily as a body of truths accredited by miracles and prophecies, authoritatively imposed by official statements of the magisterium. Instead, Christ is viewed as the key to the meaning of all history, including our own inner history and experience. The Catholic Church, even in its official teaching, in this matter comes very close to the Protestant and Anglican view of revelation, as represented by such thinkers as Richard Niebuhr, Alan Richardson, and Van Harvey.

The fundamental concept of revelation, therefore, is no longer a factor that divides Protestants and Catholics as such. Many in each confessional group would agree that revelation is an extraordinary transforming event, which, without ceasing to be mysterious and beyond human comprehension, illuminates the human situation and opens up the meaning of history and of the universe. Such an event comes upon man without his being able to control or master it; it is a gift, and from the ultimacy of its significance, confirmed by the united testimony of those who have witnessed and experienced it most closely, it may be reasonably regarded, in faith, as the self-giving of God himself. It prompts man to respond with the exclamation of Zachary

(Lk. 1:68), "God has visited his people." For the Christian, revelation occurs preeminently when it is given to men to discern the meaning and value of their personal history and that of the whole world in the light of Christ.

Taking this general view of revelation as a hypothesis, I should like to discuss some of the problems which it raises. Some of these difficulties are so acute as to call into question the very viability of revelation as a theological category. If these questions are insoluble, one is hardly justified in continuing to speak of revelation. And according to the way in which one answers them, one will have radically different concepts of revelation. I shall touch on five major problems which are currently much discussed, and give rise to sharply differing views of revelation, not between Protestants and Catholics as such, but between different groups of theologians within each of these confessional families.

1. What is the relationship between reason and revelation, between acquired and revealed knowledge?

2. In the actual historical order, is revelation always present to all men, or does it first come when man learns of some determinate historical intervention of God, such as Christians believe to have occurred in biblical history, especially in the life, death, and exaltation of Jesus?

3. Is revelation primarily and essentially an interior experience that defies external expression? Or is it a clear message that a man can communicate to others and ask them to accept?

4. Is revelation a light that enables a man to look on the data of experience in a new way, or does it, on the contrary, furnish new data and have a proper content of its own?

5. In the Christian view, did revelation come to an end with Christ or with the apostles, or is it, rather, an on-going process still occurring in our own day?

I. REASON AND REVELATION

A CCORDING to the Scholastic theory of revelation, as outlined above —especially in the manual tradition of the late nineteenth and early twentieth centuries—human knowledge is divided into two compartments. There is a lower tier of truths which man can gather on his own (and this would include some rudimentary knowledge of religious matters, such as the existence of God and of the moral law), and a higher realm of truths which are not attainable by reason but only by revelation, if God should choose to speak. Revelation, then, has the dual function of imparting doctrines (such as the Trinity and the Incarnation) which man could not gather at all by the exercise of reason, and of giving clear and easy access to truths which man could not learn on his own without great difficulty and obscurity.

On this theory, as usually presented, strictly revealed truths are in no sense acquired by the exercise of human intelligence. They are given by God. Man has the option of either accepting or rejecting them, but he does not forge them by his own mental efforts nor can he, once they have been revealed, personally verify their truth or falsity. He accepts them on the authority of the revealing God or he does not grasp them at all. When a doctrine is proposed as God's word man has, of course, the power and duty to investigate the evidences of credibility. Through external signs, such as miracles and prophecies, he may reasonably come to the conclusion that the herald who proclaims this doctrine is indeed sent by God. But at this point the task of reason is over. Faith alone can go beyond the judgment of credibility and utter the assent, "this is true."

The more one reflects on this seemingly clear dichotomy between faith and reason, the more obscure it seems to become. For one thing, it lacks any solid biblical warranty. While the Bible is full of assertions about how the "word of God" comes to prophets and others, a critical study of the biblical evidence does not justify the popular impression that a clear line can be drawn between the word of God and the word of man. God's word comes to expression on human lips, and in its content and style always reflects the personality and training of its human spokesmen. The prophets of Israel were not men who sat around idly waiting for messages from God. The greatest of them were deeply involved in the events of their time. When they declared God's will for Israel they were generally voicing their own insights—inspired insights—into the meaning of the events occurring before their eyes. God was at work in and through them, but not in a way that absolved them from the use of their own native powers of observation and reflection.

The biblical idea of God, so far as we can judge, was derived from experience and inference. The events of history taught the Israelites that Yahweh, their God, freely loved them and chose them, for all their faults, to be his own people, that he was powerful to protect them and to bring his promises to fulfillment, that he was just in his punishments, but merciful when the people repented. When the prophetic literature represents Yahweh as claiming these attributes for himself, it is using a literary form to express what the Israelites had learned from their dealings with him. Revelation, then, did not dispense the people from utilizing their mental powers, but occurred in and through their rational activity.

The same may be said, essentially, of the New Testament revelation. According to contemporary scholarship, it is highly doubtful that Jesus ever claimed messiahship or divinity for himself in precise terms. Probably he never said, "I am the Messiah," or "I am the Son of God," and certainly he would never have said, "I am God." But his disciples, seeing him in action, and experiencing his presence after Easter, came to the conclusion that in this man God had fulfilled his promises to Israel and had made himself present on earth in human form. When the early Christians applied divine predicates to Jesus, they were making inferences from the data of their experience concerning him rather than meekly submitting to what he said about himself. Their revealed doctrine did not involve a suspension of rational activity, but stemmed from an exercise of reason, critically applied to the particular situations in which they found themselves.

Can we rightly say, then, that the doctrine of the Trinity or of the Incarnation lies beyond the scope of reason? The first Christians took over the idea of God the Father from the Old Testament, which described the historical experience of Israel as the foundation for this belief. The divinity of Jesus was, for the disciples, a matter of experience, interpreted in the light of God's promises to Israel. Finally, the doctrine of the Holy Spirit was scarcely more than a statement, in Jewish religious vocabulary, of the phenomena occurring in the Spirit-filled Church. In its origins, therefore, the doctrine of the Trinity, and likewise that of the Incarnation, were not extrinsically imposed by authoritative teaching, but were derived from reflections on the data of experience. In structure, religious knowledge does not greatly differ from our knowledge of other matters, such as the character of persons familiar to us from history and experience. We do not know about other persons simply by deduction from self-evident philosophical truth, but through what they show of themselves in their actual conduct. In interpreting their words and actions, we make use of imagination and empathy. In knowledge of this sort, the dichotomy between faith and reason does not seem to do justice to the complexity of the matter.

In its struggle against aprioristic Rationalism, which would have confined reason to things knowable with mathematical certainty, the Church insisted that religious knowledge is "above reason." But this way of putting the matter is not entirely fortunate. In a certain sense, as the Modernists were not alone in contending, all human knowledge is an achievement of the mind that knows. In Blondel's phrase, nothing can enter the mind of man unless it comes out of him, as a development of his previous capacities and tendencies. Religious knowledge would be unassimilable by man unless it represented a fulfillment of his inner dynamism to understand himself in his total situation.[15] Although some of the Modernists no doubt interpreted this self-fulfillment too naturalistically, the leaders of the movement were on the trail of something very valid, that was largely overlooked by the anti-Modernist theology of the next few decades. Anti-Modernist orthodoxy often spoke as though revelation were a pure humiliation of reason—as though it were dehumanizing rather than perfective of man.

Further theological probing since the Modernist crisis has shown that we are not faced by a choice between a naturalistic immanentism and a supernaturalistic extrinsicism. According to the theology of Karl

Rahner, and many who accept his views, man is born into the world with an intrinsic ordination to union with God in Christ, and thus not in a state of pure nature. In choosing to give himself in grace through Christ, God also called men to this wonderful union with himself. If this call is not to be something that remains shut up in the divine will, but something divinely efficacious, it must leave some trace on human nature as concretely constituted. Man comes into the world as a place in which God calls him to himself. Hence, we may apply to every human being the sentence of St. Augustine's *Confessions*: "You have made us for yourself, O Lord, and our hearts are restless until they find rest in you."

Granted this intrinsic ordination to the divine, one can easily see how God's self-gift to us in revelation is simultaneously the fulfillment of an innate tendency of human nature. What theology understands as God's self-disclosure from above, may also be looked at from below, in which case it appears as the self-transcending actualization of man's vocation to union with God in knowledge and love. God's gift and man's self-realization coincide in one and the same event. The sudden breakthrough in man's quest for the divine is the work of God insofar as he is the bearer of the self-transcending movement of the world itself.[16] Man actively uses his own powers in order to apprehend what God himself is disclosing. Revelation, therefore, should not be contrasted with reason as something that begins where reason ceases. Rather, reason and revelation progress together. The highest exercise of reason occurs when man uses it to fulfill the deepest tendencies of his nature and to accede to the presence of the divine.

In speaking of faith as a self-fulfillment of reason, I am of course using the term reason with a much wider meaning than would have been admitted by those who rigidly contrasted the two forms of knowledge. For them reason meant the manipulation of clear and distinct ideas, resulting in a quasi-geometrical demonstration. But it is precisely this concept of reason which I wish to challenge. In the concrete order, reason grapples with the contingent and the ambiguous, viewed against a horizon of mystery, apart from which we would lack any framework of meaning. The dynamism of reason is constantly influenced by the divine attraction. Hence it is unrealistic to think of reason, in its concrete exercise, as the Rationalists did. Theologians who put such heavy emphasis on the contrast between faith and reason were to some extent victimized by the Rationalist concept of reason.

The Hungarian philosopher of science, Michael Polanyi, has brilliantly analyzed the inseparability of faith and reason, even in the realm of scientific investigation. The task of solving any problem, he argues, presupposes that we already possess some intimations of the "as-yet-unknown." "Our active foreknowledge of an unknown reality is the right motive and guide of knowing in all our mental endeavors. Formal processes of inference cannot thrust forward the truth, for they have neither passion nor purpose."[17] Religious faith differs from scientific faith, Polanyi contends, not so much in kind as in scope and depth. It involves the meaning of life and of the universe as a whole.[18] Religious conversion, achieved through revelation, commits and transforms the whole man in a way in which the expansion of natural knowledge does not do.[19]

Many Christians might hesitate to accept the close analogy between scientific reason and revelatory knowledge because they are accustomed to think of faith as a reliance upon testimony. We believe the articles of the creed, they would say, not on internal evidences but on the authority of the revealing God. But the notion of revelation as divinely attested truth can be misleading. Useful up to a point, the analogy between divine revelation and human testimony limps badly when pressed too far. It is quite true that we cannot base our religious beliefs solely upon the evident data of experience and rigorous inferences from these. We have to rely upon the obscure intimations of the divine presence. But the testimony of God, if we wish to use this term, is not merely verbal. Verbal attestation, as Rahner has said, "only indicates something not truly possessed and does not impart the thing itself."[20] Now in revelation which comes from grace, the reality itself, of which faith speaks, is truly bestowed, in however veiled a manner. The testimony of God is his incipient self-communication to the human spirit, which in turn adheres to him in the response of faith.

When we rely on human testimony, we can normally be certain, prior to our act of human faith, that the person on whose word we rely is really speaking. But in the decision of faith, what is at stake is not whether we are to accept what God vouches for, but rather whether he does actually vouch for that which we are being asked to believe. Hence, the decision of faith depends on the search for signs of God's self-communication in history and in our inner experience. As soon as we have succeeded in deciphering the signs, and have unequivocally accepted them as carrying a divine message, we have virtually made the act of faith. Hence, the crucial decision is not, as in human testimony, whether the word of the witness is true, but whether the divine witness is really saying what he is alleged to be saying.

In reading the signs of God's self-communication we have to employ a logic basically similar in form to that which Polanyi describes in his works on scientific method. Speaking of the discovery of scientific laws, Polanyi shows that the appraisal of order is always an act of personal assessment. In a sense it is subjective; but it is by no means arbitrary. "Man has the power to establish real patterns in nature, the reality of which is manifested by the fact that their future implications extend indefinitely beyond the experience they were originally known to control."[21]

An epistemology such as Polanyi's seems to be eminently applicable to the discernment of a divinely given pattern in the events of biblical history, which constitutes for Niebuhr and others the heart of the Christian revelation. If scientific reason operates as Polanyi describes it, there is no need to follow Niebuhr in his dichotomy between science and personal knowledge. Yet one can say, as he did, that the discovery of patterns in history is subject to progressive validation.[22] In Old Testament times the presence and activity of God began as scarcely more than an unconfirmed promise, as in the faith of Abraham. But the promise provided the key for the interpretation of history under Moses, the judges, and the monarchy. In the eyes of Christians the promises of Yahweh were surpassingly fulfilled in Christ. Throughout Church history the revelation has undergone continual confirmation and has itself been understood with greater refinement and accuracy.

Thus, the inquiry of faith, and the progress of revelation, bear significant similarities to the process of scientific inquiry and discovery. They do not differ radically in kind from the methods by which we interpret the events of history. I conclude, therefore, that there is no opposition between faith and reason as concretely exercised, or between acquired and revealed knowledge.[22a] In his search for the God of whom he previously had an obscure intuition, man is exercising faith and reason at the same time and almost in the same degree. Faith, adhering firmly, even passionately, to a meaning as yet but faintly intimated, leads the mind forward to a richer and more comprehensive grasp of the total meaning of life and history, as this meaning is given in those paradigmatic events by which God specially manifests his gracious presence and his saving purposes.

II. THE UNIVERSALITY OF REVELATION

MY second question about revelation concerns its distribution. In the opinion, or at least the imagination, of most Christians, revelation is the prerogative of certain favored groups. Many would limit it to those who have made contact with the biblical message in some form, whether in the Old Testament or the New. Jean Daniélou speaks for many when he writes in his popular booklet, *The Salvation of the Nations*:

> Thus, the essential difference between Catholicism and all other religions is that the others start with man. They are touching and often very beautiful attempts, rising very high in their search for God. But in Catholicism there is a contrary movement, the descent of God towards the world, in order to communicate His life to it. The answer to the aspirations of the entire universe lies in the Judaeo-Christian religion. The true religion, the Catholic religion, is composed of these two elements. It is the religion in which God's grace has made answer to man's cry. In other religions grace is not present, nor is Christ, nor is the gift of God.[23]

Actually views such as this, which confine revelation to one religion, whether it be Roman Catholicism or at least some variety of Judaeo-Christianity, can find a measure of support in the Bible. The only kind of revelation in which the Israelites or the first Christians were greatly interested was that which had come to them, through Abraham, through Moses and the prophets, or—for the Christians—through Jesus and the Apostles. Those outside the covenant were frequently looked upon as people without revelation. Revelation for the Israelites was normally connected with the Covenant of Sinai and for the New Testament writers it was connected with the new Covenant established through the sacrifice and glorification of Jesus.

Still one must balance against this general impression a few texts which say explicitly that God has in some way manifested himself to all peoples. Even the Old Testament speaks of God's covenant with Noah and all his descendents, which would include all men now living on earth (Gn. 9:1-17). In the New Testament, Paul says that God has manifested to the pagans his invisible attributes, including his everlasting power and divinity (Rom. 1:19-20). Later, in Rom. 2:15, Paul adds that God has written his law upon the hearts of those who have not received the Mosaic Law, in such wise that they may be justified by following their conscience.

In his preaching to the pagans at Lystra, Paul tells them that God did not leave their ancestors without evidences of himself in the regularity of the seasons and the fruitfulness of the earth (Acts 14:17). Then again, in his Areopagus sermon, as presented in Acts 17, Paul congratulates the men of Athens for being extremely religious, and adds that "what therefore you worship in ignorance, that I proclaim to you"—namely the Unknown God. This would seem to imply that God had already made himself known to them, even though only paradoxically, as one unknown. And finally there is the famous, but obscure and controverted, text in John's prologue, describing the Logos as "the light that enlightens every man who comes into the world" (Jn. 1:9). In view of texts such as these, the Christian cannot write off the opinion that God has in some way spoken to those who have never made historical contact with the biblical revelation or its derivatives.

In modern Catholic theology there is a marked tendency to hold that God somehow reveals himself to all men. Many theologians regard this as a logical conclusion from two other principles, both well attested in the New Testament—namely the universal salvific will [that God "wills all men to be saved" (1 Tim. 2:4)] and the doctrine that "without faith it is impossible to please God" (Heb. 11:6). Putting these statements together one can argue that it must be possible for all men to make acts of faith; and since faith is commonly understood as a free assent to God's revelatory word, it may be concluded that God in some way reveals himself to all men, enabling them to work out their salvation or perdition in acceptance or rejection, in obedience or disobedience.

Without necessarily endorsing this particular argument, Vatican II put its authority behind the view that God reveals himself to all. In this connection, one may consult *Dei Verbum* n. 3, which affirms that God gave his promise of redemption from the time of man's original fall into sin, and continually thereafter kept the human race in his care in order to bestow eternal life upon those who perseveringly do good in search of salvation. The Declaration on the Non-Christian Religions asserts (n. 2) that the other religions often reflect a ray of that divine Truth which enlightens all men. *Lumen gentium* declares that divine Providence does not "deny the help necessary for salvation to those who, without blame on their part, have not yet arrived at an explicit knowledge of God" (n. 16).

In yet another document of Vatican II, The Pastoral Constitution on the Church in the Modern World, we are told that "since Christ died for all men, and since the ultimate vocation of man is in fact one, and divine, we ought to believe that the Holy Spirit in a manner known only to God offers to every man the possibility of being associated with this Paschal mystery [Christ's saving death and resurrection]" (n. 22). And we are told (n. 36) that "all believers of whatever religion have always heard his [God's] revealing voice in the discourse of creatures." All these texts harmonize admirably with the very clear affirmation of the Decree on Missionary Activity (n. 7) that "God in ways known to Himself can lead those inculpably ignorant of the gospel to that faith without which it is impossible to please Him."

Hence we may conclude that, according to present Catholic teaching, all men, at least at some time in their lives, in ways known to God, receive sufficient revelatory enlightenment to be able to respond with an act of salutary faith. The Council does not try to work out a theory of when or how this enlightenment occurs. But what the Council deliberately refrained from doing by authoritative decree, theologians are implicitly invited to do by unofficial inquiry. Attempting to penetrate the how and the why, theology may construct theories which bring out the full meaning, intelligibility and credibility of the official doctrine.

In the opinion of many theologians, such an analysis may usefully take its departure from the view of Karl Rahner, already mentioned, that God's universal salvific will produces a necessary and ineradicable impression upon human nature as it is concretely realized. God's grace, destined for all men, powerfully attracts them toward the fulfillment of the destiny to which they are invited. One may think, in this connection, of Jesus' own saying, as reported in the Fourth Gospel, "And when I am lifted up from the earth, I shall draw all men to myself" (Jn. 11:32). This Christological text throws light on the statement of Paul in his sermon of Athens to the effect that all members of the human race are created in order to "seek the deity, and, by feeling their way toward him, succeed in finding him. Yet in fact he is not far from any one of us, since it is in him that we live, and move, and exist..." (Acts 17:27 f.).

If God's grace has an impact on the depths of every human spirit, we may already at this point speak of an inchoate revelation. Even before it communicates any precise information (or even if it should never do so), the call of grace alters the horizons of man's consciousness and causes him to experience the world in a new way. He can no longer look on joy or suffering, life or death, exactly as he otherwise would—for he is always tending beyond all temporal satisfactions for a union with God and a peace which this world cannot give. This orientation toward the God of grace enables one to recognize the signs of God's loving presence not only in the explicit teaching of the various religions, but in the order of nature, in the events of history, and in the particular circumstances of one's own life. To all men God shows himself in one way or another, if only as he did, according to St. Paul, to the pagan inhabitants of Lystra, "bestowing blessings, giving rains from heaven and fruitful seasons, filling your hearts with food and gladness" (Acts 14:16).

Revelation, then, comes to all men as an effective offer. The extent to which a man personally responds with the assent of faith, and places his confidence in the God of grace, depends upon his own free decision. It belongs to the mystery of sin that a man is capable of hardening his heart in unbelief. Whether one assents in faith or not is something largely hidden from the subject himself. The deep layers of our being, where God encounters us in silence, are opaque even to ourselves. Because we are not pure spirits, but spirits which come to consciousness only through contact with the surrounding world, we do not fully reflect upon our own activity. We cannot plumb the depths of our own motivations and intentions.

Since we cannot know by mere introspection whether we ourselves respond to God in faith, or whether we deceive ourselves, we cannot presume that a man who professes to be an unbeliever is not also deceiving himself. The professed unbeliever might be, beneath the surface, a man of faith.

Superficially it might seem that faith, in the sense of believing because of the authority of God, would be unattainable to those who, by a deliberate judgment, reject the existence of a personal God. But this way of looking at the matter would be too rationalistic. Faith is submission not to the idea but to the reality of the revealing God. A man with no conceptual or articulate awareness of God may, at the deepest level of his being, be assenting to God's self-offering in love. It is possible for a man to express his faith without using the word "God." He may say, for instance, that he acknowledges the supremacy of conscience, or the absolute claims of truth, or an unconditional obligation to devote himself to the true good of other men. Such a man, if he is fully sincere, would be accepting the imperious invitation of grace, and would deserve to be ranked, theologically, as a believer. Many who profess no belief in God actually adore and serve him under some other name.

Along lines such as this it is possible to see how Vatican Council II could declare that even those who have not yet arrived at an explicit knowledge of God receive the helps they need for their salvation—including, presumably, the revelation needed for a salutary act of faith. While not explicitly believing in God, they may do so implicitly by recognizing realities or values which are in fact divine. And parenthetically it may be added that some who profess to believe in God may, theologically speaking, be unbelievers. Perhaps they have set up some mental construct of their own and given it the adoration that is due only to the living God who lies beyond our highest powers of conception. An inadequate idea of God—such as many Christians have—may well be an idol.

We cannot give any kind of numerical estimate regarding the ratio between men of faith and faithless men in the world. Since the core of man's personal existence is so largely hidden, we can only hope for ourselves or others that we or they are true believers. Insofar as we subscribe to the view of Paul that the grace of God is more powerful than the sinfulness of man (cf. Rom. 5:15-19), we may surmise that the majority of men do in fact respond to revelation in sufficient measure to obtain eternal salvation.

Christianity, of course, stands before the world, and before the other religions, with the conviction that it has a definite revelation to herald. The Christian tidings are indeed a revelation, as I shall try to clarify in the following sections of this paper. But this does not mean that the men to whom the Christian evangelist is sent have had no previous experience of revelation. The history of mankind is made up of many successive layers of revelation and of faith. A man who responds to grace in a merely implicit way, as God communicates himself in an inarticulate depth-experience, already has his place among the believers. When the gospel is announced to him, it has a certain added credibility because the hearer has been prepared for it by his lived experience, familiarizing him with the God of grace. When such a person hears of God's total gift of himself through the life, death, and resurrection of Jesus, and through the outpouring of the Spirit of Christ on Pentecost, he can recognize in this message a meaningful interpretation of his own experience. For he has already responded, through the Holy Spirit, to the grace of Christ. He is therefore in a position to accept the gospel, not simply with the attitude of one coming from infidelity to faith, but as one who is passing, as Paul would say, "from faith to faith" (Rom. 1:17). Our God is one who heaps grace upon grace, revelation upon revelation.

III. INNER EXPERIENCE AND OUTWARD EXPRESSION

THE third question I have proposed to discuss has to do with the relationship between the two aspects of revelation—the inner experience (which may be called, in Rahner's vocabulary, unthematic or transcendental) and the outward expression (which may be designated as thematic or predicamental). The interrelationships between these poles can be, and in fact have been, variously conceived.

The objectivist mode of thought, which was characteristic of Scholasticism, especially in its later phases, and of the theologies of the Rationalistic period, tended to look on revelation as having some kind of objective existence in the world prior to man's conscious reception of it. Revelation was said to be present in historical events or in written records, such as the Bible. In this view the role of man as subject was simply to notice what was antecedently there and to respond to it by acceptance or rejection. This view of revelation is of course inadequate, for it rests on an untenable theory of truth. Truth of any kind has actuality only in a living intellect; it presupposes subjectivity, participation, and commitment. In a totally objectivized world there would be no truth. The objectivist theories of revelation were vitiated by the *"tabula rasa"* theory of knowledge; they depersonalized and reified the notion of truth in an unacceptable way.

The Modernists, rightly perceiving the flaws in the objectivist position, reacted with a view of truth that was, at least in tendency, subjectivist. For them revelation was a matter of ineffable interior experience. According to Sabatier, who might be classified as a Protestant Modernist, revelation is always immediate, individual, and interior. It is a prayerful experience of encounter with the infinite Spirit. The outward expressions of relevation, in this view, are not part of revelation; rather, they are an envelope in which revelation can be enclosed or— perhaps better—a wire by which it can be transmitted. For the Modernist, words and doctrines are only symbols that point to the event of revelation, and perhaps evoke it; but they cannot constitutively pertain to it.

A third position on our question would admit a psycho-physical dualism. According to this view there would be two irreducibly distinct forms of revelation: the impact of grace interiorly acting on the human spirit and the outer preaching of the word. God comes to man in either or both of these two ways. But this position is unsatisfactory since it fails to clarify the relationship between the two. If God can come interiorly by the immediate influx of grace, why should he bother to come externally through word or event? Or if men can know him through outward manifestations, why is the inner illumination of grace necessary?

The fourth position, which seems to be the correct one, would relate inner and outer revelation by appealing to some theory of mutual causality. This can be done in terms of a philosophical anthropology such as Karl Rahner's. Man, according to this view, is by definition an incarnate spirit—"spirit in the world." He acts in accordance with his nature; hence never simply as spirit or simply as body. A fully human act must be psychosomatic. The spiritual and the corporeal are two aspects of the same complex reality. The spirit is really present in the flesh by a kind of identity in difference. Since man comes to himself as spirit through his contact with the world about him, revelation must come to him in an incarnate way, through events in nature and in history. The human response to revelation is not merely a passive mirroring, but an active expression of that which has been received. Revelation exists in each individual insofar as he creatively responds by his own human activity. As in every other type of thought, so in the realm of revelation, man comes to himself as a spiritual being by expressing his thought in concepts, words, and images.

This leads to a reflection on the signs of revelation. Signs, such as miracles, are not merely extrinsic pointers to a revelation other than themselves. Rather, they are living embodiments of the revelation which they signalize, and are intrinsically related to it by a kind of reciprocal interdependence. Wherever it exists, revelation has to come to expression in signs, which sustain and intensify the inner reality, as well as betoken its presence. Revelation is preeminently expressed in personal signs, such as the fidelity of the witness, the altruism of the saint, the penance of the converted sinner.

Granted the social nature of man, expression is by its very essence communicative. As we have already said, man's revelatory encounter with God arises in conjunction with his dealings with his fellow men. There is no inner grace without the social context which theology calls "external grace." Man receives, thanks to the self-expression of revelation in others, and his own receptivity takes the form of a socially tangible and historical expression. Whenever he expresses his ideas to himself, man puts himself in a social situation; he speaks to an audience, at least a potential and imaginary one. Thus, revelation does not really come to itself in the man of faith unless it communicates itself through him to others. As Paul says, quoting the Psalmist, "I believe, therefore I have spoken" (2 Cor. 4:13). In order to be saved, as Paul elsewhere asserts, one must both believe in his heart and speak with his tongue (Rom. 10:9). The two aspects of man's response to revelation are ordinarily inseparable.

The social nature of man accounts for what may be called the ecclesial character of revelation. Revelation, insofar as it expresses and communicates itself, is generative of community; and the community, in turn, becomes the locus of further revelation. Seen in the perspective of faith, the history of mankind seems to show that while remarkable individuals may be the privileged recipients of revelation, this does not happen in a significant degree except within the context of a remarkable community. Revelation is a social phenomenon to such an extent that, at least in the Bible, it is predicated first of all of the community. The primary recipient of revelation in the Old Testament is Israel as a people; and in the New Testament the primary subject of faith is the infant Church. The Christian revelation is not entrusted to any individual, but to the Church as a corporate body, which is its custodian and herald. The communal or collegial character of revelation confirms what philosophy has to tell us of the social nature of man. God makes his great revelations when men are gathered together in his name.

If it be true that revelation does not exist without somehow coming to expression in a human and socially tangible way, it would seem to follow that revelation will inevitably give rise to some kind of communal religion. Combining this conclusion with what I have already asserted about the universal availability of revelation, we may now draw some conclusions regarding the revelatory significance of the world's religions. They are expressions and bearers of revelation, and they establish loci of further revelation.

The Old Testament is unique among religions in that it provided, so to speak, the cradle for the Incarnation. It prepared historically for the earthly life of the eternal Logos. If we look upon the religions of the world as phyla of an evolutionary tree, we can say that the Judaeo-Christian religion is the phylum in which occurred the evolutionary breakthrough, i.e., the definitive expression of revelation in Christ as God's personal Word. Viewed retrospectively from the standpoint of Christian faith, the whole history of Israel may be interpreted in terms of Christ as the goal to which it was at least unconsciously tending. Christ, as the fulfillment, influenced the whole of that history by drawing it to himself. Just as the whole process of biological evolution, from man's point of view, seems to consist of a series of experiments and tentative gropings leading toward the emergence of man, so the history of religion exhibits a similar groping toward its Christian realization.

Yet, if we are considering the revelatory significance of the world's religions, it would be too narrow to look upon all the others as unsuccessful efforts to achieve the fulfillment that was vouchsafed to Judaism alone. In view of what we have already seen about the universality of revelation, each of the religions must be judged to express some aspect of God's revelatory presence. And if it be true that the eternal Logos is the universal revealer, as a common interpretation of John 1:9 would have it, we cannot say that Christ is simply absent from the non-Christian religions. Rather, he is present in them, in an unexplicit or non-thematic way. He is the author and bearer of all the religions insofar as they mediate an authentic encounter with God.

He is also their goal insofar as all divinely inspired religion tends to the recognition of God's definitive self-gift in Christ.

In our own time there are signs of an emerging dialogue among the world religions. If this dialogue is to succeed, Christianity must be prepared to recognize the divine vocation of the other religions. Christ does not have to be brought to them from outside, for he is already present and operative in them, albeit in a hidden way.[24] They are called to come to fulfillment in him, without loss of their own distinctive character. They do not necessarily have to pass through the precise route that Judaism took in its recognition of Christ as the fulfillment of its own prophetic religion and traditions. The living Christ, rather than historic Christianity, is the definitive self-manifestation of God. All the religions, including Christianity, must tend toward him as their crown and prize.

The various religions, insofar as they objectify different aspects of the inner reality of grace, have a salutary function. The light of Christ radiates in them, too. They can be bearers of revelation to their own adherents and also, no doubt, show up aspects of man's relationship to God that have been unduly neglected in the forms of Christianity known to us. The fact that Christianity has hardly existed, during the past millenium, except as a Western religion, makes it especially important to study the non-Western religions. By assimilating the authentic values these religions have to offer, we shall not be watering down our Christianity, but on the contrary enriching it with jewels which it ought to have, but does not in fact possess because of the limited religious capacities and sensitivities of modern Western man, whose sense of religion has become in certain respects atrophied.

The contemporary state of Western civilization raises yet another question about revelation. If revelation expresses itself in religion, what is to be said of non-religious people? Is their lack of religion evidence that they have not received, or responded to, the revealing presence of God? In answer to this question we must again appeal to our distinction between the explicit and the implicit, the thematic and the non-thematic. In general, religion is the thematization of man's conscious relationship to God; it is what results when man reflects on this relationship and tries to bring it to appropriate expression. But as we have already noted, a man may have a very real and decisive relationship to God which is not religiously thematized. He may conceive of his supreme duty as service to his fellow-man, or the quest for truth, or the promotion of justice. These impulses give rise to social movements analogous to the great religions. Tillich calls them quasi-religions. World views which embody a system of values, and involve some kind of ultimate commitment, even though they are not explicitly religious and may make no mention of God, may in fact enshrine insights and orientations derived from revelation. Just as the non-Christian religions can become vehicles of the grace of Christ, even when they do not explicitly invoke his name, so the great secular faiths of mankind, such as Marxism and Utopian Socialism, may in an implicit and non-thematic way articulate man's responses to the self-revealing God. The Christian must school himself to detect the Christian meaning, the "sensus plenior," of secular humanism in its various forms.

In answer to our initial question, then, we may conclude that revelation involves both inner experience and outer expression. Neither alone constitutes the whole of revelation. Nor are the inner and the outer two unrelated types of revelation. Revelation has an inner unity, inasmuch as the experience issues from the historical situation constituted by human persons in relationship to one another. Once received, revelation expresses itself in outward forms and symbols, which bring the revelatory experience to fulfillment, sustain it, and communicate it to others. This process of revelation being relayed through symbolic expressions occurs not simply in one religious tradition (the biblical or Judaeo-Christian) but, in varying forms and degrees, in all the religions of man. Secular humanism in its various forms may be, and often is, an embodiment of revelatory insights thematized in a non-religious way.

According to Christian faith, the Christ-event of the New Testament is the supreme manifestation of God's revelatory self-communication to man and of man's response in the obedience of faith. Jesus Christ is therefore to be viewed as the source and goal of all the religions and of all authentic forms of secular humanism, insofar as this too expresses more or less accurately the meaning and value of man as he stands in the sight of God. Christianity must be on guard against looking upon itself as the exclusive self-revelation of God. As one among the religions, it must continually seek to prove its absolute value by showing its capacity to absorb all the religious truth and value in all the other religions and quasi-religions. Only in this way can it overcome its historical particularism and make itself the universal agent of reconciliation which, under Christ, it is called upon to become.

IV. LIGHT OR CONTENT?

THE vast majority of theologians in our time admit that Christianity *has* or *is* a revelation, but a growing number seem to question whether there are such things as "revealed truths." In the standard Catholic view of revelation, as I have described it in my introductory section, the idea of "revealed truths" is primary. Christianity is thought to be a revealed religion consisting of a set of objective, propositional truths resting on the authority of God as revealer. Certain doctrines are singled out as matters of divine faith, e.g., "God is three persons in one nature," "Jesus Christ is truly God and truly man." These propositions are thought to embody a truth-claim basically similar to that of philosophical statements such as "every contingent being has an efficient cause," or "man is a body animated by a rational soul." They differ from these philosophical truths not in their truth-value but in their warrants. For they are thought to rest not on experience and rational inference but on the authority of the revealing God.

Although this view has until recently been dominant in Catholic theology, and probably still is in certain seminaries and chanceries, it obviously suffers from an inordinate extrinsicism and objectivism. From all that we have said in the preceding pages it should be evident that revelation is not a set of propositional truths prefabricated in heaven and artificially inseminated into the minds of men. In the present age, it would be disastrous to seek to perpetuate the mythical or magical view of revelation, depicting it as an infusion of propositional truths into the minds of seers and prophets. We have seen that there is no strict line of division between acquired and revealed knowledge.

Once it is recognized that man is born into a redeemed universe, and that his entire spiritual life unfolds under the sign of his vocation to union with God, it becomes exceedingly difficult to delimit any precise sphere of revealed truth. But if one admits God's gracious concurrence in man's movement toward religious truth, one can say that every major advance in man's realization of his relationship to God in the articulation of the preconceptual experience of grace, is in some sense revealed. Creedal and confessional statements may be called revealed insofar as they embody a valid truth-claim which is not verifiable by objective scientific techniques or without reliance on spiritual discernment.

As ordinarily understood, revealed truth connotes infallibility. Contemporary theology is seeking to define more accurately the meaning and limits of infallibility. By and large, it is evident that human statements of religious truth are not exempt from a certain admixture of human error. Whatever truth-value may accrue to religious knowledge, thanks to the influence of the divine Spirit at work within the spirit of man, this does not magically protect the human recipient from confusion and error.

This fallibility-quotient, as we may call it, would seem to be present, not merely in the pagan religions, in which Christians are wont to find innumerable aberrations, but even in the biblical revelation. If infallibility is to be claimed for the Bible, this can hardly be on the basis of the objective accuracy of all its individual assertions. The biblical authors, in the New Testament as well as the Old, were badly mistaken about many matters, not only scientific and historical, but also moral and doctrinal. Attempts to distinguish between religious and nonreligious passages in the Bible, attributing infallibility only to the former, are unavailing. From a Christian point of view, the teaching of the Old Testament about the vindictiveness of God, the afterlife, the ethics of matrimony and war, and many other "religious" subjects is seriously deficient. Even in the New Testament there are numerous religious teachings which do not command the assent of modern Christians. The expectation of an imminent end of the world, evident in many of the earlier strata of the New Testament writings, has obviously been proved wrong, and most apologetical maneuvers seeking to evade the consequences of this fact have proved unavailing.

On the other hand, it would be irresponsible to insist on fallibility to the point of neglecting the infallibility component which is present in all revelatory knowledge, whether in the Old Testament or in the New, or for that matter in the non-Christian religions, insofar as they too contain insights achieved through the help of grace. Whenever it is given to men to see something in the light of the divine Spirit, and to bear witness to this, their statements have a certain peremptory quality. However poorly they may have registered and expressed what they discerned, it was really there, and we should ignore it at our own peril. The precise nature of what men saw remains, no doubt, a subject for continual refinement and interpretation, and for reconsideration in the light of further evidence, but no further development in understanding will result in a simple negation of what was originally stated. If we presuppose that God did show something to the Jews through their history, and to the early Christians through their encounter with Jesus, we unquestionably have something definitive, irreversible, and if you like, infallible in the Christian revelation. The Christian is committed by his faith to the fact that this is so.

The infallibility of revelatory knowledge, which characterizes the Bible as a whole, although not necessarily each of its statements taken in isolation, continues—according to Catholic belief—in the statements of the Church. It is the Church's task, through its official teaching organs, to frame formulas, appropriate for various cultures and ages, of such a nature as to let the truth of the gospel shine forth in untarnished purity, and not to succumb to the perversity of men. The official formulations to which the Church commits herself are true insofar as they are translucent to the word of God which comes to believers in and through them. The truth of these doctrinal statements is not precisely that of objective scientific statements which contain no reference to God. Using the term "myth" in a wide sense, one may admit that religious language, insofar as it refers to the inscrutable mystery we call God, is mythical.

Some would hold that modern man thinks not mythically but scientifically, and have therefore proposed a demythologizing of the religious statements contained in the Bible and in Church documents. The proposal is sound insofar as it rests upon a recognition that these statements do contain a mythic element to which the modern believer is not bound to assent as though it were a strictly descriptive factual statement. The creeds themselves are full of parabolic language. But the demythologizing program risks falling into error if it intends to eliminate the mythic dimension and to translate religious statements into objective scientific discourse.

In the rationalistic age from which we are only beginning to emerge, theology was in danger of interpreting its own task too objectively. In order not to be misunderstood, all Christian dogmas have to be interpreted from within the experience of Christian faith. They attempt to speak about the relations between man and God, and especially about the way in which God communicates his life to men through Jesus Christ and the Holy Spirit. Of these things we cannot speak in the simply objective way in which we are accustomed to talk about stones or bugs. There always has to be some reference to an experience in which we ourselves are involved, in a deeply personal way. Once this personal reference is forgotten, the gifts of God are in danger of being looked upon as mere things, and grace tends to be treated as though it were an impersonal substance. The relations between man and God are fatally misrepresented.

The custom of talking about "revealed truths" incurs precisely this danger. The data of faith are thought of objectively, as though they existed "out there," independently of the consciousness by which they are apprehended. Whatever may be the case in other areas, this cannot be so in theology. The God of faith is not just a God "out there." He is our savior; he is the life of our life. Hence faith-statements always say something about man as well as about God; their truth is saving truth. Richard Niebuhr was correct when he wrote that the sphere of revelation is "the story of what happened to us, the living memory of the community."[25]

The inseparability between the act of faith and its content could be illustrated at length, except that the theme would take us too far afield. It could be shown, I believe, that the doctrines of faith are articulations of what the act of faith, in its inherent structure, already is. Faith is not an empty sack that can be filled by anything God chooses to say.

Faith is inherently trinitarian because of the way God comes to man. Before man can respond in faith, God must first manifest himself. This he does by his Word, especially by Christ, the Word Incarnate, who is God's perfect self-realization in created form. But we could not recognize Christ as the Father's Word unless our hearts were attuned to him by the Holy Spirit. Thanks to the inward anointing of the Spirit we can say: "In your light we see light" (Ps. 35:10). Because faith is an active reception of God as He communicates himself under the twofold form of Word and Spirit—that is, objectively and subjectively—faith is trinitarian not only in content but also in structure.

The same unity between content and structure could be illustrated with regard to other dogmas. For example, the story of the Incarnation, death, and resurrection of Jesus is recapitulated in the faith-life of every believer. As St. Paul insisted, we all die in Christ, in order to be raised with him. Through the surrender of faith we die to our sinful selves, and in courageously dying with him we enter into the fullness of life.

There remains, of course, the problem what to do with traditional doctrines that seem practically unrelated to our contemporary experience. Many would feel that the question whether angels exist, or whether the world was "created in time" rather than "from eternity," and other similar questions, have little or no existential reference. I can scarcely do more at the present time than to mention the problem. By way of an answer, one might suggest that these doctrines, to the extent that they really are matters of faith, must be understood in relation to man in the present life. If they were mere information about the past, or the future, or the world beyond, without impact upon man's present attitudes and conduct, and without a point of insertion into his life-experience, they would not fall within the ambit of potential revelation. The efforts made in previous generations to frame a scientific theory of cosmic and human origins on the basis of the early chapters of Genesis has exhibited, once and for all, the futility of seeking objective scientific information through the channels of revelation.

Sometimes the question is asked whether revelation actually supplies man with any intellectual content that could not otherwise be known. As we have already seen, it is most difficult to designate any propositional statements which can be made by the light of faith alone. One could conceive of a person, applying his unaided natural powers to the data of history and experience, saying almost anything that a Christian says by faith. But if revelation reveals nothing new, is it revelation at all?

I do not believe there are any watertight creedal tests that can discern between the believer and the unbeliever. If they say the same things, they do so in a different way. The believer's speech is an expression of his personal acceptance of the inner light of grace, inviting him to friendship and communion with God. This may, and normally does, enable him to say things that presumably he would not otherwise say. It gives him a certain connaturality with the divine, and thus helps him to detect signs of the presence and activity of God in the world. It puts him in a position to see positive meaning in what Scripture and the Church have to say about the mystery of God's self-communication to man through love. When the believer speaks of these things, he is interpreting his own religious experience as one in whom the loving invitation of God makes itself felt.

In the last analysis the question whether revelation is "light" or "content" is otiose. It introduces a false dichotomy. Because we ourselves are always involved in the mysteries of which faith speaks, the light of faith is constitutive of the objects on which faith bears. The formal and material objects intertwine. Every expression of faith has a subjective as well as an objective reference.

V. CLOSED OR CONTINUING REVELATION?

THE last point which I proposed to discuss is the following: whether the Christian revelation came to an end at some determinate moment in the past (say, the Ascension of Christ, or Pentecost, or the death of the last Apostle), or whether, on the other hand, revelation is an ongoing process that will not cease until history itself comes to a close.

Some would say that, at least for the Catholic Christian, this cannot be an open question. Did not the Encyclical *Lamentabili* affirm, in opposition to the Modernists, that revelation, insofar as it constitutes an object of Catholic faith, reached its completion with the Apostles?[26] Of course the Decree did say this, but one can still raise the question as to exactly what it binds us to hold. This particular document was a syllabus of propositions culled from the writings of the Modernists, and rejected as unsatisfactory. In many cases the very terms of the formulations, being those of the Modernists themselves, were unfortunate. The Catholic is surely forbidden to hold the contrary of these propositions in the sense intended by the Modernists. Thus, in the present case, he will not feel free to adopt a free-wheeling view of revelation in which the New Testament would be treated as a mere point of departure rather than as an abiding norm. The Modernists' view of continuing revelation will most surely be rejected. But it does not follow from this that God has ceased to communicate with mankind ever since the Apostle John breathed his final sigh.

Many Catholic textbooks, going slightly beyond the documents of the magisterium, assert that revelation closed with the death of the last Apostle. At Vatican Council II the question was raised whether this statement should be inserted into the Constitution on Divine Revelation. The final declaration stated that Jesus "by His whole presence and self-manifestation, by His words and deeds, by His signs and miracles, especially by His death and glorious resurrection from the dead, and finally by His sending of the Holy Spirit, perfects revelation in completing it, and confirms with divine testimony that God will be with us to free us from sin and the shadows of death and to raise us to eternal life" (n. 4). "As a result," the Constitution continued, "the Christian economy, as the new and definitive covenant, will never pass away, and so new public revelation is to be awaited before the glorious manifestation of our Lord Jesus Christ" (*ibid.*). Some bishops proposed that this statement be amended to include an explicit affirmation that revelation "closed with the death of the Apostles." The Commission charged with the preparation of the schema refused, and replied tersely: "The truth intended by this statement is already declared, when it is said that Christ completes revelation; but the formula does not lack difficulties, and indeed from several different points of view" (*et quidem propter rationes divergentes*).

The formula which the Council refused to include in *Dei Verbum* insinuates that there was something unique about the period between the Ascension of Christ and the death of the last Apostle. This would have been a time when the deposit of faith was still being accumulated. But it is hard to see why this is so. The Council was better inspired to focus on the Christ-event, together with the Pentecostal descent of the Spirit of truth, as the period when the essential object of Christian faith was constituted. No doubt the activity of the Holy Spirit was especially intense during the early years of the Church, when so many new decisions had to be made that would establish the Church on its course through time. The Apostles' understanding of and reaction to the revelation they had received, enshrined in the New Testament, was destined to be normative for future centuries. But no one holds today that the New Testament was composed in its entirety before the death of the last of the twelve Apostles. Nor has the Holy Spirit ceased to accompany the Church with positive inspirations as it progresses through history.

There might be some justification for saying that revelation was closed with the completion of the Christ-event and the sending of the Holy Spirit by the risen Lord. At this point God had totally given himself to man as Word and Spirit, and the new and definitive covenant was complete.

Yet in another sense it is wrong to speak of revelation being closed at all. Revelation for the Christian means the active self-communication of God to man as a conscious subject, and this, as we have seen, goes on whenever God makes himself present in grace and love. When God has spoken to man through the incarnate life of his Son upon this earth, he did not fall silent and retire into some kind of Deistic lethargy. The word of God, once spoken in Christ, continues to be spoken. It is a living word which continues to come to man in new and surprising ways. According to the documents of Vatican II, God continues to speak to men through the Bible, through Christian preaching, through the example of the saints, through the voice of conscience, through the "signs of the times," and in countless other ways. All this "speaking" of God may be called revelation; it is new revelation, not in the sense that it tells us something that was in no way told to the first Christians, but in the sense that it makes that message live again for ourselves and for our day. If it were not revivified by new revelation, it would no longer be revelation at all. For a past revelation is simply an item of history unless it is still going on.

In an earlier generation, when Catholic theology was dominated by the subject-object dichotomy, it seemed easy to hold that revelation was complete in apostolic times, whereas faith, the subjective appropriation of revelation, still continues to be given. This would be acceptable if revelation consisted essentially of an objective deposit, handed down unchanged from one generation to the next. But in the view we have proposed, revelation must be understood more vitally and existentially. Revelation does not exist apart from the self-manifestation of God within the consciousness of those who are called to believe. To the extent that God continues to communicate himself in love to those whom he calls to union, he must be said to continue to reveal himself—and this revelation never occurs twice in exactly the same form. The stable dogmas and creedal formulations of the Church express the constant patterns of revelation, but they do not set forth, in an exhaustive way, its contents.

The development of dogma is a difficult question, to which no satisfactory solution can be given here, for I have barely touched on the problem in what sense dogma is revelation. In the present context I would only note that the question would be far more difficult than it is if one were to imagine that the revelation given in the first century consisted of a determinate number of propositions. It would be quite impossible to deduce all the present dogmas of the Church from statements in the Bible or verifiable tenets of apostolic tradition. On the theory of revelation we have proposed, both the statements in Scripture and the recent dogmas of the Church have to be interpreted as crystallizations of the experience of the Chrisitan community, whose faith could never be totally objectified as a collection of propositional statements.

Karl Rahner, in his discussion of the development of dogma, remarks that the closedness of Christian revelation is, in reality, a total openness. Because God has fully disclosed himself by his absolute self-communication in Christ, the Word made flesh, he cannot say anything strictly in addition to what he has already said. "The closing of revelation is not the arbitrary ending of God's speaking, which could have gone on and only as a matter of fact fell silent after some chosen utterance.... It is man's being opened up for and into the real and not merely conceptual self-communication of God [in Christ]."[27] Since the closure is really a disclosure, Christian revelation has an inner dynamism to develop. If it failed to do so it could scarcely be a genuine disclosure of the dynamic reality we call God.

In the contemporary atmosphere of rapid change and mobility, many Christians are distressed by the feeling of being compelled to adhere to a revelation completely given many centuries ago. They feel that this shackles them to the past and inhibits their free development as adult and responsible persons. Such fears are unfortunately not groundless. In many presentations, Christianity is set forth as a mere collection of propositional statements found in ancient documents, to which believers are required to subscribe. This objectivist and legalistic conception of revelation can easily have the effect of subjecting men of today to the dead hand of the past.

Rightly understood, however, the "givenness" of Christianity as an event of the past is not antithetical to its being given today. On the contrary, it is the strongest guarantee that it will still be given today and in the ages to come. We might apply in this connection what Paul says of grace: "He who has not spared even his own Son but has delivered him for us all, how can he fail to grant us also all things with him?" (Rom. 8:32). If he has spoken to our forbears in Christ, can he fail to speak to us today? Whatever "more" he has to say to us is somehow implied in, and not really extrinsic to, the Word which fully expresses his divinity. The "filling up" of revelation, by which it becomes a vital reality of our day, does not detract from, but rather proves, the sufficiency of the revelation given first of all in Christ. The knowledge that God has totally communicated himself in Christ does not make us deaf to his work today, but rather alerts us to be attentive to his voice.

To speak accurately, it might be better not to say simply that revelation has occurred or is occurring. The term does not apply with full intensity to anything in the past or the present. If we wish to be guided by the etymology of the term "revelation," which means unveiling, it scarcely describes the veiled and obscure intimations of God that are given to faith. In the New Testament, and particularly in Paul (e.g. 1 Cor. 1:7, 2 Thess. 1:7, Col. 3:4, Rom. 8:18; cf. Lk. 17:30, 1 Pt. 1:7, 13, 4:13, 5:4), it is clearly taught that the full revelation of God in Christ, and of our glory in and with him, is to take place at the final Parousia.

The faith which is given to us, and which we are able to articulate to some measure through our knowledge of what God has done in the history of salvation, does not orient us primarily to the past. Our attitude as Christians is not that of men anxiously clinging to a treasure which they already possess and are afraid of losing. Rather, the story of God's great deeds of love, as handed down to us, makes us strain forward with hope and eagerness for the fullness of knowledge and union with the God of grace. Our faith liberates us from false anxiety and false complacency; it makes us long joyfully for that moment, beyond all time as we now know it, when we shall see him as he is (1 Jn. 3:2) and when we shall know him even as we are known (1 Cor. 13:12).

NOTES

[1] New York: Macmillan, 1967.

[2] *History and Hermeneutics* (Philadelphia, 1966), p. 11.

[3] *The Idea of Revelation in Recent Thought* (New York: Columbia Paperback Edition, 1964), p. 15.

[4] H. R. Niebuhr, *The Meaning of Revelation*, pp. 3-4.

[5] Cf. the two essays of Pannenberg in J. M. Robinson and J. B. Cobb, Jr., (eds.), *Theology as History* (New York, 1967), esp. pp. 125-128.

6 "The Current Controversy on Revelation: Pannenberg and His Crittics," *Journal of Religion* 45 (1965), 230.
7 H. R. Niebuhr, *op. cit.*, p. 69.
8 *History Sacred and Profane* (Philadelphia, 1964).
9 *The Historian and the Believer* (New York, 1966), p. 258.
10 *Decree on Ecumenism*, n. 11.
11 *Constitution on Revelation (Dei Verbum)*, n. 2.
12 *Constitution on the Church in the Modern World (Gaudium et spes)*, n. 22.
13 *Ibid.*
14 *Ibid.*, n. 14.
15 *The Letter on Apologetics* (New York: Holt, Rinehart & Winston, 1964), p. 152. Cf. the discussion of Blondel's apologetic in Auguste Valensin, art. "Immanence (Méthode d')," *Dict. Apol. de la Foi Catholique*, 4th ed., Paris, 1915, vol. 2, col. 579-93.
16 This theme has been powerfully developed not only in Rahner's essay *On the Concept of Revelation* (New York: Herder & Herder, 1966), but even more explicitly in his work, *Hominization* (New York: Herder & Herder, 1965), pp. 81-93. Both essays are in the *Quaestiones Disputatae* series (vols. 17 and 13, respectively).
17 M. Polanyi, "Faith and Reason," *Journal of Religion* 41 (1961), 237-47, quotation from p. 243.
18 *Ibid.*, p. 246.
19 *Ibid.*, p. 244.
20 K. Rahner, "Considerations on the Development of Dogma," *Theol. Investig.* 4 (Baltimore, 1966), p. 13.
21 M. Polanyi, *Personal Knowledge* (Harper Torchbook Edition, New York, 1964), pp. 36-37.
22 *The Meaning of Revelation*, p. 97.
22a This statement, as I understand it, is not really irreconcilable with Vatican I's affirmation of a twofold order of knowledge (*DS* 3015); for Vatican I was using the term "reason" in an abstract sense rather than in the concrete sense explained in my text.
23 J. Daniélou, *The Salvation of the Nations* (Univ. of Notre Dame, paperback ed., 1962), p. 14. These sentences must no doubt be understood in the light of other statements in which Daniélou, even in this book, alludes to the interior and exterior self-revelation of God to every man in the world; *ibid.*, pp. 20-23. See also his *The Lord of History*, chap. 8.
24 Cf. R. Panikkar, *The Unknown Christ of Hinduism* (London, 1964) for an interesting development of this thesis.
25 *The Meaning of Revelation*, p. 66.
26 "*Revelatio, obiectum fidei catholicae constituens, non fuit cum Apostolis completa*," condemned proposition n. 21 in the Decree of the Holy Office, *Lamentabili* (*DS* 3421).
27 "Considerations on the Development of Dogma," *Theol. Investig.* 4, p. 9.

De-Judaization and Hellenization: The Ambiguities of Christian Identity

Jaroslav Pelikan

IN the modern search for the meaning of Christian identity, no issue has been more persistent than the question of Hellenization. The accusation that one's theological opponents have sacrificed the content of the faith to a Greek understanding of reality has long been a standard weapon in the arsenal of Christian polemics. Nestorius, for example, charged that the Alexandrian view of the Incarnation, according to which, by the communication of idioms, birth and suffering and death could be predicated of the Logos, had been "led astray by the mentality of the Greeks [*planomenēs kath Hellēnas dianoias*]." But it has been especially since the Reformation that theologians and historians have debated the extent of Greek influence upon the development of Christian doctrine. Probably the best-known analysis and documentation of that influence was the magisterial *Dogmengeschichte* of Adolf Harnack, whose definition of dogma read: "In its conception and in its development, dogma is a product of the Greek spirit on the soil of the gospel." More recently, the issue of Hellenization has become a lively point of controversy also among Roman Catholic thinkers, as the reactions to Leslie Dewart's *The Future of Belief* attest.

If one examines the question of Hellenization more profoundly, however, the usual discussions of it prove to be both superficial and one-sided. It is interesting, for example, that for all his criticism of the Hellenization of Christianity, Harnack attacked even more sharply the continuing authority of the Old Testament in the Church. Implicit—and sometimes explicit—in much of the criticism of the Old Testament by German scholars of the nineteenth and twentieth century is an aversion to Judaism both ancient and modern, and an effort to purge Christianity of the vestigial remnants of its Jewish heritage. This aversion, too, has a long history, and a sorry one. Christian thought must probe its relation both to Hellenism and to Judaism if it is to achieve a clear understanding of the ambiguities within its own identity, for the obverse side of any "Hellenization" to which the development of Christian doctrine may have been subject is its "de-Judaization."

The scholarly investigation of this problem is a task for various disciplines. Biblical exegesis needs to see how these and related processes are at work in the various strata of the New Testament. Historians of Judaism can add much to our knowledge by continuing research into both rabbinical and Hellenistic Judaism. Only the beginnings of research into liturgical history have illumined many doctrinal questions. Recent examinations of Hellenistic syncretism have put the question of heretical Judaism and its importance for Christian development into a new light. Hellenistic philosophy has begun to look different after the work of various historians of Stoicism and Middle Platonism. But the history of early Christian doctrine has a special stake in the question, as well as a distinctive contribution to make to any reconsideration of the issues.

I. DE-JUDAIZATION

According to tradition, only one of the writers of the New Testament, Luke, was not a Jew. As far as we know for certain, none of the Church Fathers was a Jew—although both Hermas and Hegesippus, for example, may have been. The transition represented by that contrast had the most far-reaching of consequences for the entire development of Christian doctrine.

The earliest Christians were Jews, and in their new faith they found a continuity with the old. They remembered that their Lord himself had said that his purpose was to fulfill, not to abolish, the law and the prophets; and it was useless for heretics to deny this saying. From the early chapters of the Book of Acts we get a somewhat idealized picture of a Christian community that continued to obey the Scriptures, the worship, and the observances of Jewish religious life. The members of the Church at Jerusalem, which Irenaeus called "the Church from which every Church took its start, the metropolis of the citizens of the new covenant," followed James, their "caliph," in refusing to acknowledge a fundamental cleavage between their previous life and their new status. Clearly they recognized that something very new had come—not something brand-new, but something newly restored and fulfilled. Even after the fall of Jerusalem in A.D. 70, these "Nazarenes" maintained continuity with Judaism; they "wish to observe the ordinances which were given by Moses ... yet choose to live with the Christians and the faithful." But especially in the period before A.D. 70, the tensions within Jewish thought were reflected also in the beginnings of Christian theology. The party centering in James manifested interesting analogies to Palestinian Judaism, while the "missionary party" eventually identified with Paul, as well as the Christian apologetics of the second century, reflected certain affinities with the Jewish thought of the Hellenistic Diaspora.

More fundamental than these parallels, however, is the conflict between Hellenistic Jews and Hellenistic Jewish-Christians over the question of the continuity of Christianity with Judaism. For after A.D. 70 that conflict marked the relations between Christian and Jewish thought everywhere. The extent and the scope of the continuity produced controversy between Peter and Paul, and it went on troubling the Church. Various practical solutions were designed to meet immediate problems of cultic and dietary observance, but these did not issue in a consistent way of interpreting the theological question: What is new about the new covenant? Whatever else they may mean, the differences between the way this question is answered in Acts 15 (with its crucial textual variants) and the way Paul discusses it in Galatians do suggest the continuing difficulty which the Church faced. To this extent, F. C. Baur was right in seeing the conflict over this issue as fundamental to the interpretation of the rise of Christian doctrine. The leaders of both sides were Christians of Jewish origin; despite their differing answers, therefore, they asked the question of continuity between Judaism and Christianity with a deep personal poignancy.

As converts began coming more from pagan than from Jewish ranks, however, the poignancy lessened and the obverse side of the question became more prominent. For Jewish Christians, the question of continuity was the question of their relation to their mother; for Gentile Christians, it was the question of their relation to their mother-in-law. What was offensive about Christianity in the eyes of Gentiles was, to a considerable extent, what it had inherited from Judaism. Therefore, Celsus and other pagan critics lampooned the claim that God had put in an appearance at, of all places, "some corner of Judaea somewhere"; and the Emperor Julian scorned the Jewish and Christian conception of God as "essentially the deity of a primitive and uncivilized folk," even while he chided the "Galileans" for forsaking Judaism. Not only the Gentile critics of Christianity, but also the Gentile converts to Christianity demanded a decision about just how much of the Jewish tradition they were obliged to retain. Marcion was therefore a heretical instance of what may have been a rather widespread resentment also among orthodox believers; for the Epistle of Barnabas, while not going as far as Marcion in its rejection of the Old Testament, did claim that the original tablets of the covenant of the Lord were shattered at Sinai and that therefore Israel had never had an authentic covenant with God. Tertullian's declaration, in opposition to Marcion, that "today" there were more who accepted the authority of the Old Testament than rejected it raises the question whether the number of those rejecting it may not at one time have been considerable.

This struggle over the authority of the Old Testament and over the nature of the continuity between Judaism and Christianity was the earliest form of the quest for a tradition that has, in other forms, recurred throughout Christian history. The Christian adoption of Abraham as "father of the faithful" and the Christian identification of the Church, the city of God, with the heritage of Abel are illustrations of this quest for a tradition and of its fulfillment in the Old Testament. When the Church formulated its quest for a tradition in a doctrine of correction-and-fulfillment, it was enabled to claim that "all these... going from Abraham all the way back to the first man, it would not be an exaggeration to call Christians, in fact, if not in name." That doctrine of correction-and-fulfillment likewise helped to set a pattern for the treatment of the problem of tradition in subsequent centuries. Thus, Athanasius could claim to have the tradition on his side despite the subordinationist or Modalist language of many of the Fathers; Augustine could seek to exonerate the Greek fathers of the charges of Pelagianism; the orthodox opponents of Gottschalk could seek to exonerate Augustine in turn; the argument over the *Filioque* turned on the testimony of tradition; and the Protestant Reformers could affirm their loyalty to the Catholic tradition despite their separation from Rome. All these arguments followed the outline of the appropriation of the Jewish tradition by the Christians of the first and second centuries.

Primary evidence for the development of that appropriation is a genre of Christian literature devoted to a comparison of Christianity with Judaism. Within this genre "there is no dialogue... which is conducted on quite so high a level of courteousness and fairness" in the early church as the *Dialogue with Trypho* of Justin Martyr, but Justin's treatise was only one of many. Virtually every major Christian writer of the first five centuries either composed a treatise in opposition to Judaism or made this issue a dominant theme of a treatise devoted to some other subject. Scholars are generally agreed that Justin's work represented the literary form of an actual interview, albeit one composed many years after the fact and reflecting the author's hindsight on the debate. But it is equally clear that most of the later treatises *adversus Judaeos* neither reflected nor envisaged any such interview. Rather, the dialogue with Judaism became a literary conceit, in which the question of the uniqueness of Christianity in comparison with Judaism became an occasion for a literary exposition of Christian doctrine for a non-Jewish audience of Christian readers. When, for example, Abelard wrote his *Dialogue between a Philosopher, a Jew, and a Christian,* he may have incorporated some of the subjects still being treated in face-to-face encounters between Jews and Christians, for these were probably more frequent than the present state of our sources would suggest. But Abelard's primary purpose was a dialectical one: he was writing to make Christians think, not to make philosophers or Jews accept Christianity.

Comparison of the treatises against the Jews from the first three centuries has disclosed the recurrence of certain biblical passages and conflations of biblical passages, certain historical references, and forms of argumentation. Thus, early in the twentieth century, the discovery of the long-lost text of the *Proof of the Apostolic Preaching* of Irenaeus (albeit in an Armenian version) provided additional support for the theory that there existed a compilation "of Scriptural texts grouped under argument-headings, intended to convince the Jews out of the Old Testament itself that the Old Law was abolished, that its abolition was foreseen in the Old Testament, and that its purpose had been to prepare and prefigure the New Law of Christ." This commonplace in Christian literature, aimed at demonstrating that the Church had now become the new and the true Israel, may well have antedated the Gospels themselves. From the traditional title of such treatises as Cyprian's *To Quirinus: Three Books of Testimonies Against the Jews* this set of commonplaces has acquired the title *Testimonia*. The literature of the dialogue with Judaism is thus an important source for the developing self-understanding of Christian theology, as well as for its understanding of the differences between Christianity and Judaism.

A prominent element in this literature of the dialogue is understandably the issue of the continuing validity of the Mosaic law. The Old Testament had declared that the law was as permanent as the covenant with Israel; but the Christians, "treating this covenant with rash contempt, spurn the responsibilities that come with it." This appeared to Jewish thought to be a repudiation of both the law and the covenant. Justin's reply to this charge by Trypho was a stratification of the Old Testament law. The Christians retained that in the law of Moses which was "naturally good, pious, and righteous"—usually as much as conformed to a reductionistic conception of the natural law. Thus "the providence which long ago gave the law [of Moses], but now has given the gospel of Jesus Christ, did not wish that the practices of the Jews should continue." Hence Christians were not bound by anything that had been addressed to the old Israel as a people. Such a stratification of moral, civil, and ceremonial elements in the Mosaic law proved very difficult to maintain with any consistency, and the Fathers could not make it stick. Irenaeus, for example, celebrated the superiority of Christian doctrine and life to all of the law, including the Decalogue, even though he also affirmed that "the words of the Decalogue" had undergone "extension and amplification" rather than "cancellation" by Christ's coming in the flesh.

A more effective way than stratification for coping with the law of the Old Testament was provided by allegorical and typological exegesis. Here again the Epistle of Barnabas went further than most. To the question, "Is there not a commandment from God which forbids the eating" of ceremonially unclean animals, it replied: "Yes, there is, but Moses was speaking in spiritual terms." The same was true of the circumcision of Abraham. Less drastic in his spiritualization of the Old Testament commandments, Tertullian argued that a "new law" and a "new circumcision" had superseded the old, which had been intended only as a sign or type of that which was to come. Drawing directly on sources in Hellenistic Judaism, Origen set his interpretation of the Mosaic law into the context of an allegory on the Exodus from Egypt; "with Origen the allegory of Philo [on the life of Moses and the Exodus] will be incorporated into Christian tradition, and become part of the traditional typology." A special feature of the typology of the Exodus was the anticipation of baptism by the miracle of the Red Sea; baptism was, in turn, set in opposition to the circumcision of the Old Testament. As we shall see, it is certainly an exaggeration to say that "by transforming the gospel into a New Law the Apostolic Fathers returned to the impossible situation from which Christ came deliberately to redeem," for the term "new law" and related terms such as *Christonomos* are not devoid of the evangelical content which "law" sometimes bears in the usage of both the Old and the New Testament. At the same time it is evident that as moralism and legalism manifested themselves in Christian theology, much of the edge was removed from the argument of Christian apologetics against the Jewish conception of the law.

Although the law and the prophets belonged together in the language of Jewish theology, Christian theology identified its cause with that of the prophets against the law; hence Ignatius argued that the prophets had observed Sunday rather than the Jewish Sabbath. Christian apologetics was even more assiduous in looking for proofs that Jesus was the fulfillment of the prophetic promises than for indications that he was the end of the law. The beginnings of this process are evident already in the New Testament, especially, of course, in books such as the Gospel of Matthew and the Epistle to the Hebrews, but also in Luke, the one New Testament writer traditionally identified as Greek; it is in his gospel that the risen Christ "beginning with Moses and all the prophets interpreted to them in all the [Old Testament] Scriptures the things concerning himself." The New Testament formula, "that the Scripture might be fulfilled" may sometimes refer to a result rather than a purpose, but the translation "in order that [by divine decree] it might be fulfilled" suggests that the precise distinction between purpose and result is not really applicable. Irenaeus summarized the teaching of the New Testament and of early Christian tradition generally when he declared: "That all these things would come to pass was foretold by the Spirit of God through the prophets, that those who serve God in truth might believe firmly in them."

Thus the two purposes of the *testimonia* were: to show that Judaism, with its laws, had been superseded; and to prove that "he who had been foretold has come, in accordance with the Scriptures" of the Old Testament. To this end the *testimonia* compiled (and, as we have noted, often conflated) those passages that were most readily applicable to Jesus as the Christ. The rebellion of the nations against Jahweh, as described in Psalm 2, was fulfilled in the suffering of Christ: "the heathen were Pilate and the Romans; the people were the tribes of Israel: the kings were represented in Herod, and the rulers in the chief priests." The "enthronement psalms" could be applied to the resurrection of Christ, by which he had been elevated to the status of lordship; Psalm 110 was a favorite proof text for this claim, already in the New Testament. The other favorite proof text was the description of the "suffering servant" in Isaiah. The rabbis who disputed with Origen contended that it "referred to the whole people [of Israel] as though of a single individual," but it was interpreted so unanimously and unambiguously as Christian Scripture that even Trypho was constrained to admit that the Messiah was to suffer, though not that he was to be crucified. The "coming of the Lord" in later Jewish prophecy and apocalyptic also referred to Jesus as the Christ; but now it had to be divided into two comings, the first already accomplished in the days of his flesh and the second still in the future. Beyond the difference between humiliation and glory it was not always clear what the basis was for this division, which neither Judaism nor the anti-Judaistic Marcionites would accept. The assurance with which this interpretation was set forth indicates that Christian doctrine took the Christological meaning of these passages for granted.

What the Christian tradition had in fact done was to take over the Jewish scriptures as its own so that Justin could say to Trypho that the passages about Christ "are contained in your Scriptures, or rather not yours, but ours." Indeed, some of the passages were contained only in the Christian Old Testament. So assured were Christian theologians in their possession of the Scriptures that they could accuse the Jews not merely of misunderstanding and misinterpreting them, but even of falsifying their text. When they were aware of differences between the Hebrew text of the Old Testament and the Septuagint, they capitalized on these to prove their accusation that the Jews had "taken away many Scripture passages from the translations carried out by the seventy elders." Of special importance was the Septuagint translation *parthēnos* ("virgin") in Is. 7:14, which had been adopted by the New Testament and was canonized by early Christian writers. In Ps. 22:16 there may have been two Hebrew readings transmitted in the Jewish tradition: "they have pierced my hands and my feet" and "like a lion are my hands and my feet." Christian teachers, following the Septuagint, read "pierced" and applied this verse, together with the entire psalm, to the crucifixion; their Jewish opponents "maintain that this psalm does not refer to the Messiah."

In addition to these variant readings and canonized translations there developed a group of Christian additions to the text of the Septuagint or, as Daniélou has termed them, Christian *Targumim* and *Midrashim*, which paraphrased and expanded passages from the Old Testament in ways that substantiated Christian doctrine. Justin accused the Jews of mutilating the passage, "The Lord reigned from the tree," to delete the obvious reference to the crucifixion of Christ. The Christian exegetical tradition found many other such deletions and mutilations in the Jewish tradition of interpretation. It was perhaps a part of the same process of appropriation when the Christian historian Eusebius ascribed to Josephus the *testimonium Flavianum,* confessing the messiahship and the divinity of Jesus; or when the same Christian writer supposed that Philo's *On the Contemplative Life* was describing the early Christians rather than the Jewish Therapeutae. The growing confidence with which both these appropriations and these accusations could be made was in proportion to the completeness of the Christian victory over **Jewish thought.**

Yet that victory was achieved largely by default. Not the superior force of Christian exegesis or learning or logic, but the movement of Jewish history seems to have been largely responsible for it. It has been suggested that by its rise the Christian movement deprived Judaism of some of its earlier dynamic, especially of the proselytizing zeal that had marked Jewish thought in the Hellenistic Diaspora and even in Palestine. There were several translations of the Hebrew Bible into Greek by Jews (as well as perhaps one or more by Christians). By the end of the second and the beginning of the third century A.D., when Latin gradually began to displace Greek in the western part of the Roman Empire, the situation within Judaism itself had changed. The Septuagint seems to have been called forth both by the loss of ability to read Hebrew among younger Jews in the Diaspora and by the desire to present the case for Judaism to the Greek-speaking world. But it seems that neither of these factors produced any translation of the Old Testament into Latin by a Jew; for when the Hebrew Bible began to appear in Latin versions, these appear to have been the work of anonymous Christian translators and finally of Jerome. After the sack of Jerusalem in A.D. 70 and its desecration during the following years Jewish polemic against Christianity was increasingly on the defensive, while Christian doctrine felt able to go its own way, without engaging the rabbis in a continuing dialogue. Origen seems to have been one of the few Church Fathers to participate in such a dialogue. Origen seems also to have been the first Church Father to study Hebrew, "in opposition to the spirit of his time and of his people," as Jerome says; according to Eusebius, he "learned it thoroughly [*ekmathein*]," but there is reason to doubt the accuracy of this report. Jerome, however, was rightly celebrated as a *vir trilinguis* for his competence in Latin, Greek, and Hebrew, and Augustine clearly admired, perhaps even envied, him for his ability to "interpret the divine Scriptures in both languages."

The testimony about the Hebrew knowledge of other Church Fathers—for example, Didymus the Blind or Theodore of Mopsuestia—is less conclusive. But it seems safe to propose the generalization that, except for converts from Judaism, it was not until the "biblical humanists" and Reformers of the sixteenth century that a knowledge of Hebrew become standard equipment for Christian expositors of the Old Testament.

Whatever the reasons, Christian theologians writing against Judaism seemed to take their opponents less and less seriously as time went on; and what their apologetic works may have lacked in vigor or fairness, they tended to make up in self-confidence. They no longer looked upon the Jewish community as a continuing participant in the holy history that had produced the Church. The diatribes of Chrysostom were an extreme instance of anti-Jewish prejudice among the Fathers, but even those who were less violent in their language no longer gave serious consideration to the Jewish interpretation of the Old Testament nor to the Jewish backgrounds of the New. Therefore the urgency and the poignancy about "the mystery of Israel" that are so vivid in the New Testament have appeared only occasionally in Christian thought, as in some passages in Augustine; but these are outweighed, even in Augustine, by the many others that speak of Judaism and paganism almost as though they were equally alien to "the people of God," viz., the Church of Gentile Christians.

But the "de-Judaization of Christianity" did not express itself only in the place accorded to Judaism by Christian theologians. A more subtle and more pervasive effect of this process is evident in the development of various Christian doctrines themselves. Among these doctrines, the doctrine of God and the doctrine of man both bear marks of "de-Judaization." In Judaism it was possible simultaneously to ascribe change of purpose to God and to declare that God did not change, without resolving the paradox; for the immutability of God was seen as the trustworthiness of his covenanted relation to his people in the concrete history of his judgment and mercy, rather than as an ontological category. But in the development of the Christian doctrine of God, immutability assumed the status of an axiomatic presupposition for the discussion of other doctrines. Hence the de-Judaization of Christian thought contributed, for example, to the form taken by the Christological controversy, in which both sides defined the absoluteness of God in accordance with the principle of immutability even though they drew opposite Christological conclusions from it.

Similarly, the course taken by the development of the Augustinian tradition has been affected by the loss of contact with Jewish thought, whose refusal to polarize the free sovereignty of God and the free will of man has frequently been labeled "Pelagian." But the label is not appropriate, for it can be said, epigrammatically, that Judaism has a Pelagian doctrine of man but an Augustinian doctrine of God. Augustine accused the Pelagians of "putting the New Testament on the same level with the Old" by their view that it was possible for man to keep the law of God, and Jerome saw Pharisaism in the Pelagian notion that perfect righteousness was attainable under the conditions of existence. The development of Christian theology in the East, especially in the Antiochene school, manifested other ways of transcending the antitheses prevalent in the West and of setting forth "doctrine which cannot properly be called either Augustinian or Pelagian." But it, too, formulated the question in a manner alien to the Jewish tradition—even as it sought to find the answer for the question in the Hebrew Bible.

Because the victory of Christian theology over Jewish thought came more by default than by conquest, the question of the relation between two covenants has returned over and over to claim Christian attention. The significance of Jewish thinkers for Christian theologians—for example, of Maimonides for Thomas Aquinas, of Spinoza for Schleiermacher, or of Buber for Protestant theology in the twentieth century—is not simply part of the continuing interaction between theological and "secular" thought. In spite of the philosophical cast of these Jewish thinkers, Christian theologians have hearkened to them more as relatives than as strangers. At the same time, as we have noted, the less philosophical and more biblical elements of the Jewish theological tradition have failed to play a similar role in Christian history. But whenever individual theologians have seemed to be going too far in their denigration of the Old Testament, as Marcion and the biblical criticism of the nineteenth century did, they were denounced for relegating the larger part of the Christian Bible to a sub-Christian status. One of the most reliable indices of the interpretation of Judaism in Christian thought is the exegesis of Romans 9-11. The history of this exegesis is the record of the Church's struggle to give theological structure to its intuitions regarding the relation between the covenants, or to reestablish the sense of continuity-with-discontinuity evident in the language of the New Testament about Israel as the chosen people.

It was apparently from Jewish sectarianism that some of the earliest forms of Christian heresy came. According to Irenaeus, "all the heresies are derived from Simon of Samaria," and one of the oldest catalogues of Christian heretics, that of Hegesippus as preserved by Eusebius, lists Simon first among those who came from "the seven sects among the [Jewish?] people" to corrupt [the Church] by vain teachings." Eusebius himself termed Simon "the prime author of every kind of heresy" and identified him with the Simon of Acts 8:9-25. Cyril of Jerusalem, too, called him "the inventor of all heresy." But the primary source of information about the heresy of Simon is Justin Martyr, himself a native of Samaria, although a Gentile. According to Justin, Simon was acknowledged by his adherents "as the First God," and "they say that a certain Helen . . . was the First Thought which he brought into existence." The concept of the First Thought seems to have been derived at least partly from Jewish speculations about the personal Wisdom of God. Thus "Simonian gnosis arose out of Judaeo-Samaritan sectarianism," and through it contributed to the beginnings also of Christian Gnosticism. Like other forms of Gnosticism, Simonianism was radically pessimistic in its view of the created world, thus apparently carrying the implications of the doctrine of the two spirits of the Dead Sea Scrolls all the way to the point of an ontological dualism.

Not all the heretical forms of Jewish Christianity, however, manifested this dualism. Irenaeus reports that "those who are called Ebionites agree [with Jewish and Christian orthodoxy] that the universe was made by God." Where they diverged from Christian orthodoxy was in their view of Christ, for according to Origen, there were "two sects of Ebionites, the one confessing as we do that Jesus was born of a virgin, the other holding that he was not born in this way but like other men." The first of these seem to have belonged to the orthodox Christians of Jewish origin mentioned earlier, who continued to observe the regulations of the Mosaic law even after they have accepted the messiahship and divine sonship of Jesus; it seems likely that they were identical with the "Nazarenes." The second group of Ebionites taught that though born as other men are, Jesus was elected to be the Son of God, and that at his baptism Christ, an archangel, descended on him, as he had on Adam, Moses, and other prophets. Jesus, too, was no more than the "true prophet." The distinction between Jesus and Christ was characteristic also of Cerinthus and was to figure in various Gnostic Christian systems, but among the Ebionites it seems to reflect Essene teaching. In addition, the heretical Ebionites "use the Gospel according to Matthew only, and repudiate the Apostle Paul, maintaining that he was an apostate from the Law." Their name seems to have been derived either from a founder called Ebion or from the Hebrew word for "poor." Some scholars see in the Ebionites those descendants of the Essenes who remain Christian after the year 70. Like the Ebionites, the Elkesaites regarded Jesus as "a man like every other man" and as one of the prophets; to this extent they, too, bear marks of the heretical forms of Jewish Christianity.

As we have noted, perhaps the most important implication of the discovery of the Dead Sea Scrolls for the history of the development of Christian doctrine after the New Testament is that it has made it possible to identify connections between sectarian Judaism and the beginnings of heretical Christianity. With the help of such additional sources about the history of aberrant forms of both Judaism and Christianity, the less familiar aspects of the Jewish heritage of early Christian teaching are being illumined, and it is becoming possible to check more accurately the various reports of the Fathers about the influence of heretical Jewish ideas upon heretical Christian theology. It should also become possible to determine what influences there were in the opposite direction, as Mandaism and other heretical species of Judaism absorbed elements of Christian heresy, and thus also to weigh the possible importance of both Jewish and Christian heresy for the origins of Islam.

Within the mainstream of orthodox Christianity, however, the Jewish heritage remained visible in other ways. The growth of the cultic, hierarchical, and ethical structures of Christianity necessitated the Christianization of many features of Judaism. While much of that growth does not belong directly to the history of the development of doctrine, it is important because of this "re-Judaization of Christianity." Thus Justin argued that one of the differences between the old covenant and the new was that the priesthood had been superseded and "we [the Church as a whole] are the true high priestly race of God." In the New Testament itself the concept "priest" referred either to the Levites of the Old Testament, now superseded, or to Christ or to the entire Church —not to the ordained ministry of the Church. But Clement, who is also the first to use the term "layman," already speaks of "priests" and of "the high priest" and significantly relates these terms to the Levitical priesthood; a similar parallel occurs in the Didache and in Hippolytus. For Tertullian, the bishop is already "the high priest," and for his disciple, Cyprian, it is completely natural to speak of a Christian "priesthood." And so by the time of Chrysostom's treatise *On the Priesthood* it seems to have become accepted practice to refer to Aaron and Eli as examples and warnings for the priesthood of the Christian Church. He also speaks of "the Lord being sacrificed and laid upon the altar and the priest standing and praying over the victim," thus summarizing the sacrificial language about the Eucharist which had also become accepted practice. Therefore the apostles, too, were represented as priests.

But this "re-Judaization" does not indicate any recovery of close association between Judaism and Christian theology; on the contrary, it shows how independent of its Jewish origins Christian thought had become, and how free it felt to appropriate terms and concepts from the Jewish tradition despite its earlier disparagement of them. Now that Christian theologians were no longer obliged to engage in serious dialogue with Judaism, they were able to go their own Christian way in formulating the universal claims of Christianity. Not only the Jewish Scriptures and the Levitical priesthood, but other prerogatives and claims of the chosen people were consistently transferred to the Church—both an indication and a cause of the isolation of Gentile Christian thought from either the Judaism contemporary to itself or the Jewish Christianity out of which it had originally come. The Church, therefore, was the inheritor of the promises and prerogatives of the Jews. "Just as Christ is Israel and Jacob, so we who have been quarried out from the bowels of Christ are the true Israelitic race," the "third Israel" spoken of in Isaiah. Likewise, the Church was now "the synagogue of God," "those who believe in" Christ having become "one soul, and one synagogue, and one Church." Not the old Israel, but the Church had the right to call Abraham its father, to style itself "the chosen people," and to look forward to inheriting the promised land. Indeed, no title for the Church in early Christianity is more comprehensive than the term "the people of God," which originally meant "the new Israel" but gradually lost this connotation as the Christian claim to be "*the* people of God" no longer had to be substantiated.

This appropriation of the Jewish Scriptures and of the heritage of Israel helped to make it possible for Christianity to survive the destruction of Jerusalem, and to argue that with the coming of Christ Jerusalem had served its purpose in the divine plan and could be forsaken. It also enabled Christianity to claim an affinity with the non-Jewish tradition as well as with the Jewish and to formulate such doctrines as the Trinity on a more comprehensive basis than that provided by Jewish monotheism. These and other advantages were cited by the defenders of Christianity against Judaism; they do not usually mention, even though they often exhibit, the impoverishment that came from the supposition that in the Old Testament and in the Jewish elements of the New Testament, the Christian Church had as much of the tradition of Judaism as it would ever need.

II. THE DISPUTE WITH HELLENISM

THE apologetic war of the early Church was fought simultaneously on two fronts, for the theologians also addressed themselves critically to the other chief component of their thought world, classicism. For their dispute with Judaism they had extensive precedents in the New Testament, where most of the arguments just summarized had appeared, at least in a seminal form. But the audience to which Christian thought was directed increasingly, and then almost exclusively, during the second and third centuries was one to which very little of the New Testament had been addressed. Except for fragmentary reports like those in Acts 14:15-17 and Acts 17:22-31 and discussions such as that in Rom. 1:19-2:16, theologians had almost no biblical precedent for their apologetics to pagan thought. Therefore these few passages from the New Testament have been called upon to provide the apologetic enterprise in every age with some sort of biblical justification for its work. Faced with this situation, the defenders of Christianity could take the Apocalypse of John as their model, and repudiate pagan thought with all its works and all its ways, just as they unanimously repudiated the imperial cult; or they could seek out, within classicism, analogies to the continuity-discontinuity which they unanimously found in Judaism. The theologians of the second and third centuries combined these two emphases, but in varing proportions.

This they did in a series of apologetic treatises, the most comprehensive and profound of which was probably *Contra Celsum* by Origen. Some of the elements in the Christian self-defense and self-definition against Judaism also provided ammunition for the theologians who sought to define similarities and differences between the Christian faith and Hellenism. But in other respects the two apologetic cases were radically different and the Christian writers against paganism took over arguments that had become standard in the apologias for Judaism, as well as other arguments from Greek philosophers. Here again, Justin is important not only for the intrinsic value of his treatises in interpreting the apologetic conflict of the early Church, but also for the insights his works provide into the relation between the two fronts of that conflict. Although the earliest apology for Christianity, that of Quadratus, the most brilliant apology, that of Origen, and the most learned apology, that of Eusebius, were all written in Greek, the Latin writers "Tertullian, Lactantius, and Augustine outweigh all the Greek apologists." We shall, of course, draw upon both bodies of apologetic literature in this interpretation.

Much of the attack from pagan classicism, and therefore much of the defense from Christianity, was not principally doctrinal in nature. In the correspondence between Pliny and Trajan, and in much of the apologetic literature to follow until the tracts of Julian, two of the charges that constantly recurred were those of encouraging civil disobedience and of practicing immorality. But in the midst of arguments about these charges, which are not of direct concern to us here, doctrinal issues continually arose. For example, one of the most widespread calumnies against the Christians was the charge, "most impious and barbarous of all, that we eat human flesh" or "loaves steeped in blood." The basis of this accusation was the language used about the Eucharist by Christians, who seem to have spoken about the presence of the body and blood of Christ so realistically as to suggest a literal cannibalism. In the midst of rather meager and ambiguous evidence about the doctrine of the real presence in the second and third century and well beyond that period, these slanders would seem to be an important source of information in support of the existence of such a doctrine; but it is also important for the history of doctrine that the Fathers did not defend the propriety of such language by elaborating a doctrine of the real presence.

One doctrinal element in the pagan attack was the claim that the Christians taught absurd myths. The theogonies of Hesiod and the tales of Homer had gradually been allegorized and spiritualized by the leaders of classical thought, who "ennobled what is base," until they were able to speak of "the divine" (neuter) and of "being" in language that only rarely betrayed the ancestry of their ideas in classical Greek and Roman mythology. This process of refinement and spiritualization, in which Socrates and others had been martyred for their criticism of the mythical picture of the gods, had largely accomplished its purpose by the time of the conflict between pagan thought and Christian doctrine. And just when the leaders of pagan thought had emancipated their picture of the divine from the crude anthropomorphisms that ascribed human features to the gods, the Christians came on the scene with a message at whose center stood one called "Son of God." It is not surprising, when "the most learned and serious classes ... are always, in fact, the most irreverent toward your gods," that these classes should also have been the ones who vehemently resisted this message, which seemed to be a relapse into "a physical meaning of a gross kind," the very thing from which, after such a hard struggle, they had been rescued. Therefore they lampooned such biblical narratives as those dealing with the virgin birth and the resurrection, as Athenagoras indicates when he says: "We do indeed think also that God has a Son—and please let no one laugh at the idea of God having a Son! This is not a case of the myths of the poets who make the gods out to be no better than men." Or, in the defense of Theophilus, the Christian assertion that God had a Son was not meant "as the poets and writers of myths talk of the sons of god begotten of intercourse [with women]." These and other parallels between the Christian and the pagan criticisms of ancient mythology were intended to show that, even in speaking of Jesus as the Son of God, "we tell no incredible tales when we explain the doctrines about Jesus."

Sometimes the pagan attacks struck at the very heart of the Christian gospel. Despite the ambiguity that seems to be present in the Fathers of the second and third centuries on the questions of justification, grace, and forgiveness, they did have to deal with these questions in the attacks of their pagan opponents. Celsus was the spokesman for much of paganism when he attacked the gospel of forgiveness as cheap grace and said: "Those who summon people to the other mysteries make this preliminary proclamation: Whoever has pure hands and a wise tongue.... But let us hear what folk these Christians call. Whoever is a sinner, they say, whoever is unwise, whoever is a child, and, in a word, whoever is a wretch, the kingdom of God will receive him." Julian expressed a similar judgment about the promise of forgiveness in baptism. Such attacks prompted even some fathers whose doctrine of grace was not very profound to see that if "you compare the other deities and Christ with respect to the benefits of health [or salvation] given by them," it would be recognized that "aid is brought by the gods to the good and that the misfortunes of evil men are ignored," while, by contrast, "Christ gave assistance in equal measures to the good and the evil." More perhaps than they themselves could acknowledge, these spokesmen for Christianity thus pointed to the distinctive character of the Christian message as a promise of health and rescue based not upon worthiness but upon need; here as elsewhere, the pagan critics of Christianity seem sometimes to have been more profound in their recognition of this distinctive character than its defenders.

In the same way, the pagan critics acknowledged the distinctiveness of Jesus Christ in a manner that was sometimes more trenchant than the theology of the Christian apologists, and thus called forth a more profound statement of Christian doctrine than would have appeared without the challenge. It was not only the story of the resurrection of Christ that drew the fire of pagan critics as a fable or the report of a hysterical woman, but the significance attached to the resurrection by Christian theology. Nowhere does that significance come more unequivocally to expression than in the polemic of Christian theologians against the pagan doctrine of the immortal soul. "The soul is not in itself immortal, O Greeks, but mortal. Yet it is possible for it not to die": thus Tatian voiced the doctrine that life after death was not an accomplishment of man, much less his assured possession, but a gift from God in the resurrection of Christ. Even when the apocalyptic vision had been eclipsed and the immortality of the soul had become a standard element in Christian teaching, it was always modified and held in check by this stress on the divine initiative in the achievement of the life everlasting. In these and other ways the attacks of pagan authors on the Christian message left their mark on the Church's doctrines long after their external challenge had lost its effectiveness.

The reply of the apologists to that challenge has also continued to affect the development of Christian doctrine both directly and indirectly. It was at least partly in response to pagan criticism of the stories in the Bible that the Christian apologists, like their Jewish predecessors, took over and adapted the methods and even the vocabulary of pagan allegorism. Not even the most shocking of biblical narratives could match the crudity and "blasphemous nonsense" of the Greek myths, in which the gods were depicted as being superhuman, not in virtue but in endurance, "not more superior in dominion than in vice." The apologists recited lengthy catalogs of the amorous exploits of the gods, taking care to note that these details were being quoted from the pagan authors themselves. Those who held to such shameful accounts of the divine had no right to reproach the Christian narrative of "the birth of God in the form of a man.... For it is not permissible even to compare our conception of God with those who are wallowing in matter and mud." If the myths were true, they should not be admitted in public; if they were false, they should not be circulated among religious people. A common way out of this difficulty among sophisticated pagans was allegorical exegesis. Thus a sophisticated pagan such as Celsus "claims that his own exegesis of ancient writers is in harmony with their intention of handing down the truth in veiled form, to be uncovered by philosophical exegesis, while Jewish and Christian exegesis is merely defensive"; Porphyry accused Origen of misapplying Hellenistic allegory to the Jewish Scriptures. In his reply to Celsus, Origen was willing to acknowledge at least some validity to the allegorical exegesis of the Homeric poems. Other Christian writers, however, denounced Stoic and other allegory as "the veneer of sophistic disputes by which not the truth but its image and appearance and shadow are always sought after." Simultaneously, therefore, the apologists cited the pagan philosophers against pagan religion and denounced them for the artificiality of their efforts to square their teachings with Homer and Hesiod. Seneca was "often in agreement with us"; but Socrates was in a class by himself, because he had refrained from allegorizing Homer but had banished him.

The reason for this was that Christ had been "known in part even by Socrates." As the apologists came to grips with the defenders of paganism, they were compelled to acknowledge that Christianity and its ancestor, Judaism, did not have a monopoly on either the moral or the doctrinal teachings whose superiority Christian apologetics was seeking to demonstrate. To some extent this acknowledgement was a tacit admission of the presence within Christian thought of doctrines borrowed from Hellenism. To account for the presence of such teachings in pagan philosophy, the apologists drew upon several devices. Justin, as we have seen, sought to draw a connection between the philosophers and the pre-existent Logos. It was the seed of reason in man, the *logos spermatikos,* by which pagan thinkers like Socrates had been illumined to see what came to be clearly seen through the revelation of the Logos in the person of Jesus. As the Logos had been adumbrated in various ways during the history of Israel, so also what paganism had learned about God and about the good life could be traced to the universal functioning of the Logos. The Stoics, the poets, and the historians all "spoke well in proportion to the share [they] had of the seminal Logos." But now that the seminal Logos had come in person, those who had been under his tutelage could find the fuller meaning of their intuitions. For Origen, too, the "Logos who came to dwell in Jesus . . . inspired men before that." The apologists' use of the idea of the seminal Logos in their dispute with Hellenism certainly helped to establish this idea in the Christian doctrine of Christ, but other factors were no less important.

Tertullian's explanation of the presence of noble and good elements in paganism employed the idea of natural law rather than that of the seminal Logos. For him this included knowledge of the existence, the goodness, and the justice of God, but especially the moral precepts flowing from that knowledge. This "law of nature" agreed with Christian revelation in its condemnation of moral evil. Even in his Montanist phase, Tertullian could appeal to "the law of the Creator," apparently with this "law of nature" in mind. In opposition to Jewish teaching about the law of Moses, Tertullian argued that the primordial natural law, which had been given in an unwritten form to Adam and Eve and thus to all nations, had now been "reformed for the better." Origen used the familiar Stoic distinction between "the ultimate law of nature" and "the written code of cities" to justify the Christian refusal to obey the idolatrous laws of the nations, including Rome; he was "apparently the first to justify the right to resist tyranny by appealing to natural law." But the Christian acceptance of the pagan idea of natural law did not compel a Christian theologian like Origen to be oblivious of the relativity in the laws of the nations. Most of the history of Christian thought about natural law belongs to the development of Christian social ethics rather than to the history of doctrine; but it did play a role in the effort of early theologians to deal with paganism, and it went on to "provide the daughter churches of Western Catholicism, Lutheranism and Calvinism, with the means of regarding and shaping themselves as a Christian unity of civilization." Only in the new apologetics of the Enlightenment did this definition of the natural law meet with fundamental opposition.

Perhaps the most widespread theory proposed by the Fathers to account for the truth in Hellenism was the suggestion that it had come from the Old Testament. Here they were following a precedent set by Jewish apologists. Aristobulus claimed that both Plato and Pythagoras had read Moses; Philo traced various Greek doctrines to a biblical origin; and Josephus maintained that the Jewish Bible was the source of many of the most profound insights in pagan thought. In the same spirit, Justin saw Moses as the source for the doctrine of creation in Plato's *Timaeus*, adding, however, that among Christians the confession of this and related doctrines was not confined to the learned but was present also among illiterates. Plato's *Phaedrus* was likewise traced to the Bible by Origen, who professed to have received this explanation from other writers. Theophilus of Antioch extended the claim to the Greek poets as well as the philosophers, who "plagiarized from the Scriptures to make their doctrines plausible." Minucius Felix took the various philosophical notions of the conflagration awaiting the world as proof that the "divine proclamations of the prophets" had provided the philosophers with the basis of their correct, even though "corrupted," insight. Characteristically, Tertullian, while conceding the possibility that the philosophers may have studied the Scriptures, insisted that their presuppositions prevented them from understanding biblical truth. Augustine, too, considered the possibility, which he had learned from Ambrose, that Plato had become acquainted with the Bible while both he and Jeremiah were in Egypt; later on, Augustine withdrew this explanation on historical and chronological grounds, but continued to feel that at least some acquaintance with the Bible was the only possible explanation for Plato's cosmology and ontology.

Clement of Alexandria also maintained that the doctrines of the *Timaeus* came "from the Hebrews," but he had several other explanations for the parallels between philosophy and revelation. "He begins with the possibility that the truth contained in philosophy is to be ascribed to an accident involved in God's providential economy. He continues with explanations attributing the element of truth in philosophy to the general revelation, or even making the Greek philosophers prophets similar to those of the Old Testament. And he ends by indicating that philosophy owes its existence to a reflection of the eternal truth itself, and that the philosophers have beheld God—an imperfect, vague, unclear yet true vision." It is, of course, true that many of the ideas whose similarity to philosophical teachings is a problem to Clement were found in the Hebrew Bible as a result more of eisegesis than of exegesis; thus, for example, his doctrine of creation in some ways owes more to the *Timaeus* than to Genesis, even though he claims to find that doctrine in the latter rather than in the former and therefore must explain the embarrassing parallel.

This effort to demonstrate that the truth of revelation, which was also being affirmed by the pagan philosophers, had occurred first in the Old Testament was not merely a way of finding biblical support for one or another doctrine. It was also part of the campaign to prove the superiority of Christian doctrine on the grounds of its antiquity. Antiquity was widely regarded in pagan thought as lending authority to a system of thought or belief. Celsus attacked Christianity in the name of a *philosophia perennis,* "an ancient doctrine which has existed from the beginning, which has always been maintained by the wisest nations and cities and wise men." Christ was spurned by the pagans as "only of yesterday," as one who had not "been known by name" until his own time. Or, as Arnobius paraphrases the case for paganism on the basis of its supposed antiquity, "your [i.e., the pagans'] religious observances precede the one we espouse by many years, and for that reason are truer because fortified by the authority of age." Because the Christian message was centered not simply in some "timeless truth," but in the historical events of the life, death, and resurrection of Jesus "under Pontius Pilate," it appeared to be discredited as an innovation.

But the proclamation of those events was not the whole of the Christian message; or, rather, the apologists, together with the whole Church, believed that those events were announced beforehand in the sacred Scriptures of the Old Testament. On the basis, then, of Moses and of Homer, "the one being the oldest of poets and historians, and the other the founder of all barbarian wisdom," Tatian proceeded to prove "that our doctrines are older, not only than those of the Greeks, but than the invention of letters." Tatian's teacher, Justin, who argued the case for Christian "innovations" against Judaism, had argued earlier that the Old Testament, which was "now in the possession of all Jews throughout the world," but which actually belonged to Christianity, was "of greater antiquity than the Greek writers." Expanding upon these arguments, Clement of Alexandria demonstrated, in the summary words of Eusebius, "that Moses and the Jewish race went back further in their origins than the Greeks." Tertullian exclaimed: "Moses and God existed before all your Lycurguses and Solons!" In reply to the sneers of Celsus about the recent and outlandish origins of Christian teaching, Origen, too, maintained that "Moses and the prophets ... are not only earlier than Plato but also than Homer and the discovery of writing among the Greeks. They did not say these things, as Celsus thinks, 'because they misunderstood Plato.' How could they have heard a man who had not yet been born?" Ambrose appears to have been one of the few defenders of Christianity to admit, in his dispute with Symmachus, that this argument from antiquity did not hold; for "not the antiquity of years, but that of morals is laudable. It is not shameful to move on to something better." Nor was this claim to antiquity comprised in the mind of most of the apologists by the circumstances, sometimes noted in the writings of their pagan opponents, that some of the doctrines whose antiquity they demonstrated from the Old Testament were not explicitly stated there, but had come into Christian theology by way of Greek philosophy and only then were discovered in the Jewish Scriptures.

Thus, although Clement of Alexandria told the Greeks that for the ideas in Plato's *Timaeus* they were "indebted to the Hebrews," he was himself indebted to the *Timaeus*. Nevertheless, he joined with the other apologists in defending what he understood to be the biblical view of creation against the cosmogonies of the philosophers, including the *Timaeus*. When "the chorus of the philosophers" were guilty of "deifying the universe" instead of "seeking the Creator of the universe," they needed to be told that "the sheer volition [of God] is the making of the universe. For God alone made it, because he alone is God in his being [*ontōs*]. By his sheer act of will he creates [*dēmiourgei*]; and after he has merely willed, it follows that things come into being." In opposition to the Platonic idea of the demiurge, then, Clement asserted that God himself was the one who creates [*dēmiourgie*] all things. On the basis of this and similar statements, E. F. Osborn has concluded that "Clement is the first person to state and give reasons for the doctrine of creation *ex nihilo*."

But Clement's contemporary, Tertullian, elaborated the doctrine of creation *ex nihilo* more fully, in his *Treatise against Hermogenes*. To some extent he seems, both here and elsewhere, to be dependent on Theophilus of Antioch, who had taught, in opposition to the Platonic idea for the coeternity of God and matter, that "the power of God is manifested in this, that out of things that are not he makes whatever he pleases" and that therefore "nothing is coeternal with God." Conceding that creation *ex nihilo* was not explicitly stated in the Bible but only implied, Tertullian argued from silence that "if God could make all things out of nothing, Scripture could quite well omit to add that he had made them out of nothing, but it should have said by all means that he had made them out of matter, if he had done so; for the first possibility would be completely understandable, even if it was not expressly stated, but the second would be doubtful, unless it was stated." Apologists like Clement, Theophilus, and Tertullian recognized that the coeternity of God and matter was inconsistent with the sovereignty and freedom of God. In spite of the difficulties it causes in the problem of evil, the alternatives to creation *ex nihilo* appeared to be a pantheism which taught that "God and matter are the same, two names for one thing" and a dualism that could be resolved, if at all, by denying that God the Creator "made all things freely, and by his own power, and arranged and finished them, and his will is the substance of all things."

From this it followed, according to Irenaeus, that God the Creator "is discovered to be the one only God who created all things, who alone is omnipotent, and who is the only Father founding and forming all things, visible and invisible." In answer both to mythological polytheism and to the doctrine of the coeternity of God and matter the apologists came out as the spokesmen for divine transcendence and for strict monotheism (or, in their usual word, "monarchy"). They "apply the word nearly always to the absolute monarchy of God, and its primary sense is omnipotence. But since the whole significance of omnipotence is that it can be wielded only by one ultimate power, it really comes to mean monotheism." So long as the challenge to Christian doctrine was coming from classical polytheism or from philosophical pantheism or even from Gnosticism, this stress on the "monarchy" seemed to align the apologists with the Old Testament doctrine of God, in spite of their divergence from Judaism. But when Christian thought was called upon to vindicate its language about the divine dispensation ("economy") in Christ as consistent with monotheism, it took on the far more subtle assignment of demonstrating that its doctrine of "the Trinity ... in no respect challenges the monarchy, while it conserves the quality of the economy."

In their defense of the biblical view of creation, the apologists were also obliged to take up the question of the meaning of history. Greek historical thought had been impressed by the constantly recurring elements in human history; one of the ways, though not the only way, the Greeks adopted for the interpretation of history was therefore a theory of cycles. Among the Romans, their own sense of manifest destiny prompted a revision of this theory, at least to the extent that although previous events had foreshadowed the coming of Rome, as Vergil said, the fall of previous civilizations did not indicate the inevitable course of empire, so long as Rome remained true to the ideals of its past. In declaring the loyalty of the Christians to the empire while repudiating the deification of the emperor, apologetic theologians were compelled to clarify their reasons for differing from these ideas of history. It was a necessary presupposition of the Christian proclamation that historical events were unrepeatable; otherwise "it is inevitable that according to the determined cycles Moses will always come out of Egypt with the people of the Jews, [and] Jesus will again come to visit this life and will do the same things he has done, not just once but an infinite number of times according to the cycles." In opposition to Roman claims, Tertullian asserted that "all nations have possessed empire, each in its proper time ... until at last almost universal dominion has accrued to the Romans," adding ominously: "What [God] has determined concerning [the Roman empire], those who are closest to him know."

When a theology was dominated, as Tertullian's sometimes was, by a vivid futuristic eschatology, it could share the Roman belief that the empire represented the final phase of human accomplishment, but always with the proviso that now it was time for the final phase of divine intervention. But when that intervention did not come, at least not in the form in which many had expected it, the apologists had to deal with the possibility that the world would continue even without the empire as they had known it. They often fall back upon a more general conception of "the providence of God, which regulates everything according to its season." As we noted earlier, such a view of providence, like the monotheism of which it was a corollary, seriously complicated the problem of evil and of free will, as the formula of Origen suggests: "As a result of [God's] foreknowledge the free actions of every man fit in with that disposition of the whole which is necessary for the existence of the universe." The doctrine of divine providence became the standard rubric under which theologians considered the problem of history. It remained for Augustine to clarify the Christian conviction that because of Christ and despite "all appearances, human history does not consist of a series of repetitive patterns, but marks a sure, if unsteady, advance to an ultimate goal."

Concerned as they were with ethical questions at least as much as with doctrinal issues, the apologists also sought to prove and defend the superiority of the Christian ethic. Of the devices employed in this defense, doctrinally the most important was their interpretation of the Christian gospel as a "new law." When Barnabas speaks of "the new law of our Lord Jesus Christ, which is without a yoke of necessity," he sets a pattern followed by many later theologians. Justin calls Christ "the new lawgiver," and Origen calls him "the lawgiver of the Christians"; by Cyprian's time such phrases as "the evangelical law" or "the law of the gospel" seem to have become a standard designation for the Christian message. As Moritz von Engelhardt urged, such phrases "passed over into Christian language without indicating *eo ipso* an inclination to a Jewish-Christian way of thinking. And something that could otherwise be interpreted in this sense acquires, in the context, a different and evangelical meaning." The "new law" implied new demands (the knowledge of Christ, repentance, and a sinless life after conversion) as well as new promises (forgiveness of sins and immortality). But when the Jewish context of such terms as "covenant" became less precise, "new law" also shed some of its earlier connotations.

As Christianity became more respectable socially, its apologetics became more respectable philosophically. Long after the official adoption of Christianity by the emperor and eventually by the law of the empire, Christian theologians still went on writing apologetic treatises. One of the most important works of Thomas Aquinas was his *Summa*

Against the Gentiles, when there were certainly very few "Gentiles" left in Western Europe and the pagans for whom it was ostensibly composed could not have understood it. But the tone of that *Summa,* and of apologetic treatises for some centuries preceding it, indicates that the war was decided even though it was not over. Like the "dialogues *adversus Judaeos,*" apologetics against classicism became more and more a function of churchly theology, which it continued to be in most of the great systems in the history of Christian thought until the Enlightenment, when Christian doctrine found itself on the defensive again and was obliged to reconsider the meaning of its earlier victory in the dispute with Hellenism. Then it was that the apologetic approach of works such as Origen's once more commended itself to the attention of theologians.

Meanwhile, the victory of Christian apologetics was celebrated and documented in two ways, represented by Eusebius and by Augustine. Eusebius, to whose learning and industry later centuries are indebted for much of what has been preserved about the early history of Christian apologetics, devoted a large part of his immense literary output to a defense of Christianity. His two-part treatise, the *Praeparatio evangelica* and *Demonstratio evangelica,* has been called "with all its faults... probably the most important apologetic work of the early Church." In it he summarized and elaborated most of the arguments we have been detailing here, but he also set his own work apart from that of his predecessors by criticizing their preoccupation with "dialetical arguments" at the expense of "historical facts." To redress this balance, Eusebius composed historical works, first a *Chronicle* and then his *Ecclesiastical History,* both of which attempted to prove, by means of "historical facts" rather than merely of "dialetical arguments," that Christianity and Christ possessed great antiquity and that the history of Christianity was a universal history. This he did in response to the repeated pagan charge that the Christian message was too recent and too parochial to merit serious consideration. He cast his apologetic in the form of a historical account and thus laid the foundations for ecclesiastical history. And when, in the course of his writing the *Ecclesiastical History,* the political need for Christian apologetics was removed with the conversion of Constantine, he nevertheless continued to provide the materials for the apologia to the intellectuals, which remained necessary longer than the apologia to the empire.

It was, in fact, the lag between the two kinds of apologia that provided the occasion for the definitive exposition of the Christian case against classical thought, the *City of God* of Augustine. It was an "endeavor to reply to those who attribute the wars by which the world is being devastated, and especially the recent sack of Rome by the barbarians, to the religion of Christ." As we have seen, the *City of God* repeated many of the arguments against paganism and for Christianity that had become commonplaces of the apologetic literature, but it organized them into an interpretation of world history in which the eternal purpose of God is borne by the *civitas Dei*. Some earlier apologists had argued that, far from being the threat to Rome which its opponents called it, Christianity was actually the support of righteous governments. This argument Augustine took up into his schematization of world history as a conflict between the spiritual descendants of Abel and those of Cain, claiming that the collapse of the Roman ideal was due to the failure of the empire to recognize the true source of its strength. Both in the history of his chosen people and in the lives of "holy pagans" God had made his city known among men. Its ultimate destiny was that of the heavenly Jerusalem, which, in Augustine's description at the conclusion of the *City of God,* unites and transforms many of the themes of early Christian apocalypticism. Like Eusebius, Augustine translated apologetics into history; but the history was not merely the account of the succession of the Church from the apostles, but the whole way of divine providence.

The subsequent influence of the *Ecclesiastical History* and the *City of God* helped to assure the arguments of the apologists a permanent place in the development of Christian doctrine, in addition to the importance of these treatises for other areas of Christian thought and practice. At least until the humanists of the Renaissance, Christian theologians viewed Hellenism as the apologists of the early church had taught them to view it.

III. THE CHRISTIANIZATION OF HELLENISM

THE closing of the philosophical school at Athens by the emperor Justinian in 529 is usually interpreted as a symbol of the victory of Christian theology over classical thought, when, in Gibbon's words, Christian theologians "superseded the exercise of reason, resolved every question by an article of faith, and condemned the infidel or sceptic to eternal flame. In many a volume of laborious controversy they exposed the weakness of the understanding and the corruption of the heart, insulted human nature in the sages of antiquity, and proscribed the spirit of philosophical inquiry, so repugnant to the doctrine, or at least to the temper, of a humble believer."

Such an interpretation of Justinian's decree against the Athenian academy seems to receive corroboration from the circumstance that its closing was the act more of a coroner than of an executioner. The establishment of the imperial University of Constantinople by Theodosius II, or perhaps by Constantine himself, had already transferred the center of Greek learning from Athens to the new capital of the Hellenic world, and thus the pagan school in Athens, "had already outlived its purpose" and "was no longer of great import in a Christian empire." The pagan professors emigrated from Athens to Persia, but eventually returned to the empire, having obtained a promise of safe-conduct from Justinian. Teachers of philosophy, then, were regarded as both unwanted and harmless. From that interpretation it would be an easy step, though a wrong one, to conclude that theology had eliminated philosophy from the attention of thoughtful men: "Philosophy branched off from theology. It became its handmaid and its rival. It postulated doctrines instead of investigating them. It had to show their reasonableness or to find reason for them. And for ages afterwards philosophy was dead."

It is indeed true that the formal study of Greek philosophy declined with the rise to authority of orthodox Christian theology. Thus of the writings of Aristotle only the *Categories* and *On Interpretation* had apparently been translated into Latin; not even the rest of the treatises belonging to the Organon, much less the ethical and metaphysical writings, were put into a form that would have made them accessible to Western theologians. Boethius, the translator of these treatises, had intended to render all of Aristotle and Plato into Latin, and thus "to bring them into harmony and to demonstrate that they do not disagree on everything, as many maintain, but are in the greatest possible agreement on many things that pertain to philosophy." But the two logical treatises were all that he completed, or at any rate all that was preserved, and apparently all of Aristotle that was known to the Christian West until the early part of the twelfth century. Only then did Western thinkers turn once more to a concerted study of classical philosophical systems, and then primarily as a result of external provocation as well as internal theological necessity. Even then they studied Aristotle as theologians. Thus it could seem as though philosophy and matters philosophical disappeared from the attention of Christian thinkers for half a millennium or more.

Yet this same scholar, whose translation of Aristotle delineates the end of classical thought as much as does the nearly contemporary closing of the school at Athens, was also the author of a book which seriously qualifies any such interpretation of the triumph of theology. *The Consolation of Philosophy* by Boethius, "the noblest literary work of the final period of antiquity," played a major role in the history of medieval literature and devotion. Languishing in prison, presumably for treason and for his fidelity to Trinitarian orthodoxy in defiance of an Arian emperor, Boethius turned his hand to an old genre of classical literature, the *consolatio,* which had been adapted from Greek models by Cicero. Boethius seems to have been the first Christian theologian to employ the *consolatio,* but the result is a form of consolation which pictures the operation of the divine in the affairs of men without any unmistakeable reference to the Christian view of God, either Arian or Trinitarian. The basic theme of the book is a defense of free will and of the goodness of divine providence, under whose sovereignty fate is permitted to function. In a dialogue with Philosophy personified, Boethius develops his doctrine of God as "the constant foreknowing overseer . . . the ever-present eternity of [whose] sight moves in harmony with the future nature of our actions as it dispenses rewards to the good and punishments to the bad."

So ambiguous is this doctrine of God that some scholars have found in it "conclusive proof that the author was not a practical believer in Christianity," while others claim that "the picture of God drawn there is so warm and authentic in a Christian sense that even if there were no decisive external proof available for the Christian confession of the last of the Romans, one would be justified in regarding Boethius as a Christian thinker." On the basis of this ambiguity, critical historical scholarship long doubted the traditional account that the *Consolation* was written by a Christian theologian; it maintained that the author of the *Consolation* was not the Boethius to whom five treatises on Christian doctrine, including a polemic against Nestorius and Eutyches and an influential exposition of the doctrine of the Trinity were attributed. Careful research into both the thought and the language of the Boethian corpus has demonstrated that both the *Consolation* and a least four of the theological treatises came from the same man. Proceeding from this literary conclusion to argue that in the *Consolation* Boethius was "proving as much of *fides* as *ratio* will allow him," E. K. Rand maintained that this apologetic aim "explains why there is not a trace of anything specifically Christian or biblical in the entire work." But this does not answer the question why at least one orthodox theologian, in the hour of utmost need, found solace more in philosophical contemplation based on natural reason than in the Christian revelation to which his theological works pointed and for which, presumably, he was martyred.

In many ways, *The Consolation of Philosophy* only dramatizes a more general problem. The victory of orthodox Christian doctrine over classical thought was to some extent a Pyrrhic victory, for the theology that triumphed over Greek philosophy was itself conditioned by the language and the thought of classical metaphysics. Just how conditioned it was and in what specific ways, has been and still is a matter of argument among historians and theologians. For example, the Fourth Lateran Council in 1215 decreed that "in the sacrament of the altar ... the bread is transubstantiated into the body [of Christ], and the wine into [His] blood," and the Council of Trent declared in 1551 that the use of the term "transubstantiation" was "proper and appropriate." Most of the theological expositions of the term "transubstantiation," beginning already with those of the thirteenth century, have interpreted "substance" on the basis of the meaning given to this term by such classical discussions as that in Book V of the *Metaphysics* of Aristotle; thus transubstantiation would appear to be tied to the acceptance of Aristotelian metaphysics or even physics. Yet the application of the term "substance" to the discussion of the eucharistic presence antedates the rediscovery of Aristotle; thus Ratramnus speaks of "substances visible but invisible" and his opponent Radbertus declares that "out of the substance of bread and wine the same body and blood of Christ is mystically consecrated." Even "transubstantiation" was used during the twelfth century in a non-technical sense. Such evidence lends credence to the argument that the doctrine of transubstantiation, as codified by the decrees of the Fourth Lateran and Tridentine councils, does not canonize Aristotelian philosophy as Christian doctrine. But whether it does so or not in principle, it has certainly done so in effect; as "natural law" has come to be equated with a particular ecclesiastical formulation of what ought to be natural, so "substance" has come to be defined as a particular philosophical theology has defined it.

Thus transubstantiation is an individual instance of the problem of "the Hellenization of Christianity." As we noted at the outset, the charge that one's theological opponent has subordinated the truth of divine revelation to the philosophy of the Greeks is a common one in the history of theology polemics. *The Little Labyrinth,* probably written by Hippolytus, attacked the adoptionism of Theodotus and Artemon because, among other errors, these heretics had "deserted the holy Scriptures of God" and given themselves to a study of Euclid and Aristotle. The accusation recurs in the attacks of the Reformers on medieval scholasticism, but it was with the work of Souverain, *Le platonisme devoilé,* published in 1700, that the idea of dogma as the Hellenization of Christianity became a widely circulated explanation of the development of early Christian doctrine. And in the *History of Dogma* of Adolf Harnack it became one of the most important interpretive tools for the study of the history of theology. Taken as it stands, "Hellenization" is too simplistic and unqualified a phrase for the process that issued in orthodox Christian doctrine, and Harnack himself did not use or intend the phrase with as oversimplified a meaning as has often been read into it. It certainly is true that in its language and sometimes in its ideas orthodox Christian doctrine still bears the marks of its struggle to understand and overcome classical thought, so that what later generations of the Church (including those generations that were themselves ignorant of classical thought) inherited in the dogma of the Church included more than a little of classical philosophy as well. Victory over classical thought there assuredly was, but a victory for which some Christian theologians were willing to pay a rather high price.

How high a price is evident from the writings of the apologists, as we have already seen. Even when the reader makes due allowance for the task of the apologists as the spokesmen for the Church to the Gentile world—and "due allowance" would mean more allowance than many historians of doctrine have been willing to make—the fact remains that "their attitude toward ancient culture is contradictory. On the one hand, the zeal of battle prompts them to look for contrasts and to accentuate them sharply, purposely to bring out the shadows, to create a dark background for the bright beam of Christianity, and not to be ashamed of using evil means for that end. On the other hand, the deepest contrasts are often concealed and veiled from them, because they have already taken up the gospel into the conceptual forms and ideas of the time and have blended it with them. They claim to be fighting for the new faith against the old world; in fact, they are partly continuing the battle of intellectual currents which were already at war in the ancient world, only adding to them some new issues and weapons." In various ways they joined to assert the thesis that Christ had come as the revealer of true philosophy, ancient and yet new, as the correction and also the fulfillment of what the philosophical mind had already grasped.

That thesis received its most authoritative exposition in the apologetics of Clement of Alexandria. Like other apologists, Clement has been represented as a thoroughgoing Hellenizer, who trimmed the Christian faith to suit the presuppositions of an alien philosophy, because "the tradition of the Church [was] a foreign thing to him both in its totality and in every detail." Thus his writings had been interpreted as primarily or even exclusively apologetic in intent. But the dominant theme of his authorship was clearly "the problem of training the immature wisely" in Christian doctrine and even more in the Christian life, as is explicit in *The Tutor* and implicit throughout *The Miscellanies*. But in the *Exhortation to the Greeks* Clement addressed an appeal to his philosophical colleagues to complete their world view by accepting Christ. What they had already grasped of the ultimate nature of reality he called "a slender spark, capable of being fanned into flame, a trace of wisdom, and an impulse from God." He chided them for being satisfied with a religious outlook that pictured deity as their religions did, while their philosophical outlook had far transcended these crude pictures. Their representations of Zeus were "an image of an image," but the true image of God was in the Logos; and therefore the authentic "image of the image" was the human mind itself, not the crude statues, whose inadequacy their philosophers had taught them to recognize. He portrayed in glowing terms the intellectual and moral superiority of the Christian way to anything that even the noblest paganism had been able to discover. For "that which the chiefs of philosophy only guessed at, the disciples of Christ have both apprehended and proclaimed." Therefore he appealed to them, blending Scripture and Homer: "Philosophy is a long-lived exhortation, wooing the eternal love of wisdom, while the commandment of the Lord is far-shining, 'enlightening the eyes.' Receive Christ, receive sight, receive your light, 'in order that you may know well both God and man.'" Clement did not feel obliged to refute the charges of immorality and irrationality still being directed against Christian life and doctrine. He writes as an evangelist among the Greeks.

The importance of philosophy for his doctrine, therefore, is not to be sought primarily in his complimentary remarks about the persons or even about the ideas of the philosophers, especially about Socrates and Plato, but rather in the influence of Middle Platonism for his thinking about such crucial Christian doctrines as the nature of man and the person of Christ. Man he pictured as a dual being like the Centaur of classical myth, made up of body and soul; and it was the lifelong task of the Christian "philosopher gnostic" to cultivate the liberation of the soul from the chains of the body, in preparation for the ultimate liberation, which was death. This conception appeared even in Clement's profoundest statements of the Christian doctrine of man as creature and sinner, and is reflected in Clement's accommodations to the Platonic doctrine of the pre-existence of the soul. A similar ambivalence was evident in his Christology. He repeatedly affirmed the historicity of the incarnation and the reality of His flesh; but because his definition of what constituted true humanity labored under the handicaps just described, his Christological statements frequently came to formulations that sound Docetic. It seems evident that Clement was not in fact a Docetist, but he did blur the distinction beween the Logos and the soul in a way that could lead in that direction. Not the history of the life, death, and resurrection of Jesus Christ, but the divine Logos who appeared in that history would seem to have been the motif of Clement's Christology. Hence he seems to speak with greater ease about the mode of existence peculiar to the resurrected Lord than about the mode manifest in His sufferings. One reason for this lay in Clement's concept of the resurrection itself, whether Christ's or the Christian's. Here, too, the Middle Platonic view of the immortal soul sometimes seemed to be equated with resurrection, despite other indications that the soul was not naturally immortal. This is no simple "Hellenization of the Gospel," as his polemics against Gnosticism for just such Hellenization made clear; but it is less a victory of Christian doctrine over Greek thought than it appears to be.

Origen, too, has been represented as a consistent Hellenizer; one of his pagan contemporaries said of him that "while his manner of life was Christian and contrary to the law, he played the Greek, and introduced Greek ideas into foreign fables." Until quite recently it was customary to lump Clement and Origen as "Christian Platonists of Alexandria" and to ignore the great contrast between them. Basing their interpretation of Origen largely on his *Contra Celsum* and *De principiis,* historians of doctrine neglected his massive works on the Bible. From a study of these latter it is evident that Origen relied far less than did Clement on "secret tradition" and that he was even more intent than Clement on keeping his speculations within the confines of the tradition. Therefore, the tension between biblical and philosophical doctrine is, if anything, even more acute in Origen than it is in Clement. An apt illustration of the tension is Origen's doctrine of the resurrection, to which he devoted two books and two dialogues (all of them lost, except for fragments). The doctrine of a literal resurrection of the physical body was one that was "preached in the churches" "for the simple-minded and for the ears of the common crowd who are led on to live better lives by their belief." But Origen regarded this literal doctrine as an allegory for the teaching that "in the body there lies a certain principle which is not corrupted from which the body is raised in corruption"—not the body that died, but a "body" appropriate to the new and immortal life. Origen was quite willing to acknowledge, meanwhile, that he shared the doctrine of the immortality of the soul with pagan philosophers. He also taught "that the life of the soul did not begin when the soul was joined to the body" but had preexisted and had fallen in that earlier state. To another Christian of the third century, this was "the trifling of some who shamelessly do violence to Scripture, in order that their opinion, that the resurrection is without flesh, may find support; supposing rational bones and flesh, and in different ways changing it backwards and forwards by allegorizing." Thus the pagan philosopher failed to grasp what Origen believed to be the true meaning of the Christian doctrine of the resurrection, while the Christian literalist regarded that meaning as a betrayal of the biblical message to Platonic spiritualism. Eliminating either pole of Origen's thought from his system would make him more consistent; but it would be an oversimplification and a distortion of his thought, for both biblical doctrine and philosophical concepts are essential components of his theology.

Biblical doctrines and philosophical concepts are also intermingled in the theology of Tertullian, albeit in a different proportion. His question, "What has Athens to do with Jerusalem?" and the resoundingly negative answer he repeatedly provided to that question have sometimes obscured the philosophical elements in his thought. The very issues whose significance we have examined in Origen—the resurrection and the soul—illustrate both Tertullian's aversion to philosophy and his dependence upon it. His treatise on the resurrection acknowledges some affinity between Christian doctrine and the teachings of some philosophers, but proceeds to expound various biblical passages about the flesh in antithesis to the philosophers and the heretics; he gives special attention to 1 Cor. 15. The treatise on the soul opens with a similar attack on philosophical doctrines, specifically on the doctrine of the soul of Plato, whom he later calls "the caterer to all these heretics." Once more he had to acknowledge parallels between biblical truth and philosophical speculation, but he was intent upon "freeing, on the one hand, the sentiments held by us in common with them from the arguments of the philosophers, and of separating, on the other hand, the arguments which both parties employ from the opinions of the same philosophers."

In theory, then, Tertullian owed loyalty only to the Bible and to the "most frequent admonitions" of the Montanist Paraclete; "what we are ourselves, that also the Scriptures are (and have been) from the beginning." But it was by no means obvious what the Scriptures and the tradition of the Church (or even the Paraclete) taught about the origin and nature of the human soul. Therefore, he felt obliged to "call on the Stoics also to help me, who, while declaring almost in our own terms that the soul is a spiritual essence (inasmuch as breath and spirit are in their nature very near akin to each other), will yet have no difficulty in persuading [us] that the soul is a corporeal substance." By the time Tertullian had finished vindicating the biblical doctrine of the soul against the philosophers, he had invoked not only the Stoics, but Aristotle (whom he does not seem to have cited anywhere else) and other philosophical sources ranging from the pre-Socratics Heraclitus and Democritus to the philosophical scholar of the Augustan age, Arius Didymus. For his doctrine of the resurrection and of the simultaneous origin of soul and body, Tertullian could not avoid invoking the very philosophy against whose pretensions he had spoken so violently. Thus, while Origen may be said to illustrate the modification of philosophical concepts by continuing exposure to biblical doctrine, Tertullian may be said to illustrate the continuing and unavoidable, if not always acknowledged or even conscious, influence of philosophical teaching on Christian theology. Each shows that there was indeed a victory of theology over classical philosophy, but also that the victory was by no means as one-sided as the spokesmen for Christian doctrine claimed it was.

Lest the examples of Origen and Tertullian be dismissed as unrepresentative on the grounds that both have been condemned as heretics, the unimpeachable orthodoxy of a Gregory of Nyssa may be taken as evidence for the thesis that the tension between biblical and philosophical doctrine has continued to characterize the orthodox theology of the Catholic tradition. Even if it is not accurate to maintain that his doctrine of the Trinity was rescued from tritheism by a Middle Platonic concept of essence, his view of the doctrine we have examined in Clement, Origen, and Tertullian—the doctrine of the soul and of the resurrection—reinforces the thesis, as the very title of his treatise, *On the Soul and the Resurrection,* suggests. It, too, insisted that "while [pagan philosophy] proceeded, on the subject of the soul, as far in the direction of supposed implications as the thinker pleased, we are not entitled to such license, namely, of affirming whatever we please. For we make sacred Scripture the rule and the norm of every doctrine. Upon that we are obliged to fix our eyes, and we approve only whatever can be brought into harmony with the intent of those writing." Yet Gregory, like his mentor Origen, could not altogether escape the dominance of Platonic philosophy; in form and even in content, his treatise on the soul repeatedly betrays its ancestry in the *Phaedo,* just as his mystical theology documents both his involvement in and his transcendence of Platonic thought.

Two Christian doctrines are perhaps the most reliable indices of the continuing hold of Greek philosophy on Christian theology: the doctrine of the immortality of the soul and the doctrine of the absoluteness of God—"God and the soul, that is what I desire to know," in Augustine's familiar formula. The idea of the immortal and rational soul is part of the Greek inheritance in Christian doctrine; Thomas Aquinas and Philip Melanchthon are only two of the many theologians to compose treatises *De anima* whose content was determined more by philosophical than by biblical language about the soul. Indeed, the idea of the immortality of the soul came eventually to be identified with the biblical doctrine of the resurrection of the body, one of whose original polemical targets seems to have been the immortality of the soul! The pagan or heretical equation of the soul with life and the claim of natural immortality apart from the action of God the Creator were rejected by Christian thinkers on the grounds that "the soul itself is not life, but participates in the life conferred upon it by God," by whose will alone the soul received the capacity to endure eternally. Therefore, "the soul participates in life because God wills it to live; thus it will not even have such participation when God no longer wills it to live." Tatian's statement that "in itself the soul is not immortal, but mortal" was based on his presuppositions concerning the relation between time and eternity and concerning the relation among body, soul, and spirit. Yet it did give voice to the insistence on the doctrine of the resurrection in opposition to natural immortality. The basis for this insistence was the Christian doctrine of creation. Because only God was without beginning and everything else had been "brought into existence by the Framer of all things above, on this account we believe that there will be a resurrection of bodies after the consummation of all things." Athenagoras argued at length that the confession of God as the Creator required a doctrine of resurrection as the completion of the divine purpose, and that thus "the reason for [man's] coming to be guarantees his permanence forever, and his permanence guarantees his resurrection, for without this he would not be permanent *as man.*" But the argumentation of Athenagoras, in its contrast with that of Tatian, is already an indication of the synthesis between immortality and resurrection that was to be the orthodox doctrine. Origen's speculations about the pre-existence of souls and their eventual salvation were condemned formally in 543-553, but had been repudiated by most theologians all along. Thus the doctrine of creation was defended by being distinguished from the doctrine of the fall of man: human sin and mortality were not due to some pre-historical fall of the soul and its subsequent incarceration in the body, but to man's first disobedience. Once the doctrine of the immortality of the soul was separated from the notion of the pre-existence of the soul, it could be harmonized with the doctrine of the resurrection. The treatise of Ambrose on the resurrection voiced the orthodox consensus when it argued the doctrine of immortality was incomplete without the doctrine of resurrection; resurrection thus meant the conferral upon the body of that deathless life which the soul already possessed. What the philosophers taught about the immortality of the soul was thus not incorrect but only incomplete.

The other Christian doctrine whose development was significantly affected by the continuing dominance of Greek thought was the doctrine of God. Implicit in the biblical view of God as the Creator was the affirmation of his sovereign independence: God was not dependent on his creatures as they were on him. But in their assertion of the freedom of God, the prophets simultaneously emphasized his involvement in both love and wrath with the covenant people. Therefore, the Old Testament doctrine of the sovereign freedom of God could not be synonymous with the philosophical doctrine of divine "apathy" or impassibility, which meant first of all that God was incapable of the changes and sufferings that characterize human life and feeling, although derivatively it could also mean "impassivity," that God was indifferent to the changes and sufferings of man. It is significant that Christian theologians customarily set down the doctrine of the impassibility of God as an axiom, without bothering to provide biblical support or theological proof. Even Tertullian, for all his hostility to metaphysics, argues this way against the "patripassianism" of Praxeas. For Athanasius it was "an admitted truth about God that he stands in need of nothing, but is self-sufficient and filled with himself," as it was "a principle of natural philosophy that that which is single and complete is superior to those things which are diverse." For Gregory of Nyssa the very suggestion that God could be passible was too absurd to merit serious consideration and too blasphemous to bear Christian repetition. Didymus the Blind took it for granted that the Holy Spirit, as God, had to be "impassible, indivisible, and immutable." According to Theodore of Mopsuestia, "it is well known . . . that the gulf between [the Eternal One and a temporal one] is unbridgeable"; and again "known that variety belongs to creatures and simplicity to the divine nature." Cyril of Alexandria dismissed as *lēros* and *mania*, any suggestion that the Logos, as God, could be transformed. And Apollinaris summarized the consensus of Christian theologians, regardless of party, when he declared: "Anyone who introduces passion into the [divine] Power is atheistic [*asebēs*]." Theologians who found Platonic speculation congenial and theologians who found it incompatible with the gospel were agreed that the Christian understanding of the relation between Creator and creature required "the concept of an entirely static God, with eminent reality, in relation to an entirely fluent world, with deficient reality."—a concept that came into Christian doctrine from Greek philosophy.

Nevertheless, any such concept had to be squared with the assertions of both the Old and the New Testament that God was wrathful against sin, as well as with the confession that Christ the crucified was divine. Some Christian theologians went so far as simply to identify the Christian doctrine of God with the philosophical rejection of anthropomorphism; thus Arnobius argued that God (the gods) had to be "immune to every disturbance and every perturbation," with no "agitation of spirit" or wrath. Others did not go to this extreme, but maintained that the philosophical doctrine of impassibility was not incompatible with the biblical language about the wrath of God; thus Justin refers to God as *apathēs*, but also "speaks again and again of God in the most personal language." Still others seem to have been constrained at least partly by their polemical stance to think through the relation between wrath and transcendence with more awareness of the subtlety in that relation; thus, we have noted, Tertullian contended against Praxeas for the impassibility of God, but Marcion's separation between the God of love and the God of wrath evoked from him the distinction that "God may be wrathful, but he is not irritated." The doctrine of the absoluteness and impassibility of God came to form one of the presuppositions of the Trinitarian and Christological issues; and the doctrine of the atonement of Anselm was based on the axiom "that the divine nature is impassible, and that it can in no sense be brought down from its loftiness or toil in what it wills to do."

Although the axiom of the impassibility of God did not require conventional biblical proof, one passage from the Old Testament served as the validation for Christian discussions of ontology: "the towering text," the word from the burning bush in Ex. 3:14. To Clement of Alexandria it meant that "God is one, and beyond the one and above the Monad itself"; to Origen, that "all things, whatever they are, participate in Him who truly is"; to Hilary it was "an indication concerning God so exact that it expressed in the terms best adapted to human understanding an unattainable insight into the mystery of the divine nature"; to Gregory of Nazianzus it proved that "He who is" was the most appropriate designation for God; to Theodore of Mopsuestia it was the mark of distinction between God and all his creatures; to Augustine it proved that "essence" could be used of God with strict propriety, while "substance" was not precise. From these and other sources this understanding of the passage passed into the authoritative summaries of Christian doctrine, *The Orthodox Faith* of John of Damascus in the East and the *Summa* of Thomas Aquinas in the West. It is no exaggeration, therefore, to speak of "a metaphysics of Exodus," with which a Church father such as Clement of Alexandria sought to harmonize his "Christian Platonism."

Even in the case of the theology of Clement, however, it is misleading to speak of "Hellenization." As we have seen, although theologians quoted Scripture in support of ideas originally derived from philosophy, they often modified these ideas on the basis of Scripture. The tension between biblical and philosophical doctrine is especially pronounced in those thinkers, such as Origen and Augustine, whose preserved writings include both apologies addressed to pagans and biblical expositions addressed to Christians. This would, in turn, raise serious doubt about the validity of a distinction between "apologetics" and "kerygmatic" theology historically or theologically. At most, it would appear valid to distinguish between the apologetic and the kerygmatic tasks performed by the same theologians, and in such a distinction to keep the entire picture in view, with all its tensions. It is even more a distortion when the dogma formulated by the Catholic tradition is described as "in its conception and development a product of the Greek spirit on the soil of the gospel." Indeed, in some ways it is more accurate to speak of dogma as the "de-Hellenization" of the theology that had preceded it and to argue that "by its dogma the Church threw up a wall against an alien metaphysic." For in the development of both the dogmas of the early Church, the Trinitarian and the Christological, the chief place to look for "Hellenization" is in the speculations and heresies against which the dogma of the creeds and councils were directed. Speculation there continued to be; also after the dogma had been promulgated, the question of the proper function of philosophy in the exposition of Christian doctrine remained inescapable even for theologians such as Tertullian or Luther, who strove to rule it out of court. But Christian doctrine also proved again and again that it could not live by philosophy alone, but had to turn to the word of God in the Old and New Testament.

IV. THE AMBIGUITY OF CHRISTIAN IDENTITY

THE end result of these disputes with Judaism and with Hellenism was a schematization of the relation between Christianity and other religions that assured the finality of God's revelation in Christ while acknowledging the partial validity of earlier revelations. The prophecy of Jacob concerning Judah summarized all three points, namely, the historical mission of Israel, the end of that mission with the coming of Jesus, and the place of Jesus as the divine answer to the aspirations of all nations. Justin took the prophecy to mean both that Judaism has completed its vocation and that the Gentiles now looked to Christ as the one who was to come again; he maintained that the phrase, "the expectation of the nations," proved that the passage referred to Christ rather than to Judah himself. Irenaeus saw in it the prophecy that Christ was to be "the hope of the Gentiles," and Cyprian took it as evidence that it would be the Gentiles rather than the Jews who would believe in Christ. With Justin, Hippolytus referrred it to the Second Coming of Christ. Origen summed up the meaning of the passage for the relation of Christianity to both Judaism and Hellenism: "The man who reads the prophecy with an open mind would be amazed at the way in which, after saying that the rulers and leaders of the people would come from the tribe of Judah, he also fixes the time when the rule itself is to come to an end. . . . The Christ of God, for whom are the things which are laid up, has come, the ruler of whom the promises of God speak. He was obviously the only one among all his predecessors and, I would make bold to say, among posterity as well who was the expectation of nations." The prophecy became the theme for the statements of the Christian interpretation of history, as in Eusebius, Augustine, and Sozomenus, and it has been cited to prove the finality of Jesus Christ throughout Christian history.

The finality of Christ was interpreted in various ways, but each involved some acknowledgment of the revelations that had gone before. The motif of Clement's *The Tutor* was a definition of virtue as "a will in conformity to God and Christ in life, rightly adjusted to life everlasting," but the very terminology of this definition was transposed from Stoicism; and his exposition of the Decalog as a symbol of the name "Jesus" prompted him to observe that the Greek philosophers had "caught a spark from the divine Scriptures" but had not apprehended the full truth. Both the revelation of the will of God in the Decalog and the investigation of virtue in the philosophers had been granted by God, but they now had to yield to him whose way they had prepared, the Teacher of the good and perfect life. Where the apocalyptic vision predominated, the decisiveness of Christ was seen as an explicitly chronological finality. Tertullian warned his pagan readers of the coming of Christ as judge, "which now impends over the world, now near its close, in all the majesty of Deity unveiled"; but even he had to admit, in the same paragraph, both that "in former times the Jews enjoyed much of God's favor" and "special revelations" and that the pagan "philosophers, too, regard the Logos . . . as the Creator of the universe." The coming of Christ was the last and greatest revelation of the will of God, but earlier manifestations had to be accorded at least a temporary importance.

When the cross and suffering of Christ were taken as the primary content of his uniqueness, even these new and unprecedented events were interpreted as the fulfillment of prophecy. For Irenaeus, "Christ is the treasure which was hid in the field, that is in the world . . . but the treasure hid in the [Old Testament] Scriptures is Christ, since he was pointed out by means of types and parables." But the "types and parables" were not merely the words of the prophets, who, as "members of Christ . . . set forth the prophecy [assigned him]"; but the events and persons of the history of Israel performed this function also, as when "the suffering of the Righteous One was prefigured from the beginning in Abel, also described by the prophets, but perfected in the last times in the Son of God." Thus Abel was a hero of the Christian faith. Abraham was "the chief and the forerunner of our faith," who "saw in the Spirit the day of the Lord's coming and the dispensation of his suffering"; but with that coming and suffering, the mission of Abraham had reached its goal, and it was right for his followers to "forsake their ship and their father and to follow the Logos." Some ancient Christian writers went further. Origen, defending Christ against the claim of Celsus that "Jesus' message of salvation and moral purity was not sufficient to prove his superiority among men ... [because he] should not have died," replied that "if [Celsus] considers as evil poverty, and a cross, and the conspiracy of wicked men, obviously he would say that evil also befell Socrates"; but Socrates "would not have been able to prove that he was pure from all evils," while Christ was. A comparison between the suffering of Christ and that of Socrates seems to have become a commonplace of Christian apologetics, which was thus able simultaneously to find an anticipatory parallel in pagan as well as in Jewish literature for the message of the cross and to demonstrate the superiority of Christ.

In the apologetics against paganism—although not so obviously in that against Judaism—the old age of the Christian Scriptures was a testimony to their credibility. But the argument was employed also against Judaism, for the apologists consistently maintained that the Jews did not understand their own Bible properly because they had not accepted Jesus as the Christ. The Christian attitude toward the Jewish Bible was therefore an ambivalent one. On the one hand, the Old Testament could be regarded as obsolete, now that "he for whom it had been laid up" had come; on the other hand, by means of a "spiritual interpretation," it could be claimed for the Church as Christian Scripture. The radical version of the former position seems never to have been taken by the majority of Christians. To be sure, Tertullian did make the intriguing statement that "today" there were more who accepted "our position" that the Old Testament was still a part of the Christian Bible than accepted the heretical position of Marcion and others that it had become completely obsolete and devoid of authority with the coming of Christ. But even Harnack was not prepared to conclude any more from this than "it is not altogether impossible that there was a decade during the second century in which the number of Christians who rejected the Old Testament was greater than the number who accepted it." Nevertheless, the very term "Scripture," which originally referred exclusively to the Old Testament, came to be applied—both in the singular and in the plural—to the entire Christian Bible, comprising both the sacred writings that Christianity had inherited from Judaism and the Christian writings on the basis of which the Jewish Scriptures were being interpreted. This is the valid historical development underlying Harnack's judgment that the most significant event in the history of the Church between 150 and 250 was that Christianity became a religion of two Testaments.

"The authority of the Old Testament," as Nathanael Bonwetsch observes in his comment on Harnack's statement, "was the immediate consequence of the services which the Old Testament had performed, and was still performing, for the Church." These services were manifold. To its eighteenth-century author, the theme of *Christianity as Old as the Creation* was to refer primarily to the congruence between Christianity and natural religion; but to the early Church, it meant the continuity between Christianity and the Old Testament. When Justin, disputing with Trypho, referred to the Old Testament as "your Scriptures, or rather not yours, but ours," he was voicing the almost universal Christian claim that the direct line of succession ran from the Old Testament to the Church, not to the synagogue. Adam, Noah, Abraham—"all these ... it would be no departure from the truth to style as Christians, in point of fact if not in name." A prominent token of that continuity was the worship of the Church. "None of our authorities give us clear information on the use of the Psalms and other hymns or chants in the primitive church," but we do know from Justin that "the memoirs of the Apostles or the writings of the prophets" were read in the Sunday service, and the eucharistic prayer in the Didache gives thanks "for the holy vine of thy son David, which Thou madest known unto us through Thy Son Jesus." Whether or not the liturgy of the early Church included the actual singing of the Psalms, it was certainly replete with allusions to the Old Testament, in its prayer, reading and exhortation.

Yet another service performed by the Old Testament, as we have seen, was the development of the Christian conception of the apostolic ministry into a priesthood that stood in continuity with the Levitical priesthood of the Old Testament people. Origen, for example, combines the apostolic and the priestly definitions of the Christian ministry when he says that "the Apostles and their successors, priests according to the great High Priest ... know from their instruction by the Spirit for what sins, when, and how they must offer sacrifice." Perhaps as important as the cultic and the sacerdotal services rendered by the Old Testament to the concrete life of the Church was the ethical service provided by the commandments of the Old Testament, especially by the Decalog. For despite the strictures on the Jewish law that became a stock argument of anti-Jewish polemics, the Decalog, summarized and reinterpreted by the ethical teachings of Jesus, was accorded a special place in the Church. Irenaeus said that "the words of the Decalog ... remain in force among us"; and even the Gnostic Ptolemy, a follower of Valentinus, in his letter to Flora, distinguished between the Decalog and all the rest of the law of Moses, seeing the former as fulfilled in Christ and the latter as either abolished or spiritualized. It is not clear what role the Decalog played in Christian worship (although there is some indication that it was recited at certain services) or in Christian education (although certain passages in Augustine give the impression that it was used as a basis for instruction in ethics); but it is clear that the Decalog was highly valued as a summary of the law of God, both natural and revealed.

In these and other ways, the Church took possession of the Old

Testament—or, at least, of those portions of the Old Testament that were susceptible to Christian interpretation. We have already noted the prominence of allegorical and typological exegesis in the Christian disputes with Judaism, but the "spiritual" interpretation of the Old Testament was characteristic also of the theological explanation of the Old Testament for other Christians. Most of what the Christian theologians of the second century and even of the third century had to say about the inspiration of the biblical writers pertained to the Old Testament prophets rather than to the authors of the books of the New Testament. With Philo, Athenagoras thought that the prophets "spoke out what they were in travail with, their own reasoning falling into abeyance and the Spirit making use of them as a flautist might play upon his flute"; Clement of Alexandria called the prophets "the organs of the divine voice," but distinguished between the ecstasy of false prophets and the inspiration of authentic prophets, which preserved their individuality. For Origen, the inspiration of the Old Testament precluded imputing unworthy meanings to the text; or, as he argued in another passage, "If therefore [all Scripture] is inspired by God and is profitable (Tim. 3:16), we ought to believe that it is profitable even if we do not recognize the profit."

From this Origen drew the conclusion that the profit of the Old Testament could not be found through a literal exegesis, which frequently led to absurd or otherwise unprofitable meanings. For Scripture was to be interpreted according to three senses, the literal, the moral, and the intellectual or spiritual; and the last was the perfect and complete meaning. Although the explicit discussion of his hermeneutical theories and of their application belongs to the history of interpretation rather than to the history of doctrine, the subject does bear consideration here both as part of the process by which the Christian doctrine of Scripture developed and as the presuppostion for the development of other doctrines. For, diverge though they did in so many other ways, Origen and Tertullian agreed that, in the words of Tertullian against Marcion, "heretics either wrest plain and simple words to any sense they choose by their conjectures, or else they violently resolve by a literal interpretation words which ... are incapable of a simple solution." The progressive growth of the allegorical interpretation of the Old Testament was not, as Werner maintains, a compensation for the decline in the eschatological expectation of the Church, but the explication of the Christian consensus that "the writings of Moses are the words of Christ," and that therefore the term "words of Christ" did not include "only those which he spoke when he became man and tabernacled in the flesh; for before that time, Christ, the Word of God, was in Moses and the prophets."

On the basis of this consensus it was possible to read the Old Testament as a Christian book and to see "the words of Christ" not only in such passages as Psalm 22, as was explicitly warranted by the New

Testament, but also in such books as the Song of Songs. The development of the doctrine of the Trinity, for example, was decisively shaped by the use of Proverbs 8 as a passage dealing with the relation between the pre-existent Logos and the Father. And although both the orthodox and the Arians read the chapter as a "word of Christ," Newman's generalization is probably an accurate one: "It may almost be laid down as an historical fact, that the mystical interpretation and orthodoxy will stand or fall together." When the mystical interpretation was surrendered or at least seriously qualified, as in Theodore of Mopsuestia, his opponents professed to see a causal connection between his hermeneutics and his Christology. The Christological exegesis of the Old Testament and the dogma of the two natures in Christ supported each other. The declaration of 1 Cor. 15:3-4, echoed by the Nicene Creed, that both the death and the resurrection of Christ had taken place "in accordance with the Scriptures," provided the orthodox tradition with justification for elaborating the statements of the New Testament by additions from the Old.

A good example was Deut. 28:66 LXX: "You shall see your life hanging before your eyes," which, frequently in conjunction with Jer. 11:19 and other passages, came very early to be interpreted as a reference to those who crucified Christ. The heretics who refused to see prophecies of Christ in the Old Testament claimed that "there is nothing easier than to prove that this does not refer to Christ," but was a threat addressed to Israel by Moses. But Irenaeus spoke for the orthodox tradition in challenging the heretics to show who but Jesus Christ could have been meant by such prophecies as this; and both he and Cyprian linked it with Psalm 22, Isaiah 65:2, and other standard predictions of the cross. Tertullian's version predicted the cross even more explicitly, saying: "Your life will hang *on the tree* before your eyes," which he explained on the basis of other references to the tree of the cross. Among Western writers, Novatian, Lactantius, and Rufinus all echoed the traditional usage and connected it with the stock passages from the Psalms and the prophets. Among Eastern thinkers, Athanasius and Cyril of Jerusalem quoted it as evidence of the clear language about Christ in the Old Testament. This became the standard interpretation of the passage, which both in its content and in the differences between Jews and Christians over its exegesis was seen as proof that the Old Testament had clearly predicted the coming of Jesus Christ but that Judaism had failed to understand the Old Testament correctly. The prophecies of the Old Testament were fulfilled, the religion of the Old Testament was superseded.

The attitude of the Church Fathers toward Hellenism contained a somewhat analogous judgment of its historic role; it, too, had been fulfilled but superseded. "Whatever things were rightly said among all men," wrote Justin, "are the property of us Christians." Thus Christianity laid claim to all that was good and noble in the tradition of classical thought, for this had been inspired by the seminal Logos, who became flesh in Jesus Christ. But this meant that not only Moses but Socrates had been both fulfilled and superseded by the coming of Jesus. Some ancient Christian writers were willing to concede a great deal to the preparatory work of the seminal Logos among the Greeks; others were less generous. None went so far as to designate the history of Greek thought a second Old Testament, although in some of his formulations Clement of Alexandria approached such a designation: "Before the advent of the Lord, philosophy was necessary to the Greeks for righteousness... For God is the cause of all good things; but of some primarily, as of the Old and the New Testament; and of others by consequence, as of philosophy. Perchance, too, philosophy was given to the Greeks directly and primarily, till the Lord should call the Greeks. For this was a schoolmaster to bring 'the Hellenic mind,' to Christ, as the law brought the Hebrews. Philosophy, therefore, was a preparation, paving the way for him who is perfected in Christ." Here the statement of Paul in Gal. 3:24 becomes a justification for a positive evaluation of the place of Greek philosophy in the history of salvation or at least in the history of revelation. But in other passages Clement maintains that the Greeks, unlike the Jews, had no "schoolmaster" to teach them the will of God.

Even this concession to philosophy, however, was aimed at proving that Hellenism had represented only a preparatory apprehension of divine truth. In Christian practice, classical thought continued to perform such a preparatory function. For example, Cicero's *Hortensius* "turned my [Augustine's] prayers toward Thee, O Lord, and gave me new hope and new desires." Justin had been prepared for Christian revelation by the study of Soicism, then of Aristotelianism, then of Pythagoreanism, and finally of Platonism. None had satisfied his search for truth, but each had led him progressively closer to those teachers who were "more ancient than all those who have the reputation of being philosophers," the Old Testament prophets. Various apologists seized upon various bits of evidence for the anticipation of revealed truth in the writings of the classical tradition—now Socrates, now Cicero, now other thinkers and writers. Two of the most important sources of such evidence were the Fourth Eclogue of Vergil and the Sibylline Oracles.

Although the apologetic interest in Vergil seems to have been drawn first to the *Aeneid,* it came to concentrate on the fourth of his Eclogues. This "messianic eclogue," written in 41 or 40 B.C., prophesied a golden age, the culmination of the centuries, in which the virgin would return and a new offspring, bearing a divine life, would descend from heaven to earth to rule a world transformed by his father's virtues. Augustine believed that these words really referred to Christ, even though "poetically" since the poet had actually spoken them of someone else. Jerome was not willing to "call the Christless Maro a Christian" on the basis of these lines, but *The Oration of Constantine* went much further than Augustine in claiming that Vergil intentionally made his language obscure to avoid persecution, but that he "was acquainted with that blessed mystery which gave to our Lord the name of Savior." With these credentials Vergil became the beloved poet even of Christians who were hostile to classical literature. The medieval West multiplied legends of Vergil's supernatural knowledge and exploits, and it was both for his style and for his content that Dante was able to celebrate Vergil as "my master and my author." Whether Vergil's imagery owed its origins to Hebrew messianism or not, it was "the expression of ... the profound longing for peace, the unvoiced yearning for a world governed by the goodness of God rather than the conflicting desires of men.... It was this longing that prepared the way for the expansion of Christianity," and at least in this sense the Fourth Eclogue was "messianic." But to some apologists for Christianity its messianism was considerably more explicit.

Vergil's authority was enhanced by his reference to Cuma in the Eclogue, which Christian writers connected with the Cumaean Sibyl also mentioned in the *Aeneid*. "There is no possession of the Romans, sacred or profane, which they guard so carefully as they do the Sibylline oracles," wrote Dionysius of Halicarnassus; and a modern historian has observed that "the study of the outward and inward effects of the Sibylline books is ... the real history of religion in the first half of the [Roman] Republic." Various interpolations crept into the Sibylline books already under the Roman auspices, but it was especially from Jewish and then from Christian sources that such interpolations came. Josephus cited their authority to substantiate his apologetic case for Judaism, and Eusebius drew upon Josephus. Several Christian apologists followed his lead, to the point that Celsus ridiculed Christians as "Sibyllists." Thus Justin cited the Sibyl in support of the Christian doctrine "that there is to be a dissolution by God of things corruptible." Theophilus lumped the Sibyl with the Hebrew prophets among the "men of God who were borne along by the Spirit and became prophets, being inspired and made wise by God"; the Sibyl "was a prophetess among the Greeks and the other nations," who had prophesied the eventual conflagration of the world. He quoted from the Sibylline oracles more extensively than most other Christian writers and may have been the source for some of them. Clement of Alexandria found the Sibyl "in remarkable accordance with inspiration" but did not accept her oracles uncritically. Lactantius found proof not only, as other fathers had, for Christian eschatology, but for monotheism, for the doctrine of creation, and even, by combining the oracles with Proverbs 8, for the doctrine that God has a Son; Augustine based his use of the Sibyl at least partly on Lactantius. Other apologists, too, made use of the Sibyl to corroborate Christian teaching. It was an epitome of this apologetic use when the *Dies irae* of the Franciscan

Thomas of Celano prophesied the coming of the day of wrath on the basis of the dual authority of "David and Sibyl"—a conflation which more timid medieval Christians vainly tried to mollify. Sometimes the references to the Sibyl were combined with citations of "Hystapes," a syncretistic work published under the name of the Persian magus, who thus provided additional evidence for the claim that pre-Christian paganism had not been devoid of expectations of that which had come in Jesus Christ.

This interpretation of the relation between natural and revealed religion found support in many areas of the life of the Church, as did the interpretation of the relation between Christianity and Judaism discussed earlier. The missionary practice of the Church was constrained to recognize from the outset that "God shows no partiality, but in every nation any one who fears him and does what is right is acceptable to him" (Acts 10:34-35), and that therefore the Greek did not have to become a Jew en route to the gospel. From this premise it appeared to follow that Christian missionaries should affirm whatever could be affirmed of the religion prevailing in the nations to which they came and should represent Christianity as the correction and fulfillment of the expectations at work in those nations. When Gregory I instructed the missionary Augustine to adapt both pagan temples and pagan holy days to Christian usage, he was, as Latourette has observed, "but following the practice widely current in the days when the Roman Empire was being converted." And while it may be an exaggeration to speak of this approach to the religion of the nations as "the syncretism of a universal religion," it was based on the principle that Jesus Christ is the divinely ordained answer to the needs and aspirations of the Gentiles as well as the fulfillment of the messianic expectations of Israel. Partly as a consequence of such missionary practice, a similar view of the relation between natural religion and revealed religion is evident in the development of Christian piety, as the Church led the nations through lower to higher forms of devotion and worship.

For the development of Christian doctrine, the most significant area where this ambiguity of Christian identity manifested itself was probably the relation between philosophy and theology. As we have seen, most of the generous things which the Church fathers said about paganism applied to the philosophers. Toward the religious rituals of Greek and Roman paganism, Christian apologists had only contempt. They did not, for example, elaborate on the significance of pagan sacrifices for the sacrificial significance of the death of Christ for they shared with their pagan opponents a disgust at the crudities of polytheistic practice. But they took the position that while the priests and professional religionists of the nations had been perpetuating idolatrous beliefs and practices, the philosophers had begun the process of emancipation and rationalization which Christ, the eternal Reason of God, had now consummated. Both pagan polytheism and Jewish monotheism had now been superseded by his coming. As Gregory of Nyssa summarized the case in a remarkable passage, Christian "truth passes in the mean between these two conceptions, destroying each heresy, and yet accepting what is useful to it from each. The Jewish dogma is destroyed by the acceptance of the Logos and by the belief in the Spirit; while the polytheistic error of the Greek school is made to vanish by the unity of the Nature abrogating this imagination of plurality. While yet again, of the Jewish conception, let the unity of the Nature stand; and of the Hellenistic, only the distinction as to persons.... It is as if the number of the Trinity were a remedy in the case of those who are in error as to the One, and the assertion of the unity for those whose beliefs are dispersed among a number of divinities." This is echoed by the other Cappadocians and by other theologians as well.

In the orthodox doctrine of the Trinity, then, Christianity articulated both its continuity with the Old Testament and its answer to Hellenism. Thus Augustine's *On the Trinity* first demonstrated the doctrine of the Trinity from the Scriptures, including and especially the Old Testament; and then proceeded to argue that "in the Trinity, Christian wisdom discovers that for which Classicism had so long vainly sought, viz. the *logos* or explanation of being and motion, in other words, a metaphysic of ordered process." Both the controversies over the doctrine of the Trinity itself and the irrepressible disputes over the propriety of philosophical speculation within the limits of orthodoxy were evidence that the relation of Christian doctrine to both Judaism and classical thought is a perennial issue in theology. The forms of the issue were largely set by the literature of the first five centuries, but the questions that were left unanswered in the triumph of Christian theology over both Judaism and classicism were to take their revenge by reasserting themselves with insistent force when the political, cultural, and ecclesiastical presuppositions of orthodoxy began to wither away in the modern era. Thus the problem of Christian identity compelled a reconsideration of how Christianity is related both to its Jewish and to its Hellenic heritage.

Morality: Underlying and Unchanging Principles?

Bernard Haring

My topic is: Morality—unchangeable principles for human conduct. Today, many people's religious security is shaken because they had believed in certain principles, while assuming that the whole Church did likewise. Suddenly they came to the realization that even certain zealous orthodox people no longer believed in these principles—or if they did believe, they expressed their views in new, almost unrecognizable forms. We must remember that Christian life is not to be faced exclusively through abstract principles. It is, therefore, important that today's Christian acknowledge that placing all confidence and trust in abstractions will not give him a firm basis for the Christian life. On the other hand, the Christian knows that he is faced with the living God, who has revealed Himself in Jesus Christ—the Christ who *is, was* and *shall be*—the Christ of absolute faithfulness in whom we can place our trust. This confidence is the basis for stability in Christian life and thought. Christ, who is more significant to our lives than any special form of Christian dogma, lends genuine continuity to faith. God has spoken to mankind His final word in a Christ who is both the abiding message and messenger—in a Christ, who is the way, the truth, and the life of the faithful—in a Christ in whom we have continuity. Yet, this stability in Christ does not imply immutability; rather, it implies the dynamic presence of the One who is Lord—the Lord of history—not the Lord or guardian of the dead. In this Christ, stability and genuine fidelity are based on a dynamic understanding of the word of God. If we look upon faith mainly as an assent to a collection of definitions and formulations of doctrine and of abstract principles, the present age will bring itself to an ever-increasing insecurity and frustration. Faith, understood narrowly as a mere adherence to formulations of abstract immutable principles, is not the Christian faith in its true fullness. Such a narrow faith will be profoundly shaken by doubts concerning the validity of certain principles so far unquestionably asserted and accepted as parts of the deposit of faith or the Christian tradition. Faith, in the biblical tradition and in the best of Catholic thought, is a humble and grateful acceptance of God revealing Himself, and therefore implies a complete surrender to Him.

Such a faith is concerned with essentials, rather than with speculations regarding such things as, for example, the sociology of angels, the hierarchy of spirits, or, the principle of individuation of angels. I do not doubt that other beings besides man were created by God. However, this aspect ought not to be made a keynote of faith. The essential matter is man's constant self-surrender to God, thus remaining open in order to attain an ever more perfect understanding of God's true countenance, His love for man. Such a faith is the best safeguard against false insecurity.

At any time, the real object of faith is God, who reveals Himself in His salvific will towards man. Faith is an existential "yes" to God's self-manifestation. It is the expression of perfect trust in Him. In faith, man surrenders and entrusts himself to God. Of course, faith further implies the attitude of listening, that is, the profound and sincere desire to perceive rightly what God reveals *(fides quae creditur)*. Furthermore, the essence of faith lies in its being a reminder to man, lest he forget his finite condition as a creature on this earth: "Now we see only puzzling reflections in a mirror, but there we shall see face to face. My knowledge now is partial" (I Cor. 13:12).

I. THE TRUE MEANING OF THE DYNAMISM IN CHRISTIAN ETHICS

HAVING established these matters, let us turn to the meaning of "dynamism" in Christian ethics. When dealing with the dynamics of the natural law, one must keep in mind both the necessity and immense possibility of growth and conversion. This is a gradual growth in our awareness, and concomitantly in our realization of freedom; a growth not only in experience, but also in prudent reflection on experience; a growth in achieving a synthesis through both intuition and systematic effort; a growth in achieving a synthesis in the sense of Christian existentialism. The term "dynamic" is synonymous with continuity in development and evolution. Christians believe in the oneness of human history in view of the one design of the One God. Therefore, we believers see the "dynamic" characterized by the will to fidelity towards God's design. Yet, fidelity to the living God should be carefully distinguished from fidelity to bare abstract principles in their time-bound formulation. The latter always implies an imperfect approach, an imperfect attempt of man to express something and to cling to it. Indeed, fidelity must be distinguished from a tenacious clinging to set patterns, formulations and customs which, in my opinion, represents the most striking example of a refusal of fidelity to the living God, the Lord of human history.

If we wish to understand the full implications of the dynamic aspects of Christian life, we also have to take into consideration that type of *discontinuity* which comes into human history and thought through sin and error. There is discontinuity not only in the life of the individual, but also in human history as such. We notice this type of discontinuity in the people of various cultures, and even in the life of the Church in both the Old and New Testament. There are many forms of discontinuity in the Church today—particularly, for example, a certain "triumphalism" among Catholics. The history of Israel, likewise, shows deplorable discontinuity, and sometimes hopeless discontinuity, were it not for God's mercy. It is only through God's mercy that we are not totally confused and confounded. The "dynamic" which arises from God does not exclude the possibility of a decline. The history of salvation is the history of God with man, whom He desires to see free—whom He, Himself, endowed with the gift of freedom, the ability to discern and to choose—but in a way that He does not detract from man's freedom.

The Church, especially as it embodies the right understanding of Christian morality, is often threatened by a partial disintegration through the loss of the center. In some manuals of moral theology, you find enumerated 500 and more occasions to commit mortal sin, many of them strikingly petty. This clearly indicates the absence of a hierarchy of values through the loss of the center in some manuals of moral theology. The same loss of the center was particularly noticeable in art during the last century—referred to in the famous book by Sedlmair as: *Der Verlust der Mitte* ("the loss of the center"). Even today the loss of center is a threat to the Church, as well as to the correct understanding of Christian morality. Lack of synthesis and relevance of laws will lead to partial disintegration— chiefly through the kind of discontinuity which is caused by a stubborn clinging to outdated formulations which today no longer reflect and meet the needs of man. Sin threatens the integrity of moral knowledge—both in the individual and in communities.

The "dynamic" in Christian thought and life calls for a saving discontinuity—a change or conversion for both the Church and the individual. The Council has affirmed: *Ecclesia semper reformanda*, which means that the Church is in constant need of renewal. The first or basic conversion in the life of the individual is a transition from death to life—from the state of mortal sin to friendship with God. This "first" conversion has to be reiterated after mortal sin. The "second," or continuing conversion, means purification and growth in friendship with God. Only continuous conversion (characterized by varying degrees of discontinuity in proportion to cooperation with grace) applies both to the whole Church and communities within the Church.

All these various viewpoints and facets of the "dynamic" have to be understood in the light of the historicity of man and of the Church. Historicity ought to be defined as that historical genuineness of man in which he *has* history, *is* history, and *makes* history. But man has a history only through God. Man's historicity, therefore, cannot be defined without the One who called him into being and constantly sustains him. Man has the possibility to shape history beyond material aspects through a more dynamic and more realistic acceptance and utilization of his true opportunities.

II. HISTORICITY IN AN ESCHATOLOGICAL PERSPECTIVE

THE "philosophy of history" of the last century, which had so greatly influenced the philosophy of Hegel and even more so that of Karl Marx, expressed its belief in the oneness of human history as a continuous progress. Nevertheless, this philosophical thinking could not explain the fundamental problem of continuity of life since they refused to see history in the light of God's loving design. It is striking that Karl Marx, like any number of Old Testament prophets, believed in the oneness of history and taught that the whole dialectic process is leading to the perfection of the classless society where everyone loves everybody else. He believed that increasing tensions are leading to final fulfillment in love. It seems that even today there are some people who think that increased tensions between the right and left wing in the Church will lead to genuine renewal. While we have no way of avoiding tensions, we nevertheless should try not to increase them.

In the midst of the various forms of discontinuity, an eschatological understanding disposes us to recognize the more profound continuity; namely, the beginning in the word of God—the beginning—not just in the temporal sense. We can leave open the question of a temporal beginning of the world, in the sense of the world's beginning thousands or millions of years ago. St. Thomas, in his book on the possibility of a world without a temporal beginning which he wrote "against the grumbling people" *(De aeternitate mundi contra murmurantes)*, expressed the opinion that the beginning of the world by God's word can be understood in the sense of a continuing dynamic presence of the word of God in human history. The question of a beginning of time is secondary.

Furthermore, the eschatological perspective also takes cognizance of the conflict between the followers of Adam (solidarity in sin), and the followers of Christ who have manifested the fullest extent of human solidarity (solidarity in salvation). However, the fact of our solidarity with Adam should not be carried to the implied assertion of a well-known conservative theologian in the council who, in answer to a question—why in a certain draft the name of Adam occurred more frequently than that of Christ?—responded that Adam was the first man and, therefore, more fundamental than Christ. It is an almost classical expression of desperation that reference to Adam seemed more important than reference to Christ. Likewise, in the theory concerning limbo, it seems preposterous to imply that some men would be under the impact of the first Adam without having come under the radiant influence of Christ. Every person, created according to the image of God, is truly touched by the radiance of Christ's grace. If in this perspective we consider the question of limbo, it seems quite inconceivable that some souls, without their own fault, could remain under the impact of the first Adam without having come under the saving influence of the second Adam.

Christ is the center and fulfillment of human history. Both the community and the individual receive their unifying and dynamic perspective from Christ in a way that each *kairos* is illumined and vitalized by the remembrance of the past history of salvation and by Christian hope and expectation. The *kairos* of moral and religious decision is filled with the energies of the first and second coming of Christ—the intervening time is an actual on-going coming of Christ. This eschatological view of the *kairos* prevents fragmentation and discontinuity. It means a dynamic approach which guarantees continuity and an open mind. Each moment of decision, in the life of the community as well as in the life of the individual, is a true *kairos* (in the biblical sense) and therefore receives its dynamic hope and its expectation, its beautiful and dynamic perspective, from its union with the past history of salvation.

The individual Christian, as well as the entire community, is constantly imperiled by the "dynamic" of the history of sin. Consequently, a Christian eschatological perspective implies the notion of tension and uncertainty insofar as man has failed to set all his faith and hope in Christ. An eschatological and, therefore, historical orientation, is absolutely fundamental to a true understanding of Christian morality. Over-simplification through the suppressing or deleting of some aspects of Christian morality, tends to falsify all our principles (for example, the John Birch society). Historicism lacks continuity, and therefore differs thoroughly from historicity, which is the full perspective in which we see the present issues. Historicism is another kind of pagan integration, while in historicity the vital perspectives of history are seen in an integrated perfect approach.

III. THE DYNAMISM OF DIVINE REVELATION

ONLY after a general clarification of the meaning of the "dynamic" aspect of Christian life in its eschatological perspective, are we able to approach a particular aspect essential to an understanding of Christian morality—the "dynamic" in divine revelation. The whole of

Creation is a manifestation or revelation of God's design, since all things are made by the word of God (cf. Col. 1:16; John 1:1:ff.). It is significant that in the Hebrew language the expression for word *(dabar)* signifies both "a word spoken" and an event or a deed. In God's revelation, word and event are synonymous. This biblical perspective must always be kept in mind.

A full awareness of evolution, in the whole of the universe and human history, gives a new emphasis and accent to the traditional teaching of the *creatio continua,* the continuing creation, namely, the continuous dynamic presence of God in His world. In an era of greater knowledge and a broadened outlook on the unmistakable marks of evolution, the idea of a continuing or ongoing creation receives an increasing emphasis and enthusiasm. An ever ongoing creation of the world and a humanity in evolution also implies an ongoing revelation. This, in turn, demands an attitude of constant listening on the part of man. We cannot limit God's manifestation to the words of the Bible. Such an attitude seems to place restrictions on God's revelation in action. God, who is far greater than man, constantly reveals Himself to man. The whole world cannot contain the words of God's manifestation (John 21:25). The heavens continuously proclaim the glory of God—they proclaim His ongoing dynamic presence, not by being immobile, nor by barely obeying static laws, but rather by their marvelous evolution. The evolution of the whole of the universe is closely linked with the evolution common to man. God's presence is most clearly reflected in man's progress, movement, and historicity. This truth particularly applies to a fuller understanding of man's nature and man's morality. Morality should be an "objective" response to the dynamic way in which God reveals Himself. A static concept of life and morality is not objective in so far as it does not truly respond to the dynamic presence of God. A static concept of God and creation is the chief cause of man's security complex which promotes laziness of thought. Objectivity, in the best of philosophical thought, is only guaranteed when man opens himself to the total message of the word and event with which he is faced. Man's nature is the nature of a "being-in-becoming"—it is the dynamic presence of God—a dynamic word which always spells out new avenues.

We see a continuing creation going hand-in-hand with an ever ongoing revelation in the history of the world of man; we see it in the light of that unique event in which God poured out the fullness of His love, His self-revelation in Christ. Therefore, only in the light of Christ can we truly read the book of history and perceive its dynamic direction and the genuine existential meaning of the signs of the times, the *kairos*. In the writings of the Fathers of the early Church, we see a decided Christocentric approach. It should, likewise, be our effort to lead everything to Christ, to see everything—all events of Church and world history—in the light of Christ's coming and mission.

The idea of a continuing creation, which means an ever ongoing revelation in the history of the world and of man, must be understood as part of God's completely unique revelation culminating in Christ. Only in view of Christ, and in the light radiating from Him, can we penetrate the book of history as to its dynamic direction and the truly existential meaning of the signs of the time, the *kairos*. Human history is like the sealed scroll in the Apocalypse: "Then I saw in the right hand of the One who sat on the throne a scroll, with writing inside and out, and it was sealed with seven seals.... There was no one in heaven or on earth or under the earth able to open the scroll or to look inside it.... The Lion from the tribe of Judah, the Root of David, has won the right to open the scroll and break its seven seals" (Apoc. 5:1-5).

The fact that Christ alone is the key to a redeeming perception of history and to an understanding of the concrete appeals arising from the opportunities of the present moment does not obviate the need for personal effort or dispense us from utilizing all human resources in order to come to a fuller understanding of the dynamic aspect of divine revelation. We have to make a constant effort to read in the book of history. We are to make use of all means which Divine Providence puts at our disposal. While in earlier ages a reliance on the tradition handed down from previous generations seemed sufficient and acceptable, today's Christian is in need of a continuous study of the social sciences —historical research, sociology, comparative culture, psychology, and social psychology.

It seems significant that when the Redemptorist Fathers opened the *Academia Alfonsiana,* they provided for a chair for the "Old Testament" teaching—that is, they included in the curriculum a study of the pedagogy of the Old Testament or God's wonderful dealings with His chosen people. In the light of the dynamic character of our era, we gain new appreciation of the historical, dynamic, and pedagogical character of divine revelation, especially in regard to the moral and religious invitations and commandments. It is worthy of notice that, already in the patristic age, the constant reading of the Old Testament forestalled an all too static assertion regarding the things intrinsically and absolutely evil. We see this in the approach to polygamy, divorce, slavery, and usury. A good illustration of this dynamic approach is evident in the obligatory character of the levirate marriage where the widow was given over to the brother of the deceased husband who was charged with the duty to raise offspring to his brother, regardless of his own marital status. Genesis 38 illustrates how strongly this directive was emphasized; it even received religious sanction from the covenant. In view of this fact, our missionaries, laboring in countries possessing primitive cultures, should refrain from labeling the levirate marriage a form of polygamy and, as such, intrinsically evil.

Neither the Israelites, nor the infant Church, seemed to be fully cognizant of the fact that some of the moral, ritual and judiciary laws and commandments belonged to an "interim-ethics." These laws had an appeal in a particular historical hour but yielded to a new order. This is well illustrated in the story of St. Peter and Cornelius. St. Peter at first was shocked by the invitation to "kill and eat." Peter's spontaneous response—"Far be it from me Lord, for never did I eat anything profane or unclean" (Acts 10:13-15)—indicated that he considered these regulations as abiding principles. Even St. James, in the first council-meeting of the apostles, confused vital principles with such secondary laws as "kosher" which, at that particular epoch of the Church, were not only unessential but even detrimental, since they tended to create barriers betwen Christians of Jewish and Gentile origin.

IV. DYNAMIC INTERACTION BETWEEN RELIGION AND MORALITY AND BETWEEN FAITH AND ETHICS

Not only do some men believe in a vital morality and sound ethical teaching without religious beliefs, but some theologians, ethicists and humanists even go so far as to emphatically assert that religious or dogmatic attitudes may often be stifling to genuine morality. It seems that Erich Fromm is speaking in the name of many people when in his book, *Man for Himself,* he points out that he has discussed the problem of ethical norms based on our knowledge of the nature of man, and not on revelation and man-made laws and conventions. E. Ballard also observes that there are reasons for believing that religious and theistic beliefs, like other traditions, become potent influences tending to freeze one's grasp of relevant values into routine judgment patterns of the conventional sort. Here the question arises: Is morality, in all its expressions and norms, revealed once forever? Are the moral principles simply objective truths in an inflexible form of thought and pattern?

The Christian religion is not an abstract, timeless doctrine. It is an ongoing history between God and man, and as such a constant coming of God to man, a continuous revelation and manifestation of the mystery of God's love for man and, on the part of man, a gradual grasp of God's design. It embraces the unfailing, saving action of God who, by a continuous dynamic invitation, solicits man's wholehearted response to His life-giving revelation. Dynamically and gradually, man experiences a calling to truth and sincerity of existence in complete openness and ready response—of existence called to morality. I would define morality as man's innermost self—a calling or constant openness to true continuity, newness and existential risk. God manifests His love and loving design in the measure which is in keeping with man's limited capacity and his vital needs. He does not wish man to waste his talents in self-complacency, self-pity, or frustration, but expects him to be totally open to the grace of the present moment.

Faith in God and faith in Christ was a vital reality existing long before dogmatic manuals were written, before man had a systematized expression of faith or religious thoughts. It is true that faith, which is an assent to the proclamation of Christ, finds a variety of expressions that come about as a consequence of cultural differences. We find good illustrations of this in both Roman and Hellenistic cultures. Faith can exist in vital forms even in people who are unable to express it in precise and rational concepts. Peter was not a man capable of systematic dogmatic theology, but he was indeed a man of faith, and a capable preacher and witness to the mystery of Christ. St. Paul, on the other hand, was more theologically inclined, although he did not produce a systematic, abstract exposition, but one that urges a total response to Christ in concrete situations. Faith always implies a *yes* to the love which God has manifested toward the whole of mankind and a *yes* to that all-embracing love to which God is appealing through the very revelation of His all-embracing love for men. If this affirmation is truly sincere and vital, it will contain an urgent appeal to an ever increasing understanding of the true countenance of God's own love and a fuller perception of the needs of our neighbor in the context of the present situation. It implies a constant openness to the needs and exigencies of love which will always vary according to time-bound circumstances, according to the measure of grace bestowed upon the person involved. In addition, these needs are perceived according to the sensitivity of one's own heart. Despite all differences, there is a certain continuity of ways and means in which the true countenance of love manifests itself.

Faith and hope are events of salvation through God's grace in the "here and now," but with dimensions which embrace both the beginning of all things in the word of God and the fulfillment of all hopes beyond the narrow limits of the present moment. Faith and hope, enkindled by the dynamic presence of God's love, make an appeal to each individual and each community "to use to the full the present opportunity ... not to be fools, but try to understand what the will of the Lord is" (Eph. 5, 16 ff.).

Since the object of our faith and hope is God's own love for men, as manifested in the past and present history of salvation and in a unique way in Christ, faith implies a fundamental dynamism toward ever new, genuine expressions of neighborly love and fraternal solidarity according to the *kairos,* the present dynamism of history. The whole of Christian morality is a stream of love in response to the action of God's own love in history. Formalism and all forms of escapism from the present needs and opportunities are but signs of a weakening of our faith, hope, and love. They betray the absence of genuine religion. Those who "worship the Father in spirit and truth" (John 4, 24) are bound to recognize in all men their brothers and sisters, and will use their talents received from God accordingly in meeting their fellowmen's needs.

The great prophetic tradition, culminating in Christ, had always opposed the kind of deterioration and weakening of religion which tended to freeze man's grasp of the relevant values into routine judgment patterns. The most classical example of the prophetic spirit of genuine religion in opposition to a dead formalism is found in the parable of the Good Samaritan. The formalistic priest and levite also had seen their fellowman in his pitiful forsaken condition. However, their consciousness was filled with minute legal prescriptions and traditions of their law. These same kinds of "religious" people are again seen during the passion of Christ. These men were bent to a scrupulous observance of the external ritual laws even while contriving to annihilate the Christ. They carefully "stayed outside the headquarters (of Pilate) in order to avoid defilement, so that they could eat the Passover meal" (John 18, 28). And after they had succeeded in executing their evil designs, they were most eager to fulfill the requirements of the Sabbath. "The Jews were anxious that the bodies should not remain on the cross for the coming Sabbath" (John 19, 31).

The history of religion (especially the history of the "prophets") is an ever-renewed dynamic force against that unnatural dichotomy between religion and the vital needs of men. It is a well-known fact in history that a priestly class which has lost the genuine vitality of religion will often strive for a "pure cult" without a true passionate concern for men. They will be keen to observe the Sabbath but fail to serve the poor; they will teach the "pure" doctrine by repeating past time-honored formulas, despite far-reaching changes wrought by history. Pope John XXIII—in a genuine religious or prophetic tradition —spoke against such a dichotomy: "In order that Christian teaching may influence the various spheres of human activity—in private, domestic, and social life—it is, first of all, essential that the Church keep her eyes fixed on that sacred heritage of truth handed down from the fathers. At the same time, the Church must be cognizant of the present circumstances and new conditions and forms of life which provide effective avenues for the apostolate in today's world.... Furthermore, we must be whole-hearted and fearless in tending to the mission which the present age imposes upon us.... We must remember that the deposit of faith itself, or the truths contained in our time-honored teaching, is one thing; the manner of its presentation, in full integrity and meaning, is another" (Address of Pope John XXIII at the Opening of the Second Vatican Council). It is evident, then, that religious teaching, by its very nature, is eminently and thoroughly pastoral or existential, always in touch with the changing reality of men, in order to remain faithful to the living God and to serve man here and now.

The dynamic aspects of religious morality essentially depend on the dynamism of faith and worship. However, it must be remembered that faith does not immediately and once for all transform the moral trends of man. The history of salvation clearly shows us that revelation does influence the whole thinking of men. Nevertheless, it does not merely dictate a new system of morality. Imperfect patterns of conduct are not suddenly eliminated. We find this well illustrated in Abraham, our father in faith, who acted according to his cultural heritage and environment when he took Agar as his second wife and, likewise, when he dismissed her in response to the vehement desire of his chief wife Sarah. Again, we have to see these incidents in the light of contemporary attitudes. Most likely, his actions were in agreement with the religious convictions of his day and environment, even when he willed to sacrifice his beloved son Isaac. He acted in a time in which people of his culture believed that God, under determined circumstances, could will the sacrifice of the first-born. But in the same incident we recognize a new breakthrough of religion toward a greater humanity when Abraham—in the light of faith—understands that God does not wish the sacrifice of his son as a proof of his submission and respect. Abraham showed the dynamism of his faith by acting according to the best of his insight and the culture of the time in which he lived. Abraham, in this incident, demonstrated personal growth in morality which enriched the following generations.

Rudolf Otto (in his world-famous book *Das Heilige*) has systematized the history of the relationship between religion and morals with his famous distinction between *"sakrales und sanktioniertes Ethos"*—the ethos of the sacred (religiosity of respect for God) and the inherited ethos which only receives sanction through the religious understanding of the world.

The tribes of Israel brought their traditional ethos into their covenant with God. Most of their ethos received sanction through the covenant with Yahweh, while other trends were severely excluded. In the course of the religious history of Israel, we notice, from time to time, a simultaneous decline of both moral standards and religious fervor. In God's good time, religious renewal through the prophets and priests, imbued with a prophetic spirit, led to definite cultural transformations and significant changes in the moral life and thought of God's people. In the course of the history of Israel there is definite evidence of the development toward monogamy and a deepened understanding of the dignity of woman as well as of man. However, we have to see this against the historical background. At that particular time in history, cultures revealed a definite, although rudimentary, trend towards monogamy, based on different motivations. This provides evidence that such developments, not only depend on faith or an increase of religious zeal and fervor, but likewise on cultural transformations.

Similarly, today's apparent decline of priestly and religious vocations cannot be traced merely to a decline of faith. There are many other factors in today's society that have brought a change in attitude to a religious vocation. It is a well-known fact that in Israel the idea of the covenant, with its powerful impact, was often presented under the image of a marriage. Conversely, it is worthwhile to notice that the concrete experience of family life (parental and conjugal love) had its own special influence on the mode in which the religious idea of the covenant was understood and expressed. Likewise, our personal ideas of God, to a lesser or greater extent, are colored by our cultural heritage. They certainly give evidence of a tremendous transformation when compared with those of a patriarchal society—just think of today's partnership type of marriage and the participation of women in the social, cultural and civic life. As late as 1930, the encyclical, *Casti Connubii*, taught patriarchalism as an abiding norm and condemned the activities of women outside the family as "degrading and leading to slavery."

V. A TYPOLOGY OF RELIGIOUS ETHICS

THE morality which is an integral part of the Christian religion is always a morality of love. At the very heart of faith is the truth that God is personified love. He has created man in order to have concelebrants of His own love. In the history of salvation He has manifested His all-embracing love. Religion, in its very essence, is the revelation of God's love and man's response in a faith filled with and active in love. The ethos which follows from this religious thought and attitude is the ethos of fraternal love. Everything is good insofar as it truly expresses and promotes genuine love among men.

Nevertheless, in keeping with the historical context, we find a variety of articulations, a variety of fundamental approaches that only make sense when considered in the total historical context. The root of this can be traced not only to religion itself, but to the whole reality in which man encounters God. The changing emphasis and leitmotif in religious events and approaches are likewise linked with a variety of moral demands and imperatives.

An ethics of law can simultaneously be an ethics of love. For example, the eminent role of Moses as the law-giver, who united the tribes of Israel, gave a special accent and value to the concept of law and guidance. Such an approach does not necessarily diminish the specific religious value of love, gratitude, fidelity and mercy, but denotes a line of departure in relation to which other moral values are considered. They are sanctioned by law, through the law-giver Moses, who acted with the authority of God, who deigned to reveal His will—His "law"—through Moses.

In a somewhat similar fashion we have to look upon the idea of the old Germanic leitmotif of an absolute *Gefolgschaftstreue*—an absolute and blind allegiance towards the particular prince or leader. This kind of obedience was an unquestioning one, no matter what the command implied. In such an obedience, the virtues of prudent discernment and maturity of judgment are lacking. There is the possibility of a genuine transfer from this absolute allegiance to a whole-hearted following of Christ, for He is the only one who deserves absolute trust and unconditional allegiance and fidelity. The religious "sanction" of such an ethos of allegiance to princes, and consequently a one-sided approach to the whole matter of morality (in the light of these traditional values), was greatly detrimental to the call towards Christian maturity and prudent discernment in keeping with the great commandment of love. In fact, it has led to an over-emphasis on external obedience in the religious realm that turns into "blind obedience." In early Protestantism it caused the misunderstanding of the *usus politicus legis* (an almost absolute allegiance to the political leader and unquestioning obedience to his laws and precepts in the name of religion). Likewise, the various epochs dominated by Constantine the Great, Charles the Great and Otto the Great, not only confused political and religious "power" and leadership, but gave such extensive power to the religious leaders of their respective period that they became very worldly princes of the empire. The impact of such an ethos, promoted by this type of power-seeking and career-making bishops and priests, is well-known to all historians. It is difficult to determine its extensive influence on religious and moral teachings and practices, even up to our present time. Worthy of note is the fact that in the Bible the name "prince" is used almost exclusively for the prince of darkness.

In past eras in which the great masses of people had neither an opportunity for higher education nor the required ambition towards social advancement, a certain paternalism seemed the accepted rule in both the Church and society at large—even more so if the religious leaders really cared for the welfare of those entrusted to them because this was the accepted style of life which permeated the whole culture of that period.

On the other hand, in times like the great French Revolution and even more so in our dynamic epoch, an approach characterized by a leitmotif of law or an allegiance with a paternalistic concept of obedience and authority, would greatly discredit religion and religious morality. It certainly is likely to be condemned as reinforcing the "establishment," or as clinging to the past *status quo.* In our dynamic age there exists a definite trend towards an ethos which, above all, emphasizes the virtues of maturity and social involvement for the betterment of today's "structures." Religion or faith, if rightly understood as history of salvation, as a constant call from God and man's response to this call, will be able to sanction, purify and strengthen this new ethos.

Already in the Old Testament we take notice of an encounter between religion and the Greek ideal of wisdom. St. Paul, when talking to the Jews, emphasized the real concept of law—"the law of the Spirit" and "the law of faith"—but when speaking to the Greeks, his emphasis, in keeping with the Greek mind, was on the value of genuine wisdom and love manifested in the "foolishness" of the cross.

In the Greek ethos, particularly noticeable in Aristotle, there is the fundamental idea of *eudaemonia* (self-fulfillment) in the pursuit of wisdom and in the establishment of social order. This trend, likewise, gave rise to a new code clearly evident in the writings of the Greek Fathers (Clement of Alexandria and others) and particularly noticeable in the teachings of the theologians of the Renaissance period. The theology of the Church Fathers in the first centuries essentially attempted to give an integrated outlook to wisdom as understood by the Greek philosophers and redeemed by Christ's humble wisdom, thereby giving sanction to the fundamental values of the Greek ethos of self-fulfillment while liberating it from a self-centered outlook.

In the Orient we find a deep comprehension of the values inherent in contemplation when compared with the more practical trends evident in the Roman Occident. In both instances, the Christian teaching did not merely give sanction to prevailing trends and thoughts, but asserted a purifying influence on the ethos of the current epoch. However, it should be remembered that this purifying action on the ethos can only be accomplished in terms of a clear and whole-hearted "yes" to the genuine values of a particular ethos. Unfortunately, the complementarity of the different development of the ethos, in both the East and the West, was sometimes over-shadowed by other factors, especially by narrow-minded rivalry and cultural absolutism. This becomes particularly evident in the great schism between the East and the West.

In my book *The Christian Existentialist* (New York University Press and University of London Press, 1968), I have tried to evaluate and compare the various forms of encounter between religion and the personalistic and existentialistic ethos of modern man. In genuine Christian and humanistic thought, it always has been an accepted truth that the person is the greatest value. However, in our age there is a new way of expressing the unique *I-Thou* relationship and its value in contradistinction to the anonymous in both the economic, social and political realms. Theology has to recognize the importance of the person and the value of man's innermost experiences. I do not maintain that Christians should simply become blind followers to the personalistic, socialistic or existentialistic trends of their epoch or environment. Yet, their morality will fail to exert a vital and potential influence if they fail to express the old and unchangeable truths and values in terms which are in keeping with the prevailing currents and patterns of thoughts—if they fail to utilize the fresh breeze of the spirit of a particular epoch for their sailing. Thus only will they be able to give the right kind of direction to new and vital expressions of human experience.

Modern man has a sharp and new consciousness of evolution and the constant possibility, as well as need, for progress and development. There are certain types of secular ethics which express a sharp awareness of this perspective in an almost classical manner. To quote Julian Huxley:

> The developed human individual is the highest product of evolution; the experiences which alone have high intrinsic value, such as those of love and beauty and knowledge and mystical union, are accessible only to human individuals.... I would suggest that the secondary critical point in human evolution will be marked by the union of all separate tradition in a single common pool, the orchestration of human diversity from a competitive discord to harmonious symphony.... This is the major problem of our time—to achieve global union for men.... Present-day men and nations will be judged by history as moral or immoral according to whether they have helped or hindered unification.... Our ethical principles are not just a whistling in the dark, not the *ipse dixit* of an isolated humanity but are the nature of things related to the rest of reality—and indeed only if we take the trouble to understand that relationship will we be able to lay down ethical principles which are truly adequate.... Ethics is relative to process, which is both meaningful and of indefinitely long duration.... Above all, an evolutionary ethics is of necessity a hopeful ethics, however much the justifiable hope is tempered by a realization of the length and difficulty of man's ethical task.... But as knowledge grows and our capacity of its wise application increases, that influence will certainly grow and be exerted more and more to encourage a desirable direction of our evolution (J. H. Huxley, *Touchstones for Ethics 1893-1943*, pp.254-255).

By quoting this text I do not mean to endorse or adopt the entire system of Huxley's ethics. But I am convinced that here, too, we find some fundamental values which are part of our religion as a history of salvation within the evolution of the whole world. Teilhard de Chardin has made an effort to show a Christian approach to religion in the light of our present knowledge of evolution. A great deal of work in this direction is still to be accomplished. Our ethical principles are truly ethical if they are related to the rest of reality. In my own ethical thinking, and my whole approach, I have always tried to stress the fundamental idea of a continuous conversion by placing the chief emphasis on the goal-commandments rather than on mere prohibitive laws. I have tried to elaborate a dynamic understanding of the whole morality as an ongoing call—and an ever new way of listening and responding to God's call in a particular historical moment. I realize that this is a mere beginning towards the great task still to be accomplished.

One of the chief objectives of moral theology is to help contemporary man and society to bring the essential values, needs and opportunities of man, within the radius of religion. Thus, they will become purified, activated and "sanctioned." This is not equivalent to yielding to a shapeless relativism—but rather is a faithful response in keeping with man's relativity and God's own action in the history of salvation.

Since we understand morality in this dynamic, historical and eschatological context, we place even greater emphasis than Erich Fromm on a morality based on our knowledge of the nature of man. However, this does not oppose or minimize the importance of revelation which, rightly understood, cannot prevent our arriving at a deeper knowledge of human nature. Revelation, in the broad sense, promotes, deepens and purifies man's genuine understanding of his vocation, of his calling and his destiny. Since we believe in revelation, we feel particularly obliged to listen with utmost attention to the whole reality which is sustained and illumined by the creative presence of the word of God. In our concept of revelation we include the ever ongoing work of God in human history, God's dynamic presence which gives final relevance to man's experience, to the experience of all mankind. Thus our ethos is an adoring "yes" to God's continued presence and action in the world. All human efforts to learn ever more about man's nature and destiny are to be seen as responses to the total reality of "revelation," in God's work and word in the history of salvation.

One of the chief temptations for Churchmen and ethicists is precisely their futile attempt to impose on others moral laws and imperatives without evaluating their vital meaning in past history and in the context of the present historical hour. They present just one kind of approach of past ages, one set of inflexible rules, and thus impoverish men in their total response to the situation because they possess only limited knowledge of man's true nature and experiences in a particular culture. The concrete measure of morality depends on the knowledge which the moral agent himself, in all sincerity, has acquired and is still trying to acquire.

One of the objectives for my extensive traveling as a lecturer is the desire to become familiar with men of various cultures. Moral theologians have a constant need for "listening," for "being open." In fact, to be Catholic means to be universal, which implies the desire to go beyond the narrow limits of any particular culture. We all are in great danger of a tribal existence.

There is a simultaneous pluralism in historical development and the particular ethos. This is well illustrated in the history of Israel. There, likewise, is a real, though limited (and endangered), unity in all cultures. Consequently, there is a genuine possibility for communication between the various forms of ethos.

In the Old Testament, the ancient custom of the levirate marriage was not only tolerated but even fully sanctioned by the morality of the covenant (cf. Gen. 38). Whether the brother of the deceased husband (brother-in-law) was married or not, he had the duty to raise offspring to the widow if she was childless. This was her right—it was sanctioned by law and God punished Onan with death because he refused to conform to this custom of "family-justice." Genesis 38 is very explicit about the obligatory character of the levirate marriage and its particular values. Later it came into disuse merely because of cultural transformations in Israel. But even today this same custom is deeply rooted in the traditions and the whole economic, social and cultural life of numerous tribes in Africa. Why then should the Church be so severe toward a related custom in mission countries, particularly if a sudden change may block evangelization and cause serious difficulty to many persons? A case of this nature was submitted to me while traveling in Southwest Africa during the past year. The older brother of the deceased husband was charged with the protection of the widow of his brother. Symbolic of this protection is that he build her a little house and, according to tribal custom, stay with her at least one night. In fact, the whole clan watches to see whether he performs his duty as brother-in-law. However, in our case the woman was told by the priest that she, as a Catholic, was not permitted to conform to this ancient custom. The result was that she had to hand over her three little children to the brother-in-law and she, herself, became an outcast from her husband's tribe, as well as her own, since the latter did not accept her back into its clan. Though the levirate "duty" does not realize fully the ideal of monogamy, it nevertheless can, for a certain historical moment, be the best possible solution for a people in a tribal state until the whole of the social and religious transformation permits them to find better solutions which, in their own minds, embody higher moral values. Before imposing our own ideal manner of life on primitive people, we should first allow religion to exercise its full dynamic influence and then select the values related to their own culture and consequently conducive to a desirable cultural transformation.

VI. THE NORMATIVE VALUE OF THE SERMON ON THE MOUNT

THE literary form *(genus litterarium)* of the sermon on the mount permits no doubt concerning the normative value of the sevenfold "but I tell you" (see my article in *Catholic Biblical Quarterly*, Vol. 29, 1967, pp. 375-385). It clearly illustrates a shift away from the prohibitive law. The emphasis of the sermon on the mount is on the goal-commandments. The nine times "blessed" is more than an optional piece of advice. Both the community and each individual are given the urgent invitation to pursue the path in the direction of the clearly delineated goal, namely, an absolute readiness to forgive; a complete control of all anger and ill-will, even to the point of becoming a selfless and generous instrument of peace. The sermon on the mount invites man to exercise a careful guard over his heart's desire beyond the mere avoidance of adultery; to be always ready to sacrifice the most cherished goods in behalf of genuine love and moral integrity; to be irrevocably faithful to one's spouse, in a fidelity which does not permit an easy escape in divorce. It exhorts towards absolute sincerity of heart which obviates the need for any type of oath; towards a complete trust in the power of non-violence as the collected energy of love—a love of neighbor which even embraces our enemy. Above all, the goal set for the disciples of Christ is no other than God's own merciful and compassionate love for men (cf. Mt. 5:48; Lk. 6:36).

Looking back into the history of the Church, and especially into the history of moral theology, we are surprised to see how rarely these great directives of the sermon on the mount have been taken seriously. How many unnecessary oaths have been imposed and how readily have these been justified by moralists? We realize that too little attention has been given to Our Lord's directive of non-violence—that, in reality, weapons of war were blessed all too readily by priests and dignitaries of the Church—that, despite gross evidence of national egotism, there were theories of endorsement regarding a "just war." Even after the 18th and 19th centuries, moralists of some countries were tolerant towards the institution of slavery.

Evidently, all this illustrates a partial infidelity towards the spirit of the gospel, a certain amount of discontinuity, a lack of balance. It is a sign of weakness in "religion." Yet, in my own opinion, there are other elements at work. There is present not only a partial blindness toward some of the abiding values and goal-commandments of the gospel, but also an absence of a dynamic approach attempting to understand man and man's history. In this regard, Christ's own words to His apostles are significant—He addressed them: "I would have to tell you still many things, but the burden would be too great" (Jn. 16:12).

Take for example the failure of our tradition to give attention to the command of "non-violence." In spite of much evidence to the contrary, there were many moralists, and indeed the majority of the religious elite in the Church, who tried very hard to restrain warlike nations and unscrupulous princes by carefully enunciating the required conditions for a so-called "just war." Some moralists made so many stipulations that, if princes would have paid attention to these conditions, there would have been very few or almost no wars; while other moralists, unfortunately, acted as the mouth-pieces of unscrupulous princes and therefore tended to extend unduly the "just war theory" in particular situations. Even in the Old Testament there were some rulers and men who were considered as prophets who would have liked to justify each war fought by Israel. In our days there is a great need for a growing consciousness regarding our mission to promote a non-violent approach in settling disputes among nations in agreement with the spirit of the gospel. In our present era, we certainly can no longer respect the time-honored formulas of past eras since one powerful nation has enough weapons by which the whole of humanity could be destroyed. Today we need new outlooks and approaches for the solution of issues. Therefore, the present situation urges us to give more attention to the principles enunciated in the sermon on the mount.

In the same context, namely, in view of the goal-commandment expressed in the sermon on the mount, let us approach the subject of divorce. Here, too, I feel that the question of divorce should be studied in complementarity with the oldest traditions of the Orthodox Churches or, rather, with the practice of the Catholic Oriental Churches since the 2nd and 3rd centuries. We certainly might benefit from their experiences. Nevertheless, all our efforts in settling the question of divorce, or in dealing with spouses who have remarried, must be in keeping with the goal-commandment of absolute fidelity. First of all, we should aim at better preparation for marriage by premarital instructions and counseling. We are to take seriously the goal-commandment, otherwise all our discussions and efforts in regard to divorce and remarriage become completely ineffective and even harmful. Only in a context where we truly follow the dynamics of the goal-commandment of *mercy,* of understanding people in their difficulties, can the searching about new solutions become fruitful. The attitude of simply condoning divorce and remarriage is just as heretical as teaching only the one commandment of indissolubility of marriage and thereby forgetting about the commandment of mercy. We have to teach both fidelity and mercy. Thus the Orthodox (Oriental) Churches are taking seriously the goal-commandment implied in the sermon on the mount while, at the same time, they also tolerate or permit a remarriage (a second marriage) not only in case of physical death of a spouse but, likewise, in case of "moral," "civil" and "mental" death of one of the partners of the first marriage. According to their interpretation, life imprisonment could be considered "civil" death, while mental illness, without any prospect of cure, would be equated with "mental" death. On the other hand, the Latin Church, at least after the 11th century, insisted on a strict interpretation and issued absolute legal prohibitions for remarriage unless the marriage bonds were dissolved by physical death of one of the spouses. Despite this strict interpretation in the Latin Church, the Oriental Churches remained convinced that their practices of permitting remarriage are compatible with the goal-commandments of the gospel teaching, as well as the great commandment of mercy. The question remains whether there is a clear-cut contradiction between the approaches of the two divisions of the Church and whether the issues could be studied in the perspective of complementarity, thereby arriving at a desirable synthesis. The question of paramount importance should be: how the universal Church of today could strengthen the attitude of fidelity and stability in Christian marriage and, at the same time, show merciful and compassionate understanding for the abandoned spouses? Only a study of the matter in its total context and in the light of new knowledge will bring about a more dynamic approach. We may also ask the question: to what extent can gradualism go today and to what extent should we encourage changes in our rapidly changing world?

VII. THE DYNAMIC OF NATURAL LAW

RATIONALISM has brought into the natural law doctrine an emphatically static character—a *status quo* theory or ideology. This trend also had its definite impact on Catholic moral theology. Natural law often was built more on conceptual operations than on the fullness of human experience. Today, this form of thinking is no longer acceptable, although some Churchmen are still clinging to it. We are looking upon man in an historical context of evolution and, at the same time, we show greater admiration for the fundamental unity of mankind through the various eras and cultures. Natural law teaching, without a real grasp of moral values in the different situations and circumstances, is *time-bound*—marked by the epoch in which it is formulated.

Modern natural law thinking does not start with abstract formulations but, rather, with a scientific investigation into all kinds of human experiences. The empirical sciences—sociology, psychology, comparative culture, ethnology, anthropology, etc.—precede the effort of a comprehensive phenomenology. A possibility of a systematic approach is likely only with increased knowledge derived from these empirical sciences. The inductive method of reasoning does not exclude deductions and speculations, rather, both the inductive and deductive methods of reasoning can aid us in our endeavor to find a solution. Yet, all speculation without a firm grasp on reality appears unacceptable to modern man. At one time when the famous philosopher Hegel explained his abstract theory, Heinecke, one of his students, questioned him by saying: "Does your teaching not contradict reality?" Hegel's answer was: *Umso schlimmer für die Wirklichkeit* ("the worse for reality")—in other words, reality would have to conform to our speculations.

By no means are we suggesting that one ignore the teaching of the magisterium of the Church in regard to natural law. We see in the magisterium of the Church a stream of human traditions and a combined effort to judge and to illumine our human experiences and thoughts by the light of reason and in the light of the gospel. Naturally, the efficiency of the magisterium is endangered if temporarily dependent on the narrow circle of a particular school of thought—on one system of theology. In matters of natural law, the teaching office of the Church has to gather all the available human experiences. It is quite significant that the papal commission assigned to study the question of "birth control" consisted of both men and women, two-thirds of which are lay people representing all walks of life and modern sciences. The theologians, though predominantly chosen in view of their more conservative thinking, represented various theological schools and cultural backgrounds. Such a pooling of experiences and opinions is far more important today than at any previous epoch in the history of the Church. It therefore came as a shock (like an earthquake) when, finally, the encyclical *Humanae Vitae*, July 29, 1968, ignored the findings and proposals of the large majority of that commission and returned to a biological concept of natural law. Natural law means, by definition, what is plain and open to the eyes of reason as a result of shared experiences and insights. It cannot be imposed when no convincing reasons, or even erroneous reasons, are given.

The Pope is the supreme teacher of dogma and morals in the Church, but he is also supposed to be—in an outstanding way—a "listener" and a "learner." Either he learns from the few who surround him—maybe from an inbred group in a non-collegial exercise of authority, or he makes fullest use of all the shared experiences and insights of the whole Church, in a collegial exercise of authority. The Pope has the all-important office of bringing the gospel, or "good news," to all men by means of all the various channels through which the Holy Spirit wishes to teach men—he has to listen to all.

In my opinion, natural law ought to be equivalent to the shared personal experiences and insights of all men into the changing realities and the abiding vocation of men—not isolated individuals—but, rather, men living in community. Indeed, though man himself is a changing reality, his essential nature remains *un*changed as he goes through the different epochs of history—the ice era, the stone era—he always remains man endowed with intellect and free will. Yet his whole being—his psychological pattern, his way of reasoning, his way of experiencing, etc.—is always related to the world around him and, therefore, affected by relationships to the surrounding environment. Therefore, natural law ought to be explained as man's conception of his identity as a human being, his capacity for knowledge, his sincerity of conscience, his perception of God's call in the special circumstances of the particular hour; the natural law is man's capacity to love and to reciprocate love, to experience and to communicate his own experiences and insights to others, to enter into meaningful relationships with other men by sharing their joys and sorrows. This is a very dynamic process. Furthermore, man is not only greatly dependent on his environment but, in turn, is able to affect and shape it even far beyond his own epoch, beyond the narrow confines of his own lifetime. Man has a deep concern for freedom. Man is not only variable in his biological constitution, but also in his God-given endowment of intellect and free will, of conscience and the capacity of love, since these are subject to influences arising from his particular historical hour.

Historicity is part of man's "nature," not only in the sense of something additional to nature but, rather, as part of his human existence and deeply interwoven with all human expressions. There is a certain relativity which, however, must be distinguished from relativism. I strongly assert man's relativity but exclude any total relativism.

Historicity implies the law of growth. It belongs to the nature of the individual person to have a history which begins with the day of his conception and unfolds unto the last day of his life—unto death. In this history of the individual there are the decisive moments of opportunity where man can make giant strides toward shaping his future, built on the heritage of his environment and ancestors. There, too, are many moments in the life of each individual where acceptance of the inevitable seems the only choice. In a similar sense, humanity, as such, has its phases of development which can be compared to childhood, adolescence and adulthood, although never in an absolute sense.

Natural law is not something static or something merely added to revelation in the specifically Christian sense. Therefore, man's capacity for reflection over past human experiences must take cognizance of the stupendous experience which in the Incarnation has entered into human history. Yet, these religious values are not equally accessible to all men. The Church, herself, gives evidence of definite fluctuations. There are moments in the Church, or at least in part of the Church, where stereotyped rules obscure the *kairos,* the signs of the time—while, on the other hand, there are epochs in which false securities are broken by a truly prophetic spirit, thereby giving way to new horizons. It is impossible to expect a perfect balance between the various values endorsed by different approaches and particular forms of ethos.

Therefore, perhaps we ought to realize that we cannot simply and passively rely on what the magisterium has told us for the past thirty or forty years. We must go far beyond the limits of analyzing teachings of the magisterium as expressed in encyclicals, papal discourses, and pastoral letters. To act otherwise would not only imply lack of responsibility, but also a real disservice to the magisterium. The Church's very doctrine on natural law expresses a warning in this regard. The magisterium has no monopoly in the field of natural law since natural law implies the spontaneous manner in which the human person— within the community and within the concrete situation—can understand what is good and what is evil. Natural law—by definition—is that part of moral knowledge which is "visible to the eye of reason" (see Rom. 1:19). However, this does not mean an acquisition by abstract reasoning but, rather, an existential access by experience and common effort of reflection.

VIII. THE CHANGING IMAGE OF THE CHURCH

VATICAN II unambiguously marks a definite shift in the self-understanding of the Church from a more static to a more dynamic age. In today's Church there is a new emphasis on the pilgrim aspect, on the call to penance and to constant renewal, a keen and humble awareness of imperfections, as well as the universal call to holiness. The Church also realizes that the most deadly danger would be the wrong kind of immutability which would classify her among the "establishments"— that is, among the immobile, outdated institutions no longer concerned for the real opportunities, the real needs and the real welfare of men—incapable of fulfilling her original mission. It would imply a serious accusation of infidelity if she would cling to antiquated structures and modes of thought. This would be an isolation from the historical context. The Church is affected by the rapid pace of human history and development. "The human race has passed from a rather static concept of reality to the more dynamic, evolutionary one" (*Gaudium et spes,* Art. 5). Human progress and evolution can exert its beneficial influence on the Church provided it is stirring her up to find a fuller understanding of her own dynamic aspects with which her divine Founder has endowed her. We are referring here not only to the dynamic aspects of our human society, but also those of the divine foundation, the Church. In early Church history, many members, even in the college of the apostles, had a rather Jewish image of the Church—holding on to many sacred traditions of the Mosaic law. This caused great turmoil and dissension in the primitive communities of the early Church until the Jewish image of the Church was finally replaced by that of the Church universal. This, however, was realized only after a painful process of self-evaluation (cf. Gal. 2:11-14).

The entrance of the Roman empire into the realm of the Church—or the Church into the realm of the empire—seriously affected the understanding of the Church in her true nature and identity. There was considerable conflict between the image of the Church produced by Constantine's alliance between the throne and the altar—between earthly power and the Church. Due to this, the image of the Church became identified with the party in power. This unfortunate alliance came to a climax and a practical encounter between Innocent III and St. Francis of Assisi. Their confrontation was one of love and, therefore, conducive towards the betterment of the Church. It was the most effective non-violent attack on the triumphalism in the Church and an all too earthly understanding of Messianism (cf. Mt. 16:21-23).

The great schism between the Orient and Occident, as well as the strifes resulting from the Reformation and Counter-Reformation, had a lasting (and often restricting) impact on the image and self-understanding of the Church. All these fluctuations of emphasis were reflected in the whole of the ethos, as well as in the teaching of moral theology. I have treated the theme of the interdependence between the self-understanding of the Church and the Christian morality in view of an ecclesiology of Vatican II in my article: "Christian Morality as a Mirror-image of the Mystery of the Church," in: *Proceedings of the Eighteenth Annual Convention of the Catholic Theological Society of America* (June 1963), pp. 3-24. This study should be widened by a typology of the interdependence through all the history of the Church and of the moral theology.

Throughout all these changes, the Church's identity remained, although at times it appeared disturbed. We should not expect to see this identity of the Church in a continuity of formulations expressed in customs, laws and definitions. A good example of a certain discontinuity is the Bulla *Unam Sanctam* of Boniface VIII which certainly cannot be compared in content or style with the Gospel of Saint John. In fact, the identity of the same Church includes discontinuity through human weakness; it includes both fortunate and unfortunate adaptations to the spirit of the epoch and at times, through God's merciful faithfulness, the discontinuity of courageous reforms and conversions. All this has to be evaluated against the great varying cultural background of the whole Church. It found reflection in the approach to moral teaching, including the fundamental forms of ethos, the shift of emphasis, the partial blindness, etc. In view of this undeniable fact, it would be *un*-theological and *non*-theological to consider only the sources of the magisterium over the past hundred or fifty years of the Church and to act as if the past epoch were the final stepping stone, as if all matters were settled once forever. Without the ever changing self-understanding of the Church over the past century, the Church of today would be a mere establishment of frustration. Indeed a theology which fails to take into consideration a constantly changing self-understanding of the Church seems like an ostrich. Most of the moralists have not yet tried to treat moral theology in the full perspective of the history of salvation, including the whole history of Christianity and the history of the different images of the Church.

For many, the sudden awareness of the problematic could become a temptation to overlook the true identity of the Church amidst all the turmoil of changes, amid the various forms of discontinuity and of failures. It would be fallacious to preserve and to protect the identity of the Church and her doctrine by clinging to outdated formulas. At the same time, we must guard against the fallacy of concentrating on various forms of discontinuity and thereby ignoring the basic continuity evident in God's design and the history of man.

Many of the changes in the Church which we witness today, particularly the changes in attitude and shifting emphasis regarding certain precepts, can be more fully understood when we consider the truly pastoral character of the teaching office of the Church. Her teaching ought not to consist of abstract statements of theoretical expositions but rather pastoral approaches to man's needs, opportunities and problems. Her role is truly pastoral. By paying attention to this aspect, for instance, John Noonan in his book, *Contraception, A History of its Treatment by Catholic Theologians and Canonists,* comes to grips with fundamental facets of the whole historical problem. However, it is true that in the past the Church often had to wrestle over long periods of time till She came to a clear understanding of certain issues which later on appeared self-evident.

IX. WHAT IS THE ABIDING REALITY IN CHRISTIAN MORALITY?

THE dynamism of modern society and culture is greatly imperiled by the loss of the center, by a loss of identity, by a lack of continuity of life. Moral theology has an urgent mission to serve mankind and the Church by finding and preserving ever better—not continuity of form—but the continuity of life which, in the final analysis, is fidelity to the living God, the God of history and Father of Our Lord Jesus Christ.

Only One is immutable, namely, God. He does not change His mind. However, we should not confuse immutability with immobility. Human history has a marvelous unity in the design of God. Nevertheless, it is difficult for us to reconcile continuity and this oneness of the design of God for mankind with the evident discontinuity brought into this world by sin. Yet, in spite of all, we know that the continuity of the plan of salvation in Christ will remain forever.

In Christ, human history has found its Alpha and Omega. Christ made no attempt to answer beforehand all the questions which would arise after His ascension. The fact is clearly expressed in the doubts and hesitations which arose within the apostolic community when they were faced with new dimensions of universality. Christ came to manifest the genuine countenance of love in all His words, deeds and actions. Therefore, everything we know has to be measured against the background of our knowledge of Christ. To know Him is the most basic guarantee of continuity in Christian morality. If we do not turn to Him but merely rely on abstract principles, then continuity is greatly threatened.

Although Holy Scripture is in truth a great treasure, it nevertheless may at times be difficult to ascertain which of the biblical doctrines are of permanent validity for all times and circumstances. While there are many time-bound guidelines, the Bible presents a definite image of Christ and of man's vocation to genuine love. Any kind of situation ethics which asserts that there are no abiding values beyond the bare abstract principle of love is an affront against Christ and Holy Scripture. Christ has not come to bring men a formalistic and abstract principle of love—He rather came to manifest and make fully visible the true countenance of love—a goal to be achieved by all men. This love is infinitely more than an abstract principle, or a vague sentiment or an unworkable definition.

There are certain attitudes, sentiments, and actions which are in striking opposition to Christ's teachings regarding genuine love. In Gal. 5 and Mt. 6-7, Holy Scripture concentrates on the criteria for the discernment of spirits, and discernment between true love and its counterfeits and enemies. The harvest of the selfish nature cannot be reconciled with the harvest of the Spirit (Gal. 5:19-23).

In addition to Holy Scripture, we find orientation and guidance from the writings and deeds of the saints—not necessarily canonized saints. I like to place the emphasis on saints who are synonymous with the great religious and moral geniuses of all times and nations, who in union with Christ and His gospel, give us ample orientation towards a genuine Christian life.

Modern history and our present dynamic society do not only confront us with a wider knowledge of the ethos of our time, but also grant us ever new possibilities to gather all the treasures of human experiences from past epochs and cultures. Today, more than ever, there is a striking awareness that humanity cannot survive unless we protect and foster some common moral values, e.g., the dignity of each human person, the freedom and sincerity of conscience, the necessity of patient dialogue, the solidarity of the whole human race, the importance of the stability of marriage and family, and social justice to the underprivileged. There is an increasing awareness concerning a scale of values in vital questions. There is common agreement regarding the principles on which every reasonable man will agree—and which were enunciated by the council document, "The Church in the Modern World" (Art. 35), namely, "Man is more precious for what he is than what he has." It is impossible to exhaust the far-reaching implications of social justice but we exclude categorically some dangerous attitudes and practices which are evidently irreconcilable to this principle.

One of the most fundamental rules for true ecumenical dialogue is a whole-hearted concentration on those truths which unite us. Furthermore, our effort towards dialogue and unity will be conducive towards a more balanced view for both the individual, the Church and the world-at-large. Many people tend to become disturbed by an attitude which places emphasis on controversial issues and on conflicting views and beliefs. While they become absorbed in the things which divide and separate, they tend to lose the necessary faith and confidence in the continuity and unity of life. Due to a decided pluralism in both the contemporary Church and secular society, we are more than ever before faced with countless changes which demand an adjustment on our part. The most wholesome way to balance the problem of adjustment consists in an approach which carefully weighs all controversial issues while chiefly concentrating on points of consensus of opinion and complementary views.

BIBLIOGRAPHY

Baumgartner, H. M. *Die Unbedingtheit des Sittlichen*. München, 1962.
Burgh, W. G. *From Morality to Religion*. London, 1938.
Garnett, A. Campbell. *Religion and the Moral Life*. New York, 1955.
Häring, B. *Das Heilige und das Gute Religion und Sittlichkeit in ihrem gegenseitigen Bezug*. Krailling vor München, 1950.
———. "The Normative Value of the Sermon on the Mount," *Catholic Biblical Quarterly*, XIX (1967), 375-385.
MacIntyre, A. *Secularisation and Moral Change*. London, 1967.
Schlick, M. *Problems of Ethics*. New York, 1930.

Schneider, H. W. *Moral for Mankind.* Columbia, 1960.
Wagler, R. *Der Ort der Ethik bei Friedrick Gogarten: Der Glaube als Erämchitgung zum rechten Unterscheiden.* Hamburg-Bergstedt, 1961.
Williams, Gardner. *Humanistic Ethics.* New York, 1951.

EDITOR'S NOTE: This article has been reworked in light of the publication of the Encyclical *Humanae Vitae*, issued two months after this lecture was delivered.

Scriptural Basis for Secularity

Eugene Maly

FROM April of 1943 to April of 1945 Dietrich Bonhoeffer was in Nazi prisons in Germany, a period climaxed by his execution by hanging. During this time he wrote a number of letters that have since proved a fecund source for theologians in the discussion of secularization.[1] It is generally agreed that the process of secularization has been hastened radically in our century by the advances in technology and man's consequently increasing ability to control his environment and, in fact, the universe. But it is only in recent years that theologians have begun to formulate a theology of secularity. The significance of Bonhoeffer is that he put into words the process that had been taking place by asking probing questions of contemporary Christianity: "What is the significance of a Church (church, parish, preaching, Christian life) in a religionless world? How do we speak of God without religion? How do we speak ... in secular fashion of God? In what way are we in a religionless and secular sense Christians, in what way are we the *Ekklesia*, 'those who are called forth,' not conceiving of ourselves religiously as specially favored, but as wholly belonging to the world? ... What is the place of worship and prayer in an entire absence of religion?"[2]

Bonhoeffer himself had no final answers to these questions. But he made several observations that justified asking them. For example, writing just a little over a month after he had posed the cited questions, he noted that "The movement beginning about the thirteenth century ... towards the autonomy of man (under which head I place the discovery of the laws by which the world lives and manages in science, social and political affairs, art, ethics and religion) has in our time reached a certain completion. Man has learned to cope with all questions of importance *without recourse to God as a working hypothesis.*"[3]

It was shortly after this that he wrote the sentence that was to cause so much controversy, "... the only way to be honest is to recognize that we have to live in the world *etsi deus non daretur.*"[4] Some of the discussion has centered around the translation of the Latin phrase. Did Bonhoeffer mean "as though God did not exist," or "even if God does not exist"? The question of grammar aside, it seems impossible to interpret Bonhoeffer in the latter sense in view of his own attitude throughout his last years (on his last day in prison he was seen deep in prayer), in view of the general context of the letters (the reference above, for example, to a God as "a working hypothesis" is an indication of what he is talking about), and, finally, in view of the immediate context of this letter. He goes on to speak of God "... teaching us that we must live as men who can get along very well without him."[5] Bonhoeffer was no "death-of-God" theologian in the strict sense, even though he may have prepared the way for their emergence by his observations.

This overly brief survey of Bonhoeffer's thought should at least provide a starting-point for our presentation as it did for the great debate that followed in the years after World War II. There were a few attempts to synthesize the debate in some kind of systematic form. Although these were of the *haute-vulgarisation* type, they had an enormous influence on the thinking public and so spurred the professional theologians to take up the problem more seriously.

One of these was Bishop John A. T. Robinson's *Honest to God,* published in 1965.[6] Almost half the book is devoted to a consideration of the idea of God and how modern man can speak meaningfully of him. This is, of course, at the heart of the problem and forms the framework for the consideration of other aspects of theology, such as Christology, worship and morality, which the bishop takes up in the remainder of the book. Obviously, radical questions were being asked, and the tentative (it is good to emphasize the adjective) conclusions were persuasive enough to touch off a flurry of reaction. While Bishop Robinson's account might be described as the report of a personal experience of Christianity in a secularized world,[7] it is much more than that. It is an honest attempt to face difficult questions, made by a competent scholar, even though his competence is, admittedly, a limited one.[8]

A more systematic treatment of secularization in a more defined area was Harvey Cox's *The Secular City,*[9] where the social implications of secularity for the Christian individual and for the Church are strikingly propounded. No other book on the subject has had such an impact on modern Christian society, at least here in the United States. Cox deals, as anyone involved in the resolution of this problem must, with two questions, those of theology and sociology. The latter includes especially the phenomenon of urbanization that has characterized modern American culture. Here Cox is at his best, which probably explains the attention given his book especially by college students. The theological aspect is weaker, although the author clearly is aware of the theological issues involved. Nevertheless, the attempt to provide in the first chapter, for example, a biblical basis for secularization must be judged as much too general and over-simplified. It is not likely that Cox himself intended more than this, given the greater emphasis on the sociological aspect and given the reading public he had in mind. At any rate, much serious work remains to be done in the theological area and this paper is an attempt to explore the biblical basis in greater detail.

Perhaps the most serious attempt to approach the problem from the theological point of view is Eric Mascall's *The Secularization of Christianity*.[10] Here we find, first of all, a presentation of the fundamental dichotomy that exists between "the changeless and the changing."[11] There follows a critique of two of the more radical proponents of the secular, Dr. Paul M. van Buren and Bishop Robinson.[12] Final chapters confront the fact of modern scientific growth and its impact on the supernatural,[13] and the very particular question of miracles in the gospels.[14] There is no doubt in my mind that this is a brilliant analysis of the problem and that it does have much to offer for one interested in the speculative aspects. Because, however, of the density of Mascall's reasoning and especially because of the Scholastic mold in which his reasoning is cast, it is not likely that the study will have an impact parallel to that of the more radical theologians. It is felt, therefore, that a fresh examination of the biblical literature might provide a more suitable basis for further theological development. It is with that in mind that the following study is undertaken.

We must begin with a clear understanding of what we mean by the terminology involved, particularly by the term secularity. The word is here meant to describe the autonomy of man and all of nature.[15] As a Christian theist, I understand this autonomy as relative, not absolute. Admittedly this is a crucial point in the contemporary discussion and a word deserves to be said about it.

In the strictest etymological sense the expression "relative autonomy" would have to be considered self-contradictory. But even in the order of natural, as contrasted with transcendent reality, we do speak of a relative autonomy, wherein that which enjoys autonomy is successfully integrated into another higher order or relationship without suffering any diminution of its basic independence. Thus, in the area of biblical studies, the science of textual criticism, operating completely within the framework of its own laws, can be integrated into the higher science of exegesis. The integration not only does not mean a tampering with its own autonomy, but also confers an added dignity to the science by reason of the new relationship.

In an approach to the problem that borders closely on our own, H. de Lubac has some observations that should prove helpful here. His concern is with the precise relationship between nature and the supernatural, which can be seen as another way of expressing the integration of the autonomous into a higher order. He shows that theology has always been concerned with this relationship, but that the truly traditional theology has proclaimed, not a separatist thesis of nature and the supernatural, but an integrated one. It is only in relatively recent times that the separatist thesis gained ground. Some proposed this with the concern to give "the autonomy of nature and natural philosophy their due. Others did so in the name of a purer orthodoxy: rightly wanting to condemn the excesses which sought to deny something of the Creator's sovereign freedom and the complete gratuitousness of his gift, they did not realize that they were in fact falling into the opposite error and watering down the traditional idea."[16]

He goes on to show that a separatist thesis can be seen as responsible, in part at least, for the inroads of a pernicious secularism:

> While wishing to protect the supernatural from any contamination, people had in fact exiled it altogether—both from intellectual and from social life—leaving the field free to be taken over by secularism. Today that secularism, following its course, is beginning to enter the minds even of Christians. They too seek to find a harmony with all things based upon an idea of nature which might be acceptable to a deist or an atheist: everything that comes from Christ, everything that should lead to him, is pushed so far into the background as to look like disappearing for good.[17]

In the context of this theological development we can see how important it is for the Christian theist to speak of a relative autonomy.

An immediate reaction to this could be that ambiguity is being deliberately introduced into the discussion. For the absolute secularist the word "secular" is taken at what is considered its fullest value, understood in the sense of absolute autonomy. For such there can be no question of an integration into a higher order. Ultimately, this suggests the inability to cope with, in the sense of making meaningful to a fully human life, the concept of transcendence. It is this same inability with which the "death of God" theologians have struggled, as Macquarrie[18] and Richards[19] have both brought out in their studies of this problem. It must be admitted, then, that there is a difference, and a quite profound one, between the Christian theist's and the absolute secularist's understanding of the word "secular."

(Parenthetically, we can add here that the notion of "relative autonomy" may not be as foreign to the absolute secularist as we think. In a study entitled "Marxism and the Philosophy of Man," Adam Schaff argues for a "relative autonomy" with regard to the *individual*: "But when the individual is treated as the starting point of our analysis we must not forget that his autonomy is only *relative*. This is not a mysterious monad of will and consciousness, isolated and deprived of contact with others; this is a *social* individual, because, unable to live without society, he is—since the moment of birth—shaped *by society* and is its product, physically and spiritually."[20] Admittedly, the integration of an individual autonomy into society is not the same as integration into a transcendent order, but the analogy is present and should prove helpful toward an understanding of what is meant. Further clarification may be had by pursuing the notion of Christian secularity.)

There is a reason for our use of the word "secular" despite the ambiguity that is or may be thereby introduced. It is that we might affirm, with as much vigor as possible, a reality that the secularists have repeatedly claimed that we deny and that many Christians themselves have falsely interpreted. That reality is precisely the secular, the world in the totality of its being. It is a reality that biblical religion sees only as a *bonum,* the object of divine love and consequently the legitimate object of human concern. It is because there has been a misunderstanding of this is the past, as is illustrated in the pejorative overtones that the very word "secular" has even today in the minds of many Christians, that it is necessary now to restore a properly biblical conviction by the vigorous assertion of secular value. Perhaps, if the biblical view can provide some fresh insights into this contemporary problem, the introduction of the ambiguity will have been justified.

Intimately associated with the modern Christian attitude toward the secular is the interpretation of eschatology, and for that reason something should be said about it here. By eschatology is generally meant the understanding of the final goal of creation, the doctrine of the *eschaton.* Throughout the greater part of the Old Testament period eschatology was conceived of in a community and cosmic sense. In other words, creation's final goal would be the perfect reign of God among his people, enabling them to achieve full community with themselves and with all of nature. The prophetic announcements of the new heaven and the new earth were the apocalyptic expression of this cosmic community. Such a conviction necessarily presupposed a positive regard for the secular reality.

It was towards the end of the Old Testament period that an individual eschatology was introduced to the Jewish people. We find expressions of it in the Wisdom of Solomon where we read that "the souls of the righteous are in the hand of God" (3:1a), that "the righteous live forever, and their reward is with the Lord" (5:15) and in the story of the seven Maccabean brothers who attested, in the face of death, to their belief in personal resurrection to new life (2 Macc. 7). Jesus was heir to this conviction of individual eschatology as seems clear from his answer to the Sadducees who denied the resurrection and who questioned him about the woman married successively to seven men.

But it would be an unfortunate and unjustified interpretation of the New Testament to say that community and cosmic eschatology were denied or even ignored. In the first place, this was so firmly imbedded in the Jewish mentality that we would need a clear denial on the part of Jesus or of his early followers to think that this conviction did not live on. Moreover, it forms the necessary background for the concepts of the Kingdom of God and of the Church. In the Christian faith individual eschatology must be seen and interpreted in the context of community and cosmic eschatology.

The history of Christian theology would reveal that a proper balance between individual and community eschatology was not always preserved. Individual or personal salvation has been and still is at times preached as the almost exclusive concern of Christianity. We might ask whether this distortion of the New Testament message has been a factor in Martin Buber's evaluation of the emergence of Christianity. He writes: "The stream of Christianity, flowing over the world from the source of Israel and strengthened by mighty influences, especially the Iranian and the Greek, arose at a time in Hellenistic civilization, and especially in its religious life, when the element of the people was being displaced by that of the individual. Christianity is 'Hellenistic' insofar as it surrenders the concept of the 'holy people' and recognizes only a personal holiness."[21]

There is little doubt that an individual eschatology in an exclusivistic sense removes the individual from his community and cosmic framework and inculcates or at least encourages a disdain for the world as secular reality. Many writers have already noted the presence of this tendency in such a popular devotional book as the *Following of Christ*. What has happened is that a horizontal eschatology, in which fulfillment comes through time and history and through *this* world, has given way to a one-sided vertical eschatology in which time, history and the secular are only the incidental but restricting vesture to be discarded when the fullness of reality is had. A glance at the conventional textbooks on theology should confirm this analysis, since under eschatology the emphasis is given to the fate of the individual in death, judgment, heaven or hell. Consequently, a restoration of the balance of the eschatological picture will go hand-in-hand with a proper evaluation of the secular.

The secularity debate has, almost by definition, raised the problem of the sacred and profane. It hardly needs saying that there has been much misunderstanding of these terms. Those writing professionally on the subject have not always had the same precise meaning in mind, which has probably contributed to the misunderstanding. For this reason I would like to make clear my own understanding of the terminology involved before getting to the heart of the discussion.

It is a commonplace that the one factor making the greatest contribution to the development of secularity has been the rapid advances in technology and, in general, in all those sciences that manifest man's increasing control of the created universe. Total secularity is properly had only with total control, a stage obviously not yet realized. But such control is not absolutely inconceivable, whence the possibility of speaking in terms of total secularity. In other words, it is recognized now that there is no area in the created universe that enjoys some kind of special status, a "holy" place that is altogether beyond the probing fingers of scientific men. The whole of created reality is therefore said to be "profane."

This recognition of the profane can, first of all, be contrasted with primitive man's concept of the universe about him. It was, of course, the pre-Copernican, three-tiered universe of the heavens above, the earth, the Sheol, or the underworld, below. Within this universe certain areas were considered to be so linked with the transcendent order of the gods that they totally escaped man's control. Biblical man shared this conviction, although it was considerably affected, as we shall see, by Israel's conception of Yahweh. What is important for our purpose is that an underlying conviction of "holy" areas accounts for much of the conceptual and terminological framework in which the Scriptures are presented. The holy garden protected by the cherubim with flaming sword, the "awesome place" that was the scene of Jacob's vision, the mysteriously burning bush—these are some of the more spectacular expressions of the mentality.

Another illustration, and one which focuses more directly on the issue of autonomy, is found in the book of Job. After Job's frustrating dialogue with his friends, he appeals to the divine Judge for a hearing. The answer comes in the form of a theophany in which a long series of questions is directed to the plaintiff. As is evident from the reaction of Job, they are intended to emphasize man's inability to pierce the mystery of divine transcendence. By an overwhelming listing of the "holy" areas of the universe man is made more conscious of the transcendent reality. Job's problem about the mystery of suffering, while it is not directly answered, is swallowed up in the surpassing mystery of God himself.

The questions designed to express this transcendence are interesting. Among them we find these:

> Have you entered into the springs of the sea,
> or walked in the recesses of the deep? . . .
> Have you comprehended the expanse of the earth? . . .
> Where is the way to the dwelling of light,
> and where is the place of darkness? . . .
> Have you entered the storehouses of the snow,
> or have you seen the storehouses of the hail? . . .
> What is the way to where the light is distributed,
> or where the east wind is scattered upon the earth? (38:16-24)

For ancient man these questions could only be answered in the negative; man's autonomy could not even be conceived to extend this far. Modern man, on the other hand, would give an affirmative reply to all these questions. The springs of the sea and the recesses of the deep, the storehouses of snow and hail are no "holy" places defying his control.

The term that I would use to express this primitive conception is "sacral." By it I mean the description of these areas of the created universe that were conceived to have been invested with numinous power and that modern man has exposed as being just as much subject to his control as any other. It is here where the process of secularization or desacralization properly unfolds.

This recognition of the profane or secular must be related to the conviction of divine immanence that underlies the whole of biblical religion. By divine immanence is meant the identification of the transcendent Lord with his creation in a saving presence. The Incarnation is the supreme manifestation of such immanence. But it is manifested in varying degrees throughout the whole of biblical history. It is important, in this regard, to note that biblical studies have shown that Israel conceived of divine saving immanence as being manifested from the very moment of creation, whence the axiom that ktisiology presupposes soteriology. A clear indication of this conviction, which can be demonstrated in several ways, is found in Paslm 136 where Yahweh's covenant love, his *hesed,* is extended to the creative activity of the beginning (vv. 5-9).

It is the conviction of this saving presence that demands, for the biblical theist, the integration of autonomy into a transcendent order already described. It is here that I use the word "sacred." It would describe created reality inasmuch as it has been affected by the divine saving immanence. And since, as we have just seen, that extends to all of creation, we must conclude that the terms sacred, profane and secular are coterminous but have distinct nuances. "Sacred" designates created reality as integrated into the higher order, "secular" as autonomous and "profane" as desacralized.

As will be made clear, the process of secularization is also the process of historicization. In other words, events are seen, not as the predetermined repetition of the mythical acts of the gods, but as the once-for-all unfoldings of the historical process. This is especially important for the comparison of Israel's literature with that of her pagan neighbors. We shall have more to say of this later, but it was felt that it would be helpful to make the point now, even if only briefly.

What follows consists of two parts. In the first I will point out those passages and themes in the Old Testament which clearly reveal the process of secularization taking place, whether in contrast to the mythological beliefs of Israel's pagan neighbors or in contrast to her own mythological expression in more primitive documents. The second part will consider the underlying biblical bases for secularization. I do not presume to offer any radically new interpretations of the biblical texts. The modest hope is that a consideration of them in the light of our contemporary development might aid in the more fruitful discussion of the problem of secularity.

The first great breakthrough in secularization in Israel's history came with the breakdown of the tribal amphictyony as a highly influential force on Israel's life and the emergence of a sophisticated, secular civilization under David and Solomon. In his *Old Testament Theology* von Rad describes this breakthrough and pinpoints the signs.[22] We can first say a word about some of the historical events that manifested the new spirit.

Von Rad points out that in the case of David's election as king three arguments are adduced for his choice: his blood relationship, his military prowess and, lastly, his designation by Yahweh.[23] The secular element receives the greater emphasis. This takes on added significance when we compare this scene with that of Saul's choice (1 Sam. 10). The activity of the spirit of God in Saul's favor (recalling the strongly charismatic element in the period of the judges) is the major witness to his candidacy, and the final determination is made by lot. The only secularizing element in the account (and this does represent some evolution from the period of the judges) is the subsequent acclamation by the people.

The emergence of prophecy in Israel at the time of the rise of the monarchy is not necessarily connected with the latter phenomenon, but it does represent a similar thrust in the direction of desacralization. Scholars have pointed out that dissatisfaction and disaffection with the morally defunct priesthood of the day and, in particular, with the corrupt practices of the Elides (cf. 1 Sam. 2:12-17; 8:3-5) catapulted the ecstatic prophets into prominence. This meant that the word of Yahweh was no longer confined to the cult but was now brought out into the everyday life of man. An incident recorded in 1 Kings 19:11-13 highlights this development. The prophet Elijah is told to stand upon the mount of Horeb and there he experiences successively a strong wind, an earthquake, a fire and finally "a still small voice." It is in the last that the prophet recognizes the special saving presence of Yahweh. By this story the author warns against associating the divine activity too exclusively with the awesome and the unusual and insists on associating it with the seemingly insignificant. While this represents a remarkable spiritualization of religion, by the same token it implies that all of secular reality is affected by the divine immanence.

It is in the literature that the age produced that we can detect the most significant signs of secularization. This literature was not, of course, a *creatio ex nihilo*. It was produced by collecting and editing a number of traditions that had been originally attached to local shrines and tribal centers. There they had served a cultic, aetiological or even mythological purpose. By being separated from these centers they lost their former significance and were reinterpreted as part of an ongoing history.[24] The reinterpretation was intended to explain the Davidic monarchy and its meteoric emergence on the world scene. Thus, while it remained theological inasmuch as the explanation rested on Yahweh's mighty deeds, the new direction was clearly one of desacralization.

Von Rad rightly emphasizes the significance of a transition from a conception of events as "basically episodic and isolated" to a comprehensive survey of all preceding history. In his own words, "This ability to deal with extensive complexes of connected history and not just episodes must be regarded as one of the most momentous advances in man's understanding of himself, since its effects upon the spiritual development of the whole of the West are incalculable."[25] The Elijah incident mentioned above is illustrative of what has happened. Yahweh was conceived to have acted not just in the dramatic, a conception which would favor a distinction between the sacred and the secular, but in the whole of history and in the whole of man's life. It means that the profane has significance and can be treated with all seriousness by a man of God. "Unquestionably we have here to do with the traces of an Enlightenment on a broad basis, an emancipation of the spirit and a stepping out from antiquated ideas."[26] We shall note later the contrast with the common pagan conception of the secular.

Ever since the last century when the first major discoveries of extrabiblical literature were made, it has been the fashion for commentators on the early chapters of *Genesis* to emphasize the elements in common between Israelite and non-Israelite stories of origins. This was received with great hesitation by many who feared that the unique character of biblical literature was under attack. In response to this reaction and in order to counter it, Catholic exegetes spoke more freely of the mythological features of the stories. A serious effort was made, and made successfully, to have myth adopted as one of the biblical literary forms.

While this insistence may have been necessary in the light of the cultural background of most Bible readers, it has had its unfortunate consequences. One of these was to overemphasize the mythological elements and to underplay the secularizing elements. On the popular level, that has led to an almost total dismissal of the stories as having any relevance today. And even on the scholarly level Catholic exegetes especially still seem to be captivated by the mythological. The presence of mythological elements should actually have been a presupposition of our investigation, not a later and painful discovery. If this were so, it is not likely that we would have applied the term "myth" to any of these stories at all.

Let us now concentrate our attention on some of the texts to see the secularization process at work. The Yahwist's history, since it is a product of the period of empire, can be presumed to reveal the new mentality in one of its earliest expressions. And we can go to the paradise story of Genesis 2-3, since this would generally be thought to contain the strongest mythological elements. These are undoubtedly there. But does a comparison with the creation myths of Israel's pagan neighbors reveal any striking differences?

One appears in the conception of the garden itself. Some years ago John L. McKenzie noted, "No Mesopotamian account is as anthropocentric as the Paradise story (of Genesis); this is one of its most striking and distinctive traits."[27] It is its strongly anthropocentric character that precludes the "garden of Eden" from being equated with the mythical gardens of Mesopotamian literature. It is true that in the Gilgamesh epic a single pair, Utnapishtim and his wife, are made by the gods to reside "at the mouth of the rivers,"[28] a reference to the dwelling place of the gods. But it is clearly implied that they could enjoy the privilege only on the condition of being raised to divine status: "Hitherto Utnapishtim has been but human. Henceforth Utnapishtim and his wife shall be like unto us gods."[29]

In other words, the Yahwist has demythologized the garden by making it a garden of man, not of the gods. The quite profane remark that man was put in it "to till it and keep it" (Gen. 2:15) adds a further secularizing note. It is an echo from the everyday life of the ordinary Israelite who made his living from the soil. We can contrast this with the ancient Akkadian picture of man being created and then "charged with the service of the gods that they might be at ease."[30] Thus, while a mythological motif lingers on in the reference to the trees in the garden (2:9), the comment of von Rad that "the mythical is almost completely stripped away"[31] can be accepted.

Dennis J. McCarthy makes a similar observation in his remarks on the Yahwist's primeval history.[32] His purpose is to show that J was not too concerned with the *origin* of the world, but with its ordering. This depends on the watering of the ground by rain and its cultivating by man. Above all, there is no indication at all of a *Chaoskampf* which features so much in the pagan stories of origin.[33] He concludes: "Thus the evidence hardly indicates a need for demythologizing in the sense of a working away from a belief in the *Chaoskampf* and all its characteristic apparatus. The evidence is that such 'demythologization' was there from the first because Israel was interested in historical, not cosmic origins, and so it could use the mythic themes without hazard."[34]

A further historicizing element is detected in the remark that the garden was planted "in Eden" (2:8). Speiser notes that "the term is used here clearly as a geographical designation."[35] The geocentric orientation, like the anthropocentric, is a secularizing tendency; it is one more attempt to link the garden with what Israel knew of geography and so with her own dim, historical origins "in the East." It is not entirely unlikely that the garden be seen as "an archetype of the world," "an epitome of the earth itself."[36]

A still more extensive use of geography for desacralizing purposes is found in the passage dealing with the four rivers that are constituted of the one that "flowed out of Eden to water the garden" (2:10-14).

Admittedly the passage is an erratic piece as far as its literary connection with the rest of the story is concerned. But that does not affect the point we are making. Nor does the fact that it is not always possible to determine the precise geographical areas embraced by the four rivers. Almost certainly the author intended references to rivers that were actually known in antiquity. This is evident in the case of the last two named, the Tigris and the Euphrates. It can be presumed in the case of the other two.[37] The significance of this is well put by von Rad in his remark, "Now suddenly we find ourselves in our historical and geographical world!"[38]

Rivers, and waters in general, played an important role in the mythologies of the Mesopotamian and Nile valleys. And there is little doubt that the authors of our Genesis stories were influenced by this fact in their own reconstruction of primitive history. But we find a completely different direction taken by the biblical and non-biblical authors in their portrayal of the role. In the *Pyramid Texts* of Egypt the primaeval waters are referred to as Nun. The descriptions indicate that it was the inundation of the Nile river that was the basis for the conception. But Nun quickly loses its identification with historical and geographical reality in the text's "extravagant declaration that the king was born in Nun ... (suggesting) that Nun was regarded as the original creative principle. In other texts of various periods Nun is referred to as the 'Ancient' and the 'Father of the gods,' and is specifically described as the father or Atum or Re."[39] The loss of identification with secular reality was a deliberate measure on the part of the ancient author in his desire to mythologize that reality. Much the same can be said of the two bodies of water that are featured in the *Enuma Elish,* Mummu-Tiamat and Apsu. The former represents the salt waters of the sea and the latter the fresh waters of the rivers and lakes. We are possibly justified in considering the "commingling" of these waters "as a single body"[40] a veiled reference to the emptying of the Tigris and Euphrates into the Persian Gulf. But once again that geographical basis has been almost completely swallowed up in the mythological features that are dominant. Secular reality has lost its interest for the author who is solely concerned with the mythical acts of the gods.

It is precisely this secular reality that our biblical author, on the other hand, is concerned to restore. Rather than becoming less and less recognizable, the geographical and historical bases become more and more recognizable, even though the author's limited knowledge and dependence on existing literary traditions did not enable him to be completely successful. The significant point is that the direction of his interest was not mythological but geographical and hence secular. J. P. Audet, in an article in *Nouvelle Revue Théologique* concerning this passage in Genesis, remarked, "Strange geography, but strange only for the geographers."[41] Underlying the remark is the relatively recent discovered awareness of mythological features that do color the description. In the light of our observations here, however, it would be more to the point to remark, not on the strangeness, but on the conventionality of the passage. And just because of the author's obvious secularizing tendencies, it might be well to deny this story the designation of "myth."

One more example from the Yahwist's reconstruction of prehistory can be given. It is the story of the tower of Babel in Genesis 11:1-9. The theology of the passage needs little comment. It pictures the climactic stage in the story of man's alienation from God and from his fellowman, the stage that prepared the way for the call of Abraham and the beginnings of a people of God. But the author's use of the tower story has its own significance. It is Speiser's contention that the original inspiration of the passage was a literary and not a monumental one, and possibly the reference in the *Enuma Elish* to the building of the city and the temple.[42] At any rate, it was at the temple that the rites of the New Year festival were celebrated, in which the primordial victory of Marduk was re-enacted. The celebration was the very heart of the Babylonian mythology and it is natural to suppose that our Yahwist author was well aware of this. Is he, then, issuing a polemic against the whole mythological conception? This is the considered opinion of some. "The cosmic significance of the ziggurat is fully recognized, but at the same time is exposed as a human attempt at self-realization on a superhuman level . . . Babylon, centre of the universe, becomes the centre of confusion, the very point from which mankind is scattered abroad, the place and the sign of God's judgment upon man's attempt to be like God (v. 9)."[43] The process of desacralization takes on cosmic dimensions and so prepares for the completely secular, though still sacred, unfolding of human history.

We have concentrated our attention on just a few texts from the early chapters of Genesis. But it is felt that these have something special to say about the author's purpose. It would be in this primeval history, beyond not only the author's personal memory but also the national memory of his people, that we would normally expect a mythopoeic tendency to assert itself strongly. It is just the opposite that occurs. This suggests that in his later history, which deals with what we know as historical times, the Yahwist will continue and even accentuate his secularizing tendencies. Nor are we disappointed. In his presentation of the patriarchal narratives we can note his exploitation of the common, at times even bawdy, events in which his ancestors are involved. Moreover, when he does introduce the divine activity in those places where he is not dependent on pre-existing material, there is a simplicity about it that contrasts sharply with the overwhelming theophanies of other stories. One of the most majestic passages in all of the patriarchal narratives and the one most fraught with significance for all that is to follow is the call of Abram from Mesopotamia. Yet it is told with a simplicity that would seem to belie its importance (Genesis 12:1-4).

The Yahwist, of course, was not the only one, even though he was the first of whom we have record, to desacralize and thus secularize history. We can note in the Priestly story of creation, for example, a similar urge to describe the creative activity in a way that will make it meaningful for the everyday life of the Israelite. The six-day workweek with one day of rest was certainly providing a demythologized framework to the story, regardless of the liturgical overtones. It has long been noted that the sun and moon are not directly named in this account in order to avoid any possible reference to the Mesopotamian gods with the same names. Similarly, the "great sea monsters," the *tanninim* that rivaled the gods of the ancient pagans, are thoroughly demythologized and mentioned along with "every living creature that moves" (1:21). A. van der Voort notes that only in this verse and in the one referring to man's creation (1:27) does the author use the expression *wayyibra' 'elohim,* suggesting his deliberate intention to group these sea monsters, under a very vague generic term, among other creatures.[44]

The same author goes on to point out the evolution of the concept of these mythological beings within Israel. Reminiscences of the ancient struggle between them and the pagan gods are found in such passages as Isaiah 51:9; Psalm 74:13 f.; etc., and are there used to accentuate the power of Yahweh. In other places, such as Ezekiel 29:3, the great dragon becomes simply a metaphor for the Pharaoh of Egypt.[45] In other words, an examination of a concept such as this would illustrate the development of Israel's secularizing tendency from the earliest period down to at least the immediate postexilic period. Throughout, the mythological terminology continues to be used, but its role is increasingly one of emphasizing the power of Israel's God and hence of secularizing the mythical.

In a recent publication, W. F. Albright discusses these same *tanninim* in the context of the first creation story. After noting the long and complex history of this account and indicating that its extant form was reached in the seventh century B.C., he compares its canonical form with Canaanite and Babylonian versions of the story. Whereas in the latter:

> the dragon or dragons of chaos preceded the regnant divinities, in Gen. 1 the monsters are created by God himself. We read in verse 21 that "God created the sea-monsters" (Heb. *tanninim*), using the plural of a word which in Canaanite was employed in the singular for the dragon of chaos which was destroyed by a god at creation. It follows that there was originally a statement in verse 2 mentioning specifically and succinctly the triumph of God over the great Deep (*Tehom=Acc. Ti'amat*), which was later deleted. In any case it is obvious that the pagan archetype was thoroughly demythologized at some stage in the history of Gen. 1. There are many other cases of demythologizing in the cosmogonic narratives

of Genesis as well as in the Patriarchal stories. In later Israel the tendency to eliminate polytheistic references was spasmodic, depending presumably upon periodic reform movements and efforts to eliminate remaining traces of paganism. It may confidently be stated that there is no true mythology anywhere in the Hebrew Bible. What we have consists of vestiges—what may be called the "debris" of a past religious culture.[46]

We have inserted this rather long quotation, not only because it deals with the precise image which we have been treating here, but also because it is a confirmation of an observation made above, namely, that the term "myth" cannot be properly applied to the Bible at all. We might note also that Dr. Albright refers to the mythological elements or vestiges that are found in the Scriptures as the "debris" of a past religious culture, a term used independently by this writer in a paper delivered at St. Louis University in the fall of 1968. "If we do find illustrations of the sacral, or mythological, in the Scriptures, as in the case of Job, these must be seen as the debris of a mentality already shattered by a new outlook but not yet cleared by the necessary applications of that outlook to all aspects of reality. Only a post-Copernican world view would make that possible."[47]

Crucial to the discussion at this point is the precise understanding of the word "myth." It is obvious that I have had a definite meaning in mind since I have rejected it as a properly biblical literary *genre*. Moreover, from all that has been said thus far, it is clear that I have connected the term with a process of sacralization which is just the opposite of the process of secularization that we find operative in the Bible. Because of the contemporary insistence on demythologizing the Scriptures, however, and because of the diverse meanings given to the word, even by current authors, it is most important that we make very clear the meaning intended here.

Since I find myself in agreement with Dr. Albright's conclusion stated above that there is no true mythology anywhere in the Hebrew Bible, it could be supposed that his definition of myth would be an acceptable one. In the book referred to he does not undertake a formal study of the word; in the context of the passage quoted he does make this important statement:

> Since no religion can exist without the use of concrete language and symbolism to express the ineffable, it is, of course, impossible to eliminate all "myth" in the post-Platonic sense without destroying the best part of our religious heritage. When I use the term "demythologizing" I am using it in the sense of eliminating specifically polytheistic elements in the narratives of Genesis as well as poetic survivals or pagan borrowings in Old Testament literature.[48]

Thus, for Albright, myth is associated with a polytheistic world-view that is consciously rejected in the canonical Scriptures.

We shall consider here, principally, two studies on the subject of myth, one by the well-known anthropologist, Mircea Eliade,[49] the other by the biblical scholar, Brevard Childs.[50] The viewpoint of the former will be necessarily broader than that of the latter and will thus serve as a convenient background for our biblical study.

Although he begins the opening chapter of his book with the precise question we are asking, "What exactly is a myth?"[51] Eliade never does propose a clear definition. Rather, he describes various elements that constitute a myth in order to determine whether there are myths in the modern world. From these descriptions it is possible to derive some important insights. He rejects, first of all, the very general definition given by the liberal theologians of the past century, which was that myth described anything opposed to reality.[52] Since reality, for so many of them, was restricted to observable data or rationalization, myth was unimportant for them. This is significant because, for many of our Christian laity today, there is present, though perhaps unconsciously, a similar mentality. Myth is something that is simply "not true," and when it is applied to the Scriptures, they see this as an undermining of their inspired character. This is one more reason, if a pastoral one, why the use of the term should be carefully studied.

One of the basic elements that Eliade sees as constituting a myth is its exemplary or archetypical character. By this is meant that in the course of history an event described in a myth will be repeated because of the power inherent in the mythical event itself. Obviously, in this sense myth is not at all opposed to truth or reality; rather, it is conceived to describe *absolute truth*.[53] Succeeding events will derive their validity as true to the extent that they are assumed into the mythical pattern. It is clear, too, that a mythical event occurs at the beginning of time, or better, in a special time that is beyond the calculations of man. Finally, it must be concluded that the protagonist of the myth must be a divine being or, at least, a "superman" capable of investing events with mythical power. Thus, we can say with Eliade that "a myth is a *true history* of what came to pass at the beginning of Time, and one which provides the pattern for human behaviour. In *imitating* the exemplary acts of a god or of a mythical hero, or simply by recounting their adventures, the man of an archaic society detaches himself from profane time and magically re-enters the great Time, the sacred time."[54]

It is not easy to determine which elements Eliade considers to be essentially constitutive of myth. Since he goes on to speak of modern myths, and since modern Western man is no polytheist, he cannot be thinking of a polytheist mentality as the necessary mental framework for thinking mythologically, although he would, presumably, consider this to be an essential aspect of the primitive concept. In order to make his application to the modern world, he extracts from the primitive concept that which he believes to remain valid for today, thus giving myth a somewhat broader meaning. He sees it as an "expression of *a mode of being in the world.*"⁵⁵ He goes on to apply this, in one case, to Marxist Communism where he finds what he calls "one of the great eschatological myths of the Middle Eastern and Mediterranean world, namely: the redemptive part to be played by the just (the 'elect,' the 'anointed,' the 'innocent,' the 'missioners,' in our own days by the proletariat), whose sufferings are invoked to change the ontological status of the world. In fact, Marx's classless society, and the consequent disappearance of all historical tensions, find their most exact precedent in the myth of the golden age which, according to a number of traditions, lies at the beginning and the end of History. Marx has enriched this venerable myth with a truly messianic Judaeo-Christian ideology; on the one hand, by the prophetic and soteriological function he ascribes to the proletariat; and, on the other, by the final struggle between good and evil, which may well be compared with the apocalyptic conflict between Christ and Antichrist, ending in the decisive victory of the former."⁵⁶

It hardly needs stating that this broader concept of myth, which is decidedly not tied to a cyclic concept of history nor to the pagan, polytheistic mentality, is not the one which we have had in mind in our references to the biblical break-through above. Later on, we shall have occasion to take up this subject of the meaning of history once again and shall indicate the peculiar character of the biblical understanding as underlying the process of secularization. In other words, we do combine the concepts of sacral and mythical for reasons that we shall see shortly. For the time, however, we can note the suggestive comparison made by Eliade and others between Marxist Communism and the Messianic Judaeo-Christian ideology. This eschatological orientation of history, which is at the heart of so much of the contemporary theology of hope, is understood by some communists as including an *absolute* future.

It is here where, quite frankly, I find difficulty in reconciling Eliade's analysis of Marxism and his note of repristination or repetition of the *Urzeit* which he seems to attach strongly to the concept of myth. For the modern commentators on Marx, if there is any absolute, it is not an absolute past which provides the pattern for the unfolding of history, but an absolute future. In an article summarizing Ernst Bloch's theology of hope, K. Heinitz writes,

> Bloch's concept of the hoped-for utopia is not one of repristination ... Bloch asserts that "God should no longer be thought of as "above" man, but as "before" man in his development. God is before, in front of, man on each "utopian" rim or brink of his development of human possibility.⁵⁷

We can see how radical this is for the discussion of secularization. It has been our contention thus far—and we shall offer more arguments—that the Bible has initiated the process of secularization by its anthropocentric, geocentric and historocentric orientation. There are no absolute divine actions in a timeless past which unconditionally fix the pattern of human behaviour. There *are* divine acts, but these are in historical time and they provide meaning for the development of a future not yet achieved. The one absolute existing from the beginning is God.

Bloch, and the communists, would carry secularity beyond even this by asserting *no* absolute from the beginning. "Bloch hopes that man will achieve 'transcendental immanence without transcendence.' "[58] Accordingly, the demythologization process must be carried even further, so that the last myth, that of an absolute God at the beginning, is destroyed.

Eliade, of course, would not subscribe to this conviction. It was merely his discussion of the meaning of myth that was the springboard for our further consideration of Marxist communism. We can now return to the question whether myth includes, necessarily, the note of repristination or return to the *Urzeit*. By extending the term to include Marxist communism, it would seem that it does not, at least in Eliade's view, since, according to the communist theoreticians, there is no absolute beginning to which there can be a return. And yet, if we can appeal to Eliade's own writings, there seems to be a constant insistence on this in his speaking of myths. For example, in the preface to the book referred to above, he writes,

> The Myth defines itself by its own mode of being. It can only be grasped, as a myth, in so far as it *reveals* something as having been fully manifested, and this manifestation is at the same time *creative* and *exemplary*, since it is the foundation of a structure of reality as well as of a kind of human behaviour. A myth always narrates something as having *really happened*, as an event that took place, in the plain sense of the word....[59]

Again,

> There is no myth which is not the unveiling of a "mystery," the revelation of a primordial event which inaugurated either a constituent structure of reality or a kind of human behaviour... It can establish itself as a myth only to the extent that it reveals the existence and the activity of super-human beings behaving in an *exemplary manner*....[60]

While it is myth in this sense that has been the object of this paper, it is difficult, in my mind, to reconcile this with any eschatological view of reality, whether it be Judaeo-Christian or Marxist communist.

Turning now to Childs' study,[61] we find a clearer exposition of the different definitions of myth and an understandably greater emphasis on the biblical problem. Childs proposes, first of all, the very broad definition which became the foundation for much of the later studies on the Bible and mythology. According to this, myth is "a necessary universal form of expression within the early stage of man's intellectual development, in which unexplainable events were attributed to the direct intervention of the gods."[62] New Testament scholars are aware that Rudolph Bultmann adopts a quite similar understanding of myth, which is most important to keep in mind if we are to evaluate properly his bent for demythologization.

But, as Childs notes, such a definition is not phenomenological but historic-philosophical, whereby a judgment on the material is implicit and the risk assumed "that false categories, unsuitable to the subject, are forced upon it."[63] In other words, a distinction between the natural and the supernatural is presupposed as part of ancient man's mentality, or at least is forced upon him. Moreover, it is assumed that modern man can readily determine when ancient man was speaking of the one or the other.

A more refined definition, in accord with the developments in form-criticism, presents the myth as "a literary form concerning stories of gods."[64] If this is taken in a polytheistic sense, as it generally was, then myth could not be a part of the canonical, biblical literature which is monotheistic. The definition is not, however, too satisfactory because of its great emphasis on the *literary expression* and because it fails to get to the heart of mythopoeic man, to an understanding of his mentality.[65]

Childs goes on to study myth as an insight into reality in order that he might propose a phenomenological definition. He is very close to Eliade here, on whom he depends to some extent. He shows how primitive man felt impelled to project some kind of order on created reality about him:

> In the plastic form of a myth a principle of organization is found which creates out of the chaos of particulars a unity. The unique character of the myth is found in the fact that the shaping of this raw material takes place on the plane of personalized powers in which the elemental impressions of nature are transformed into stories of gods.[66]

Another decisive element in the mythopoeic mentality is seen to be the retrojection of the established order to some primeval event.[67] This, I am inclined to believe, is an essential characteristic. It is an emphasis made, as we have seen, by Eliade, despite the difficulty experienced in applying the concept to Marxist communism. It is repristination, or return to the primordial times marked by the exemplary actions of the divine beings.

After these considerations and a brief study of the myths of primitive religion and of ancient Egyptian religion, Childs proposes this summary which can be offered as a phenomenological definition, at least a tentative one: "Myth is a form by which the existing structure of reality is understood and maintained. It concerns itself with showing how an action of a deity, conceived of as occurring in the primeval age, determines a phase of contemporary world order. Existing world order is maintained through the actualization of the myth in the cult."[68] It is, basically, this understanding of myth that we have had in mind in our examination of the biblical material.

It should be clear how intimately associated with the problem of secularity this question of myth and the mythopoeic mentality is. We will see something of this later in our consideration of the notion of history. Childs shows how the anthropologist, R. Pettazzoni, has worked out the distinction between truth and falsity as proposed by a myth; it is a distinction that would justify our rejection of myth as part of the canonical Bible. According to the ancient mentality, a myth was "true" if it depicted the sacral or "holy," if it dealt with those primeval acts on whose pattern the present world order was established. A myth was considered "false" if it dealt with the "secular," with those phenomena that had no relationship to the archetypical acts of primeval time.[69] As we have seen thus far, and as we shall see further, biblical "revelation" is concerned precisely with the "secular."

Having made clear what is our understanding of the word "myth," an understanding which we believe to be consonant with the phenomenological approach of modern scholars, we can now proceed to a further examination of the secularizing process in the Old Testament. The examples that follow deal with a different kind of material, for the most part, but add new dimensions to the nature of the break-through initiated by the biblical authors. The first involves a text dealing with exclusively Israelite tradition. It concerns the sealing of the covenant between Yahweh and the people after the entrance into the promised land. It is found in Joshua 24. Scholars are agreed on the existence of several layers of redactional material here. In the passages concerning the witnesses to the covenant, in v. 22 we read that the people themselves are designated the witnesses. In v. 26a we read that Joshua "wrote these words in the book of the law of God." Some commentators see this as a later scribal addition made when the Torah had reached a quasi-canonical status and began to be considered the definitive norm, and therefore "witness" to Israel's actions. In v. 27 Joshua is said to designate a large stone as the witness to the covenant. This doubtless belongs to the most primitive stratum when objects of nature served a sacral purpose. The later, probably Deuteronomic author, whose concern is with the freedom of Israel to choose its own gods, makes the persons themselves witnesses against themselves. Here especially we can see a secularizing tendency in the stricter sense of asserting the autonomy of man. It belongs to a period when the role of sacral objects had lost some of its momentum.

In the first part of this article we recalled the lack of an individual eschatology in most of Israel's history. In other words, they simply had no firm convictions concerning existence in another life. There are, of course, the references to Sheol, the abode of the dead, but it is not conceived of as a place of reward or punishment. The author of Ecclesiastes put it most forcefully in these words: "Whatever your hand finds to do, do it with your might; for there is no work or thought or knowledge or wisdom in Sheol, to which you are going" (9:10). The passage is particularly revealing since it emphasizes the need to make the most of the present reality, and the reason given is the lack of any conviction about future *life*. No stronger affirmation could be made of the value of the secular.

The question can legitimately be asked whether Qoheleth can be said to be within the mainstream of Israel's tradition. He certainly is to the extent that we find no cult of the dead in any earlier stage of Israel's authentic tradition. (The calling forth of the dead Samuel by the witch of Endor is acknowledged as a perversion of Israelite religious practice.) This lack is in strange contrast to the elaborate cult of the dead developed among Israel's neighbors, especially in Egypt. It is a telling witness to Israel's stubborn refusal to escape the present reality, to deny the secular.

But it would be myopic, at the same time, to consider this lack of conviction about an after-life in isolation. Israel, as we have already pointed out above, had a strong sense of cosmic and community eschatology. It is argued here that a strongly historic or secular eschatology provides a much firmer basis for an appreciation of secular reality than would a secularist concept of history that has no transcendent goal. In other words, the hope of the secularist is a restricted one; it can be spelled out in clearly defined terms. For the biblical eschatologist, hope is expressed in and through the secular but transcends its present manifestation. It is also argued that the introduction of an individual eschatology into the already existing framework of community and cosmic eschatology does not at all compromise this understanding of secularity but serves, rather, to particularize it. Commenting on this paradox of the secular and the eschatological in Israel's religion, Jürgen Moltmann remarks, "In this enigmatic fact that Israel's religion of promise clings with obstinate exclusiveness to the historic and this-worldly fulfillment of the promises, we have the presupposition for understanding the resurrection of Christ as the resurrection of the crucified one and not as a symbol for the hope of immortality and for the resigned attitude to life that goes along with it."[70] In other words, we can say that resurrection is the affirmation and transcendent continuation of this life and of secular reality, not its negation. For the Christian theist this is the necessary climax of Old Testament revelation.

The biblical theme of "rest" can also be seen as another expression of eschatological secularity. The theme has its roots in the very real world of a pilgrim people, a people looking for surcease from the fatigue and dangers of the wilderness wandering. Already in 1933 von Rad sketched the significance of the theme in Deuteronomy, where "rest" is presented as "the altogether tangible peace granted to a nation plagued by enemies and weary of wandering."[71] In a sense, Deuteronomy sees the "rest" as something already granted to Israel, and so it is possible to speak of a realized eschatology of the Old Testament. But the exhortatory fervor with which the author urges Israel to be loyal to Yahweh and the insistence with which he invokes the once-for-all events of Mt. Horeb bear witness to the expectation of a "rest" not yet granted.[72] Still it is a this-worldly expectation as any Israelite hope had to be. The future gift of God will fulfill and not negate the secular.

In his commentary on Genesis 1-11, Zimmerli compares the "rest" of God in 2:2-3 with the "rest" of Israel in Deuteronomy. In the latter, he writes, it is the *politische Mensch* who speaks; the Deuteronomic "rest" is had when all enemies have been defeated and when Israel can live in security in the land flowing with milk and honey.[73] The Priestly author sees a more profound possession of that "rest" in the Sabbath observance. He has spiritualized but not thereby desecularized the concept. It remains within the context of Israel's work-a-day world. It is, therefore, a misunderstanding of the Priestly author's theology to revise the Massoretic text, as is done in the Confraternity translation in imitation of the Septuagint and other ancient writers, and to read, "On the *sixth* day God finished the work he had been doing. And he rested on the seventh day from all the work he had done" (2:2). Such a reading would establish a dichotomy between the six work days and the seventh day, a dichotomy that would be understandable only in the context of a vertical eschatology which prescinds from the secular. For the Priestly author, it is insisted, the "rest" of God *is* the completion of his creative activity, the eschatological fulfillment of created reality. Correctly, therefore, does the Massoretic text say that God completed his work on the *seventh* day, the day of "rest."

We have some evidence that the two concepts of "rest" in Deuteronomy and the Priestly author are complementary and not contradictory in the fact that the author of Hebrews in the New Testament juxtaposes the two references and sees them as both contributing to a Christian conception of the "rest."[74] "This rest (of Hebrews) is an eschatological expectation, a fulfillment of the prophecies of redemption, an entering into that rest which there has always been, from the beginning, with God. In the fulfillment of this hope the whole purpose of creation and the whole purpose of redemption are reunited."[75] We can recall here the distinction we made at the beginning of our discussion between the autonomy of created reality and its integration into a higher transcendent order. The Priestly author saw the work of creation as a soteriological act which would reach its climax, not in the denial of creation but in its completion in the "rest" of God. The author of Hebrews explains that his soteriologico-creative activity is fulfilled in the God-man, Jesus Christ.

Biblical secularity, it can be repeated, is not that of the secular humanist. This is quite obvious from all that has been said thus far. What we are attempting to show is that biblical religion does not, as did the pagan religions of Israel's neighbors, desecularize reality in order to find an adequate expression. The divine order, which is the proper object of religion, is presented as consonant with and even necessary for a true estimate of created reality. This is so even in that aspect of religion where the transcendent might threaten to annihilate the secular completely, that is, in ritual worship. For the ancient pagans, ritual was an escape from reality. Through it pagan man felt himself integrated into the mythical life of the gods, into a mythical time that was not subject to human calculation. Because of the importance of this for understanding the totally different direction taken by Israel, it is necessary to say something here about the ancient pagan concept of history and of ritual worship.[76]

The gods of primitive man were generally associated with the phenomena of nature, and usually with those phenomena whose more awesome aspects, eternally manifested, impressed the primitive mind as being expressive of divine qualities. Thus the re-occurring rain storm was seen as the reflection of the storm god, the mighty river as the river god, and so on. The earthly reality, in other words, was a reflection of the heavenly reality. Hence, by the observation of the earthly phenomena were they able to create their heavenly pantheon. By the same means these people were also able to determine the various activities of their gods. What happens in nature must happen because the gods themselves so act. The apparent death of nature in the autumn of the year must be caused, they reasoned, by the death of the god of nature, and its regeneration in spring was similarly attributed to the divine regeneration.

Since their reconstruction of the heavenly reality was based on those phenomena which occurred with some regularity and which could thereby be examined with greater precision than those events which occurred only once, it is understandable that a greater emphasis was placed on the former while the latter were practically ignored as being meaningless. The divine activity, consequently, was associated only with the eternally re-occurring event of nature.[77]

But this activity of the gods was presumed to take place in a special kind of time that was not (as mentioned above) subject to human calculation. We would call it mythical time, but for the pagans it was the sacred time. In this sacred time there takes place, for example, that titanic struggle between the gods and the forces of chaos which result in the ultimate victory of the former and in the eventual act of creation which, it must be noted, was not considered to have taken place in historical time, but in that mythical period that is beyond natural reality. This act has its counterpart in the annual renewal of nature in the spring of the year. Again, in mythical or sacred time there takes place the *hieros gamos*, or the sacred marriage between two divine beings which is the ultimate explanation of the fertility of the earth. In short, it was in this special time that all of those heroic deeds of the gods are enacted which alone give an explanation to the recurring phenomena of nature, to the endless repetition of nature's cycles.

Ancient man felt that he could reproduce this sacred time in his own life by ritual means. By the performance of a ritual act, or by giving ritual importance to any act which could be found to have a divine archetype, i.e., one that had been performed by the gods or heroes *in illo tempore,* such as hunting, fishing, generation, war, sacrifice, archaic man experienced this special time. His act coincided with the mythical act and he thus reverted to the mythical epoch of the gods. Now he truly existed, now he achieved the fullness of his being.[78]

Profane time, on the other hand, was that experienced by man in the performance of any other acts which had no divine archetype, for which no mythical exemplar could be found. Such were especially those acts or events which took place only once and were not repeated. These had no real meaning. Man, in this state, was not really being, he was "becoming."[79] Understandably ancient man preferred the existence in mythical time and abhorred profane time.

With this outlook on events it is clear that primitive man could not conceive of any goal in history, any destiny that had not already been achieved. The goal of life, rather, consisted in preserving, as best he could, the *status quo,* which meant, in the last analysis, the preservation of the endless cycle of nature.

We can, perhaps, understand this whole process more clearly if we examine one of the most common ritual practices among the peoples of the ancient Near East, i.e., the New Year festival. Although there were wide variations concerning the beginning of the new year and the actual length of the year, there was the common notion that each new year represented a complete regeneration of time, a repetition or reflection of the mythical act of creation. A new beginning was made through a victory over the forces of chaos and the old time was abolished.

In particular we can note that, in the celebration of this festival, there was represented, first of all, the return to the primordial chaos that existed before the archetypal or mythical act of creation. This was represented by the total subversion of order, in which laws were abolished, orgies of all kinds were indulged in, slaves became masters, a "carnival" king was enthroned, the true king "humiliated." Then the struggle between Tiamat, the mythical goddess of chaos, and Marduk, the creator god, took place in a ceremony in which several actors reactualized the passage from chaos to cosmos. Finally, the festival concluded with a hierogamy, or sacred marriage, in which the true king performed the marriage act with a temple prostitute, thus giving symbolic expression to the regeneration of the cosmos and of time. In the course of the twelve-day festival the creation epic, the *Enuma Elish,* was solemnly recited in the temple, providing a liturgical voice for the mystical drama being enacted.[80]

This rather long description can be justified, it is hoped, by the great stress that is seen to be placed by primitive man on the dehistoricizing and therefore desecularizing of reality in worship. It is in complete contrast to the historicizing element in Israelite worship. The Hebrew verb *zakar* and the noun *zikkarōn* are frequently used in a cultic context. It has been the common explanation of scholars that these words indicate more than simply mental recall, "remembering." According to Ringgren they mean "the re-evoking of events so that they are made 'real' to the participants, whose life and action they can influence."[81] But the important point is that the events re-evoked are historical, not mythical. Numerous parallels can be shown to exist between the Hebrew Passover, for example, and the Babylonian *akitu* festival which we described above.[82] "The key element of the Israelite festival, however, has no parallel: the focal point of the Passover is an event thought to be historical, understood in 'mythological' categories as an act of God."[83] Kraus also noted that "Myth destroys history, and magic replaces a faith in God which was interpreted in Israel in an eminently personal way."[84] Worship in Israel was not an escape into mythical time, but an assertion of historical reality.

In a fairly recent monograph on the word "to remember" in the Old Testament, the German Willy Schottroff has proposed an explanation of the term as used in Deuteronomy that would further emphasize the secular "now" of the liturgy instead of a mythical *in diebus illis*. The word appears in Deuteronomy in tight association with the warning to follow the covenant stipulations. And these stipulations, in the Sinai covenant code as in the ancient Near Eastern treaty forms, are based on and derive their validity from some saving act of the initiator of the covenant, the great king, or, in the case of Israel, Yahweh. The Deuteronomist, then, is recalling the saving event, not to "renew" it or make it active here and now, but to inculcate covenant loyalty and the practice of those stipulations which must direct their lives in the present. In this understanding, the once-for-all character of the historical event is more clearly preserved.[85] This is a significant point in any discussion on secularity, since the absolute secularist would demand that a historical event exhaust its historicality in the historical moment of its happening.

Whether Schottroff's thesis will be accepted by the scholarly world remains to be seen. In my own opinion, the present reality, in some sense, of the past historical event seems to be emphasized by the Deuteronomist, as for example in his repeated use of the expression "this day" in referring to that event. Also, the thesis would have some repercussions on the understanding of the Christian celebration of the Lord's supper which is also a "memorial," although the Christian theist who accepts the Incarnation in its strictest sense would insist that the liturgical celebrations of the Old and New covenants cannot be exactly paralleled. At any rate, in any understanding of the details of the biblical ritual, there is a decisive difference from that of the ancient pagans. Pagan man escaped time and history in the liturgy; biblical man plunged more deeply into them.

We are approaching one of the bases for Israel's secularizing tendency when we consider the name of Israel's God. It was, as we shall see, the conception of God that influenced Israel's attitude to history. Hence, some insight into that attitude should emerge from the understanding of the divine name, since in Hebrew mentality, as is well known, the name stood for the person, describing his nature, his attributes or his mission.

We are a far way today from that philosophical explanation of the name Yahweh as revealed to Moses (Ex. 3:14) which held for an identification of the divine essence and existence. (Some basis for this might be found in the Wisdom of Solomon's translation of *ho ōn* [cf. 15:1], but the author is doubtless influenced by the Platonic philosophy of his day.) Even Albright's explanation of it as a Hiph'il causative form, suggesting God's creative activity,[86] has been apparently losing ground to a more existential one. Already in 1952 Martin Buber had proposed such an explanation:

> ... the deepest basis of the Jewish idea of God can be achieved only by plunging into that word by which God revealed Himself to Moses, "I shall be there." It gives exact expression to the personal "existence" of God (not to His abstract "being"), and expression even to His living presence, which most directly of all His attributes touches the man to whom He manifests Himself.[87]

John Courtney Murray developed this same idea suggesting this translation of the Hebrew phrase, "I shall be there as who I am shall I be there." The central portion of the expression retains something of the ineffable character of God's name, but the remainder is a strong assertion of the Lord's presence in history.[88]

Most recently Jürgen Moltmann dismisses the essentialist interpretation of the name in favor of the existentialist, but he gives it a future orientation in line with his theological position. "His name is a wayfaring name, a name of promise that discloses a new future, a name whose truth is experienced in history inasmuch as his promise discloses its future possibilities."[89]

In all of these explanations what is important is that the God of Israel is seen as affirming secular reality by asserting his presence in it. And it is the conviction of the Christian secular man that this divine acceptance of the world increases the secular potential rather than denies it. J. B. Metz indicated the full meaning of this divine acceptance by the coming of Jesus Christ: "To sum up, we can say: Through Jesus Christ, God's infinite 'Yes' to the finite world enters history (cf.

2 Cor. 1:19 f.). In this infinite Yes, the finite as such wins a presence, and a power which it could never have achieved of itself, since its own Yes to itself can never be more than finite."[90] We would add, then, that what was achieved in a climactic way in the Incarnation was already initiated by the saving immanence of Yahweh in the Old Testament, an immanence pointed to by his name.

If secularity is equated with autonomy, as has been our position, then we should be able to find more than a process of desacralization in the Scriptures; we should also expect strong statements on man's independence, or autonomy. The most frequently cited text in this regard is the passage in Genesis 1:26-28, where man's dominion over all the earth and everything in it is boldly asserted:

> Then God said, "Let us make man in our image, after our likeness; and let them have dominion over the fish of the sea, and over the birds of the air, and over the cattle, and over all the earth, and over every creeping thing that creeps upon the earth." So God created man in his own image, in the image of God he created him; male and female he created them. And God blessed them, and God said to them, "Be fruitful and multiply, and fill the earth and subdue it; and have dominion over the fish of the sea and over the birds of the air and over every living thing that moves upon the earth."

This is a clear affirmation of man's autonomy and, if we can translate the primitive concept of "earth" into the post-Copernican concept of "universe," it is one of the stronger expressions of secularity in the Bible.

These verses of Genesis gain greatly in significance when seen in the context of Psalm 8, which many exegetes consider a commentary on the passage in Genesis or at least containing a reference to it. (Much depends, of course, on the dating of both pieces as far as dependence is concerned, but no one would deny a relationship of some kind.) The psalm is a magnificent hymn or praise of God; this is its major emphasis, as the inclusion of vv. 1 and 9 indicates. The point must be kept in mind for a proper evaluation of the statement of human autonomy, as we shall see shortly. First, let us briefly consider the pertinent verses:

> When I look at the heavens, the work of thy fingers,
> the moon and the stars which thou hast established;
> what is man that thou art mindful of him,
> and the son of man that thou dost care for him?
> Yet thou hast made him little less than God,
> and dost crown him with glory and honor.
> Thou hast given him dominion over the works of thy hands;
> thou hast put all things under his feet,
> all sheep and oxen, and also the beasts of the field,

> the birds of the air, and the fish of the sea,
> whatever passes along the paths of the sea. (vv. 3-8)

While there is no doubt that the author is astonished at the dominion given man by God, there is equally no doubt in his mind about the fact of that dominion over the rest of creation. The question that most readily comes to mind is whether the fact of dominion must be vastly tempered by the reality of man's fallen state. Franz Delitzsch raised this question in the light of Genesis 3, where the perversion of man's glorious state is described.[91] A certain polarity has, as a matter of fact, been introduced into the consideration of man by the realization and candid formulation of his sinful condition by the Yahwist, as well as by other sacred authors. This polarity runs through the whole of the Bible, even through the New Testament where it has, in fact, been intensified by the eschatological fulfillment wrought by Jesus Christ. And Christian theology has continued the polarity by emphasizing now the one, now the other aspect of man.

To my mind, however, Kraus is perfectly correct when he says that man's guilt is as little in view here in Psalm 8 as it is in Genesis 1, whence it would be false to the author to interpret the verses concerned in the sense of a primitive condition later annulled by sin. "Rather, all that is said in Gen. 1 and Ps. 8 about man's eminence refers to an absolutely valid constitution of God's that cannot be annulled."[92] This is substantiated, it would seem, by the fact that the final editor of the book of Genesis, who was quite aware of the Yahwist's story of sin, had no hesitation in adding the Priestly author's story of creation without qualification. In other words, he would appear to say, as does the psalmist, that God's gift, while it may not always be correctly used by man, as the story of mankind in Genesis 3-11 graphically portrays, is an unretractable gift that man can always claim.

What is stated in Psalm 8 about man is said, it must be noted, about man in general, "the son of man," an expression used to bring out the frailty of the human condition. But it is precisely this frail human being, or *Menschlein* as Martin Buber has translated the phrase,[93] that is extolled as "little less than God."[94] When we contrast this with the general ancient Near Eastern picture of human autonomy, the biblical emphasis is considerably heightened.

Kraus notes two characteristics of ancient Near Eastern anthropology. The first is that only the king is man in the fullest sense. "In ancient Sumer he is called *lugal*—'the great man.' The king stands in the closest relationship to the gods. He is begotten by the heavenly powers, nursed and raised by the goddesses. The divine king alone bears the radiant crown of the heavenly world. He can be designated as the 'image of the gods.' The Egyptian king was formed by the gods 'according to their own beauty.' The divine king, therefore, is the perfect man...."[95] The second characteristic is the relative unimportance granted the individual man. Any participation by him in the world of the gods is only indirect or relative. While there are references to man's divine race and origin, these appear in the myths as "gloomy forebodings" and "stand in sharp contrast to the self-criticisms as they otherwise appear in the cultic hymns."[96] In the light of such an anthropology we can only be more impressed by the biblical image of the "son of man" who is made a "little less than God" and given dominion over the rest of creation. Psalm 8, therefore, stands out as a forceful expression of human secularity or autonomy.

But, as we have insisted, it is a relative autonomy. For a necessary component of this autonomy is the fact that it is a gift of God: "*thou hast made him little less than God.*" This, as numerous commentators on the psalm have noted, distinguishes biblical anthropology from that of Hellenism, whose classic expression is found in Sophocles' *Antigone*: "Many great things abound, but nothing is greater than man" (332). The psalmist, on the other hand, precludes any self-deception on the part of man by placing these verses on man's glory and dominion firmly within the context of God's transcendent glory and dominion.

> The difference between the Greek and biblical estimates of man is demonstrated by the very fact that in the Old Testament human dignity has no value of its own, but has value only because it is a gift from God... *In spite of* (italics added) his insignificance man has been appointed by God to have dominion over the earth. The poet pursues this thought in great detail in order to be able to grasp to the fullest extent the grandeur of that miracle. The Lord of the universe has entrusted man even with the divine function of governing... According to the Old Testament faith, man has not gained power over Nature by means of a titanic rebellion against the Deity, but he receives dominion over "the works of his hands," as a commission given to him by God; and it is *God's* will that all things be subject to man, and it is by virtue of *God's* might that all things are subject to man. It has not come about by chance that the aforementioned Greek interpretation of culture, which made man entirely dependent of his own strength, ended in tragedy, whereas the biblical interpretation still represents even today the religious foundation on which all truly creative culture can be built.[97]

Autonomy or secularity, in the biblical sense, is necessarily integrated into the transcendent order of God's covenant love.

A similar though more primitive expression of this autonomy of man is found in the Yahwist's story of creation. All are acquainted with the account of God's intention to make man "a helper fit for him" (Gen. 2:18). We read that God, in pursuing this intent, created all the beasts of the field and birds of the air, "and brought them to the man to see what he would call them; and whatever the man called every living creature, that was its name. The man gave names to all cattle, and to the birds of the air, and to every beast of the field..." (2:19-

20). According to primitive mentality, to bestow a name is to exercise dominion and authority. It may also contain the idea that man "must accept and establish his lordship by his own free acts."[98]

(We can add here, incidentally, that the Pastoral Constitution on the Church in the Modern World offers a rich commentary on the mandate in Genesis, explaining it in a way that is consonant with both autonomy and integration.[99] The entire document is conceived on the basis of an anthropocentric approach that is fully in accord with the contemporary emphasis on secularity. Note such statements as these: "According to the almost unanimous opinion of believers and unbelievers alike, all things on earth should be related to man as their center and crown" (#12) and "... there is a growing awareness of the exalted dignity proper to the human person, since he stands above all things..." (#26). Moreover, the word "autonomy," or its equivalent, is used in a number of places to describe the role of man in creation.)

The texts of Genesis are obviously important and no exact parallel to them can be found in the extra-biblical literature of the ancient Near East. They are, therefore, illustrations of the unique dignity seen by the biblical authors to be inherent in man. The conviction of this dignity would have influenced greatly the secularizing process, as we have already seen in the case of Joshua 24, and as is reflected in the distinct role given to women, such as Sarah, Miriam, Deborah and Hannah in the history of salvation. The process would reach its climactic development in the Pauline anthropology where no distinctions remain to hinder man's proper exercise of his dignity.[100]

Closely bound up with this autonomy and contributing to its meaning in the biblical view is the freedom in which man is constituted. We have already referred to this briefly in our comments on Joshua 24. This freedom is inextricably linked up with the covenant between Yahweh and Israel, a covenant whose literary expression has been found to have particular parallels in the treaties between the Hittite emperors and their vassal nations. In other words, a relationship is founded between two responsible parties and, even though the covenant is conditioned on Israel's response, there is no blind destiny forcing Israel into the contract.

Israel's understanding of covenant freedom cannot be understood outside the context of the sanctions—the curses and blessings—which are a constant element in such treaties. An elaborated form of them can be found in Deuteronomy 28. In these we can see an exposition of what modern, secular man would have to agree is the fullest manifestation of secular reality, the object of the exercise of his autonomy, a fullness of being in all its dimensions. What is distinctive in the biblical view, of course, is that fullness of being is predicated on integration into the order of the covenant, an integration which, just as it presupposes man's response in freedom, also does not diminish the exercise of that freedom. The Deuteronomist was heir to the prophetic reaction to a *do ut des* conception of the covenant; it is impossible that he would have proposed now a magical or automatic bestowal of blessings or curses in violation of that freedom.

In the light of what we have said, there can be found in Israel's theology of freedom, covenant and sanctions a basis for the distinctions made at the beginning of this paper. The secular represents the autonomy of man expressed most surely in that free response to Yahweh as a result of which he achieves a fullness of being. There is no sacral reality which automatically assures blessing or curse outside the framework of freedom. But freedom is exercised most profoundly and most properly in responding to a transcendent Lord's saving presence in created reality, therefore in acceptance of a sacred reality. In such free response and acceptance man achieves perfect secularity, the full autonomy of his being that manifests itself ultimately in the fullness of all being, of all profane reality. In this sense can it be said that Jesus Christ, who freely and totally accepted the will of his Father and who manifested this by the fullness of being that he brought to others, depicted by the evangelists in his miracles, and to himself, realized in resurrection, was the perfect secular man.

NOTES

[1] Dietrich Bonhoeffer, *Letters and Papers From Prison*, London, 1953.
[2] Bonhoeffer, *op. cit.*, p. 92.
[3] Bonhoeffer, *op. cit.*, pp. 106 f. (italics added). This is an important observation of Bonhoeffer's and should be kept in mind for our later discussion of terminology.
[4] Bonhoeffer, *op. cit.*, p. 121.
[5] Bonhoeffer, *op. cit.*, p. 122.
[6] John A. T. Robinson, *Honest To God*, London, 1963.
[7] Cf. J. Lawrence in *Honest To God and the Debate*, London, 1963, p. 155.
[8] Cf. the remarks of H. McCabe, O.P., in *Honest To God and the Debate*, p. 166.
[9] Harvey Cox, *The Secular City*, New York, 1965 .
[10] E. L. Mascall, *The Secularization of Christianity*, New York, 1966.
[11] Mascall, *op. cit.*, pp. 1-39.
[12] Mascall, *op. cit.*, pp. 40-189.
[13] Mascall, *op. cit.*, pp. 190-212.
[14] Mascall, *op. cit.*, pp. 213-282.
[15] It is interesting to note that, in an article devoted to the discussion of academic freedom in the universities, Leslie Dewart uses as the title of his study, "Autonomy: The Key Word in Secularism." Cf. K. T. Hargrove (ed.), *The Paradox of Religious Secularity*, Englewood Cliffs, N.J., 1968, p. 177.
[16] H. de Lubac, *The Mystery of the Supernatural*, New York, 1967, p. xi.
[17] de Lubac, *op. cit.*, pp. xi f.
[18] John Macquarrie, *God and Secularity*, (*New Directions in Theology Today*, Vol. III), Philadelphia, 1967.

[19] Robert L. Richards, S.J., *Secularization Theology*, New York, 1967.
[20] Cf. Erich Fromm (ed.), *Socialist Humanism*, Garden City, N.Y., 1966, p. 144.
[21] Martin Buber, *Eclipse of God*, New York, 1957, p. 105.
[22] G. von Rad, *Old Testament Theology*, Vol. I, New York, 1962, pp. 36-68.
[23] *Ibid.*, p. 39, n. 4.
[24] *Ibid.*, pp. 38 f.
[25] *Ibid.*, p. 50.
[26] *Ibid.*, p. 53.
[27] "The Literary Characteristics of Genesis 2-3," *TS*, 15, 1954, p. 549.
[28] *ANET*, p. 95.
[29] *Ibid.*
[30] *ANET*, p. 68.
[31] *Genesis*, Philadelphia, 1961, p. 76.
[32] D. J. McCarthy, S.J., "'Creation' Motifs in Ancient Hebrew Poetry," *CBQ*, XXIX, 1967, 3, pp. 87-100.
[33] McCarthy, p. 90.
[34] McCarthy, p. 100.
[35] *Genesis (The Anchor Bible)*, New York, 1964, p. 16.
[36] *Christianity in World History*, Edinburgh, 1964, p. 71.
[37] Cf. comment by Speiser, *op. cit.*, p. 20.
[38] *Genesis*, p. 77.
[39] S. G. F. Brandon, *Creation Legends of the Ancient Near East*, London, 1963, pp. 17 f.
[40] *ANET*, p. 61.
[41] *NRT*, 79, pt. 1, 1957, p. 37.
[42] *Genesis*, p. 75.
[43] Van Leeuwen, *op. cit.*, p. 78.
[44] A. van der Voort, S.C.J., "*Génèse I, la á II, 4a et le Psaume CIV*," *RB*, 58, 1951, p. 325.
[45] *Ibid.*, p. 326.
[46] W. F. Albright, *Yahweh and the Gods of Canaan*, Garden City, N.Y., 1968, pp. 184 f.
[47] "Scripture and the Nature of Man" (to be published).
[48] Albright, *op. cit.*, p. 184.
[49] M. Eliade, *Myths, Dreams and Mysteries*, London, 1960.
[50] B. S. Childs, *Myth and Reality in the Old Testament*, (Studies in Biblical Theology, No. 27), London, 1960.
[51] Eliade, *op. cit.*, p. 23.
[52] *Ibid.*
[53] *Ibid.*
[54] *Ibid.*
[55] *Ibid.*, p. 24.
[56] *Ibid.*, pp. 25 f.
[57] Kenneth Heinitz, "The Theology of Hope, According to Ernst Bloch," *Dialog*, 7, 1968, p. 37.
[58] *Ibid.*, p. 38.
[59] Eliade, *op. cit.*, p. 14 f. (italics his, as always, unless otherwise noted).
[60] *Ibid.*, p. 16.

[61] Cf. note 50.
[62] Childs, *op. cit.*, p. 13.
[63] *Ibid.*, p. 14.
[64] *Ibid.*, p. 15.
[65] *Ibid.*, p. 15.
[66] *Ibid.*, p. 18.
[67] *Ibid.*
[68] *Ibid.*, p. 29.
[69] *Ibid.*, p. 20.
[70] *Theology of Hope*, London, 1967, p. 208.
[71] G. von Rad, "There Remains Still a Rest for the People of God: an Investigation of a Biblical Conception," in *The Problem of the Hexateuch and Other Studies*, Edinburgh, 1966, p. 95.
[72] Von Rad, *op. cit.*, p. 95.
[73] W. Zimmerli, *1. Mose 1-îl, Die Urgeschichte*, I Teil, Zurich, 1943, p. 121.
[74] Cf. Zimmerli, *op. cit.*, pp. 121 f.; von Rad, "There Remains...." p. 102.
[75] Von Rad, *ibid.*
[76] The following eight paragraphs are taken from a lecture given by the author at the Athenaeum of Ohio and printed privately.
[77] Cf. M. Eliade, *Cosmos and History*, New York, 1954, pp. 30 f. Much of this is based on Eliade's study.
[78] *Ibid.*
[79] *Ibid.*, pp. 34 f.
[80] *Ibid.*, pp. 55 ff.; for a fuller treatment, cf. H. Frankfort, *Kingship and the Gods*, Chicago, 1948, pp. 313-333.
[81] H. Ringgren *Israelite Religion*, London, 1966, p. 187.
[82] Some of these parallels can be found in Ringgren, *op. cit..*, p. 188.
[83] *Ibid.*
[84] H.-J. Kraus, *Worship in Israel*, Richmond, 1966, p. 21.
[85] Cf. W. Schottroff, *"Gedenken" im Alten Orient und in Alten Testament*, (*Wissenschaftliche Monographien zum Alten und Neuen Testament*, 15. Band), Neukirchen-Vluyn, 1964, pp. 117-126.
[86] W. F. Albright, *From the Stone Age to Christianity*, 2nd ed., Garden City, N.Y., 1957, pp. 15 f. It should be noted, however, that Dr. Albright vigorously champions his interpretation most recently in *Yahweh and the Gods of Canaan*, pp. 168 ff.
[87] *Eclipse of God*, pp. 61 f.
[88] J. C. Murray, S.J., *The Problem of God*, New Haven, 1964, p. 10. The author gives an analysis of the three parts of the expression which would be helpful in the contemporary discussion. He writes: "The text, thus understood, contains a threefold revelation—of God's immanence in history, of his transcendence to history, and of his transparence through history."
[89] *Theology of Hope*, p. 30.
[90] "A Believer's Look at the World," in *The Christian and the World, Readings in Theology*, New York, 1965, p. 78.
[91] Cf. H.-J. Kraus, *Psalmen, Biblischer Kommentar Altes Testament*, Neukirchen Kreis Moers, 1958, p. 72.
[92] *Ibid.*, p. 72.
[93] Cf. A. Deissler, *Die Psalmen*, I. Teil (Ps. 1-41), Düsseldorf, 1964, pp. 46 f.

[94] The word *elohim* is variously translated, as "God," "divine being," "angels," etc. We have adopted the translation of the RSV as more in line with the Priestly author's emphasis in *Genesis* 1:26-28.

[95] Kraus, *op. cit.*, p. 73.

[96] *Ibid.*

[97] A. Weiser, *The Psalms*, Philadelphia, 1962, pp. 144 f.

[98] G. Montague, S.M., *The Biblical Theology of the Secular*, Milwaukee, 1968, p. 17.

[99] Cf. Part I, chapter III.

[100] Cf. Gal. 3:23-29.

Jewish-Christian Dialogue: Early Church versus Contemporary Christianity

Walter J. Burghardt

As I see it, a potentially fruitful approach to the Christian-Jewish problematic should have for its springboard the factual present, dares not disregard the pertinent past, and must look creatively to the future. In consequence, I shall develop my argument through three main sections. First, I shall summarize the situation of the contemporary Jew in America. Second, I shall sketch some shadows from the distant past which helped create our frightening impasse, and some light from the recent past which augurs the dawn of a different future. Third, I shall affirm and briefly explain a handful of propositions which seem to me not simply defensible but indispensable if we are to have a creative, fruitful, even orthodox Christian theology of the Jew. I shall close with several questions to my Jewish brothers and sisters—not to harass them, but to make it possible for me to understand them as they understand themselves.

I. THE CONTEMPORARY JEW IN AMERICA[1]

IN the United States there are close to 6 million Jews, a litttle less than 3% of the American population, almost half the total number of Jews in the world. At least 75% are native-born, so that divisions based on immigration are rapidly becoming extinct, and approaches to self-identity are shaped less than ever by European experiences. Almost half live in the greater metropolitan area of New York City, 70% in the Northeastern States, 90% in or around the larger cities—so that the American Jews have become what Americans on the whole are becoming, a suburban-urban people. And they are well educated: in 1960, for example, 62% of Jews between 18 and 25 were in college or graduate school, compared to 26% of the general population.

The result of urbanization and education is reflected in the high position of Jews in America's middle-class economy. Per capita, Jews earn more than any other religious or ethnic group except Episcopalians. They far outstrip Catholics and Protestants in the white-collar occupations (78%, 33%, 32% of each group respectively) and in the professions (18%, 9%, 10%). Jews provide America with 16.3% of her doctors, 10.9% of her lawyers, 8% of her college graduates.

"One might expect," Rabbi Arthur Gilbert muses, "that a people who embraced America with such love, whose values relate with such affinity to those that provide America her uniqueness and greatness, who have distinguished themselves so brilliantly in the cultural and educational and economic life of this country, would be held in the highest esteem. Not so...."[2]

The obstacle is the pervasive presence of anti-Semitism. On the whole, the Jews have not been accepted by the social leaders of American society. Social-distance scales reveal that their fellow citizens rank Jews only above Mexicans, Japanese, Negroes, Czechs, Armenians, and Russians. A recent sampling of 1152 city and country clubs disclosed that 66% practiced discrimination on religious grounds. Some private employment agencies discriminate against Jews. And there are the endless anti-Semitic incidents: violation of cemeteries, desecration of synagogues, flaunting of swastikas, and so on.

Many sociologists agree that anti-Semitism is presently on a downgrade in America. They point to an amazing drop in anti-Semitic attitudes. Thus, whereas in 1940, 63% of Americans found "objectionable qualities" in Jews, by 1962 the number had decreased to 22%. But still the Jews on the whole remain uneasy. They admit that there is relatively little of the traditional "Christ-killer" cry; but they point out that the antipathy is more subtle, more refined—as in the deliberate exclusion of Jews from critical areas of social existence. They find it significant and discouraging that the mid-40's was the highest point of American anti-Semitism; Hitler's inhuman genocide won little or no sympathy for Jews in the United States.

Nor is it clear what lies behind the recent decrease in anti-Semitic attitudes. Is it the new ecumenical atmosphere, or is it rather an ever-increasing secularization of American society? Is it because Jews are less Jewish and Christians are less Christian? One development is startlingly clear: the young Jew is more secure, less suspicious. Jewish teen-agers, more than their parents, affirm the importance of Jewish survival, less often insist on remaining Jews because of the Christian world's hostility, have a deeper conviction that Judaism should be perpetuated for its heritage and the unique contribution it can make to society, are less likely to attribute anti-Semitism to jealousy or religious bigotry. "The majority of teenagers believe that prejudice results from ignorance and that better education and the expansion of our democratic institutions are the solution to the problem. They are more optimistic and less skeptical, less fearful and more trusting than their parents."[3]

What can be said about the religious character of American Jews? Four sets of facts merit mention. First, there has been a fantastic growth in synagogue affiliation. The young Jew is more inclined to define his Jewishness in religious terms and to view the synagogue as the basic institution of identification and affiliation. Second, there is a deepened commitment to Jewish education. Jews in America today maintain the largest voluntary system of education ever achieved by any Jewish community in Western civilization: 600,000 students are enrolled in 3,000 Jewish educational units involving 17,000 adult teaching positions. Third, there is serious criticism of curriculum, a serious effort to update it: for example, to confront the distinctive world view and the ethical approach of biblical Judaism with contemporary research and new conditions. Freedom of inquiry is held precious and is encouraged. Fourth, it can be argued that while Catholics are trying to accept a secularization process within their religion, Jews are anxious to bring more religion into their secularity.

What is puzzling to many Jewish observers is whether all this is evidence of a new religious vitality, or a sanctified overlay on an American form of secular religiousness. Ethnicity has given way in America to religiosity; but while religion is required in America as a vehicle of identification and belonging, it is too often a religion without content, personal involvement, faith, and commitment. Still, as Gilbert sees it, each of Jewry's religious communities houses a sizable remnant whose religious quest is profound and sincere. Moreover, Jewish laymen are asking questions that the rabbis are not capable of answering. "For me this is a sign that God is breaking through the fixed institutional forms of the Synagogue. His presence is stirring hearts and minds and we have reason to expect, therefore, a genuine renascence of religion in the years to come."[4]

Many Jews, but not all, support and participate in the interreligious dialogue of our day. Such involvement has impelled them to a deeper commitment to Judaism, the while it has stimulated them to raise many of the gut questions Christians are asking: What can we believe about God? What is the relationship between Judaism and Christianity? Highly important is the motivation behind this involvement: in part at least, the growing realization that "we have reached that point in world history where men will either accept their neighbor as brother, or destroy themselves."⁵ In this connection Gilbert recalls the Hasidic tale translated and repeated by Martin Buber:

> A young student after much anguish knocked on the door of his rabbi. He cried out: "Rabbi, I have eyes to see, ears to hear, and a mind to understand, yet I do not know for what purpose I was created or what meaning there is in my life." The rabbi answered: "Foolish one, neither do I know the purpose of existence, but come let us break bread together."

Finally, many a Jew has discovered that he must re-evaluate his pre-Auschwitz optimism. "For some the survival of Jews from the crematoria is a sign of God's benevolence, a testimony to His active and transcendental presence, a witness to the meaning of Jewish particularity. But for other Jews, God died in Auschwitz, strangling, gasping for breath along with His people."⁶

II. THE DISTANT AND RECENT PAST

So MUCH for the situation of the contemporary Jew in America. I shall now sketch some shadows from the distant past which helped create our frightening impasse, and some light from the recent past which augurs the dawn of a different future.

I shall not attempt the impossible task of reviewing the history of Christian-Jewish confrontation. I shall go back to the era I know best, the early patristic age, the first two postscriptural centuries, because here is where the lines of division were clearly drawn, here is where certain attitudes hardened which were to be programmatic for the future. As I read the evidence, three reasons more than any others motivated the Christian antagonism towards the Jew: (1) Christians were convinced that "the Jews" were responsible for the crucifixion of Christ; (2) Christians were convinced that the Jews as a people had been rejected by God; (3) Christians were convinced that Jews were responsible for the persecution of Christians by the Roman state. Each of these reasons calls for brief documentation, from different decades and from various areas of the Christian population.

The first reason for early Christian antagonism towards the Jews: Christians were convinced that "the Jews" were responsible for the crucifixion of Christ. Not solely responsible, of course; but still genuinely responsible. The texts are fairly frequent and they are unambiguous. Not all need be cited, but some should be, if only to concretize what can be dreadfully abstract, to hear from their own lips how some early Christians felt.⁷

The earliest Christian apology preserved through the ages stems from about the year 140, from a native of Athens named Aristides. In his search for the true religion via the correct concept of God, Aristides pays tribute to the Jews, as over against barbarians and

Greeks, for their purer conception of the divine nature and for their superior standards of morality. And still he insists: "God came down from heaven ... clothed Himself with flesh from a Hebrew virgin ... was born of the race of the Hebrews ... was pierced by the Jews and died and was buried."[8] The pertinent point here is an early Christian paradox: Aristides was not personally hostile towards Jews, but he was convinced that "the Jews" shared responsibility for the crucifixion of Christ—on the basis of what sounds like a creedal formula of his day.

A decade or two later, Justin Martyr, most competent of the second-century apologists for Christianity, refused to concede what he called a Jewish objection based on a Christian belief: that because Christ's crucifixion was necessary in God's design, the responsibility cannot be laid at anyone's door. No, says Justin: "although he suffered for mankind according to the will of the Father Himself, it was not in obedience to the will of God that you made Him suffer."[9]

Irenaeus of Lyons, in the last quarter of the second century, spoke with even greater clarity. The first of Christian theologians, he is strong indeed in his interpretation of the crucifixion. The Jews who killed Christ he compares to Cain, in that "they put the just one to death" and "their hands are full of blood." Oh yes, their action fits into God's plan of redemption, but this does not lessen their responsibility, does not deliver them from God's wrath. They dealt with Christ as they did because they did not believe in Him. They took Him prisoner and they crucified Him; for it was they who compelled Pilate against his will to deliver Christ to death. For this rejection of Christ all the Jews were responsible: the people because they did not know Him, the priests because they attacked Him.[10]

Hippolytus, writing from Rome in the early decades of the third century, claimed that it was not only the Pharisees who refused to believe in Christ; all of the sons of Israel saw God in this world and failed to put their faith in Him. In this attitude towards Christ, the Jews dishonored God the Father and severed themselves from God's mercy. The Jews killed Christ, were responsible for His death. Why did they kill him? Because they were disappointed in Him, the man they imagined had come to create a community on earth alone. Types of the fratricidal Jews were Cain and Esau; a sign of the Passion and its perpetrators was the paschal lamb killed by the Jews each year.[11]

In the middle of the third century Origen, most prolific and creative of the early Greek theologians, continued this line of thought. That the Jews crucified Christ is, he insisted, a matter of public Christian confession. Greater responsibility indeed falls on the rulers, on the priests, scribes, Pharisees; but it was "the people" that killed Christ. Try as they might to shed their guilt, either on the ground that they were not free agents because Christ's death had to happen in harmony with God's knowledge and will, or on the ground that Christ actually suffered no pain because He went to His passion willingly and with resignation, it still remains true that the Jewish people were responsible for the death of Christ.[12]

In this connection the New Testament Apocrypha are fascinating and important. These works have not been recognized by the Christian Church as inspired documents; within Catholicism they do not have the same value as the writings of the orthodox Fathers; but still they are indispensable as evidence. For the Apocrypha are often an effort to fill up the gaps in the canonical literature; they stem from the people and are destined for the people; and so they are at once more representative of the popular mentality and more influential in their appeal than the works of the theologians.

One example must suffice. The *Gospel according to Peter* stems from a writer with obvious anti-Jewish sentiments; it evidences an anti-Jewish feeling in Asia Minor before the rebellion of Bar-Cochba that is hard to estimate but cannot fail to trouble a Christian heart. It stems from a milieu that stressed the role of the Jews in the death of Christ according to the plan of God. Pilate and the Romans are exonerated; Christ is judged by the Jews, delivered by them to execution; in all the scenes of the Passion the executioners are the Jews. Even Christ's prayer for His executioners is omitted.[13]

There is evidence, from the Apocrypha, of sufficient wisdom within much of the Christian populace to distinguish Jewish authorities from the common people. On broad lines, however, I think it can be said that the masses of Christianity saw the Jewish people contemporary with Christ as (*a*) unbelievers (*b*) responsible for the crucifixion. Harshness and vehemence are relatively rare, but the basic sentiment is unmistakable: the Jewish people of Jesus' time shared in the guilt of His death.[14]

With these convictions, is it strange that Christians of the first three centuries were antagonistic to Jews?

A second reason for early Christian antagonism towards the Jews: Christians were convinced that the Jews as a people had been rejected by God; they had lost their precious prerogative, had ceased to be the people of God. Having rejected God, they have in turn been rejected by God.

In the theology of Justin, for example, the Christians are now the people of God; they have taken the place, the rights, the privileges of the children of Israel. They have inherited the promises made to Abraham and his heirs—promises that can no longer be fulfilled in the Jews. The Christians are now the true Israelites. From the Old Testament itself he concludes that "there were two seeds of Judah and two races, as there are two houses of Jacob: the one born of flesh and blood, the other of faith and the Spirit."[15] Rejected for their sins, however, the Jews were not forsaken: they could still be saved, if they became part of God's new people. They did not really know God, because they did not really understand the Scriptures; they did not understand the Scriptures, because they did not apply the Scriptures to Christ.[16]

Not much later, basically the same doctrine of rejection appears in Irenaeus. One text in this regard is particularly expressive of his mind —and especially pertinent because it stems from a work which reveals how Christianity was preached in Lyons during the last two decades of the second century:

> But Moses also says in Deuteronomy that the Gentiles are to become "the head," and an unbelieving people "the tail" [Dt. 28:44], and again says: "Ye have made me jealous with what were no gods, and have angered me with your idols; and I will make you jealous with that which is no people, and will anger you with a foolish nation" [Dt. 32:21]. Because they had left the real God and were giving service to unreal gods, and they had slain the prophets of God and were prophesying for Baal, to whom the Chanaanites had an idol; despising also the real Son of God, they rejected Him, but were choosing Barabbas, a robber taken in murder, and they denied the eternal king and were acknowledging the temporal Caesar as their king—God was pleased to grant His inheritance to the foolish Gentiles, and to those who were not God's citizens, and know not who God is. Since, then, life has been given to us through this calling, and God has restored again in us Abraham's faith in Him, we should no more turn back, I mean to the former legislation....[17]

Hippolytus writes in a familiar strain, but at times with harsh accents. The strain is familiar: the Jews, in their lack of faith, put Christ to death, and they are being punished accordingly. Glorious in their election, in being a chosen people, a holy race, they have proved false to their calling. Here the accents are harsh; for the Jews are depicted as wicked in proportion to their prosperity, stubborn and cunning, with no fear of God or shame before men, without understanding or gratitude, in love with this world, with an ungodly self-reliance. In consequence of their iniquity, they were justifiably rejected.[18]

Clement of Alexandria, sometimes called "the first Christian scholar," discusses the Jews in a vein rather distinctive in this period, an approach expected of a scholar: an effort to be objective, a calm reasonableness. His references to the Jews, however, are only occasional, rather incidental. And here he does no more than continue the theology of the past: (a) the past history of the Jews, their rejection of Christ, merited for them the punishment of God; (b) Christianity continues Judaism by replacing and supplanting it.[19]

Origen, with his intense love for Scripture, speaks in high terms of the role of the Jews in God's plan for humanity, of their past glory, of their future salvation. Nevertheless, his theological position is quite harsh. Jerusalem was destroyed, the Jews were dispersed, their condition is humble, they are in darkness, they will continue to live as fugitives and exiles, subject to their enemies and deprived of the salvific hope that comes from holy men—all because they sinned, specifically in putting Christ to death. They have been repudiated by God, are no longer His people.[20]

With these convictions, is it strange that Christians of the first three centuries were antagonistic to Jews?

A third reason for early Christian antagonism towards the Jews: Christians (not all, but in significant numbers) were convinced that Jews were responsible for the persecution of Christians by the Roman state. Not solely responsible, not even primarily responsible, but still responsible, in that Jews at times instigated persecution, at times concurred in persecution, at times applauded persecution. The texts that count for evidence are numerous enough; I shall highlight this aspect of the problem by focusing on one piece of vivid testimony, the *Martyrdom of Polycarp*.

The *Martyrdom* is a letter from the Christian community of Smyrna in Asia Minor to the Christian community of Philomelium in Greater Phrygia. It recounts in detail the hunt, capture, and death by fire of a single individual, Polycarp, Bishop of Smyrna and perhaps the most significant Christian in Asia Minor. The date of the letter is 156, the same year Polycarp was put to death. Though usually listed in the category "acts of the martyrs," the document does not reproduce official court proceedings but the reports, recollections, and even prejudices of eyewitnesses.[21]

From the narrative we gather that the persecution in Smyrna had first resulted in the death of several Christians. The pagan populace, surprised and disappointed at the courage of these martyrs, clamored for the blood of Polycarp, head of the Christian community. The policemen began to search him out, found him at a farm not far from the city, tried to persuade him to say "Caesar is Lord." Failing in this, they brought him to the arena, where "the uproar was so tremendous that no one could be heard." In the arena the proconsul commanded Polycarp: "Swear by the Fortune of Caesar; revile Christ." The old man replied: "For six and eighty years I have been serving Him, and He has done no wrong to me. How, then, dare I blaspheme my King who has saved me?" The proconsul sent his herald to the center of the arena to proclaim three times: "Polycarp has confessed to being a Christian." And at this point in the account comes the first of three phrases that are of high significance for the Jewish-Christian problematic:

> Upon this announcement of the herald, the whole multitude of heathens *and of Jews* living at Smyrna shouted with uncontrolled anger and at the top of their voices: "This is the teacher of Asia, the father of the Christians, the destroyer of our gods! He teaches many not to sacrifice and not to worship!"[22]

It was decided to burn Polycarp alive. Quickly the crowds gathered logs and firewood from the shops and the baths. And at this point in the account comes the second phrase that is of high significance for us: "And the Jews, too, *as is their custom,* were particularly zealous in lending a hand."[23]

Polycarp was fastened to the pyre, hands behind him, and the fire was lit. As the story has it, the fire would not consume him, simply surrounded his body as with a wall; so the people commanded an executioner to run a dagger through him. The Christians naturally wanted to reclaim his body; but Nicetas, father of the police chief, pleaded with the magistrate not to surrender it. If you do, he predicted, the Christians "will abandon the Crucified and worship this man in good earnest." And at this point comes the third phrase of high significance:

> This he said *at the urgent representations of the Jews,* who were again on the alert when we intended to take him out of the fire. They did not realize that we shall never bring ourselves either to abandon Christ ... or to worship any other.... When the centurion noticed the contentiousness of the Jews, he declared the body public property and, according to their custom, burnt it.[24]

Given the high position Polycarp occupied in the ecclesiastical life of second-century Syria, and given the (presumably) wide circulation of the letter describing his death, the document must have exercised a powerful influence in fanning anti-Jewish sentiment among Christians in Asia Minor and Syria. More sobering still, the antagonism must already, antecedently, have been bitter indeed, when the writer(s) could affirm not only that the Jews played a part, a loud and angry and influential part, in the persecution of Polycarp, in his death, but that this sort of activity was habitual with them; this is the kind of thing they used to do.

The accusation that Jews were prominent in the persecution of Christians was not confined to the *Martyrdom of Polycarp;* it recurred time and again in the course of the first three centuries. It emerged soon after 150 in Justin, who charged the Jews with "killing and punishing us"—for example, in the guerilla war against the Romans from 132 to 135.[25] It was repeated around 204 by Hippolytus, who charged bluntly that "the Church is oppressed and distressed by Jews."[26] It cropped up about 213 in the uncompromising North African controversialist Tertullian, who saved at least one of his lapidary phrases for the Jews: *synagogas Iudaeorum fontes persecutionum* ("the synagogues of the Jews, the fountainheads of [the?] persecutions")— perhaps in reference to the original opposition of Jews to the apostles in the time of the New Testament.[27] It was reflected in the middle of the third century when Cyprian, Bishop of Carthage, told Pope Cornelius that Jews as well as Gentiles "threaten" the Christians.[28] And near that same mid-century the progressive Origen, in the most famous apology before Nicaea, compared his Neoplatonist adversary Celsus to the Jews:

> He seems to have behaved in much the same way as the Jews who, when the teaching of Christianity began to be proclaimed, spread abroad a malicious rumor about the gospel, to the effect that Christians sacrifice a child and partake of its flesh, and again that when the followers of the gospel want to do the works of darkness they turn out the light and each man has sexual intercourse with the first woman he meets. This malicious rumor some time ago unreasonably influenced a very large number and persuaded people knowing nothing of the gospel that this was really the character of Christians. And even now it still deceives some who by such stories are repelled from approaching Christians even if only for a simple conversation.[29]

With such convictions, is it strange that Christians of the first three centuries were antagonistic to Jews?[30]

To complete this distressing picture, one ought to present more profoundly than I can do here the reasons which motivated Jewish antagonism towards Christians in the early centuries of our common era. A first reason may have been the early Jewish tradition about Jesus, as this can be recaptured from rabbinical literature. The evidence, however, is difficult to interpret, and I content myself with the sober conclusions of a scholar who after forty years limited drastically the number of passages that assuredly speak of Jesus: "[These passages] inform us of a person who was called Jeshu Hanotzri, who had disciples, in whose name his followers cured or attempted to cure sick persons, who practiced magic and deceived and led astray Israel, and who was tried and put to death for so doing."[31] There was indeed in the rabbinical schools a tradition about the historical Jesus of Nazareth, but the contents of that tradition were very meager. The rabbis of the second and third centuries "were quite aware that Jesus had lived and taught, but they attached very little importance to that fact, and took but slight interest in him."[32] One might plausibly argue, therefore, that the rabbinical attitude towards Jesus was calculated to engender in the Jewish people not hostility towards Christians but curiosity or indifference.

A more likely source of Jewish antagonism is the early rabbinical attitude towards Jewish Christians. Since the word "Christians" does not occur in the Talmud, a crucial issue is the meaning of the word "Minim." Does it mean (or at least include) Judeo-Christians, or Gentile Christians, or Gnostics? The problem is unsettled and unsettling, especially since the Minim, as a potential peril to Judaism, were regarded with aversion, hostility, dread, even at times hatred. Without arguing the case here, I see the following affirmations as historically defensible. (1) It is dangerous to speak of Minim as if it referred to a particular system or a precise tendency, as one might speak of Pharisaism or Essenism. (2) Minim covers quite different realities according to different times and places, and it is not always possible to clarify the exact usage. (3) The Minim are sometimes Judeo-Christians, but not necessarily to the exclusion of Gnostics, given the presence of Gnostic currents within Jewish Christianity. (4) Almost certainly Gentile Christians were included among the Minim; the term did not imply of necessity an ethnic bond with Israel. (5) Essentially religious in meaning, Minim was applied quite early not only to obviously apostate Jews but to Christianity of all nuances, regarded as a gigantic apostasy from Judaism.[33]

A further reason for early Jewish antagonism was the Christian position during the revolt of Bar-Cochba. The situation has been summed up by Salo Wittmayer Baron:

> Jewish patriots ... doubly resented Christian enmity in the midst of their war for survival. They could forgive the Christians' removal to Pella during the Great War, when so many loyal Jews were pro-Roman or pacifist, and when even R. Johanan ben Zakkai was smuggled out of the besieged city. Now, however, such fundamentals of the Jewish faith as circumcision, Sabbath observance, and public assemblies for study were at stake. [Justin's assertion that Bar-Cochba had ordered "that Christians alone should be led to cruel punishment, unless they renounced Jesus Christ"] had a fairly authentic ring. It evidently was but a theological reformulation of what had probably been Bar-Kocheba's military measure against a dangerous "Fifth Column," easily understandable under the existing emergency. Whether or not they were generally considered spies and Roman partisans, the refusal of all Christians to participate in the struggle, indeed their gloating over the political downfall of Judaea—whose very name soon went into disuse among the Romans, pagan and Christian alike—opened an unbridgeable gap between the mother and daughter religions.[34]

A final reason for (perhaps more accurately, a result of) early Jewish antagonism towards Christians lay in an increasing policy of segregation: for example, the fact that many rabbis insisted on closing the avenues of Jewish learning to non-Jews. In these circumstances it was inevitable that voluntary ghettos should grow up, especially where Christianity had made or was making deep inroads into the Jewish community.[35]

The early Christian-Jewish situation was indeed tragic; for it involved mutual antagonism, profound suspicion, increasing isolation. And the tragedy has been compounded over the centuries: every Jewish ghetto ever structured by Christians; every forced baptism; every crusade to liberate the holy places; every Good Friday pogrom; every portrait of Shylock exacting his pound of flesh; every accusation of deicide; every Dachau and every Auschwitz; every death for conscience' sake; every back turned or shoulder shrugged; every sneer or slap or curse.

From my standpoint, however, the early Christian tension carried within it intimations of hope and resolution; for the tension was not racist or economic, but primarily theological (e.g., the issue of Christ) and historical (e.g., the Bar-Cochba revolt). It is my contention that in our time these theological and historical issues are beginning to be faced with unparalleled frankness, openness, and creativity—an approach which augurs the dawn of a new day. The springboard for a new Catholic vision is Vatican II's "Declaration on the Relationship of the Church to Non-Christian Religions," specifically the section on the Jews (no. 4).

Not that all Jews were enthusiastic over the Declaration. First, there were Jews who opposed the document, even resented it—because the news media gave the impression that the Council had "absolved" the Jews of guilt for the crucifixion, or because Vatican II "backed and filled" over its statement for several years, or because the document reveals no note of contrition or repentance for the past. Second, there were Jews who were indifferent to the document, because it was too little and too late: for its political and civic salvation, the Jewish people of the Western world looks to the secular powers, not to a Christian community outdistanced by history and capable of no more than pleasant rhetoric. Third, there were Jews like Rabbi Marc Tanenbaum who "welcomed the Declaration as an important contribution to improve the future relations between Catholics and Jews."[36] They saw the final text as a compromise document less warm and generous than an earlier draft, were therefore somewhat disappointed; and still "in the view of this group, seen in the perspective of 1900 years of Christian-Jewish history, this Declaration represents an incredible achievement."[37]

In the course of his insightful and at times passionate critique of Vatican II, Tanenbaum has a paragraph programmatic for the future:

> During the course of the deliberations of Vatican Council II in connection with the "Jewish Declaration," the contradictory and at times confused views expressed with regard to the inclusion or elimination of a passage in the third version of the text relating the question of the conversion of the Jews brought into sharp focus the fact that the Catholic Church has done very little serious thinking about the place of Jews and Judaism in the divine economy. That episode alone underscored the need for Catholic theologians and scholars to develop a theology of Israel and the synagogue in salvation history that has some correspondence with the historic realities of the present-day living Jewish people. At the same time, the bewildering and bewildered response of many Jews to Vatican Council II, whose attitudes toward present-day Christians are based on old-world memories of Christians as persecutors, threw into sharp relief the critical need for Jews to develop a theology of Christians and Christianity

that is consonant with the realities of an emerging "new Christian" society that is struggling in unparalleled fashion to uproot anti-Semitism and to restore her traditions to biblical modes of thought and practice.[38]

III. TOWARDS A FRESH THEOLOGY OF THE JEWS

RABBI TANENBAUM'S trenchant paragraph leads logically into my third and most crucial section: the beginnings of a fresh Christian theology of Judaism. Happily, Tanenbaum's call for such a theology is confirmed by a moving plea for a new Christian-Jewish relationship from a top-flight Scripture scholar, the Lutheran Krister Stendahl:

> It is clear to me that Christian theology needs a new departure. And it is equally clear that we cannot find it on our own, but only by the help of our Jewish colleagues. We must plead with them to help us. And as far as we are concerned, it is not a dialogue we need; we are not primarily anxious to impart our views as they impart theirs. We need to ask, in spite of it all, whether they are willing to let us become again part of their family, a peculiar part to be true, but even so, relatives who believe themselves to be a peculiar kind of Jews. Something went wrong in the beginning. I say "went wrong," for I am not convinced that what happened in the severing of the relations between Judaism and Christianity was the good and positive will of God. Is it not possible for us to recognize that we parted ways not according to but against the will of God?[39]

The paragraph moves me and it puzzles me. I agree that "Christian theology needs a new departure." I agree that "we cannot find it on our own," that we need "the help of our Jewish colleagues." I too am convinced that "something went wrong in the beginning." I too suspect that "we parted ways against the will of God." But moved as I am, I am equally puzzled. I cannot agree "it is not a dialogue we need." Precisely because I need "a new departure," precisely because I suspect that our severance was not divinely willed, precisely because I must search for what Dr. Stendahl called "the lost alternatives,"[40] for these reasons I need dialogue. I have to ask the Jew, not simply whether he is willing to let me become again part of his family, but what this means—to him and to me. And so, at the risk of making a major mistake, I am going to institute dialogue with the Jew—in two stages. In the first place, I shall affirm and briefly explain a handful of propositions which seem to me not simply defensible but indispensable if we are to have a creative, fruitful, even orthodox Christian theology of the Jew. In the second place, I shall put several questions to my Jewish brothers and sisters, to make it possible for me to understand them as they understand themselves, and so to make sense out of the affirmation that we Christians are "relatives who believe themselves to be a peculiar kind of Jews."

I begin with my affirmations. First, I affirm without reservation that the Jews were chosen by God as His special people, His people of election. A covenant was made with Israel, with the Jewish people—a covenant guaranteeing that through this select segment of humanity would come to man, to the world, a unique message, a unique Scripture, a unique Messiah, a unique redemption.

Second, I affirm without reservation that Israel did not cease to be God's people after the death of Jesus. This is Paul's own doctrine: "What if some were unfaithful? Does their faithlessness nullify the faithfulness of God? By no means!" (Rom. 3:3-4). "God has not rejected His people whom He foreknew" (Rom. 11:2). In Paul's view, as expressed in his letter to the Christians of Rome:

> The vocation of this people of God is continuous, irrevocable, indestructible. The Jews are and remain God's chosen and beloved people. The new brotherhood in the Church does not destroy the old (9:3). To the Jews...belongs "the sonship"...to Israel belongs "the glory": the glory of the presence of God with his people; and "the covenant"...and "the giving of the law"...and "the worship"...and "the promises"...and "the patriarchs"...; and finally, far more important than all the others, "the Christ," the Messiah, Jesus Christ, born of Jewish flesh and blood, belongs first and foremost to the people of Israel....[41]

Israel, therefore, is still God's first-born son, has the presence of God, retains the covenant, a true worship of the priestly nation, the promises of God's grace and salvation; to Israel belong its ancestors in the one true faith and the Christ. I must hold that all these still belong to the Jews, even though the vast majority of Jews rejected and continue to reject Jesus as Messiah.

Third, as a Christian, with my own vision of God's promises, I must affirm that if it is true that Israel remains God's people, it is equally true that the Gentiles have been incorporated into God's people. From a rejected people, the Gentiles have been made into a chosen people. Not by any righteousness of ours; solely by God's free election. Israel has not been rejected; the covenant has become universal.

Fourth, as a Christian, with my own vision of God's promises, I must affirm that God's promises reached a certain definitive term in Jesus. Here, of course, is the stumbling block. I mean the affirmation of Jesus "that he was really the eschatological event foretold by the prophets—that is, the coming of Yahweh himself, under a form unexpected but nevertheless real."[42] Here, on the level of doctrine, of belief, here is the scandal and the dividing line. So sympathetic a Jew as Schalom Ben-Chorin has told us gently but firmly:

> We must then question, in the light of the Bible, whether the message of the Old Testament which the New Testament claims has

been fulfilled, has in fact been fulfilled in history, in the history lived and suffered by us and our ancestors. And here, my dear Christian readers, we give a negative reply. We can see no kingdom and no peace and no redemption. The dawning of the kingdom of God, the "malchuth schaddaj," still lies hidden in the future, whether near or far, at a time which both Christians and Jews believe can be determined by no man.[43]

Christianity believes that redemption has come in Jesus, but has not yet been definitively accomplished; Judaism sees as yet no redemption whatsoever.

Fifth, I affirm without reservation that "the Jews"—then, now, or at any time—cannot be called guilty of Jesus' death. There is no such thing as a collective responsibility of the Jews, then or now, in the crucifixion of Christ. Such responsibility is historically and theologically untenable. (Even the individual participation of Jews in Jesus' death is historically difficult, if not impossible, to reconstruct.) Such collective responsibility has been officially denied by the Second Vatican Council[44] —not because the Jews needed somehow to be absolved of guilt, but because Catholics in untold measure needed to be told what genuine Catholic doctrine is and demands.

Sixth, I affirm without reservation that at various stages of her history the Christian Church has been responsible for injustice to the Jew that cries to heaven, perhaps not for vengeance, but surely for mercy. Not a collective responsibility; but the Church has been responsible in the sense that so many Christians have been responsible. Christianity is not guiltless, because in the matter of the Jew so many Christians have been small and self-righteous, clannish and self-centered; because so many Christians have tyrannized when strong and temporized when weak; because so many Christians are as biased and anti-Semitic as their unbelieving neighbors; because so many Christians in their attitude to Israel are what St. Paul said of the godless: they are "ruthless, faithless, pitiless" (Rom. 1:31).

Seventh, I affirm without reservation that Israel has a God-given role to play in human history. Not simply the Jew who was, but the Jew who is and the Jew who will be. Israel is a mystery, yes. We do not know the intimate story of what happened in those dark, confusing decades early in the first century of our Common Era. We have a handful of facts, a headful of theological interpretations. We know that, at a given moment, a new thing sprang forth from the Jewish people—the thing called Christian. And from that time forth we have the paradox of continuity and cleavage, of theoretical love and actual hostility.

Despite the mystery, however, it can be and must be affirmed that Judaism has a mission. I do not think we are yet in a position to define it in relation to Christianity. The Christian, for all his firm commitment to Christ, has to be incredibly careful how he uses the word "conversion" in reference to the Jew—or even whether he may use it at all. In any event, I see *a* mission of the Jews on two levels: faith and life—age-old affirmation and centuries-old suffering.

On the level of faith, I submit that Israel's mission involves the "Guiding Principles of Reform Judaism" adopted in 1937:

> 1. [Judaism's] message is universal, aiming at the union and perfection of mankind under the sovereignty of God.... Judaism welcomes all truth, whether written in the pages of scripture or deciphered from the records of nature.
> 2. The heart of Judaism and its chief contribution to religion is the doctrine of the One, living God, who rules the world through law and love. In Him all existence has its creative source and mankind its ideal of conduct. Though transcending time and space, He is the indwelling Presence of the world. We worship Him as the Lord of the universe and as our merciful Father.
> 3. Judaism affirms that man is created in the Divine image. His spirit is immortal. He is an active co-worker with God. As a child of God, he is endowed with moral freedom and is charged with the responsibility of overcoming evil and striving after ideal ends.[45]

On the level of life, I submit that Israel's mission involves what it has involved since the covenant was sealed: a unique witness to fidelity and love, to God and man, through all her infidelities, through all her crucifixions. For the Jewish people has been par excellence the suffering servant. In fact, from the twelfth century on, the more common view of Jewish interpreters has seen in the servant of Isaiah 53 the Jewish people as a whole, or at least the righteous element among them; and in the suffering of the servant, not only the agony of the Captivity, but all the sufferings of the Jewish people to the time of the particular rabbi discussing the text. In this way Israel will continue to be a living, striking witness to the reality of the living God.[46]

On these levels of faith and life, Israel and the Church are surprisingly one. As Hans Küng has put it:

> Like Israel and following Israel the Church sees itself as the journeying people of God, constantly being delivered from bondage, constantly wandering through the wilderness of this age, constantly maintaining the tension between thankful commemoration and hopeful expectation and preparing itself for its entry into the promised land, the messianic kingdom, the goal that always lies in the future.[47]

Eighth, I affirm without reservation that God continues to reveal Himself to and through the Jews, the here-and-now, twentieth-century Jews. Catholics have implicitly denied this. The denial lies hidden in our age-old concept of revelation. Gabriel Moran has put it pungently:

> Because revelation is conceived to be something that came in the past and stopped, then the Old Testament [our irritating expression

> for the Hebrew Scriptures] cannot be anything but old. Despite all our contrary pleas, the Old Testament becomes that part of revelation that was supplanted or at least completed by the New Testament. It was once the revealing God at work but now it has been fulfilled. In this conception the Jewish people were once the bearers of revelation, but now they are an incongruous remnant. This line of thinking is very strong among Catholics despite the insistence of St. Paul (Rom. 11) and Vatican II that God has not revoked the promises to his people....[48]

No, revelation has not been simply sealed and delivered. God is still revealing Himself—revealing Himself to and through contemporary man, revealing Himself to and through the contemporary Jew. God reveals Himself in the lives of Christians and Jews. Once I admit this (as I must), then I must ask myself "with candor where the most striking witness to the suffering servant of Yahweh has been found in the twentieth century."[49] In fact, I would say that no group, no nation, no religion has borne such ceaseless, consistent witness to the suffering servant as the Jewish people since the twilight of our common fourth century. In the eloquent (if chronologically exaggerated) words of André Chouraqui:

> We have passed through twenty centuries of history with our hands empty, unarmed, while maintaining the most resistant of spiritual presences. Confronted with all the empires, all the nations, all the Churches, all with weapons, organized armies and means of pressure, of which we felt the weight, a small group of unarmed men were able to survive every persecution and triumph over every temptation and obstacle only by the sole virtue of their spirit. Is there not here an extraordinary testimony for our century of violence?[50]

Yes, the Catholic especially might ponder the implications of his traditional argument for the truth of Catholicism from the continued existence of the Church: by all odds, by every human calculation, she should have perished. The same can be said, perhaps more emphatically still, of the Jews: by all odds, by every human calculation, the Jewish people should have perished. The unrecognized factor is: God is here. He *is* here, and He *speaks* to and through the Jew, His suffering servant.

So much for my affirmations. The questions I must put to the Jew are basically three—each an effort to define the Jew as he defines himself. The questions stem from the fact that Jewish religion has traditionally been characterized by the alliance of a God with a people in a country. In the effort, then, to define who a Jew is, there are three elements: a God, a man, a land. Let me take each one of them separately —not that they can be divorced in concrete living, but in an effort to achieve a certain measure of clarity.

First, God. (I am not going to try to probe His nature; for, believe it or not, even to a Christian, God is mystery.) I take it that the

Hebrew Testament and the Hebrew law rest on certain fundamental notions: "the notion of a personal and transcendent God, bearer of a law of love and of holiness, who offers to the people of Israel and to humanity a covenant, an alliance."[51] How important, then, to the idea of Jewishness is the covenant concept? To be genuinely a Jew, must a man be committed to the covenant? Must Yahweh be his God? Is there a contradiction in the expression "atheistic Jew"? Put another way: What is the abiding "message" of Israel, the witness to God's truth which every Jew must incarnate at the peril of ceasing to be a Jew? *Is* there any such message, such witness? Need it have some relation to the Hebrew Scriptures, to the God of Israel? Put another way: To be a Jew, is it sufficient to believe in *man?* Take the sentence of Chouraqui: "The Jew who is the furthest away from the Word of God, by the simple fact that he exists as a Jew, remains faithful, although sometimes involuntarily and unconsciously, to the covenant of Abraham and to its permanence."[52] Do we have a concept here analogous to the "anonymous Christian"?

In this context, must a Jew say a total no to Christianity on peril of ceasing to be a Jew? More concretely, must a Jew reject Jesus—and this in virtue of his understanding of the covenant, on the level of Judaism's spiritual message—simply, because Yahweh would not be Yahweh? And if this is the basis, must a Jew who accepts Jesus, either as prophet or as Messiah or even as Son of God, cease to be a Jew?[53]

The covenant relationship is with a people. And this raises a second question, if I am to understand what it means to become again part of the Jewish family: Does the term "Jew" correspond to something ethnic?

I know there is no question here of a physiological type that can be called Jewish. I am told that the proof of this lies in Israel.

> There we find Jews who have come from 102 countries, from all the continents and from all types of civilization. It is sufficient to walk through the streets of Jerusalem, Tel-Aviv or Haifa to be clearly aware that no Jewish type exists. The only typology that stands out from this conglomeration, this assemblage of men who have come from all over the world, is the human type. You will find in Israel all types of men. [The type here is] attached to a cultural and historical tradition.[54]

This is indeed true, but only up to a point. Does not Jewish tradition itself emphasize a descent from Abraham? Is there an ethnic aspect to Judaism that cannot be compensated for, substituted for? Or is it all a matter of a cultural and historical tradition? Concretely, is it possible for *me* to really become a Jew? And if it is, what would this "conversion" involve?

Put another way: Are we back to the first question, to the alliance, to Yahweh, to sacred history? Must we say with Daniélou that "an unbeliever cannot understand what a Jew is"?

> Sartre is absolutely incapable of understanding what a Jew is; since the ideas of a sacred history, a choice by God, a revelation, are wholly foreign to him, he necessarily overlooks what causes the Jewish people to be an exceptional people. This is also why atheistic Jews are incapable of saying what they are.[55]

To focus the question: Did Paul cease to be a Jew when he became a Christian? *He* did not think so: "I myself am an Israelite, a descendant of Abraham, a member of the tribe of Benjamin" (Rom. 11:1). But this view of things may well be tied to Paul's view of what it means to "belong to Israel": "For not all who are descended from Israel belong to Israel, and not all are children of Abraham because they are his descendants.... It is not the children of the flesh who are the children of God, but the children of the promise are reckoned as descendants" (Rom. 9:6-8).

My third question touches an extraordinarily delicate issue: Are the message and the people inseparable from the land? The question is highly important for a Christian theology of the Jew. Can I define the contemporary Jew without relation to contemporary Israel? I feel quite sure I cannot define him without reference to the country before Christ, to the Holy Land as it formed him before the Common Era— and even into the early centuries C.E. The neuralgic question is: Is there an indissoluble relationship between the Jew *now* and the Holy Land *now*? And if there is, can we define or describe that relationship?

The issue has immediate relevance. I know how hurt, even perhaps angry, so many Jews were when Christian leaders did not denounce the Arabs, did not fly to the Jewish cause, in the crisis of June 1967. And my reading of the pertinent literature forced a sharp issue before my eyes. For many Jews, it was not merely or primarily a political question: elementary justice had been violated. It was also, perhaps primarily, a theological and religious question: this is not just *any* land; this is land without which the Jew is not a Jew. Am I wrong in my reading? If not, where does the Christian blindness lie?

At this point I find that a paragraph from Hans Küng's *The Church* captures my present frame of mind—my admiration and my uncertainties. He writes:

> This weak people which has survived the centuries, this decimated people which is now starting life anew, stronger than ever, has always been a riddle to the world and often to itself. What are these Jews? A race, and yet, as a result of frequent intermingling and the fact that it has no indisputable distinguishing features, not a race. A linguistic community, and yet, since only part speaks Hebrew, not that either. A religion, and yet, since many Jews have become

completely secularized or been baptized, not a religion. A State, and yet, since a vast majority is not citizens of this State, not that either. A people, and yet, since a majority has become assimilated into other peoples, not a people. Thus the Jews are a puzzling fated fellowship, mostly accepted by individual Jews, but rejected by some; this enigma is perhaps an indication of the hidden *secret* of the Jews. Their secret, which believing Jews and believing Christians alike accept, is their vocation to be a people of God in the midst of other peoples. This vocation was never questioned, even at a time when the Church regarded Israel as no more than an outmoded earlier form of the true people of God. . . .[56]

NOTES

[1] For the following information on the American Jew I am indebted to Arthur Gilbert, "The Contemporary Jew in America," *Thought* 43 (1968), 211-26.

[2] *Ibid.*, p. 214.

[3] *Ibid.*, p. 219.

[4] *Ibid.*, p. 224.

[5] *Ibid.*, p. 226.

[6] *Ibid.*, p. 225.

[7] In gathering some of the patristic material in the following pages I have been greatly assisted by the dissertation of Robert Wilde, *The Treatment of the Jews in the Greek Christian Writers of the First Three Centuries* (Washington, D.C.: Catholic University of America Press, 1949).

[8] Aristides, *Apology* 2 (*Texte und Untersuchungen* 4/3, 9-10). For a discussion of the Syriac translation and of the Greek and Armenian fragments, cf. Wilde, *op. cit.*, pp. 93-96.

[9] Justin, *Dialogue with Trypho the Jew* 95 (*Patrologia Graeca* 6, 701; tr. Thomas B. Falls, in *The Fathers of the Church* 6 [New York: Christian Heritage, 1948], 298).

[10] For the pertinent texts of Irenaeus, cf. Wilde, *op. cit.*, pp. 152-54.

[11] For the pertinent texts of Hippolytus, cf. Wilde, *op. cit.*, pp. 160-61.

[12] For the pertinent texts of Origen, cf. Wilde, *op. cit.*, p. 187.

[13] Cf. the fine edition and translation of Léon Vaganay, *L'Evangile de Pierre* (Paris: Gabalda, 1930).

[14] Cf. Wilde, *op. cit.*, p. 225.

[15] Justin, *Dialogue with Trypho the Jew* 135 (*Patrologia Graeca* 6, 789; tr. Falls, *op. cit.*, p. 358).

[16] Cf. Wilde, *op. cit.*, p. 129.

[17] Irenaeus, *Proof of the Apostolic Preaching* 95 (tr. Joseph P. Smith, in *Ancient Christian Writers* 16 [Westminster, Md.: Newman, 1952], 105).

[18] For the pertinent texts of Hippolytus, cf. Wilde, *op. cit.*, p. 165.

[19] Cf. Wilde, *op. cit.*, p. 180.

[20] For the pertinent texts of Origen, cf. Wilde, *op. cit.*, pp. 190-92.

[21] The text I am using is Funk-Bihlmeyer, *Die apostolischen Väter* 1 (2nd ed.; Tübingen: Mohr, 1956) 120-32. I have availed myself of the excellent translation by James A. Kleist in *Ancient Christian Writers* 6 (Westminster, Md.: Newman, 1948), 90-102.

[22] *Martyrdom of Polycarp* 12, 2 (Funk-Bihlmeyer, p. 126; *ACW* 6, 96).

[23] *Ibid.* 13, 1 (Funk-Bihlmeyer, p. 127; *ACW* 6, 96).

[24] *Ibid.* 17, 2 and 18, 1 (Funk-Bihlmeyer, pp. 129-30; *ACW* 6, 98-99).

[25] Justin, *Apology 1*, 31 (*Patrologia Graeca* 6, 376-77).

[26] Hippolytus, *Commentary on Daniel* 1, 21 (*Die griechischen christlichen Schriftsteller der ersten drei Jahrhunderte* 1, 33).

[27] Tertullian, *Antidote against the Scorpion's Sting* 10, 10 (*Corpus christianorum, Series Latina* 2, 1089).

[28] Cyprian, *Letter 59*, 2 (*Corpus scriptorum ecclesiasticorum Latinorum* 3/2, 667).

[29] Origen, *Against Celsus* 6, 27 (*Die griechischen christlichen Schriftsteller der ersten drei Jahrhunderte* 3, 97-98; tr. Henry Chadwick, *Origen: Contra Celsum* [Cambridge: University Press, 1953], p. 343).

[30] The ascertainable facts on Jewish participation in early harassment of Christians might be summarized as follows: (1) In Palestine there were some effective measures, but by way of exception, when the Jews had some influence and/or power: e.g., Stephen, James, and the victims of 135. (2) In the Diaspora it may be that Jews helped to spread some of the well-known calumnies; probably they had no more significant role than to share the general pagan reaction to Christianity, at times to rejoice in the repression of Christianity. (3) With regard to Polycarp's charges, it would appear that at worst individual Jews were involved. Not impertinent here is the preoccupation of the author(s) to show the parallelism between the martyrdom of Polycarp and the passion of Christ. Cf. Marcel Simon, *Verus Israel: Etude sur les relations entre chrétiens et juifs dans l'empire romain (135-425)* (Paris: E. de Boccard, 1964), pp. 148-51.

[31] R. Travers Herford, "Jesus in Rabbinical Literature," *Universal Jewish Encyclopedia* 6 (1942) 87. Herford recalls explicitly (p. 88) that in his *Christianity in Talmud and Midrash* (London: William & Norgate, 1903) he gave "what he then thought to be a safely warranted list of references to Jesus. He would not now admit all contained in that list." In particular, he withdraws the assumption that when Balaam is mentioned, Jesus is usually meant. The statement that Jesus "was a revolutionary" he corrects (as an error in translation) to say that Jesus "was one for whom aught in his favor could be said." He admits now as "doubtful and probably unfounded" the following references: Jesus born out of wedlock; Jesus a magician who brought magic out of Egypt; Jesus, under the name of Balaam, put to death by Phineas the Robber, thought to be Pontius Pilate, at the age of thirty-three; Jesus, under the name of Balaam, excluded from the world to come.

[32] Herford, *art. cit.*, p. 88.

[33] Cf. Simon, *op. cit.*, pp. 216-22, 238.

[34] Salo Wittmayer Baron, *A Social and Religious History of the Jews* 2 (New York: Columbia University Press, 1952), 132.

[35] Cf. *ibid.*, pp. 148-49; also Baron's splendid summary of the early situation, pp. 169-71.

[36] Marc H. Tanenbaum, "The Declaration on Non-Christian Religions: A Jewish Viewpoint," in John H. Miller (ed.), *Vatican II: An Interfaith Appraisal* (Notre Dame: University of Notre Dame Press, 1966), p. 362.

[37] *Ibid.*, p. 363.

[38] *Ibid.*, p. 365.

[39] Krister Stendahl, "Judaism and Christianity: A Plea for a New Relationship," *Cross Currents* 17 (1967), 453.

[40] *Ibid.*
[41] Hans Küng, *The Church* (New York: Sheed and Ward, 1968), p. 141.
[42] Jean Daniélou, in *The Jews: Views and Counterviews. A Dialogue between Jean Daniélou and André Chouraqui* (Westminster, Md.: Newman, 1967), p. 33.
[43] Quoted by Küng, *op. cit.*, p. 149.
[44] "Declaration on the Relationship of the Church to Non-Christian Religions," no. 4.
[45] *Universal Jewish Encyclopedia* 6 (1942), 242.
[46] Cf. Walter J. Burghardt, "Israel: A Light to the Gentiles?" *The Pulpit* 37 (1966), 52-54.
[47] Küng, *op. cit.*, p. 148.
[48] Gabriel Moran, "The God of Revelation," *Commonweal* 85 (1967), 501.
[49] *Ibid.*
[50] André Chouraqui, in *The Jews: Views and Counterviews* (n. 42 above), p. 51. Chouraqui is an Algerian Jew who was personal assistant to Ben-Gurion from 1959 to 1963 and became assistant mayor of Jerusalem in 1965.
[51] Chouraqui, *op. cit.*, p. 20.
[52] *Ibid.*, p. 50.
[53] Küng, *op. cit.*, pp. 147-48, quotes two moving passages from Martin Buber and Schalom Ben-Chorin that reveal how Jesus has once more become a matter of concern for leading Jewish thinkers.
[54] Chouraqui, *op. cit.*, pp. 13-14.
[55] *Ibid.*, p. 16.
[56] Küng, *op. cit.*, p. 139.

Developing Moral Teaching

John T. Noonan

CONCERNING Christian moral teaching, two hypotheses may be advanced. One view perceives it as perfectly stable; the other, that it proceeds by revolutionary jumps. Each of these hypotheses is a myth. Pure stability is achieved only by what is completely inert; revolution is achieved only by wiping the past clean. Moral thought is alive, and its categories, problems and responses are rooted in what has gone before. The myth of stability is precious to one kind of mind, the myth of revolution to another, but both stability and revolution are seductive substitutes for reality.

In reality, only change exists, which may be purposeful or arbitrary, comprehensive or choppy, evolutionary or atomic. If change is arbitrary, choppy or atomic, there exists movement but nothing more. If there is change which is purposeful, comprehensive, evolutionary, there unfolds a potential—a development. To find not merely movement but development in the successive statements in time of Christian doctrine requires, perhaps, faith in addition to reason; but Christian moral doctrine, I believe, is characterized by the kind of change which deserves the appellation, development.

I. THE CONSTITUENT ORGANS OF DEVELOPMENT

IN Christian moral teaching there appear several alternative sources from which development flows. One is the plain letter of the Bible; another, the latest statement of a Pope or a bishop; yet another, the written or oral word of leading theologians. If the letter of the Bible alone could be taken as a guide, one would have to embrace the myth of stability; if the last word of the contemporary theologian were decisive, one would be in a revolutionary situation; if the last statement of a Pope were final, one would be stopped at what the myth of stability would point to as unchangeable, until another Pope spoke differently and the myth of revolution treated the new statement as a radical reversal.

It is a mistake to suppose that the text of the Bible has ever stood viewed as a thing apart; it has always been interpreted. It is a mistake to suppose that the modern theologians can formulate their positions without reference to the Bible and the hierarchical authorities of the Church; they are nourished from these disparate founts. It also seems a mistake to suppose that the Pope can act independently of the Bible and the theologians; he should not be viewed as a head disconnected from the body. To emphasize unduly one or another of these organs of teaching is a kind of surrendering to myths. In reality, the Bible as the word of God, the Pope as the head of the Church, the bishops joined with the Pope in the exercise of collegial responsibility, and the theologians as men especially skilled in the language, concepts, and logic of religion, interact with one another. Doctrine develops in this interaction.

It may be asked if the development of speculative dogma is different from the development of moral doctrine. I should suppose that there were aspects of the two which were properly distinguishable. In particular, it would seem that the experience of the Christian community played a larger and more decisive role in moral development than it properly could play in the development of speculative dogma.[1] The experience of Christian community is yet a fourth element, in addition to the Bible, the hierarchy, and the theologians, affecting the development of moral thought.

By experience, of course, I do not mean simply *any* experience. It is clear that the repeated failure of Christians to love their neighbors as themselves does not alter the fundamental commandment of the Lord. Nor do I mean personal experimentation in a way contrary to what has already been determined as the law of the community. I mean the experience of members of the community sincerely attempting to live lives as fully as possible in accordance with the commandments of love. A privileged place in this testimony belongs to the kind of experience which is incorporated in the liturgy and is repeated in liturgical re-enactments.

It may be further supposed that experience is the test of ideals and that if ideals cannot be achieved by a normal person in the world as he finds it they should be abandoned as unrealistic. Such a view of experience appears to underlie a good deal of sociological writing and to explain the attention given, for example, to the two Kinsey reports. But such a view is possible only by means of a myth of "the world as it is" and "the normal person." In fact, the world is very little given; what it is depends on what people make of it. If ever the world as it was had been taken as the norm, we would never have gone beyond the early superstitious cultures of the Mediterranean worlds. The Christian, in particular, cannot receive the world as static, but must contemplate it in a perspective in which grace builds on nature and elevates it so that the virtues of men may be realized.

In speaking of experience, too, it would be a mistake to rate personal experience too highly. There exists a kind of mystique of experience which supposes that one is incapable of judgment unless one has had the experience. The inadequacy of this view is demonstrable when crimes are considered which everyone would agree were reprehensible without the experience of having committed them. To take an obvious example, few persons have to commit murder in order to judge that murder is wrong. The principle suggested by what is clear in the case of great crimes is that personal participation is not the ordinary and necessary condition of moral judgment of an act.

What seems to be necessary is attention to the statements of those who have had an experience which they claim as beneficial. Such testing cannot be the single decisive element, and such testimony must be scrutinized for the elimination of selfishness or self-deception. Yet if statements are made in good faith by those seeking to live Christian lives, their experience must be accorded some attention.

In an ecumenical age, the experience of non-Catholic Christians also cannot be entirely neglected, for it has value as testimony to the reasons and desires of men living in a redeemed universe. There are, I would like to suggest, hierarchies of experience. The experience of a primitive tribe is not worth as much as the experience of a developed civilization, and the experience of the unbaptized cannot for Christians be put on a plane with the liturgy.

If a rule is given in the Christian community, it may be asked how it ever can change unless someone undertakes the experience of breaking it and reporting on this experience. Much depends on the spirit in which the rule is broken. Few laws are so absolute that no occasion will occur where someone in completely good faith believes that the law permits an exception. In the passing of these exceptions into a new rule, development without conscious defiance of the law can, and frequently does, occur. In addition, there are cases, on the whole not frequent, where prophetic insights lead persons to see a law as unjust and in good faith to break the law. By either route, that of exception or conscientious disobedience, experience is obtained which is of significance for moral development and which is achieved without subjectively sinful violation of enunciated rules.

Most of the experience of the community is accessible only through history, and this fact imposes a special burden upon the historian. His task is to put particular written evidence of past beliefs into the contexts from which they came, and in doing so, reach the experience of the past community. If he fails in this task, the written records are apt to be used as inert texts which can be moved about like children's building blocks to form any and all possible childish combinations. It is only by the rigor of historical discipline that the written texts can be confined to the situations from which they arise in order to reveal their meaning. Only in context can the writings of the past constitute an index of past belief.

To insist on the necessity for a historical understanding in order to get at the essential elements of Christian experience is not to say that the historian is king. There are no kings—neither the historian, nor the modern theologian, nor the Pope, nor an individual Christian is free to state the belief of Christians as though he were "above" the Church. All of them are engaged in the process of interaction, and none is free to disregard the other or to act as if he were absolute. Certainly it is alien to Catholic teaching that new revelation will be given to or by the Pope. The Pope acts with the assistance of the Spirit to discern what has already been revealed to the community which is the Church. In this process of interaction, the only supreme norm is that set down by the "Dogmatic Constitution on Divine Revelation" on the Second Vatican Council: "The office of authentically interpreting the word of God, written or contained in tradition, has been granted only to the living Magisterium of the Church. This Magisterium indeed is not above the word of God, but ministers to it, teaching only what is contained in tradition to the extent that, by divine commandment and with the assistance of the Holy Spirit, it listens to it with fidelity, and from this one deposit of faith draws all these things which it sets out to be believed as divinely revealed."[2]

The course of development of moral thinking is not necessarily to substitute an easier rule for a harder one or a harder rule for an easier. For example, the moral law now forbidding a Christian to hold slaves might be considered as harder in its restriction on the freedom of some people to treat others as they liked, but easier in holding that all persons must be safeguarded from being treated as property by others. But while "easier" or "harder" are inappropriate terms for measuring development, it may be advanced at least as an hypothesis that the direction is to give greater responsibility to the individual person and to measure his duties to others in increasingly personal terms. We may further believe that, as the leaven, which is the gospel, penetrates the world, the direction of development is toward an increase of charity.

As illustrations of what I have said in generalities, I shall now examine two topics of moral teaching, first the development of teaching on usury and secondly the development of teaching on the purposes of marital intercourse.

II. THE DEVELOPMENT OF TEACHING ON USURY

BY the end of the twelfth century there was an absolute prohibition on making a profit on a loan or seeking anything beyond the principal in a loan.[3] Such profit was usury, such seeking was the sin of usury, and the mere hoping for such profit constituted the mortal mental sin of usury.[4] Usury was condemned by general councils of the Church, by the Popes, and all of the theologians and canonists with the consent of all of the bishops.[5]

The twelfth century rule was the culmination of centuries of interaction of the kind I have described. The Bible itself had provided a number of explicit textual condemnations of the sin.[6] The New Testament reinforced the Old with the expressed words of Christ, "Lend freely, hoping nothing thereby" (Luke 6:35). The Fathers of the Christian Church had meditated on these texts in the light of their experience of the evils of lending in the Roman Empire. They had concluded that usury was indeed a great social plague and a serious invasion of the love of one's neighbor.[7]

The teachings of the Bible and the Fathers had been further reflected upon by the bishops who met in local councils in the West in their countries after the fall of Rome. On the basis of their experience of money-lending in a totally agricultural economy they again found apposite the biblical injunctions and the harsh denunciations of money-lending by the Fathers.[8] Finally, all of these sources had been reflected upon by the Popes of the twelfth century and drawn upon by them to formulate the strict ban of profit on a loan. Their teaching was definitively expressed as the universal law of the Church in Chapter 19 of Book V of the *Decretals* of Gregory IX. This final achievement was not the work of the Popes alone, but of the Popes aided by the best theorists of their day, men such as Raymond of Peñafort and William of Auxerre who were the leaders in the newly beginning sciences of canon law and theology.

For a period between 1200 and 1500 the usury prohibition was relatively stable although exceptions were being found to its absolute range.[9] In the sixteenth century the prohibition underwent a major transition. In the course of this century the theologians argued that while it was a sin to take any profit on a loan, it was entirely Christian to make a moderate profit on the personal, guaranteed, and mutually redeemable annuity, or on the sale of foreign exchange which was to be repaid within several months, or on investments in partnerships where both the return of principal and a profit were guaranteed.[10] With the development of these several contracts by which profit in a credit transaction might be legitimately obtained, the usury rule was effectively emptied of its old meaning and given a new meaning—it became a prohibition against excessive profit in credit, not a prohibition of any profit.

The new theological opinion was partly the result of new analyses—the theologians took some of the principles of their predecessors as to annuities, insurance, and partnership and applied them in an innovative way to pure credit situations. The new opinion was partly the result of new attitudes by the theologians to the experience of Christians—there were repeated insistences that it would not do "to damn the whole world" or to say that every Christian engaged in banking was committing mortal sin; there was willingness to accept the testimony of those Christians who made lending their business and who said in good faith that they saw no incompatibility between their making a profit and the commandments of Christ.[11] The new opinion was partly the result of economic change, economic and social circumstances —in the sixteenth century, Europe had entered what is usually termed the commercial revolution, and the old agricultural economy was being replaced by one in which there was economic growth so that the use of money could have a value greater than zero. The combination of the new environment with the new attitudes and the new analyses led to the repudiation of what had been the consistent and uncontested teaching of the Popes, councils, bishops and theologians.

The development process itself was not easy. Three papal bulls—*Cum Onus* and *In Eam* of St. Pius V, and *Detestabilis Avaritia* of Sixtus V—attempted to stem the change of rule and to condemn the theological theories which supported it.[12] However, neither the bankers engaged in lending at a profit nor the theologians were daunted by the papal pronouncements made by the Popes in their role as vicars of Christ proclaiming what they took to be the divine and natural law. There was a furious controversy between laymen and bishops, bishops and theologians, Jesuits and Jesuits.[13] After twenty years of confusion the answers were clear. The papal statements were reduced to purely ecclesiastical law by the theologians, and then, as purely ecclesiastical law, were said to be binding only in countries where they were accepted, though no such countries were discovered.[14] In retrospect, the papal function appeared to have been to summarize and recall the old principles at the time when the theologians and the experience of the Christian faithful were adopting new combinations of principles which made the old absolute rule on usury obsolete.

The course of development was not easy also because no one articulated a theory of change which distinguished between permanent values which were preserved and the rule which changed. It was not until the eighteenth century that an Italian layman, Scipio Maffei, put forward a theory which showed that the basic values taught by the Church in the case of usury were justice to one's neighbor and charity in distress and that these values survived although the old usury rule was abandoned.[15] Even the eighteenth century was too early for this theory to be accepted at the papal level, and it was repudiated by Maffei's friend, Benedict XIV.[16]

Only in the nineteenth century did it become a commonplace of theology textbooks that the nature of money had changed permitting a change in the rule.[17] This explanation was not, in fact, accurate. The nature of money as conceived by the medieval theologians was a good which was consumed in its first use. Money is always consumable as long as it is viewed primarily as a medium of exchange, and money was as much a consumable in first use in the nineteenth century as in the twelfth. The explanation was wrong, but the textbooks in their attempt to find an explanation at least acknowledged that a major change had occurred. It was by then clear to everyone that the old prohibition of profit on a loan was completely dead.

If the usury history is looked at as a whole, what is seen to have occurred is that the basic values of justice and charity were protected for centuries by a rigid prohibition of profit on a loan. The rigid rule was derived from the Bible and justified by experience with the evils of money-lending. It worked with reasonable effectiveness in an agrarian economy. It was eventually eroded, but the basic values it had served were eventually served in time in a better way without the absolute rule. The development focused on the responsibility towards a borrower; for the fixed admonition to seek no profit it substituted his conscience formed by Christian values. The theological analysis moved from a focus on the act of lending and the nature of money—both conceived of as sterile—to the requirements of justice and charity in the interaction of two persons.

III. THE PURPOSES OF MARITAL INTERCOURSE

THE development of doctrine on the purposes of marital intercourse was somewhat different, because there were no express scriptural texts to provide immediate guidance. Neither the Old Testament nor the New Testament have anything to say explicitly on the purposes of intercourse in marriage. What they do is to present a combination of positive values which are stressed together with a series of rules prohibiting certain practices. As far as a starting point in Scripture was concerned, the Bible provided values and rules which, meditated upon, led to the express formulation of doctrine.

The great positive value stressed by the Old Testament is the goodness of procreation. Marriage is viewed as blessed if it is fertile, and sterility is viewed as a curse. Man's joyful cooperation in the work of God in bringing new beings into the world is a repeated theme of this part of the Bible.[18]

The gospels have nothing whatsoever to say on procreation, but they do appear to assume the existence of a society in which children are still procreated (Jn. 16:21). Only in the anti-Gnostic text of 1 Timothy 2:15 is there anything referring to the value of childbearing. What the New Testament stresses is other values—in particular the holiness of marital love as a symbol of the union of Christ and the Church (Ephesians 5:25-33). While the Old Testament accepted intercourse outside of marriage as permissible in the case of slave concubinage (Genesis 30:3) and viewed adultery as a sin committed by a married woman but not by a married man, the New Testament is clear as to the equality of sexual right of man and woman and insistent in teaching the sexual intercourse is lawful only within marriage (1 Corinthians 7:3-4). The rules set out in the New Testament on sexual intercourse are designed in part to protect embryonic life from destruction (Galatians 5:20; Apocalypse 9:21)[19] and in part to protect the sanctity of intercourse (1 Corinthians 6:9-18; Romans 1:24-27). The Christians could learn from the New Testament when combined with the Old Testament that procreation is good, that innocent life may not be taken even in the womb, that there is a personal dignity of each spouse which must be respected by the other, and that marital sexual love is holy.

The early Christian communities, however, were beset by a questioning of the meaning of marriage and a search for the measure of sexual behavior for persons who were assured of their own eternal life by a Messiah who had risen from the dead. The Jewish reason for procreation seemed to be confined to the perpetuation of the Jewish race until the Messiah had come; this reason was now obsolete.[20] The Greek reason for procreation appeared to be a desire to obtain a kind of pseudo-immortality in one's descendants; this reason, too, appeared obsolete to those assured of their own immortality in the light of the resurrection.[21] The inadequacy of the old reasons for procreation was emphasized by the New Testament emphasis on the value of virginity.[22] Hence, the Christian Right asserted that the only proper conduct for any Christian was total sexual abstinence.[23] The Right was joined by the Christian Left in repudiating marriage as an obsolete institution. The Left, instead of valuing virginity, put its emphasis on liberty. Experience was valued for its own sake. Freedom, especially sexual freedom, was highly prized. From the point of view of the Left, marriage was regarded as an unnecessary restriction on Christian freedom and procreation as an unnecessary burden.[24]

For over a century the debate as to the meaning of marriage affected the Christian communities.[25] A *via media* was sought by the founder of the first school of Christian theology, Clement of Alexandria. He turned to the best pagan philosophy of his day, Stoicism, to find a rationale for marriage. Following one strand of Stoic thought, he taught that marriage was right because it was natural, and it was natural in that the generative organs were made for generation. Consequently, a Christian acted virtuously if he married to procreate and if in marriage he had intercourse for the purpose of procreation.[26]

The Stoic rule or the Alexandrian rule on the purpose of intercourse, emerged, then, from a century of confusion and debate. It offered a rationalization for the central Christian institution of marriage, although it did so in terms which were not expressly biblical. As a kind of intellectual justification, fully in accord with the best contemporary thought, it apparently satisfied a need for rationalization that had been strongly felt. To the Right, the rule said that while Christ had set an example, it was an example that need not be followed by all men in derogation of their common humanity. To the Left, the rule said that while Christ had superseded the Mosaic law, he had not abolished human nature and that there was a measure for human morality in human nature. Coming at the end of a serious division in the Church, the rule found widespread acceptance as a theory of the proper measure of marital behavior. It was accepted by the greatest of Greek theologians, Clement's disciple, Origen;[27] and it was to be accepted by those who were to be the masters of Western moral thought, St. Ambrose, St. Jerome, and St. Augustine.[28]

The rule of Alexandria, born in the midst of an internal crisis, became fixed in Christian thought in the fourth century in the face of external competition, the competition provided by the Manichees who attacked the good of procreation itself. On the basis of their theology of the origin and destiny of man, the Manichees viewed procreation as the greatest of sins and resolutely taught, "You shall not procreate."[29] As Augustine, once himself a Manichee, said to them, they preferred prostitution to marriage because prostitutes were certain to take steps to prevent conception.[30] In contrast to this radical rejection of procreation, the Catholics, Augustine said, valued intercourse in marriage only for the purpose of procreation.[31]

In the centuries between the fall of Rome and the revival of theological science in the West, no great stress was put on the purposes of marriage, although the Augustinian current survived. In Ireland, for example, there is no trace of the Augustinian rule in the penitentials prepared by the Irish monks.[32] When theological science began to flourish again in the twelfth century, the Church was faced with what appeared to Western theologians as a reincarnation of Manicheism, the Cathar Church, which also radically denied the good of procreation.[33]

In the twelfth century, in the Western conflict with the Cathars, all of the Augustinian texts on the procreative purpose of intercourse were refurbished. They entered into the mainstream at a formulative moment. They formed a central part of the nascent canon law in Gratian's sections on marriage.[34] They formed a central part of the nascent study of theology in the *Sentences* of Peter Lombard.[35]

There were theological critics of the procreative purpose.[36] There was also a split between the opinion of the theologians and the living life of the Church. If the Alexandrian-Augustinian rule had been rigidly applied, it would have been morally impossible for the sterile or those past the age of childbearing to marry, because it would have been morally impossible for them to have intercourse without sin.[37] However, the Church never forbade marriage to the sterile or the aged, and the liturgical practice of marrying such persons provided a different testimony from that of theological opinion.

There was also inconsistency within the structure of the Augustinian argument. Bowing to the text of St. Paul (1 Cor. 7:3-4) which stated that each spouse had an obligation to have intercourse with the other, the major theologians taught that there was an obligation to respond to a spouse's request for intercourse even though the purpose was not procreative.[38] Hence, it was possible for one spouse to be committing a sin in seeking nonprocreative intercourse and the other to be acting virtuously in responding. This highly artificial view of marital relations was a perpetual difficulty and reproach to the Augustinian account.

It was not, however, until the sixteenth century that appeal began to be made to the experience of married Christians. Then theologians like the Scot John Major asserted that the Augustinian rule actually encouraged adultery because it gave the impression that nonprocreative intercourse in marriage was as much a sin as intercourse outside of marriage. Major could see no more harm in seeking pleasure in marital intercourse than in seeking pleasure in eating an apple. The teachings of the saints on the subject, he added, must be interpreted restrictively "lest we damn all spouses."[39]

The full weight of theological opinion did not begin to shift until the beginning of the seventeenth century. Then under the aegis of the remarkable Thomas Sanchez, the great Spanish Jesuit specialist on marriage, the theologians turned from the Augustinian account and recognized a plurality of legitimate functions in marital intercourse.[40] The simple old measure which identified virtue with procreative intent was gone. With the abandonment of this clear and easy measure a host of problems, which seem typically modern, were created. Papal authority intervened to condemn the opinion that intercourse "for pleasure alone" was lawful in marriage.[41] The theologians responded to this papal edict by saying that the condemned opinion referred only to pleasure-seeking which deliberately excluded all other purposes.[42]

It was not, however, until the nineteenth century that it was suggested that one of the purposes of marital intercourse could be the fostering of conjugal affection and the expression of conjugal love. This suggestion was the work of the French writer of theological manuals, Jean Gury, who built timidly on a suggestion made by Sanchez, which Sanchez himself had confined to sexual acts in marriage short of intercourse.[43] Gury's suggestion was well received by a few theologians, mostly German, but did not receive widespread acceptance in nineteenth century theology.[44]

The emergence of love as a factor in the nineteenth century theology of marriage may be accounted for in part by environmental changes which presented as a social ideal the notion that marriage should be the free choice of relatively adult persons. The older practice of the leading class in European society to marry under a large degree of parental control and to marry girls at very young ages was now undermined by the general ideal of marriage by choice. The culture's ideal of marriage for love, which became general in the twentieth century Western world, underlay the support given in the twentieth century to Gury's idea. His views were now taken up by the German layman Dietrich von Hildebrand in 1925; and they were restated and synthesized by the German secular priest Herbert Doms in *Von Sinn und Zweck der Ehe*. In Doms' masterful summary there was presented for the first time in Catholic thought, a non-Augustinian account of the purposes of marriage which emphasized personal interrelations in intercourse and justified the practice of the Church in marrying the sterile and the aged.[45]

Official reaction of disapproval to Doms' book was reflected in a Holy Office decree of 1944;[46] but by 1949 Doms' ideas had been sufficiently absorbed by the Jesuit adviser of the Pope, Francis Hürth, for them to appear in a statement of Pius XII.[47] The Pope used them to reject artificial insemination, which, he said, did not recognize the personal values of intercourse; but although used in a somewhat negative way, Doms' ideas were now being recognized at a high enough ecclesiastical level to encourage their widespread acceptance within the entire Catholic community.

In the 1950's Doms' ideas were nuanced and refined by the leading moral theologians, particularly Bernard Häring and Joseph Fuchs.[48] The fruit of this theological activity of the 1950's was the decree adopted by the Second Vatican Council in its "Pastoral Constitution on the Church in the Modern World," *Gaudium et Spes*.[49]

Here, for the first time, a general council of the Church considered the purposes of marital intercourse. It refused to say that there was a primary and a secondary purpose, as the conservative fathers of the council urgently asked.[50] Instead, it taught that the procreation and education of children was one end of Christian marriage and that children were "the supreme gift" of Christian marriage. At the same time the Council taught that Christ had commended a special love between spouses and that love was "perfected and expressed in the proper work of marriage."[51]

In this recognition of marital intercourse as a perfection of Christian love, the Council had traveled very far from the Alexandria of Clement. The path it had taken had been reached by theological hypotheses and argument, by papal condemnations and by papal teachings, and by the reflection of theologians on the experience of the Christian faithful and the testimony of the Christian liturgy—all of these factors seen in the light given by the Old Testament and the New.

IV. RULES AND VALUES

It is sometimes supposed that the usury prohibition changed because it depended on conditions external to man which changed, while a prohibition having to do with the sexual faculties of man could not change because the biological character of man does not change. As the history of the teaching on the purposes of marital intercourse illustrates, this simple distinction is simply fallacious. The prohibitions having to do with the sexual faculties of man have changed as well as the prohibition on profit in transactions of credit.

The simple distinction proposed might have been possible if restricted by an impossible hypothesis to prohibitions concerning acts or thoughts of man which are unaffected by his environment. But, in fact, human beings are not pure spirits independent of their surroundings, and even the form of their thought depends on their interactions with other human beings. In the particular case of man's sexual faculties, the teaching in the past has depended on medical and biological knowledge, and it has depended on social mores. Clearly, for example, the teaching on the role of love in marriage was immensely affected by the change in the pattern of selection of partners in marriage. Clearly, the elimination of a large slave population, legally incapable of marriage, affected the teaching on relation between the sexes. Clearly, the opening up of education to women and increased education for everyone affected the degree to which personal responsibility could be stressed in sexual relations. The teaching on the purposes of marital intercourse developed, in part, in response to changes in the culture.

The static myth of moral doctrine supposes that the rules have never changed. This account is seen as fantasy once the actual teaching is looked at. Those who espouse the static myth are helpless to account for the changes that have in fact occurred in regard to usury or in regard to the purposes of marital intercourse.

The static myth supposes that the Church is a kind of machine placed on earth by God as a prodigy to be marveled at by men because it remains the same machine. As a machine, it does not respond to its environment and it has no internal principle of life. It goes on endlessly reduplicating the same patterns. If a part wears out, it may be replaced, but the same pattern will always be cut.

This static model is a view of the Church taken by some persons within it and by some of its critics without.[52] Although the motives of these persons are different, as some act from fear and some from hostility, their vision is the same, a lifeless and remarkable monster.

An account of moral doctrine in the Church which looks at what has actually occurred is forced to make distinctions. The distinction which seems most persuasive to me is between rules and values. The rules can and have changed. The values as they relate to the fundamental good of man cannot change. This distinction cannot, perhaps, be absolute. The emphasis placed on values in rules affects their realization. Yet if one considers the history, it is plain that while the rules do change, there are a thrust and a commitment to certain goods; such a thrust and a commitment are never abandoned.

In the case of the usury prohibition, the fundamental values were justice and charity. In the case of the purposes of marital intercourse, the values were the goodness of procreation, the inviolability of innocent life, the personal dignity of the spouses in their interrelation, and the sanctity of married love. In different ways, in different cultures, the theological teachings and the rules developed sought to serve these values.

A model of moral development which makes a distinction between rules and values is also a model of an organic institution. An organism, unlike a machine, does respond to its environment, and to that extent changes. It also has an internal principle of life, and to that extent it grows.[53] This growth, this purposeful unfolding, is development.

The organic vision of the Church is that proposed to us by the gospel when it tells of a mustard seed which has grown into a tree.

NOTES

[1] St. Pius X, *Pascendi dominici gregis*, Acta sanctae sedis 40.604 (1907).

[2] Second Vatican Council, *Dei verbum*, Acta apostolicae sedis 58.822 (1966).

[3] Gratian, *Decretum* D. 88, c. 11, *Corpus juris canonici*, ed. E. Friedberg, Leipzig (1879-1888); Gregory IX, *Decretales* V. 19, *Ibid.*, Vol. II.

[4] Gratian, C. 14, q. 4, dictum post c. 10; Urban III, *Consuluit*, *Decretales* 5.19.10.

[5] Second Lateran Council, canon 13, *Porro detestabiles*, in Karl Joseph von Hefele, *Histoire des conciles*, trans. H. Leclerq (Paris, 1907-1938), V, part 1, 729; Third Lateran Council, canon 25, *Quia in omnibus* in *Ibid.* V. part 2, 1105; Alexander III, *In civitate*, *Decretales* 5.19.6; Urban III, *Consuluit*, *Ibid.* 5.19.10; Thomas Aquinas, *Summa theologica* 2-2. 78.1; Hostiensis, *Summa aurea* (Venice, 1579) 5, *De usuris*.

[6] *Psalm* 14.5; *Exodus* 22.25; *Leviticus* 25.35-37; *Ezekiel* 18.8.

[7] St. Gregory of Nyssa, *Homily*, *Patrologia graeca* (ed. J. P. Migne, Paris, 1857-1866) 54. 671; St. Ambrose, *De Tobia*.

[8] Franz Schaub, *Der Kampf gegen den Zinswucher, ungerechten Preis, und unlautern Handel im Mittelatter: Von Karl dem Grossen bis papst Alexander III* (Freiburg in Br., 1905), pp. 37-39, 58-66, 121-122, 178.

[9] As to these exceptions, John T. Noonan, Jr., *The Scholastic Analysis of Usury* (Cambridge, 1957), pp. 100-134.

[10] On the annuity contract, Domingo de Soto, *De justitia et jure libri decem* (Lyons, 1569) 6.5; on foreign exchange, Cajetan, *De cambiis* 6-7, *Scripta philosophica: Opuscula oeconomica socialia* (ed. P. Zammit, Rome, 1934); on the secured partnership or triple contract, Navarrus, *De usuris* 14, *Opera omnia* (Venice, 1618) Vol. 1.

[11] E.g., Navarrus, *De cambiis* 15, 22, *Opera*, Vol. 1; Luis de Molina, *De justitia de jure* 2.405.5, *Opera omnia*, Vol. 2.

[12] Pius V, *Cum onus*, January 19, 1569, *Bullarium romanum*, VII, 737 ff.; Pius V, *In eam*, January 28, 1571, *Ibid.* 880; Sixtus V, *Detestabilis avaritia*, *Ibid.* VIII, 783-785.

[13] Ernest Joseph Van Roey, *Le contractus germanicus*, Revue d'histoire ecclésiastique III (1902), pp. 901-946; Peter Canisius, *Epistulae et acta* (ed. O. Braunsberger, Freiburg im Br., 1896-1922), IV, 563; V, 529, 535-536; VI, 410, 416; VII, 671-672.

[14] Franz X. Zech, *Dissertationes tres, in quibus rigor moderatus doctrinae pontificae circa usuras a sanctissimo D. N. Benedicto XIV per epistolam encyclicam episcopis Italiae traditae exhibetur* (Venice, 1762), 3.2.8. 263, reprinted in J. P. Migne, *Theologiae cursus comple-*

tus XVI (Paris, 1841); cf. Bernhard Duhr, *Die Deutschen Jesuiten, im 5% Streit des 16 Jahrhunderts, Zeitschrift für katholische theologie* (1900), p. 20.

[15] Scipio Maffei, *Dell' impiego del denaro, libri tre* (Rome, 1746), pp. 75-147.

[16] Benedict XIV, *Vix pervenit*, *Theologiae cursus completus* XVI, 1059.

[17] E.g., Jean Gury, *Compendium theologiae moralis, De contractibus* 2.6.3 (Tournai, 1852).

[18] *Genesis* 9.1; *Exodus* 23.26; *Deuteronomy* 7.13-14; *Ruth* 4.11; *Job* 1.2, 42.13.

[19] The key term in these passages in *pharmakeia*, the use of drugs destroying embryonic life; the term is usually mistranslated in English as "sorcery."

[20] Eusebius, *The Gospel Demonstration*, 1.9, *Patrologia graeca* 22.77-81.

[21] St. John Chrysostom, *On Those Words of the Apostle "On Account of Fornication"* 3, *Patrologia graeca* 51.213.

[22] *Matthew* 19.12, 22.30, 1.18-25; *Luke* 1.30-37, 18.29, 20.34-36; *Apocalypse* 14.1-5.

[23] See Clement of Alexandria's account of his opponents, Clement, *Stromata* 3.6.48-49, *Die griechischen christlichen Schriftsteller der ersten drei Jahrhunderte* (Leipzig, 1897-) (henceforth *GCS*) 15. 218-219, 236, English translation in John Ernest Leonard Dulton and Henry Chadwick, *Alexandrian Christianity* (London, 1955). On the contemporary usage of "left" and "right," François M. M. Sagnard, *La Gnose valentinienne et le témoignage de S. Irénée* (Paris, 1947), pp. 544-545; cf. Matthew 25.33.

[24] See Clement's descriptions of men of the Left in *Stromata* 3.1.3, 3.2.8, 3.4.25-30.

[25] Traces may be found as early as such New Testament documents as *Apocalypse* 2.6, *Jude* 4 and 11, *2 Peter* 2 and 3.

[26] Clement, *Stromata* 3.11.71.4; Clement, *The Teacher* 2.10.95.3, *GCS* 12.214. For Stoic statement of the rule see Musonius Rufas, *Reliquiae*, ed. O. Hense (Leipzig, 1905), sec. 63.

[27] Origen, *Third Homily on Genesis* 6, *GCS* 29.47.

[28] Ambrose, *Expositio Evangelii secundum Lucam* 1.43-45, *Corpus scriptorum ecclesiasticorum latinorum* (hereafter *CSEL*), 324: 38-39; Jerome *In epistolam S. Pauli ad Galatos* 5, *Patrologia latina* 26.443; Augustine, *De bono coniugali* 6.6.10.11, *CSEL* 41. 194, 203.

[29] See John T. Noonan, Jr., *Contraception: A History of Its Treatment by the Catholic Theologians and Canonists* (New York, Paperback edition, 1967), pp. 137-145.

[30] Augustine, *Contra Faustum* 22.80, *CSEL* 251. 682-683.

[31] Augustine, *op. cit. supra*, n. 29.

[32] *The Irish Penitentials*, ed. Ludwig Bieler (Dublin, 1963).

[33] Eckbert, *Sermones contra Catharos*, *Patrologia latina* 195.102.

[34] Gratian, *Decretum* 2.32.2 and 7.

[35] Peter Lombard, *Sententiae* (ed. Fathers of the College of Bonaventure, Quaracchi, 1916), 4.31.

[36] Alexander of Hales, *Summa theologica* (Quaracchi, 1930-1948), 2-2, 3.5. 2.1.3.1.

[37] The point is noticed by Charles Billuart, *Summa Sancti Thomae hodiernis academiarum moribus accommodata* (Paris, 1827-1831), *De bonis et actibus matrimonii* 2.2.

[38] Thomas Aquinas, *In sententias Petri Lombardi* 4.31. 1.2 (*Opera omnia*, ed. Maré and Fretté, Vol. 10).

[39] John Major, *In quartum sententiarum Petri Lombardi* 4.31 (Paris, 1519).

[40] Thomas Sanchez, *De sancto matrimonii sacramento* (Venice, 1737), 9.8.

[41] Holy Office, Decree of March 4, 1679, *Enchiridion symbolorum definitionum et declarationum de rebus fidei et morum*, ed. H. Denzinger, rev. Adolf Schónmetzer (Barcelona, 1963), n. 1159.

[42] Dominic Lindner, *Der Usus Matrimonii* (Munich, 1929), pp. 186-191; St. Alfonso de' Ligouri, *Theologia moralis* 6.882, 927 (Rome 1947).

[43] Gury, *Compendium theologiae moralis, De matrimonio*, n. 688.

[44] Johannes Becker, *Die moralische Beurteilung des Handelns aus Lust, Zeitschrift für katholische Theologie* (1902), 679 ff.; Noonan, *op. cit. supra*, n. 30, p. 586.

[45] Doms, *Von Sinn und Zweck der Ehe* (Bieslaw, 1935); English translation, *The Meaning of Marriage* (New York, 1961).

[46] *Acta apostolicae sedis* 36.103 (1944).

[47] Pius XII, Address to the Fourth International Congress of Catholic Doctors, *Acta apostolicae sedis* 41:559 (1949).

[48] Bernard Häring, *Das Gesetz Christi* (Freiburg im Bresgan, 1957), English translation, *The Law of Christ* (4th ed.) 2.2.4.3.2.3a; Joseph Fuchs, *De castitate et ordine sexuali* (Rome, 1960) 2.4.1.

[49] Second Vatican Council, *Gaudium et spes*, secs. 49-51, *Acta apostolicae sedis* 58.1069-1072.

[50] John T. Noonan, Jr., *The Church and Contraception: The Issues at Stake* (Glen Rock, 1966), p. 32.

[51] Second Vatican Council, *Gaudium et spes*, sec. 49, *Acta apostolicae sedis* 58.1070.

[52] E.g., the hostile account of the change on usury given by Andrew White, *The History of the Warfare of Science with Theology in Christendom* (New York, 1922), Vol. 2, p. 264.

[53] Pius XII, Address "*Vous avez voulu*," to the Tenth International Congress of Historical Sciences, September 7, 1955, *Acta apostolicae sedis* 47.672-685 (1955).

Evolution of the Human Soul

Eulalio Baltazar

THERE are two parts to this presentation: the first is an attempt to show the intrinsic temporality of the human soul and its orientation to eternity seen as the fullness of time; the second, an explanation of the origin of the human soul by evolution rather than by immediate creation. The first part is a necessary step to showing the soul's origin by a temporal process. Implicit in our exposition and argument is a philosophic pattern of thought we call *process thinking*. Ultimately, the validity of our presentation depends on the validity of process thinking.[1]

I. THE TEMPORALITY OF ETERNITY AND OF THE HUMAN SOUL

BECAUSE of a radical shift in modern man's outlook and valuation from the timeless and suprahistorical or other-worldly, to the timely and this-worldly, our traditional view of God as immutable and of man as having a soul that is destined for the timeless and other-worldly, have come in for some hard criticisms, not only from non-Christians but from Christians as well. And just as a current theological reflection on God has concentrated on making him immanent and this-worldly, so philosophical anthropology has had for its program the historicizing of man.

My general aim is to show that man totally belongs to the universe; that he is not a foreigner to it, which seems to be the general impression one gets from the doctrine of the immediate creation and infusion of the human soul. If man's soul is not evolved, then man does not really belong to this world; he cannot, as a result, give himself fully to the building of the earth. Christian humanism becomes a farce. To show that the human soul must have been evolved, it is necessary first to show that the human soul is temporal in structure, function, and orientation. But for the strength of our contention, it is also necessary to show that God's eternity which is the goal of the human soul, is not the absence of time but the fullness of time. In the traditional view, God's eternity seen as timelessness and the immediate creation and infusion of the human soul go hand in hand. To deny one is also to deny the other. Hence, our double task of showing both God's temporality and the soul's evolution.

With respect to God's eternity as the absence of time, it is difficult to see how God can really be in the secular and temporal world. We have moved far from classical theism and from Barthian and Bultmannian theologies of other-worldliness which isolated God from the world, science, and evolution. The recent effort of the death-of-God theologians, however, of affirming temporality and secularity at the expense of God himself have proved abortive, for they have sacrificed transcendence for the sake of immanence. The direction theology must take to reconcile immanence and transcendence, it would seem, is to adopt the eschatological or processive outlook in which transcendence is located up ahead instead of up above.

With regard to anthropology, modern philosophy has taken a direction similar to that taken by modern theology of doing away with the object they are trying to explain. Thus, just as some secularist theologians tried to do away with the notion of God as being intrinsically other-worldly, so some modern philosophers have done away with the soul as also being intrinsically other-worldly. As a substitute for the soul, modern philosophy speaks instead of transcendental consciousness, of freedom and of the person.

The basic objection to the spiritual soul is expressed very well by Robert Johann when he observes that "one of the difficulties with a spiritualist anthropology is its tendency to make man a stranger in the world. For some thinkers, to hold that man is spirit, albeit *embodied spirit,* is to hold that he has access to another world besides this one, another world that is his true home. As spiritual, man may be *in* the world but is really not *of* it. He is only 'passing through.' "[2] Thus, the body-soul dualism would seem to compartmentalize human life. There is the outer life of the body which is concerned with time and the inner life of the soul concerned with eternity.

Another reason why some Christians have given up the body-soul dichotomy is because of their belief that it is Hellenic, the implication being that what is Hellenic is underdeveloped and infantile. Some of the de-hellenizers have had recourse to the Scriptural view of man which sees him as a whole, either as sinful or fleshly, *(sarx),* or as spiritual or a man of God *(ruach).* However, while Scripture avoids the dualism, it does not answer the question we are concerned with, namely the ontological make-up of man, irrespective of whether he is a believer or not. The scriptural view is set in the context of belief, not of philosophy.

Now from the philosophic point of view, the distinction between the spiritual and material dimensions of man is not necessarily Hellenic, as long as we do not see them in terms of the categories of matter and form. We can look at the body and soul as two aspects of one and the same reality, or to use Teilhard's phrase, as the *within* and the *without,* or as the radial and tangential energies of man. Modern philosophy, such as existentialism, cannot go on ignoring the reality of the soul, for sooner or later, the need for transcendence and the problem of the after-life will bring it up. We cannot go on saying the soul is dead, any more than secularists can go on proclaiming the death of God.

The true direction of Christian renewal, it seems, is to present both God and the human soul as this-worldly, instead of other-worldly and this can be done, we believe, through the use of process thought which leads to the notion of evolutionary time. Now, this effort is not a minor form of surgery on the doctrinal corpus of traditional thought; it is a major one. For traditional theology is founded on the basic premise that the timeless is better than the temporal, the immutable than the mutable, the suprahistorical than the historical.

What we are asking the reader to do is nothing short of a *metanoia,* a radical change in thought pattern from the metaphysical and timeless to the processive and temporal. This is not easy, for confining ourselves to the problem of eternity and the human soul alone, we have been conditioned for centuries to think of God's eternity as timelessness, and of the human soul as orientated to timelessness. Traditional philosophy has built up proofs to show the soul's intrinsic independence from matter by the fact that the intellect, which is a power of the soul, is able to abstract universals. The intellect is shown as a faculty of timelessness, and this abstractive ability is given as the distinction between man and brute who has only sense knowledge which shows that its animal soul is material, totally immersed in time. The human soul's immortality is founded on its immateriality. Again, the premise or assumption in traditional metaphysics is that the temporal is allied with the material, while the spiritual is necessarily supratemporal.

Now, what we would like to show is just the opposite, namely, that the material is allied with the timeless, while the spiritual is allied with the fullness of time. We would like to demonstrate that because God is Spirit, his eternity is the fullness of time and because the human soul is spiritual it is also oriented towards the fullness of time. The intellect in this case is a faculty of time so that man's highest function is to be a gatherer of time, that man fulfills himself by incarnating himself in time rather than by withdrawing from time, and that therefore human labor which is concerned with the temporal is not only humanizing but divinizing. Our first step then is to show that time is of greater value than timelessness. If we can show this, then it is not illogical and inappropriate to attribute to God's eternity the character of temporality and to the human soul too.

It is necessary to do some psychoanalysis, so to speak, of our mind

—trained to think that timelessness is of greater value than the timely—in order that we might be disabused of the false assumption that this proposition is an absolute truth when as a matter of fact it is the length of the tradition that has given it the force of a dogma.

Plato and Aristotle were the sources of our view that the timeless and the immutable are better than the temporal and the dynamic. The reason for this is that they saw only the evidence of the destructiveness of time. They were unaware of the evolutionary view that time in its evolution is creative of novelty; hence, that it is positive rather than negative. Because they were unaware of evolution, they could not see that timelessness in an evolutionary context is non-being rather than being. In the context of growth, to have no time means death or non-being, for to have no time means to have no future, and for the present to have no future means the cessation of growth or death. In evolution, timelessness is equated with death, with a museum piece, a fossil. The timely is equated with life, hence with being.

Perhaps it is necessary at this point to substantiate our assertion that for Plato and Aristotle, the timeless is better than the temporal. Thus, for Plato, in the *Timaeus* (37d), time is but the moving imitation of eternity. This means that things in time are impermanent, mere shadows and copies of the unchanging eternal ideas that dwelt in the other-worldly realm. Neo-Platonism too saw the real as the timeless and the unreal as the temporal. Thus Plotinus in the *Enneads* (3:7,7) says that time is the measure of degradation or fall of the sensible world from the region of timelessness or from the One. The farther man progressed into the future, the greater the multiplicity and contingency, because unity was found at the Alpha or beginning.

Curiously, by way of digression, we might note that our traditional theology situates the state of innocence in paradise at the beginning and that from this exalted and perfect state, there was a fall. In line with evolution, however, it is difficult to see how man could have been perfect in the beginning. Rather, the movement in accordance with the evolutionary process would be an upward one, hence, from the imperfect to the perfect. The assumption here is that the beginning of evolution is the region of multiplicity, contingency and great randomness, while the future is the region of unity, of maturation and the fullness of being, hence, of perfection. Accordingly, in line with the evolutionary framework, some modern theologians are now beginning to situate paradise at the end, as an eschatological ideal rather than as an existent primordial state.[3]

To come back to our review of the Greek view of time, we also find Aristotle calmly and dispassionately affirming, as befits the scientist that he was, the negative character of time. Thus he says: "It is in time that all is engendered and destroyed.... One can see that time itself is the cause of destruction rather than generation.... For change itself is an undoing; it is only by accident a cause of generation and existence."[4] He continues: "For we are wont to say that time wears, that all things age in time, all is erased by time, but never that we have learnt or that we have grown young and handsome; for time in itself is more truly a cause of destruction, since time is the number of movement, and movement undoes that which is."[5]

There are those who would claim that Aristotle had a notion of evolution or that, at least, it is possible to understand evolution within his philosophic framework in terms of the category of act and potency. But as J. H. Randall, Jr. says,[6] Aristotle had an idea of development but applicable only to particulars or individual patterns of growth; the species, however was fixed. And other experts on aspects of Aristotle's thought like M. Greene,[7] O. L. Reiser,[8] E. Mayr,[9] and G. G. Simpson,[10] have shown that Aristotle's thought pattern is not merely non-evolutionary, but it is opposed to the temporal in its very theory of scientific knowledge and understanding.

Thus, for Aristotle as it was for Plato, the timeless was the object of knowledge and understanding. For Plato one withdrew from the temporal by a process of *anamnēsis* or reminiscence; for Aristotle, the timeless essence was abstracted from particulars. Both in science and in metaphysics, the Aristotelian tradition considered time and space as an obstacle to true knowledge. In his *Physics,* Aristotle proceeds to abstract from space and time in order to arrive at the species. *Scientia est de universalibus.* The human soul, seen as the substantial form of the body, was accordingly seen as timeless, which thus serves as foundation for the knowledge of the transcendent and timeless God. In Scholasticism, the soul as "form" mirrors the timelessness of the divine.

Raymond Nogar observes that "philosophical traditions prior to Hegel's attempt to discover the timeless amidst the timely and to throw human understanding open to the divine. Perhaps it is correct to say that this is also the main thrust of the thought of Hegel."[11] Nogar continues: "the timely was merely the jumping off place; it was the timeless and the divine which received the attention of the Greek traditions, and in their wake the Christian philosophic traditions down to our own day."[12]

But it was not only the scientific and the philosophic that was affected by the Hellenic pattern of thought which gave preference to the timeless. Also the theological was affected. As St. Thomas himself insisted, it is false to suppose that false notions about the created universe will not lead one into error in philosophy and theology.[13] There are those of his followers, however, who think that all they have to do is to excise the antiquated scientific part of the Aristotelian system, while leaving the philosophic intact. Again, this thinking proceeds from the system and is perpetuated by the system which leads one to believe, that metaphysics, being an abstraction from time, is thus unaffected by time. What is forgotten is that no man can absolutely transcend history; that all philosophies are products of their age and culture, and so are all theological formulations.

We might propose a maxim, namely, that as the physics, so the ontology and the theology. The scientific view of the ancient and medieval tradition was Ptolemaic: the earth was at the center of the universe and around it were the sun and other heavenly bodies. This geocentric pattern was analogically represented at the anthropological level, where man's soul as the supreme substantial form was at the center, and around it were lesser substantial forms varying in their degree of immersion in time and contingency; but the human soul consorted with the pure forms or with the timeless and eternal. Aristotle gave philosophic expression to this picture by giving us the categories of substance and accident. Substance in relation to accident was the principle of permanence; accidents were contingent. Again, the mental pattern is reproduced in which the timeless or permanent was placed at the center, while at the periphery were placed the contingent accidents as satellites. The same pattern was reproduced in Christian theology. As F. Crowe, S.J. observes, ". . . medieval theologians took over Aristotelian philosophy, which had already integrated the mathematical and physical sciences, and added theology to obtain a coherent and closely-knit view of the universe."[14] Again we have a Ptolemaic view in which theology was placed at the center, its truth being the *substantia fidei*, (the substance of the faith), while philosophy was considered the *ancilla theologiae*, (handmaid of theology), and its metaphysical truths aided the understanding of the truths of the faith. Farther outside the select circle of the theologian and the metaphysician was the sphere of lowly science with its contingent and particular truths. The Scriptures were seen as possessing the universal truths from which the contingent truths of science could be judged. We need not retell the unfortunate incidents that this mind-set produced in the course of human history.

With the thought pattern that the timeless was of greater value than the temporal, God's eternity could not very well be equated with time. To express God's eternity, it had to be portrayed as the absence of time. It is thus impossible for time and eternity to have any relationship. As Louis Bouyer points out, "in Greek thought, eternity and time cannot possibly be reconciled. The two notions can be said to characterize two universes parallel to one another. Eternity is a characteristic not only of immutable, but of purely ideal realities. Time belongs exclusively to the world of matter and change."[15] Oscar Cullmann has the same observation:

> For Greek thinking in its Platonic formulation there exists between time and eternity a qualitative difference, which is not completely expressed by speaking of a distinction between limited and unlimited duration of time. For Plato, eternity is not endlessly extended time, but something quite different; it is timelessness. Time in Plato's view is only the copy of eternity thus understood.[16]

If time and eternity are thus irreconcilable, then how can we have the foundation for any analogy between God and creature? How can God create time if his eternity is the absence of time? Important as this philosophical problem is, it is not as significant for many compared to the effect the Greek view of time had on Christian spirituality. "For the Greeks, the idea that redemption is to take place through divine action in the course of events in time, is impossible."[17] Cullmann continues:

> Redemption in Hellenism can consist only in the fact that we are transferred from existence in this world, an existence bound to the circular course of time, into that Beyond which is removed from time and is already and always available. The Greek conception of blessedness is thus spatial; it is determined by the contrast between this world and the timeless Beyond; it is not a time conception determined by the opposition between Now and Then.[18]

According to Cullman, this Greek view of redemption as a withdrawal from time has come down even to our day: "Far and wide, the Christian Church and Christian theology distinguish time and eternity in the Platonic-Greek manner."[19]

Now, as long as Christian thinking has not made the shift from the timeless to the timely at the philosophic and theological levels, then man's humanization as an immersion in the temporal has no justification. For if God's eternity is the absence of time, then how can involvement in time achieve for me eternal life? No, I think the medievals were logical in withdrawing from time or simply waiting for the after-life. As long as we go on speaking of the soul's orientation as towards the timeless, then there is no foundation for serious engagement in the secular. It is hard to see how Teilhard's complaint that Christians lend themselves only to secular tasks is not justified. Thus he notes:

> The great objection brought against Christianity in our time, and the real source of the distrust which insulates entire blocks of humanity from the influence of the Church, has nothing to do with historical or theological difficulties. It is the suspicion that our religion makes its adherents inhuman.
> 'Christianity,' so some of the best of the Gentiles are inclined to think, 'is bad or inferior because it does not lead its followers beyond humanity, but away from it or to one side of it. It isolates them instead of merging them with the mass. Instead of harnessing them to the common task, it causes them to lose interest in it. Hence far from exalting them, it diminishes and distorts them. Moreover don't they admit as much themselves? And if one of their religious, or one of their priests, should happen to devote his life to what is called profane research, he is very careful, as a rule, to recall that

> he only lends himself to these secondary pursuits for the sake of conforming to a fashion or an illusion, to prove that Christians are not the most stupid of men. When a Catholic works with us, we invariably get the impression that he is doing so in an insincere way, condescendingly. He appears to be interested, but in fact, because of his religion, he does not believe in the human effort. His heart is not really with us. Christianity creates deserters and false friends; that is what we cannot forgive.'[20]

We can not answer this justified complaint of Teilhard, nor can we have a valid theology of the secular until we can show the intrinsic temporality of the human soul.

Even Vatican II in its document on the Church in the Modern World manifests still the dualism of traditional anthropology for it oscillates between insistence on collaborating in earthly progress, on the one hand, and the building of the heavenly Kingdom, on the other. Karl Rahner observes this uncertainty in the document. Thus, he asks: "Is the world which man himself creates only the 'material' for his moral testing, remaining in itself morally indifferent? Will the world simply disappear when the definitive kingdom of God arrives?"[21] If so, says Rahner, then we must "allow ourselves to be asked by Marxism how seriously we really take the world that is committed to our making. Is it ultimately only indifferent material on which we exercise our virtues?"[22] To these questions, the document has not given a clear answer. The vagueness in the document is ultimately the failure to attain an anthropology that is this-worldly. For human effort to make sense, for the spiritual transformation of the earth to have meaning, man must be totally structured for the temporal, and eternity, too, must be seen as temporal.

Let us then show first the temporal character of eternity, and we have no better place to find this than in the Scriptures. There, we observe that God's eternity is seen in terms of the category of time rather than the timeless. As the *Vocabulary of the Bible* notes:

> The eternity of God is first manifested in the fact that he was and acted before all things and all life: before the individual life (Jer. 1:5), before the people of Israel, before the created world (Ps. 90:2). Likewise He is the One who will be after all created existence. He is the "alpha and the omega, the beginning and the end" (Rev. 21:6; cf. 22:13). His divine time overflows, holds together, and envelops all other times.... The eternal life of God does not of course cease to have its specific dimension within the period between the creation and the last judgment. God is "He who is and who was and who is to come" (Rev. 1:4; 4:8).[23]

Thus, the Scriptures speak of God's divine time which overflows and holds together and envelops all other times. He contains all times, since he is spoken of as "he who was and who is and who is to come."

Furthermore, it is in the *kairos* or sacred time that God is present. And in the New Testament and in our liturgy, the deepest levels of reality and the deepest mysteries of the Faith, namely, the Incarnation, the passion, death and resurrection of Christ, are shown not as timeless but as temporal stages of the redemptive process: the Incarnation being a birth, the passion and death, being a dying of the 'seed,' and the resurrection being a germination or rebirth into eschatological time or the New Age. And Christ himself is seen as God's supreme *Kairos* or the fullness of time (Gal. 4:4).

Primitive Christianity saw God's eternity in terms of the scriptural view. Thus, as Cullmann notes:

> Primitive Christianity knows nothing of a timeless God. The "eternal" God is he who was in the beginning, is now, and will be in all the future, "who is, who was, and who will be" (Rev. 1:4). Accordingly, his eternity can and must be expressed in this "naive" way, in terms of endless time.[24]

Of course, when Christianity was preached to the Greeks, God's eternity could not very well be shown as the fullness of time, for to the Greeks, the fullness of time would mean the fullness of contingency, particularity and the absence of intelligibility, and is synonymous to prime matter. Today, however, we can go back to the scriptural view that God's eternity is the fullness of time. But an acceptance of the scriptural view entails a radical change in our thought pattern and our philosophic understanding of time. The task then we must now do is to get a proper understanding of time, so that we can peaceably attribute temporality to God and to the human soul.

In the ordinary mind, time is equated with contingency and succession, with what is imperfect, unfinished, and unintelligible. Thus, to speak of God as the fullness of time would be to attribute contingency and imperfection of God; and to speak of the human soul as temporal, as having evolved is to equate it with lower forms of soul which are seen as being immersed in time and in the material. We must therefore get away from the naive common sense view of time as temporal succession or as the measure of motion before and after, to use the Aristotelian definition of it. For as a great Scripture scholar observes:

> The attitude of Western man to linear time is, generally speaking, naive; time is seen as an infinitely long straight line on which the individual can mark such past and future events as he can ascertain. This time-span has a midpoint, which is our own present day. From it the past stretches back and the future forwards. But to-day one of the few things of which we can be quite sure is that this concept of absolute time, independent of events, and, like the blanks of a questionnaire, only needing to be filled up with data which will give it content, was unknown to Israel.[25]

The true concept of time that I would like to propose is that of evolutionary time. Now, evolutionary time is not a straight line that goes on and on; it is not a succession of moments each of which appears momentarily and is lost forever. It is false to imagine time like a string of beads, each one of equal value as the other. No, a time that evolves carries the past over into the present, and the present is itself carried over into the future, so that the future is heavy with the present and the past. The future is the fullness of time of the present and the past. Time is not an absolute container; it is one with the thing which evolves, so that as the thing matures, time also matures. Time therefore is not wholly horizontal; it ascends ontologically. In its first stages, time grows, but once it has reached its maturation point, time ceases to grow; for when one has reached the fullness of growth, then there is no longer any contingency, for there is no longer any growth. The fullness of time is equated with maturity; lack of time with immaturity, and total lack of time, with death. To illustrate evolutionary time, let us take the seed as an example. The seed which is outside the ground has no time, because it is not growing. And if it stays in this state, it will soon shrivel up and die. Its existence is towards death. But once the seed is planted and begins to germinate, then it has time. We start counting the time till it begins to bear fruit. Fullness of time is thus equated with maturity or the fullness of growth.

The fullness of time is also equated with the fullness of experience and the fullness of identity. Thus, an infant who does not have as much time as the adult does not have as much experience. And having lesser experience, it has lesser being. Again, because the infant does not have a past, it does not have a sense of duration and permanence as the basis of its identity.

Fullness of time is also to be equated with the fullness of knowledge and the fullness of activity. The infant which does not have its future, is lacking in experience and knowledge of itself. But as it possesses more time, it also attains to greater knowledge. Attaining greater knowledge, it is better able to direct its activity and gain mastery of itself, its goals. The infant attains the fullness of activity to the degree that it possesses time not only at the level of the physical, developing the use of its physical organs as they are more and more differentiated, but above all at the level of conscious and moral activity, attaining the use of reason and proper direction of life.

Thus from our brief reflection on time as evolving, as maturing, we can say that time evolves from multiplicity and chaos, from transiency and contingency to unity, non-contingency and immanence. What is true of our analysis of individual cases of growth is even more true in the case of the evolving universe taken as a single process of evolution.

The evolutionary process evolves from matter to consciousness. If we were to use the Teilhardian terminology, we would say that the evolutionary process has stages: first, the evolution of matter or cosmogenesis; second, the evolution of life or biogenesis; and third, the evolution of consciousness or noogenesis. Now, what is often not realized by the Hellenic mind is that self-consciousness or intellection is not so much a transcendence from time as the possession of fuller time. In its hierarchy of being, traditional Hellenic thought would place, at the top, eternity as timelessness, and, at the bottom, the fully temporal. The place one has in the hierarchy is measured by the degree that one transcends time and materiality. Accordingly, God is placed right at the top as Supreme Being because his eternity is sheer timelessness; angels are next, for having no bodies, they are outside temporality, their existence being midway between eternity and temporality, hence, an aeviternity (a term that is compounded of *aevum* and *eternitas*); below the angels is man because although possessed of a body, he has a soul which partakes of eternity since it is intrinsically independent of time and matter. Below the spiritual soul are the material souls of brutes and plants which are intrinsically dependent upon time and matter; and finally, at the bottom is located matter itself because it is totally immersed in time.

But an awareness of evolution or, at least, of a dynamic view of reality, which the Scriptures presuppose, and which the ancients and medievals did not have, contradicts the norm of timelessness as the measure of one's position in the hierarchy. Rather, one's position is in direct proportion to one's possession of time so that the greater the time the higher one's place. In terms of growth or evolution, the fullness of growth or being would coincide with the fullness of the possession of time or maturity, while lack of the fullness of growth would coincide with the lack of the fullness of time. In other words, lack of time is equated with immaturity, imperfection, while fullness of time is equated with maturity and perfection. Accordingly, God is ranked first, not because his existence is a timelessness nor because it is the fullness of growth, but because he is the source of all growth, the Ground, as it were, of evolution, hence, the source of all time, his existence being endless time, as the Scriptures say. And at the bottom of the hierarchy, we would place matter, not because it is totally immersed in time, but, paradoxically enough, because it possesses the least time. This is so because evolution being the growth toward the fullness of maturity is also a growth towards the fullness of time. Now, since matter is the starting point of the process, it possesses less time than consciousness which emerges later in the process.

We could verify that matter possesses less time than consciousness in another way. Obviously, both matter and consciousness possess time because both of them are in process of evolution. But matter possesses time mainly externally and in a transient way, so to speak, in the sense that time is not interiorized; it is not inner directed. Consciousness, on the other hand, possesses time in a conscious way; time doubles up upon itself, so to speak, and is able to grasp itself immanently. Time is thus interiorised and is inner directed. More concretely, we can see that the animal possesses time in a fuller way than a stone or a plant, and that for this reason it is on a higher evolutionary level. The stone possesses time purely cosmologically, because time is not possessed as living time; the plant possesses time not only cosmologically but also biologically. It belongs to a higher evolutionary level, the biosphere. The animal possesses time in a fuller way than either the stone or the plant because through conscious memory it can somehow possess the past. A dog can remember its master and recognize him; it can remember being whipped and learn from its mistake. So that animal consciousness possesses not only the present, but somehow, the past.

Comparing human consciousness with animal consciousness, we observe that, contrary to the traditional view in which human consciousness is less immersed in time than animal consciousness, the reverse is the case. Thus, human consciousness can penetrate into the past farther and more profoundly through paleontology, archaeology, history, etc., than animal consciousness can. Human memory can bring back an individual's past more vividly and in greater detail and make use of the past in a constructive way that no animal memory can. Such a use and possession of the past implies a greater possession and mastery of time than a mere reproduction of the past by animal memory.

But what is most distinctive of man, what clearly distinguishes him from the animal is man's ability to foresee, that is, to anticipate the future. Traditional thought has not realized the significance of man's ability to foresee because of its philosophic and theological anthropology, which was blinded by the *a priori* assumption that timelessness is of greater value than the timely. Consequently, man's ability to foresee was ignored as of no great significance, while the supposed ability of the intellect to abstract a timeless essence from contingent particulars was emphasized as most distinctive of man, and as the basis of difference between man and brute and also as making man a little less than the angels.

The ability to abstract "universals" is really a tenuous basis for distinguishing man from brute, for recent research has shown that animals have rudimentary intelligence, that they can learn. What is clearly a valid and empirical basis for distinction is that of all the animals, man alone can foresee. By foresight, we mean much more than conceptualization, for this attains only the present such that the rational activity involved is one of seeing, not foreseeing. By foresight we mean activities like prediction, forecast, creative imagination, prophecy —activities that have the dimension of futurity in them. Philosophically, we can reduce foresight to the activities of belief and hope.

Because man alone can foresee, he alone can plan and direct his present activities with a future goal in mind. Man alone can fear death because he can grasp it as a future event; man alone can be anxious because he grasps the future as uncertain. We can sum up man's possession of time by saying that he alone of all the animals possesses historical time; he alone inhabits the noosphere. Because of his greater ability to possess time, man is superior to the animal; in fact he is an ex-animal.

In traditional thought, the proof for the transcendence of the human soul from time and hence its immortality is the supposed ability of the intellect to abstract "universals" which are believed to be outside temporality. This so-called immaterial activity of abstraction and conceptualization implies that the source of this activity, the soul, must likewise be immaterial and if so immortal. Upon closer analysis, however, using the evolutionary point of view, we find that the ability to attain "universals" is rather a manifestation of man's ability to possess all of space and time, the ability to be present to the past, present and the future. The term "universal" is really just another name for the common evolutionary origin and term of a group or species. In other words, the basis for similarity or "universality" as a common factor possessed by individuals in a species is really their common evolutionary origin or dimension. Thus, this and that individual are called men because they belong to, or possess, the same evolutionary dimension—the historical dimension or the noosphere. Hence, so-called "universals" are not supratemporal; rather, they are temporal or evolutionary in meaning and origin.

We can also deduce that the intellect is a faculty of time rather than of timelessness from the fact that man is evolving, or, to use the scriptural phrase, that man is a wayfarer. If this is the overall situation of man, then we would expect that all his powers and faculties would be ordained for the attainment of the future. Consequently, the intellect's purpose ultimately is one of foreseeing, i.e. of direction towards the future. In scriptural language, the intellect is a light that lights the darkness of the future. The intellect reads the signs of the time. Its proper function is to be predictive and prophetic rather than purely metaphysical, existential, or empirical, i.e., merely seeing. The intellect is processive and pragmatic, rather than static and contemplative. And the will also is orientated towards the future, hence to time. It is a power for situating us in the true course towards the future goal, not a faculty for transporting us out of time.

We said earlier that man's activity of foreseeing is summed up in the activities of belief and hope. This is so, for as Jürgen Moltmann very well observes, belief makes us recognize the future, while hope opens the future for us.[26] Belief and hope are what distinguishes man from animals and the rest of the infra-human level. Man is not so much a conceptual or seeing animal, but a believing and hoping creature. He is a *homo credens et sperans*.

Thus far we have explained that human consciousness is intrinsically temporal, being ordained towards the possession of time. In the highest activity of man, that of belief and hope, we can see especially clearly the temporality of human consciousness, for belief and hope have the intrinsic dimension of the future in them. We can therefore conclude that the human soul must be intrinsically temporal for the human soul is ultimately the source of belief and hope. It is through belief and hope that the human soul is reborn into a new dimension of evolutionary time. Psychology confirms our analysis that the human soul is intrinsically temporal for as Carl Jung has found from his life-long work with peoples of both sexes and of different religions and cultures, at the level of what he calls the collective unconscious, there are archetypal symbols: the feminine symbol and the child symbol which signify the deep desire of the soul to give birth to something new.[27] Thus the soul is processive in character. This observation is also confirmed by the Christian faith which sees redemption as a process of birth and rebirth of man at the spiritual level.

If the soul is intrinsically temporal, how then are we to show the immortality of the soul? We already said earlier that lack of time, as in the case of the seed outside the ground that begins to shrivel up, is death. Fullness of time means unending life, immortality, because when one has fullness of time, then one cannot die, for death is the dispossession of time. Now, the ability precisely of human consciousness to attain the past, the present and somehow the future, is an indication of the orientation of the human soul towards immortality as unending time. Incidentally, this orientation towards the possession of all of time is the basis for spirituality and not the ability to transcend time. For consider that spirituality is total immanence where there are no parts outside parts. Now, one who possesses a part of time, such that the past and the future are fused into a single present becomes immanent, hence, spiritual. Farthest from the spiritual is the material, precisely because matter is unable to gather time by unifying past and future. It is because matter is timeless, so to speak, that it is not spiritual, that is, self-conscious.

Our conclusion that the human soul is intrinsically temporal elucidates the scriptural view that God's eternity is endless time. For if God made man in his image and to be united with his eternity, then God would not structure the whole of man for time if his eternity were the absence of time.

In terms of the evolutionary framework, God would no longer be situated outside history, in some suprahistorical and timeless region, but in the Absolute Future, for the Absolute Future is synonymous with Fullness of Time. From our human point of view, of course, the future is not yet. But it does not follow that God as Absolute Future is a not-yet in himself, for being the source of all maturation, he cannot in any way be immature. Thus, God is a not-yet-for-us, not because he does not have the fullness of time, but that we do not have the full participation in his Fullness of Time. In this sense, God is He-Who-is-to-Come.

Given the position of God in the Absolute Future, it follows that all evolving reality tending towards God must be intrinsically temporal for the only way to attain the Future is through the present and the only way to participate in God's Fullness of Time is to be structured for time. Thus, the wayfarer, the pilgrim-Church and the cosmos groaning to be delivered—all are structured for time.

Christianity seems thoroughly temporal and processive rather than supratemporal or perhaps static. What are revelation and faith but greater and more powerful lights than reason to illuminate a way towards the Absolute Future, the land of truth? And did not Christ, the center of the Christian faith, say of himself: "I am the Way; I am the Light." What is sin in Scripture but a missing of the way (hattah). And what is the Sacrament of penance but a means of restoring us into the right path ? What is the Church but the prolongation of Christ who is the Way, the eschatological sign that shows the world the path to the Future? What is the Eucharist but a continuation of the manna in the desert, hence, food for the journey into the future? What is the liturgy with its cycles but a means of growth, a participation in future time or eschatological Christian time, so that we attain to the highest evolutionary dimension, the Omega Point who is Christ, the Fullness of Time? With the processive and evolutionary structure of the economy of salvation, it would be the height of absurdity to think that the human soul for whom salvation was principally designed was not processive or evolutionary in structure and orientation.

If we look back at the static formulation of our traditional theology and philosophy, we are amazed at the ingenuity of the human mind in giving a wonderfully coherent philosophic and theological synthesis of the dialectic of withdrawal from time. We have the substantialization of the faith; we have the immutability instead of the evolution of dogma; the triumphal instead of the pilgrim Church; the timelessness instead of the temporality of eternity; the intrinsic independence of the intellect and of the human soul from matter instead of their oneness and solidarity with the evolving cosmos; the liturgy as withdrawal from temporality instead of a celebration of eschatological time, etc.

Comparing the processive and evolutionary view of man with the existential, we make the observation that, curiously enough, the latter is other-worldly, for it separates human temporality from the evolving cosmos. It is basically anti-scientific and anti-evolutionary. But in the processive and evolutionary view, man unifies in himself the whole evolutionary process that came before him. Through the human soul, man is able to unify the past, present and future. Man is the future of the whole infra-human level of evolution, and as their future, he is the fullness of time or eternity, so to speak, for the infra-human level.

With man totally temporal in both body and soul, there is a foundation for full involvement and engagement in the temporal. Work becomes humanizing. But in the metaphysical view in which the soul is seen as atemporal, man cannot totally give himself to the building of the new earth. With the processive view of man, we can have an answer to the Marxists that we Christians are equally serious and totally devoted to the progress of the earth. Our belief in God is not antihumanistic because our going to God who is the Absolute Future is not a departure from time but a participation in the Fullness of Time.

II. THE EVOLUTION OF THE HUMAN SOUL

IN the first part of this presentation we tried to show that the human soul is intrinsically temporal and processive in structure, function and orientation. Here in the second part, we would like to explore the possibility, both philosophic and theological, of the evolution of the human soul.

There are many difficulties involved in the attempt. On the level of the philosophic, for example, there is the problem of causality. How can the spiritual soul which is of a higher order of reality than matter come from the lower, namely matter? How can what is material produce what is immaterial? The seeming impossibility of resolving this philosophic difficulty is one of the reasons why traditional thought cannot accept the evolution of the human soul.

On the level of the theological, the constant doctrine of the Church as found in *Humani generis* says on this matter: "The Magisterium of the Church does not forbid that the theory of evolution concerning the origin of the human body as coming from pre-existent and living matter—for Catholic faith obliges us to hold that the human soul is immediately created by God—be investigated and discussed by experts as far as the present state of human sciences and sacred theology allows."[28] Thus, with regards to the origin of man, only a moderate evolution is allowed, that is, the evolution of the human body, but not of the human soul. Again, in the allocution of Paul VI to a group of theologians,[29] it is stated that no other reservation for the application of evolution to man is made except the immediate creation of each and every human soul.

We have in the papal declarations, it would seem, a stumbling block to the possibility of the human soul's evolution. However, Karl Rahner expresses the attitude of many theologians engaged in this particular problem when he states "that the 'peace' established between sacred theology and the present-day scientific theory of man's evolutionary origins, hominization, by the declaration of the Church's Magisterium under Pius XII and by a correct interpretation of the Genesis account, is not the end and solution of a comprehensive set of problems, but is only the basis and pacific condition of a genuine encounter between the various branches of study concerned with man."[30] Following this advice, Karl Rahner himself and other theologians like Peter Schoonenberg,[31] Piet Smulders,[32] A. Hulsbosch,[33] M. Flick and Z. Alszeghy,[34] J. de Finance,[35] and Robert North,[36] have gone beyond *Humani generis,* by presenting us with a new and deeper understanding of creation and evolution.

Most of the recent efforts to relate the origin of the human soul more closely to evolution have been instigated largely by Teilhard de Chardin's evolutionary view which would seem to derive the human spirit from pre-living and preconscious matter by way of evolution. Rahner[37] and North who are the pace setters on the new thinking on the origin of the human soul try to show by the resuscitated and refurbished Scholastic notion of concursus that God cooperates in evolution. Such a procedure, however, requires a radical redefinition of the term concursus, so as to make it to mean God's act of creation. But such a redefinition really destroys the distinction between creation and concursus in the Scholastic context. For in Scholastic thought,[38] creation in the strict sense is the production out of nothing of the various substances that constitute the universe. It is on the level of *esse*. Concursus, however, is on the level of *operatio,* that is, once God has created the universe out of nothing, he then continues to influence it, first by preserving it in being (conservation in *esse*) and secondly, by concurring in its operation (concursus in *operando*.) God's concursus, then, does not deal with creation. It cannot therefore explain the origin of the human soul. Furthermore, concursus is basically a static notion. It does not explain God's immanence and presence in evolution. I believe that one has to get outside the Scholastic framework to explain the creative causality of God in the evolutionary process. This task will be attempted later.

But whatever the method used for explaining God's causality in the evolutionary process, the result that I would propose here on the origin of the human soul is similar to those proposed by Rahner, North, Hulsbosch, Smulders and Schoonenberg. Anyone who reads their writings on the matter will observe that while the traditional terminology, "the immediate creation of the human soul,' 'is retained, this is interpreted to mean practically, "evolution." In other words, creation is now interpreted as progressive or evolutionary rather than immediate. Robert Francoeur best sums up the position of these theologians on the new understanding of creation when he says that "creation equals evolution for evolution is only God's way of creating in time."[39]

Our approach then for explaining the origin of the human soul is processive. From this processive point of view, my basic criticism against the formulation of *Humani generis* is its non-evolutionary framework.[40] I do not question the formulation as such. As long as one stays within the static framework, there is no way of explaining the origin of the human soul but to say it was immediately created by God. Hence, the formulation, given the context, is irreformable, although no explicit definition has been made by the Magisterium. However, the encyclical has not said that there is only one framework possible for expressing and understanding the origin of the human soul.

Within the evolutionary frame of reference, it is perhaps possible to say that the human soul evolved. It is our hope that in the future the official Church will adopt the processive or evolutionary pattern of thinking.

Accordingly, at the present time, it is our judgment that the formulation of *Humani generis* is but a midway point between the previous official position of absolute denial of any form of evolution and a future one of complete acceptance of evolution, given the actual evolution in the Church's position. As Zoltan Alszeghy says,[41] the first official stand was that of the Provincial Council of Cologne in 1860 in which evolution was considered "completely contrary to Scripture and faith." Likewise in the Vatican Council I, May, 1869, the same position was reaffirmed. After Vatican I, the Holy Office stated that opinions which hold that the body evolved were judged untenable since they were contrary to sacred Scripture and sound philosophy. Next, in 1909, the Biblical Commission also looked with disfavor on an evolutionistic explanation of hominisation. It asserted that the special intervention of God interrupted the series of created causes in order to fashion the body of the first man and woman. What this meant, observes Alszeghy, was that the origin of the human race was isolated "from the context of total evolution, thus destroying its immanent intelligibility which constitutes the principal attraction of an evolutionistic view of the world."[42] But finally, in *Humani generis,* a retreat was made from the absolutistic stand against evolution, for at least here, discussion on the origin of the human body from pre-existent and living matter was permitted. And lastly, in the allocution of Paul VI perhaps a little more relaxation is made in that reservations are withdrawn from applying evolution to man except that of the immediate creation of each and every human soul. We believe that this last position is itself merely the beginning of a further evolution in the Church's position.

Alszeghy explains some of the factors involved in the changed attitude of the Church toward evolution. First there was the change in the manner of presenting evolution. A hundred years ago, "evolution was the instrument of atheistic and materialistic propaganda, hence to accept evolution in the form of that time really constituted a danger to faith."[43] Today, however, with the increasing evidence for evolution, it has become more convincing, for we see that it is not necessarily atheistic or materialistic. The second reason was the progress made in exegesis. This enabled us "to avoid searching the word of God for the revelation of a scientific theory on the origins of living beings."[44] And thirdly, a deeper understanding of the nature and meaning of creation made us realize that creation and evolution are not necessarily incompatible.

But the Church's present position has not solved our problem, which may be expressed in the words of Werner Bröker: "Is it theologically and absolutely necessary to maintain the anthropological dualism of body and soul, and in such a way that what constitutes the human, the spiritual dimension or the soul, must be excluded from the evolutionary process?"[45]

In order to advance beyond the position of *Humani generis,* it is necessary to go beyond the philosophic understanding of evolution which formed the basis of the formulation. For it would seem that implied in the formula "immediate creation of the human soul," is the assumption that to accept the evolution of the human soul would mean the "de-substantialization" of living things, the levelling out of all essential boundaries up to the mind of man. Secondly, its formula seems to be based on the premise that the acceptance of evolution would imply the "de-finalization" of man, for the theory of natural selection, it would seem, would deny any direction and teleology to evolution, and affirm instead that evolution is governed purely by chance. The result of the acceptance of the evolution of the whole man, given the above premises would be that man is a product of chance, reducible to matter so that his uniqueness and essential difference from the infra-human levels is denied, and lastly that his orientation to God is an illusion. Given these fears, it is understandable that the encyclical would isolate the human soul from the evolutionary context by assigning its origin to a special creative act of God that is distinct from the evolutionary process. By the formula, "immediate creation" man's uniqueness is safeguarded, his orientation to God is clearly shown. But I believe that we can equally safeguard man's uniqueness and his origin and end as divine by saying that the human soul evolved.

First of all, for the Church to accept evolution more favorably, it must not leave evolution merely to the study of naturalists, materialists and positivists. It must not be on the defensive about evolution and over-react just because Marx and Engels were enthusiastic about it, seeing in it the destruction of faith in God and the spirituality of man.[46] Evolution, as we mentioned earlier, is not necessarily atheistic or materialistic. Teilhard de Chardin has shown that it need not be so, and a man like Roger Garaudy has applauded the Teilhardian worldview which presents religion and evolution as not necessarily incompatible and which furnishes a basis for Marxist-Christian dialogue. But the official Church has not looked with favor on Teilhard de Chardin.

The main obstacle to accepting the evolutionary outlook, however, is the static thought-pattern which the official Church still adopts. One cannot understand evolution properly as long as one tries to understand it in terms of static categories. The philosophic attitude towards evolution still predominant in the official Church is that expressed by Jacques Maritain when he said:

> I do not question that St. Thomas made no systematic use of the

idea of development or evolution in the modern sense of these words. For for one thing, that idea itself is neither enlightening nor fertile except in the context of an ontological analysis of reality.... To enclose a metaphysics in a compartment of history is not a way to give evidence of a sense of history; and it is no proof of philosophic sense to think that there is nothing more in a metaphysic than the scientific imagery which, in a given era, permitted it to exemplify itself in the plane of phenomena, which plane never confined it.[47]

Thus, for Maritain, evolution is purely on the phenomenal level and as such, it cannot take the place of metaphysics. It is for this reason that in his latest book, *The Peasant of the Garonne,* he calls Teilhard's evolutionary world-view fiction theology. It is this pattern of thinking, too, which considers evolution purely phenomenal as opposed to the substantial or metaphysical, that would lead one to conclude that the soul could not possibly be evolved since the soul as substantial form cannot come from a process that is purely on the phenomenal level.

Evolution as process is, however, not phenomenal. For in evolution, we are speaking of the emergence of new beings, new species which obviously are not purely phenomenal, but quite substantial. In evolution, we are on the level of *esse,* not of *operatio.* We are speaking of the evolution of species, not merely of the activity of a perduring species. In order to see better that evolution is on the level of the substantial, not phenomenal, it is necessary to realize that what we call substance from a common sense point of view is really process from a wider time perspective. Thus, from the very small time perspective of common sense observation, we do not observe evolution. The experience we get is the permanence of things. We see hills, valleys and mountains as models of changelessness. This experience of permanence is the foundation for the category of substance. But from a very wide time perspective of say a billion years, what was seen as substance in the common sense point of view is really process in the evolutionary perspective. Evolution is not the activity of a substance; it is the substance itself that is in process. Philosophically, then, it is justified to situate the soul within the evolutionary context.

The next static philosophic category that has to be given up in order to understand evolution properly is the category of act and potency. To many, the Aristotelian category of act and potency is well able to explain evolution, so that they do not feel the need to adopt an evolutionary point of view since they suppose their outlook is already so. But evolution is a creative process in which new levels of being are produced that were not precontained in the beginning. Act and potency, on the other hand, presupposes that there is nothing really new under the sun; no novelty, no creativity, for what is actualized is already precontained in the beginning potentially. No, the hylomorphic theory of prime matter and substantial form cannot explain the dynamics of evolution. This is also the observation of Robert O. Johann:

> Anyone who sees in hylomorphism the ultimate explanation of the material universe will inevitably find an evolutionary theory to be self-contradictory. For in the hylomorphic perspective, development must necessarily be conceived in terms of the transformation of an ultimately passive subject, prime matter. The transformation of such a subject, however, immediately entails an appeal to a cause already possessing, formally or eminently, the perfection which matter is to acquire in the process. Since matter is only the passive substrate of the change and therefore contributes nothing in the line of formal perfection to the process, the appearance of new perfection in matter must of necessity be attributed to the influence of a cause, which already has it itself and which is said to "educe" the same from the potency of matter. Such a theory, of course, makes an evolutionary conception of the world impossible.[48]

It is not only the hylomorphic theory that is the implicit framework of *Humani generis,* but also the Hellenic notion of substantial and accidental change. Evolution is not accidental change for we are here on the level of *esse,* not *operatio.* But neither is it substantial change, since substantial change means the sudden and instantaneous substitution of one substantial form by another. But in evolution, the emergence of a new form, like a new species, is by a temporal process. This temporal process, we cannot emphasize often enough, is not on the level of accidental change for we are dealing here with the emergence of new beings or new species which obviously are not on the level of accidents. Substantial change and accidental change cannot explain the kind of change that takes place in evolution. To say that the human soul evolved is false if it is understood as taking place either by substantial or by accidental change.

Whatever be the nature of the causality of evolution, a Scholastic philosopher and theologian might argue, it would still make the evolution of the human soul an impossibility. For if evolution were the emergence of new and higher forms of being from the lower, then this is to say that the principle of causality is false. In other words, one can not produce what one does not have (*nemo dat quod non habet*). How can the lower produce the higher? The only possible explanation for the emergence of new and higher beings, it would seem, is the postulate of a divine intervention through direct creation. The human soul could not have been evolved.

A proper understanding of the causality of evolution does not preclude divine causality as a factor. From the scientific point of view, divine causality must be ruled out methodically since it is empirically unverifiable. But it is inadequate to see evolution as a purely natural process and to assimilate it within the context of an Aristotelian natural order.

From the philosophic point of view, it is necessary to postulate divine causality to explain how the higher can come from the lower.

As Teilhard de Chardin observes, in an evolutionary context of evolving species, God is more imperiously demanded than in the context of fixity of species. Nicolas Corte observes that it is not necessary to believe in Teilhard's "Omega Point" to see philosophically the need for God in the evolutionary process:

> Without committing ourselves to such a decided opinion, we may be allowed to suggest that the theory of evolution is not only not opposed to the idea of God, but necessitates it even more than the theory of the fixity of species. Indeed the believer in the fixity of species may be brought to admit that the world is eternal, that it has been "fixed" once and for all without the possibility of change, and that any movements that may be observed in it are mere appearance, repetition, "tautology" so to speak. Evolution without a beginning is as self-contradictory as a square circle. If it actually had no beginning, it must, from all eternity, have had an eternity behind it; in other words it must have exhausted all its possibilities of development.
> Furthermore, if evolution, inasmuch as it is not yet finished, must have had a beginning, it requires, in order that it may begin, the intervention of a creator.[49]

Again, we can philosophically deduce the need of God in the context of evolution by a reflection on the necessities of growth. Whatever grows needs a "ground." The seed needs a ground in order that it grow and germinate. One cannot just leave a seed on the table and expect it to germinate; it must be planted. The seed is not its own ground. Again the fetus is not its own womb. So, too, the universe as something that grows requires its "ground" and we call this transcendental ground, God. Also, if the universe is in process of maturation, then, again, it needs its 'ground,' as source of its maturation and fullness. We must note here that we are not deducing the need for God from a scientific concept of evolution.

It is insufficient for theology to base its stand on the origin of the soul on a narrow concept of evolution and to conclude that to admit the evolution of the soul is to say that its origin is from chance or from a source other than God. A philosophic understanding of evolution as process shows that the universe is not an Aristotelian natural order able to evolve itself. No, evolution needs God as Ground. And we must repeat that we take issue here with Rahner who explains God's causality as that of concursus. For we are not dealing with the activity of God on the level of operation. The best phrase that would characterize God's causality is that used by Teilhard, "creative union";[50] namely, that for God, creating is the same as uniting. The metaphor of God as Ground of evolution helps to show the meaning of creative union, for the more the seed unites itself with the ground, the more it differentiates itself. With God present in the evolutionary process as Ground, it is not therefore impossible to show how the higher can come from the lower. This problem becomes impossible to solve only within the static world-view of a self-sufficient universe. We must give up this view to understand the causality of evolution. With God present in the evolutionary process, it is not metaphysically impossible to say that the soul evolved. We are also able to conclude that evolution is not mere chance occurrence, although this conclusion would be valid from the scientific point of view and method, and that it has a direction and goal, although science cannot establish this point.

But even with the presence of God in the evolutionary process as evolutor, it does not seem possible that the immaterial soul can come from matter or that what is intrinsically independent from matter could be intrinsically dependent upon it for its origin, or, to express the problem another way, how the supratemporal or timeless world of spirit can come from the temporal and contingent world of matter. The source of the difficulty is the false assumption that matter and spirit are two entities, totally exclusive of one another. However, as Rahner observes, "It is clear that spirit and matter cannot be thought of side by side, alien and heterogeneous like two particular objects of our experience which are met with next to one another in their difference as mere brute fastcs."[51] From the Christian point of view, even matter, as Rahner points out, following Augustine, is somehow spiritual, for it is also a manifestation of the Logos, Christ, who incarnated himself.[52] Thus, says Rahner, "It is evident that Christianity, by reason of certain of its elements ... positively requires this kinship and mutual relationship of finite spirit and matter in respect of origin, history and goal. It does not simply permit us to conceive it."[53] What follows from this is that on the side of finite spirits, like the spiritual soul, there is an "intrinsic ontological kinship in nature" to matter, observes Rahner, so that the difference between them is a difference in "densities."[54] Matter in this case, Rahner concludes, is "solidified" spirit.[55]

Thus, Rahner's study on the relation between matter and spirit confirms the view of Teilhard that matter is pre-conscious, that it is somehow psychic. And we might add too from our previous analysis of the human soul as intrinsically temporal that there is an intrinsic temporal kinship between matter and the human spirit for both have the dimension of time, the distinction being the qualitative difference in the possession of time. The intrinsic temporal relationship between matter and spirit is to me the crucial point to establish in order that we can establish philosophically the possibility of the temporal emergence of the human soul from matter. There may be an ontological kinship that is intrinsic as Rahner observes, but as long as an intrinsic temporal kinship is not established, then the possibility of an evolutionary unity and continuity cannot be grounded. As long, however, as traditional thought continues to think of spirit as belonging to the world of the timeless while matter belongs to the world of time the possibility of evolution of spirit from matter is *ipso facto* ruled out.

But even with the theoretical possibility of spirit evolving from matter explained, there is no empirical evidence to support the view, it would seem. For there is no evidence of any psychism or rudimentary consciousness in matter to lead us to suppose that matter could have evolved into the psychic and spiritual. A similar difficulty is voiced by many in the case of the claim that life comes from non-life. There is no evidence at all in the atom or molecule to lead us to believe that life could have come from it. First of all it is necessary to realize that matter as we have it today is not matter billions of years ago. There has been a cosmogenesis or evolution of matter itself. Secondly, evolution being an irreversible process, the conditions at the beginning could not be exactly duplicated today. However, the possibility of life coming from non-life has been shown in the scientific laboratory.

But in the case of matter being preconscious, it seems quite difficult to perceive any rudimentary form of thought. The difficulty is not in matter itself but in our demand that matter be thinking. There is the naive and unreflected view that if the conscious spiritual soul evolved from matter then matter itself must somehow be conscious. This demand manifests a misunderstanding of the process of evolution. Evolution does not follow the principle of identity which rules our common sense way of reasoning but the principle of paradox. Let me illustrate the difference by a concrete example. Thus, to see the full grown oak at the beginning, it would be foolish to use the principle of identity by demanding that the origin of the full grown oak be identical in form to it, the difference merely being in size. To demand that the origin of the full grown oak be a miniature oak is to rule out the possibility of accepting the non-oak form of the acorn as the origin of the full grown oak. But this is actually what we are demanding of matter, namely, that for it to be the origin of consciousness it must have the form of consciousnesss, that is, it must be thinking, the difference merely being one of degree. Evolution postulates precisely that for the possibility of evolution, the beginning cannot already have the form at the end, for then, there would be no need of an evolution. But if we must accept evolution, then there has to be an evolution of form. Now, if we apply the paradoxical mode of thinking to the evolution of consciousness, we would expect that for consciousness to evolve to its present form as thinking, then it cannot already be thinking at the beginning for we would then be ruling out the need for its evolution. If consciousness evolved to the level of thought, then at the beginning it must have been unthinking or unconscious. Similarly, if life evolved, then at the first stage of its evolution it must have been non-life. So it would be contrary to the very meaning of evolution to demand that matter already possess some rudimentary form of thought before we can accept that the spiritual could have evolved from it.

So far we have been exposing several philosophic assumptions that hinder the acceptance of the evolution of the human soul. Another false philosophic assumption that needs to be exposed, is responsible for the conclusion that to accept the evolution of the human soul from matter is to destroy the soul's spirituality and to reduce it instead to materiality. Hence, it is understandable that the official guardians of the Church cannot yield to any small opening, and the acceptance of the evolution of the human soul would seem to be such an opening that would inevitably land us into materialism. We admit that at the present time, when a true philosophic understanding of evolution is not had by many, the danger of Christians interpreting the evolution of the human soul as an acceptance of materialism is quite real. For the dialectical materialists do reduce everything evolved to matter itself as the ultimate principle of intelligibility. It is my opinion, however, an opinion that I share with Leslie Dewart, that, paradoxically enough, dialectical materialism is basically static in outlook in that it is the last logical development of Aristotelian thought. To reduce everything that evolves to the beginning is really a static view of process and of evolution. This means that there could not be more at the end than at the beginning; this means that everything that emerges is already precontained in the beginning. Actually, it is the Aristotelian category of act and potency all over again.

Following therefore the principle that everything that evolves must be reduced to the beginning as its principle of intelligibility, it means that the soul which evolved from matter cannot but be material. The soul must therefore be immediately created, not generated, to show and preserve its spirituality. There are two false presuppositions in the position. First, it is presupposed that evolution is purely a material process. Secondly, it is presupposed that what comes after in the evolutionary process must be reduced to what came before. In an evolving universe, however, it is not the end that is reduced to the beginning, but the beginning reduced to the end. For in evolution, one starts with imperfection and ends in perfection; one begins with becoming which terminates in being; one starts with what is immature, unfinished and ends with what is mature, finished, fully evolved. We reduce the infant to the adult, not the adult to the infant.

The principle of intelligibility in evolution is the end, not the beginning. If we want to know what a developing thing is, we wait for the end which reveals it for what it is. In the case of a developing seed, we know the seed only by the fruit. This is also the scriptural principle of intelligibility when it is stated that by their fruits you shall know them. In other words, we reduce the seed to the fruit. We call the seed by its fruit and so with all the other evolutionary stages that precede the fruit. Thus, we call the seed, say, an *apple* seed, the seedling an *apple* seedling, and the plant an *apple* plant. In other words, it is not the seed that explains the seedling, the plant, the fruit. We do not call the fruit a *seed* apple. The fruit is simply called apple; it needs no modifier for it is the principle of intelligibility of the process; it points to itself for meaning.

Now, in the evolutionary process, as Teilhard has shown, the evolution of matter leads to spirit. By the laws of the evolutionary process and of growth, spirit is the fruit of the process, consequently, it is matter that must be reduced to the spiritual, rather than the spiritual being reduced to the material. The meaning of matter is in spirit, and not the other way around. If, however, evolution were seen statically, as the activity of the universe seen as substance, then, obviously, evolution as an activity must be reduced to its beginning, as activity is reduced to substance. But in evolution, substance or being comes at the end of the process. What comes before is becoming so that becoming terminates in being and is reducible to being. Matter, then, is a dimension of spirit, a manifestation of spirit, rather than spirit being a manifestation of matter. Matter, to use the word of Teilhard de Chardin, is preconsciousness, or that of Rahner, is "frozen" spirit. Evolution is not purely a material process because matter is not an entity distinct from spirit, as in the case of the Hellenic view in which the distinction is static and spatial. In the evolutionary view, matter and spirit are but two aspects of one and the same reality. To use Teilhard's explanation, spirit and matter are the within and the without of things, the radial and the tangential energies of evolution. Evolution is psychic transformation or the evolution of consciousness or of spirit, according to Teilhard de Chardin, and this conclusion is justified, because, as we said earlier, a process is named after its goal. By the law of complexity-consciousness in which a more complex organization implies a greater concentration of consciousness, we can see that cosmogenesis or the evolution of matter tended to more complex arrangement in the cell with a corresponding increase in psychism. As the cell evolves to form multicellular organisms, there is also a corresponding increase in consciousness as manifested in the development of the nervous system and the cephalic region, the brain. The evolution results in the production of greater being, such that there emerges the human soul.

Along with the intellectual fear of materialism is a more deeply rooted fear—the psychological—which fears any contamination of the spiritual and angelic soul by matter. I strongly suspect that there is a tinge of Manichaeism in the insistence that the human soul be immediately created and infused rather than being evolved. There is a strong flavor of the other-worldly and angelic, of the Platonic and Hellenic. It reflects a basic attitude conditioned by centuries of Hellenic thought that matter is evil, that the world is profane; it reflects the traditional spirituality of withdrawal from time. But in the evolutionary view of reality, it is not so much spirit that is dragged down to the level of matter as matter that is raised up to the level of spirit.

In Teilhard's evolutionary view which is basically Pauline and Johannine, the universe is undergoing spiritual transformation. Matter is thus being spiritually transformed. Furthermore, by reason of the Incarnation, says Teilhard in *The Divine Milieu,* nothing here below is profane for those who know how to see.

Nor should there be fear that the soul by being closely united to the universe would lose its supernatural orientation or that it would share the destruction of the earth. The assumption is false that the destiny of the earth is destruction, not consummation. As Teilhard has shown, the whole evolutionary process is not only the evolution of consciousness; it is much grander, it is a Christogenesis. And in saying this, Teilhard is merely echoing the Pauline and Johannine view that the whole universe from creation on to the New Creation is Christian. Christ is cosmic, according to Paul as found in Colossians and the other captivity epistles. Christ was there already in creation, for creation was the first stage of the covenant; it was seen as a prefiguring of the baptism of Christ on the cross. So creation itself is not a cosmological order but part of the supernautral and redemptive order. David Stanley in fact observes that for the Scriptures, there are not two orders: a cosmological and a soteriological as in the Scholastic system.[56] No, from the point of view of the New Testament the whole process from creation to the New Creation is Christian. Then, why should we be afraid to situate the human soul within this process and say that it emerged from the process? Why are we afraid to say that the soul is naturally Christian, as Tertullian, with great insight, said long ago?

Another objection to accepting the evolution of the human soul is the fear that man's uniqueness and essential difference from the souls of brutes would be dissolved. For then the human soul would be material like the animal soul; it would be temporal; the foundation of immortality which is intrinsic independence from matter would be absent. With regard to this latter problem, we have shown in the first part that intrinsic independence from matter is not a proof of immortality, but rather the loss of the chance of any immortality, for the Christian faith bases eternal life on the resurrection of the body, not on the immortality of the soul. Our chance of participating in the resurrection of Christ and the same may be said for the whole universe which is groaning until now to be redeemed is in the possession of matter. Our creed speaks of the resurrection of the body, not the immortality of the soul. We should rather be interested in our theology in showing the intrinsic relation of the human soul to the universe than showing its independence, for it is this world, this universe that Christ came to redeem. The possession of time, the fullness of time, is the basis for redemption, for eternal life. The process of redemption is the redeeming of time. Time because of sin is destructive; it ends in death, barrenness. So we need to redeem the time by making it participate in Christian time through participation in the temporal process of Christ's death and resurrection prolonged in the liturgy. The human soul has to be intrinsically temporal; it has to be intrinsically structured for time, if it is to participate in the temporal process of redemption; if it is to participate in Christian time.

The liturgy with its cycles is a temporal process; it is the highpoint of the rhythm of growth of the universe. The universe is structured for it, because the universe is temporal; it is in process of being reborn as evolution shows and as St. Paul notes in Romans. It is time that redeems, not a departure from time as in the Hellenic view. The liturgy is not a dialectic from time to timelessness; rather, it is a dialectic from barrenness or lack of time to the fullness of time. Thus, the advent season is the time of planting of unredeemed time of our activities and labors; passiontide is the time of death of the negativity and destructiveness of time; resurrection is the time of rebirth of true or eschatological time; and pentecost is the age of growth till the next advent which is the second coming or parousia. Now, how can the human soul be redeemed if it were not, like the universe, structured for this temporal process of growth and redemption? No, the human soul is part of this material universe; its destiny is in it.

The human soul does not lose its uniqueness and identity in the context of evolution because evolution of its very nature is a differentiating process. The evolutionary universe seen as a process of creative union does not dissolve the soul in the totality of matter like a drop of water in the ocean. The union is not the union of two substantial parts in which the identity of the parts are lost for the sake of the identity of the whole. No, in evolution, union is based on love. The whole universe as Teilhard observes is unified through love. And love as an evolutionary reality differentiates.

We can also use the analogy of the seed and the ground to show that union differentiates. The more the seed unites itself with the ground, the more it differentiates itself. So, too, the union of the human soul with the material universe does not mean loss of identity for it. In fact, the human soul gives the evolutionary process its uniqueness, for in evolving towards the human soul, the universe becomes personalized. As Teilhard observes, the whole universe is a personalizing universe.

Again, a study of the evolutionary process shows that there are various evolutionary stages or time dimensions. Quantitative increase reaches a point at which moment there is a sudden qualitative difference. These critical thresholds mark a radical change such that we have spheres or stages that are essentially and qualitatively distinct: there is the geosphere, the biosphere, the noosphere, etc. Man is distinct because he alone possesses the historical dimension; he alone inhabits the noosphere. Evolution is not pure quantitative increase, not a smooth straight line of unilinear progress. Rather, there are plateaus which mark new creative stages in the process.

Thus, with evolution, so explained, there is no reason why we cannot say that the human soul evolved. The reason why we hold on to the formula can only be extrinsic, namely, the hang-up on safeguarding the reputation of the official Church of not falling into mistakes too often. But the Church is also an evolving reality; it is an *ecclesia semper reformanda*. As Vatican II says, the Church is holy, but its holiness is imperfect. It made mistakes in the past, but the guardians of the Church seem to have little faith that in saying the Church was mistaken in such and such a formulation or stand, the doctrine of infallibility would not be jeopardized. But it is false to prevent one area of theology from developing just because another area is underdeveloped. In connection with the development of our understanding of infallibility, I believe that process thought can help.

In conclusion, we think that in the evolutionary framework, to say that the human soul was evolved is quite justified and not contrary to faith nor a danger to it. For we safeguard all elements of the faith that the old formula was designed to safeguard, plus the most important bonus of making man this-worldly in his totality. We save man's uniqueness; his spirituality; his orientation to God.

It is a grander view and a greater manifestation of God's omnipotence to see the human soul as already in preparation at the beginning of the evolutionary process some ten billion years ago. We can appreciate more fully how momentous, how precious is this human reality composed of body and soul that I have. In it are contained the endless gropings, struggles, and work of billions of years. In it lies the hope and destiny of the whole universe; it is indeed a microcosmos. Man can see himself as a whole brother of the infra-human levels, and can realize that the foundation for his responsibility to the whole universe is not merely an external juridical decree made by God to him that he master and care for the universe and be head of all creation, but from an ontological and real foundation in which he is evolutionarily one with the whole of creation.[57]

NOTES

[1] For an elaboration of process thought, see my book, *Teilhard and the Supernatural* (Baltimore: Helicon Press, 1966), Part II.

[2] See his article, "Matter and Spirit," *America*, July 10, 1965, p. 52.

[3] See Ben van Onna, "The State of Paradise and Evolution," *Concilium*, 26 (New York: Paulist Press, 1967). See also A. Hulsbosch, O.S.A., *God in Creation and Evolution*, trans. M. Versfeld (New York: Sheed and Ward, 1965), Ch. 3. Again, Piet Schoonenberg, S.J., *Man and Sin*, trans. J. Donceel (University of Notre Dame Press, 1965), pp. 194-95.

[4] *Physics*, IV, 222b.

[5] *Ibid.*, 221a.

[6] *Aristotle* (New York: Columbia University Press, 1960), pp. 129, 138, 237.

[7] See *A Portrait of Aristotle* (Chicago: University of Chicago Press, 1963).
[8] See his article, "The Concept of Evolution in Philosophy," in *A Book That Shook the World* (Pittsburgh: University of Pittsburgh Press, 1961).
[9] See his *Animal Species and Evolution* (Cambridge: Harvard University Press, 1963), pp. 4-6.
[10] See his *This View of Life* (New York: Harcourt, Brace and World, Inc., 1963).
[11] See his article, "The God of Disorder," *Continuum*, (Spring, 1966), 107-108.
[12] *Ibid.*, p. 108.
[13] *Summa Contra Gentiles*, II, 3.
[14] See his "On the Method of Theology," *Theological Studies*, 23 (1962), p. 638.
[15] See his *Dictionary of Theology*, trans. C. Quinn (Desclee Co., Inc., 1965), p. 144.
[16] See his *Christ and Time*, trans. F. V. Filson (Philadelphia: Westminster, 1950), p. 144.
[17] *Ibid.*, p. 52.
[18] *Loc. cit.*
[19] *Ibid.*, p. 61.
[20] See *The Divine Milieu* (New York: Harper & Brothers, 1960), pp. 37-38.
[21] See his article, "Christianity and the New Earth," *Theology Digest*, 15 (Winter, 1967), p. 278.
[22] *Ibid.*, p. 279.
[23] Ed. J. J. Von Allmen, (London: Lutterworth Press, 1958), p. 424.
[24] *Op. cit.*, p. 63.
[25] Gerhard Von Rad, *Old Testament Theology* II, trans. D. M. G. Stalker (New York: Harper & Row, Publ., 1965), p. 99.
[26] See his *The Theology of Hope*, trans. J. W. Leitch (London: SCM Press, Ltd., 1967).
[27] See his book, *Psychology and Religion* (Yale University Press, 1938), pp. 1-77.
[28] See the commentary of A. C. Cotter, S.J., *The Encyclical Humani Generis* (Weston: Weston College Press, 1951), p. 41. See also DS 3895-3897.
[29] See *L'Osservatore Romano*, July 16, 1966, p. 1.
[30] See his book, *Hominisation* (New York: Herder & Herder, 1956), p. 45.
[31] See his book, *God's World in the Making* (Pittsburgh: Duquesne University Press, 1964), Chs. I & II.
[32] See his book, *The Design of Teilhard de Chardin*, trans. A. Gibson (Westminster: The Newman Press, 1967), pp. 45-85.
[33] See his book, *God in Creation and Evolution*, trans. Martin Versfeld (New York: Sheed and Ward, 1965), Ch. 3.
[34] See their book, *Il Creatore* (Florence: Fiorentina, 1959), pp. 285-88.
[35] See his book, *Existence et liberté* (Paris, 1955), pp. 258-66.
[36] See his book, *Teilhard and the Creation of the Soul* (Milwaukee: The Bruce Publishing Co., 1967).
[37] Piet Smulders and Peter Schoonenberg borrow many of their ideas on the problem of hominisation and the origin of the human soul from Rahner. For other commentaries and explanations on Rahner's ideas on the subject, see, e.g., Joseph Donceel, "Causality and Evolution,"

The New Scholasticism, 39 (1965), 295-315; Herman Ebert, "The Hour of Transcendence," *Philosophy Today,* 8 (1964), 71-83; Heinrich Falk, "Can Spirit Come from Matter?" *Thought,* (1967), 541-555.

[38] See for example Joseph Pohle, *De Deo Creante et Elevante* (St. Louis: Herder, 1912), p. 61.

[39] See his article, "The God of Disorder II: A Response," *Continuum,* 4 (1966), p. 269.

[40] As Fr. Avery Dulles, S.J., mentioned in his talk here at the Theology Institute, it was the conservatives who prevailed upon Pius XII to issue *Humani generis.* "As it turned out," observes Father Dulles, "*Humani generis* was perhaps the last great effort to contain Catholic theology within the categories of classical scholasticism." See Dulles, "The Meaning of Revelation," in this volume, *The Dynamic in Christian Thought,* ed., Joseph Papin, pp. 52-80.

[41] See his article, "Development in the Doctrinal Formulation of the Church concerning the Theory of Evolution," *Concilium,* 26 (New York: Paulist Press, 1967).

[42] *Ibid.,* p. 28.

[43] *Ibid.,* p. 31.

[44] *Ibid.,* p. 32.

[45] See his article, "Aspects of Evolution," *Concilium,* 26 (New York: Paulist Press, 1967), pp. 23-24.

[46] *Op. cit.,* p. 73.

[47] See his book, *Existence and the Existent,* trans. Galantière and Phelan (New York: Pantheon, 1948), pp. 45-46.

[48] See his article, "The Logic of Evolution," *Thought,* 36 (1961), pp. 611-612.

[49] See his book, *The Origin of Man,* trans. Eric E. Smith (New York: Hawthorn Books, Publ., 1958), pp. 130-31.

[50] See *L'Union créatrice,* 1917, in *Ecrits du temps de la guerre,* 1916-19 (Paris: Grasset, 1965).

[51] *Op. cit.,* p. 61.

[52] *Ibid.,* p. 60.

[53] *Ibid.,* p. 61.

[54] *Ibid.,* p. 56.

[55] *Ibid.,* p. 57.

[56] See his article, "The New Testament Doctrine of Baptism," *Theological Studies,* 18 (1957), p. 179.

[57] If our position is correct, viz., that the human soul evolved, then, in the future we should no longer speak of the evolution of the soul, but, rather, of the whole man. The title of our paper, however, is appropriate in the context of an evolution in Christian anthropology.

The Institutional Church

John L. McKenzie

DEFINITION

THE phrase "institutional Church" has suddenly come into common use; and while most of those who use it have a common understanding of what is meant, the term retains a disagreeable vagueness because its antonym, the "non-institutional Church," lacks a clear definition. Are we to think of the eschatological Church, the celestial Church, the spiritual Church, the ideal Church? If we are thinking of such terms, we deal with terms which designate no reality within our experience and comprehension. Furthermore, the term "institutional Church" is often employed in a pejorative sense; it means the concrete Church with its imperfections and failures. By implication the imperfections and failures are attributed to its institutional structures. This attribution may possibly be found in fact, but it should not be assumed without examination; and it is simply not true that there is nothing wrong with the Church except that it is institutional. In any hypothesis institutional structures are also a part of the good of the Church, a component of its strength. At this moment in history our evaluation of institutional structures in the Church seems ambiguous in the extreme.

We may reach a clearer understanding, and hopefully, a sounder evaluation of the institutional Church if we distinguish between the abstract and concrete. The institutional Church in the abstract can only mean institutional structures in the abstract. It becomes at once apparent that the abstract institutional Church is an ideal which does not exist in reality and never has existed. The abstract institutional Church is not found even in the New Testament. By definition the abstract is abstracted from time, from space, from history. Nor is the abstract institutional Church a Platonic idea, existing "out there" in some immutable form. The abstract institutional Church is an idea of what Church structure ought to be. The idea is formed from several sources: the New Testament, the historical experience of the Church, the mission of the Church, the practices of the Church. Since all of these factors, including the interpretation of the New Testament, vary constantly with historical experience, there is no single clear idea of what the Church ought to be which persists throughout its history; and by this I mean an abstract idea of sufficient clarity to form a basis for institutional structures. For instance, no modern Churchman would conceive institutional structures in terms of the "two swords" of Boniface VIII. The abstract idea of the institutional Church does not create concrete structures. If the Papacy and the episcopacy were conceived strictly in the terms of an abstract structure based exclusively on the New Testament, they would have a form far different from the form in which they now exist.

In the concrete the institutional Church is easy to identify; it means the hierarchy and the clergy. It is a defect of the institutional Church, which we shall touch later in this paper, that the laity are really unstructured. In common language "ecclesiastical" is often synonymous with "clerical," or even with "hierarchical." There is an established idiom in the English language in which one who enters the ministry is said to enter the Church, or the service of the Church. The institutional Church includes all those whose sociological definition is "professional religious persons," those for whom the Church is a profession in the same way in which medicine or law or business are professions. The profession is one's major occupation by which one gains a living. Discussion and criticism of the institutional Church are discussion and criticism of the hierarchy and the clergy; this implies rather clearly that the critics do not recognize the laity as pertaining to the institutional Church.

It is evident that this concrete existent reality is not the abstract ideal institutional Church; but it is not uncommon that defenders of the institutional Church, in an excess of zeal, make this identification. The concrete institutions represent the movement of the Church in history towards an ideal which it never achieves. We have already remarked that the Church's perception of its own ideal is modified as it proceeds through history. It can lose sight of its ideal either by identifying the contingent historical institutions with the ideal or surrendering to history and refusing to move any further towards the ideal. It is the abstract institutional Church which permits, rather demands, that the concrete institutional structure be continually modified in an unremitting movement towards the abstract ideal. The Church must know both what it is and what it must become; failure to know the first is unrealistic, failure to know the second is complacency. The Church has experienced both in the course of her history; and it takes a severe shock, as a rule, to move her out of unrealism or out of complacency.

Hence discussion and criticism of the institutional Church seem necessary and inevitable; for the concrete institutional Church never reaches the abstract, and nothing but discussion and criticism will keep it moving towards the elusive abstract. But discussion and criticism of the concrete institutional Church mean discussion and criticism of the hierarchy and clergy, for they are identified with the institutional Church. Surely one would think first here of self-criticism; and the history of the Church exhibits ample instances of self-criticism of the hierarchy and clergy. The same history exhibits ample instances of the refusal of self-criticism, of determined and often successful efforts to silence self-criticism. But the history of the Church does not show that discussion and criticism of the institutional Church have been restricted to the hierarchy and clergy. Laymen have sometimes spoken when few of the hierarchy and the clergy were able and willing to speak; and their criticisms, rejected or suppressed at the time, are now recognized as genuine contributions to the growth of the Church. Such discussion and criticism will continue as long as there are any in the Church who cherish a vision of the abstract institutional Church. Their vision may be cloudy and erroneous in detail, but it does impel the Church to move; complacency with the concrete structures immobilizes the Church as far is it is possible to do this.

It is deplorable that criticism of the institutional Church has been and still is so often expressed in personal attacks upon the hierarchy and the clergy. The Catholic must be wary of imitating Jesus in his invective against the scribes and Pharisees. Yet he did deliver invective against them—and the invective of first-century Palestine is not in all respects a model of style for twentieth-century polite discourse. One may say at least that Jesus did not find direct personal criticism beneath his dignity; and this criticism was delivered against those who, in words attributed to him, occupied the chair of Moses. Does the chair of Peter or the chair of a diocese except its possessor from similar criticism, when the basis of the criticism is judged to be as secure as the basis of the criticism of Jesus? I have said that the Catholic must be wary in forming this judgment; and Paul may have been hasty in calling the high priest a whitewashed wall because he did not hear Paul's case according to the Law. Certainly Jesus presents in the process of fraternal admonition a way of discussing and criticizing which can be combined with Christian love. But when the concrete institutional Church is identified with "the Church" of Matthew 18:17, then the concrete institutional Church is not subject to fraternal admonition.

Criticism of the institutional Church sometimes seems to approach the point at which it is regarded as a corruption of the Church which is ineradicable by its nature. Effectively this would mean that the institutional Church is a foreign element in the body of Christ which infects the Church with weakness and disease, and that the Church will not attain good health until this foreign body is ejected. This position is supported by the criticisms with which we shall deal later, as well as by the evident contrast between the complex institutions which the Church has evolved and the simple structure of the New Testament Church. Here a few principles must be recalled. The Church is a society in any idea of its reality, and a society demands institutional structures. The structures may fail to move the society towards its end; if they fail, the society will suffer revolution or collapse. But if the society survives revolution, it emerges restructured. An unstructured group is a horde with no purpose and no direction; it has no power beyond the sum of its individual power units. A society is not maintained simply because of community of interest. Shoppers in a large store have a community of interest, but this interest can be served only by a socially organized store or market. Without this structure the shoppers could not pursue their interests.

The most incisive critic of the institutions in recent years has certainly been Charles Davis. He has clearly and firmly rejected the institutional Church, and he has substituted for that rejection no restructuring of the institutions. He believes that the Church of the future will be non-institutional, a pure community of faith with no officers and no authority. He observes that the institutional Church has defined itself in purely sociological terms. This definition, he says, fails to define the Church, and he must reject it. At the same time he must reject the institutional Church, because one who accepts an institutional Church must accept the definition which the official Church gives of itself. The argument is not without suasive force; and one who takes it up must appeal to some "non-institutional" and non-existent Church to support his position. I have so appealed to the abstract and ideal structure, which is no more immutable than the concrete existing institutional Church, for it is an idea in the minds of men which grows or is perverted by historical experience. Hence the official Church is unable to define terminally the abstract reality of the Church. Nor can the official Church define terminally the concrete institutional Church, because it cannot do this without arresting history, which is impossible. This does not mean, unfortunately, that it cannot make the attempt.

For me at least the thesis of Davis runs directly into the hard rock of social reality. I am as convinced as Davis of the novelty of the Christian fact and the unique nature of the Christian society; but I do not believe that the Christian society's unique nature can be preserved if it ceases to be a society, which means institutions. I am quite convinced, for reasons which I cannot present in rigorous logic, that the Church of the future as Davis sees it would endure a very short time before some of its members said, "We have to organize." One may include this tendency in the demonic in man if one wishes; but I have not seen that Christianity has exorcised this demonic quality, nor do I believe it is intended to exorcise it. Christianity appears as a society from its very beginnings, and not merely as a movement or a community of pure faith.

We shall leave it to the sociologists and the political scientists to analyze the role which institutional structures play in giving a community identity and self-consciousness. That the role is highly important needs no demonstration, and it does not appear what would serve this purpose in the unstructured Church of the future. I do not dispute that institutionalization also contributes to an excess of self-consciousness, leading to self-righteousness and elitism. The community may be so sharply defined that it is not only clearly distinguished from non-members but hostile to them. It is not disputed that Roman Catholicism has sometimes exhibited these features. But Roman Catholicism has in its constitution and its teaching elements which forbid it to turn into Pharisaism; and it is not clear that these elements would be better preserved in an unstructured Church.

I accept, then, the necessity of institutions arising from the social nature of man. What form the institutions of the Church must take is determined by the mission of the Church; it must have those institutions which it needs to accomplish its task. This appears to stand in opposition to the rather common theological teaching that the institutions of the Church are determined by the institution of Jesus Christ. The institutions in question can be only the Papacy and the hierarchy; the claim of institution by Jesus Christ is not made for other parts of the structure. The claim is not disputed by pointing out that the resemblance between the historic Papacy and episcopacy and anything in the New Testament is quite remote at best; clearly the Church has felt empowered to modify these institutions, and it must be supposed that they were modified according to the Church's consciousness of its mission. The mission of the Church, like its institutions, appears in the abstract and in the concrete. The Church has never fulfilled its mission in the abstract; at any given moment in history its mission exists in the concrete, with the limitations placed upon it by a contingent understanding of its mission and its contingent resources. The Church of the Middle Ages could scarcely be said to be deeply aware of its mission to Moslems. In our generation there is a new awareness of the mission which can be illustrated by the ecumenical movement. Recognition of the bankruptcy of divided Christianity grows day by day. With this recognition there grows the recognition that the concrete institutional structures are not adapted to reunion, indeed may be the single most serious obstacle to reunion. The new awareness is shown in the use of the word "reunion" to designate the mission rather than the old word "conversion."

For several centuries the theological definition of the mission of the Church has been put in terms of the threefold office of teaching, sanctifying and governing. This definition is basically biblical, but only basically, and itself exhibits the development in the consciousness of the mission of which I have spoken. One need do no more than consult the concordance of the New Testament to discover that "teaching" and "doctrine" do not occupy the place in the New Testament which they occupy in the recent Church. Where the modern Church speaks of teaching, the New Testament speaks of proclaiming the good news; and these cannot be reduced to the same thing. Plainly, then, the development of doctrine has given the teaching office a dimension which it did not have in the early Church. Assuming that the development of doctrine was inevitable, this growth was also inevitable. But if the teaching office assumes dimensions which suppress the office of proclamation, then certain questions are in order about the Church's understanding of its mission. In particular it can be asked whether doctrine can be imposed in the same way in which the gospel can be imposed, although imposition is hardly the word for the New Testament proclamation. The gospel is imposed in the sense that once it is heard, neutrality becomes impossible. One becomes either a believer, or a disbeliever; one cannot remain a non-believer. When this is transferred to doctrine, a manifest difference appears between the officer who is the apostle of the gospel and the officer who is the custodian of sound doctrine.

The office of sanctifying has always meant in the concrete structure the administration of the Sacraments. By a somewhat inexplicable turn it is this office which has recently been most closely examined and most extensively modified. The ritual of the Sacraments has been for many centuries a strictly sacerdotal office in which the laity were passive recipients of the grace of the Sacraments. It seemed that very suddenly the Church as a body became aware that this sacerdotal monopoly was not actually fulfilling the mission of sanctifying. There was a wide demand for closer participation of the laity in the sacred, a demand which has not yet been entirely satisfied; but the direction of the trend is evident. In this office it has become apparent that the entire membership of the Church must share actively in the fulfillment of the office. May we suggest that the same principle may be extended to the other two offices? The sanctifying power of the Church is felt to expand to something closer to fullness when it is the visible power of the whole Church, when the social character of the Church is expressly recognized, than was possible when the sanctifying power was exhibited only in the performance of sacerdotal ritual.

It is the office of governing which has been the object of most discussion and criticism. Our interest here is in the evident proliferation of the structure of ecclesiastical government since New Testament times. Here too the modification has happened because the understanding of the mission has changed. To trace the process by which closer and closer control was thought necessary is beyond our power here; and I do not know whether any one has ever investigated this phenomenon thoroughly. Some would say that it is no more than another textbook example of creeping bureaucracy. There is no question that creeping bureauracy is characteristic of human society; but in the Church it has ecclesiastical roots and takes ecclesiastical forms, and these should interest the theologian and Church historian. It is not merely a question of growth in numbers, or even of complexification of the works of the Church, although this last factor is of importance. Not until the Pope became a civil sovereign did he need a minister of state and a minister of defense and a minister of internal security. But the New Testament Church, which was recognized as a single Church, was an association of local Churches. It was felt that each Christian could experience the fullness of Christianity in the local Church. I am not sure that the modern Catholic would say the same thing about his parish. The difference can easily be traced to the proliferation of the structure of government. The Pope and the bishop are not experienced in the local parish, and therefore the Catholic doubts that he really experiences the fullness of the Church there. He feels more like a customer in a rural branch of a large retail store. For the full line you have to go to the downtown store. But the local Church could be operated according to the simple structure of the New Testament Churches. It is not so operated because it has become what I likened it to, a branch. Evidently the Church has long felt that the mission is better accomplished if it operates branches.

The proliferation in the office of governing illustrates a feature common to all the three phases of the mission; and this is a large number of specialized offices with specialized functions. We need not discuss the operation of Parkinson's Law in the Church; this law has always operated and will always operate. Our concern can be again with the peculiarly ecclesiastical features of the operation of the law. Modern governments and corporations try to counteract the law by "streamlining" their operations. There has been no serious effort to streamline Church government. If one examines in detail the offices and functions which appear in Roman Catholicism, one is compelled to ask regularly whether this or that office is ecclesiastical. A competent judgment about this question is not possible to the casual observer or even to the student. But the casual observer and the student know that the tendency to multiply offices and functions beyond need and utility is pervasively human; and he wonders whether a serious examination of the governing structure of the Church would not disclose that too many of its members are engaged in administration. He will be impelled to say that we cannot talk honestly about the shortage of priests as long as this cumbersome structure is sustained. He may ask whether the Church has engaged in too many non-ecclesiastical activities. The concrete structure, we have insisted, is contingent; and none of these offices in its present form is demanded by the abstract mission.

We have to ask whether the institutional structures are adapted to the mission of the Church; but here we encounter the fact that the emergent conception of the mission still lacks the clarity which would lead to modification of the structures. I believe one can call the conception of the Second Vatican Council emergent; certainly those who have written on the mission of the Church since the Council have taken the documents of the Council as points of departure, not as terminal declarations. We have already noticed that they cannot be terminal declarations. The Council itself suggested no real modification of the structures; such suggestions would almost certainly have been premature. It did suggest a number of practical changes which, if taken seriously, would lead to modifications beyond those which can be foreseen. It is possible to suggest that the traditional threefold mission of teaching, sanctifying and governing is no longer a suitable designation of the mission.

Let us begin with the easiest, the mission of sanctifying; there has already been a serious modification in the understanding of this part of the mission. There is certainly growing restlessness with the mission of teaching and governing. It is important that the Second Vatican Council did not employ the traditional form of dogmatic decrees; this suggests that the Council as a whole felt that this traditional form was not an apt vehicle for what it wished to say. What, then, does teaching mean in the contemporary Church? Will the teaching of the Church in the future return to something more like the apostolic proclamation? The Council likewise opened the way to a new idea of Church leadership which many have explored. Unless the institutional Church arrests studies of the teaching and governing authority, these explorations will continue; and such a suppression could hardly occur in the contemporary Church. The ideas of mission and structure have already reached the point at which such an interposition would be regarded as hopelessly archaic.

Words are important; and the three words of the traditional mission have acquired such a weight of implication from long-standing practice that they may not at all describe the mission of the Church in the decades and centuries which lie in the future. I shall not attempt to redefine the mission; I think such a redefinition will come only from the collective faith and experience of the whole Church. If it recognizes itself as the living Christ, it must understand that it is not faithful to its identity by adopting features which are contrary to the reality of the historical Jesus, that is, the Jesus of the gospels. The Church will have to return to the New Testament, not to slavish imitation and archaism, but to the New Testament experience of Jesus. From this experience the apostolic Church was expected to form a Church and a proclamation of the gospel which would reach the men of their world. They could do this because they were men of their world, fully acquainted with the human condition of the Mediterranean basin of the first century of this area. Jesus himself belonged to this world; he was not a foreign figure. It is the mission of the Church to show that he belongs to the world in any time and place. I have no hesitation in saying that the Church has long been proclaiming a set of doctrines about a European Christ. I do not hesitate to say that in modern times it has presented a middle-class Christ. In both instances it exhibited what the Vatican Council called triumphalism. It has claimed an authority over minds and wills which Jesus never claimed for himself, and which the apostles did not claim in his name. Yet within the understanding of the threefold mission, sanctified by the experience of several centuries, these lapses were not seen to be contrary to the mission of the Church.

To return to Charles Davis: the institutional Church, which is a means by which the Church asserts its identity, is also a means by which the Church becomes uncertain about its identity. Those who believe in the Church believe that it never knows its identity perfectly, but that it has charismatic resources which enable it to retain its identity when it seems to be in danger of losing it. It is a struggle which is never completely won and never totally lost. The institutional Church can never be destroyed; neither can it be frozen, which is another form of destruction. The Church will grow because it is alive, and no institutional structure can arrest the growth.

SOME POINTS OF DISCUSSION AND CRITICISM

UP to quite recent years no Catholic criticized the institutional Church, either in the abstract or the concrete. Such criticisms were uttered only by Protestants and agnostics or by discontented ex-Catholics who had severed themselves from the Church. The institutional Church in the abstract was seen as the bride of Christ, spotless and without wrinkle, no more open to criticism than Jesus himself. The abstract Church in the concrete was idealized as the living body of Christ, as Jesus present and active in the world. It was recognized that the members of the institutional Church were men with human faults; but the desire to present the concrete Church as the historical realization of the abstract kept Catholics from mentioning these defects even to each other. The Reformers had criticized the Church and had left it; and this seemed to be the proper action for the critic. There had been Popes like Alexander VI; but Catholics felt that if Alexander VI had lived in the twentieth century, criticism of him would have been improper. The Church is holy mother, and a man does not criticize his mother, although in fact many men do.

The change in this attitude within the last few years has been recent and disturbing. Journals, even official Catholic journals, have been remarkably free in their criticism of the institutional Church, not sparing bishops and priests by name. There are few features of the institutional Church which have not been submitted to examination and objection. That there have been some harshness and unfairness in the criticisms must be admitted; there are few areas of human discourse in which criticism is carried on without some degree of harshness and unfairness, and this development is not alarming. The writings of theologians and journalists have reached a wide public, and the criticisms then become topics of discussion in classrooms and conversation pieces in homes and other places where people meet socially.

Why has this change in attitude occurred? One is tempted to say that it is due to Pope John's celebrated call for *aggiornamento,* for bringing the Church up to date. I would think of this rather as something which released a force already existing. The response would never have been so vigorous had the criticisms not already been formed in the minds of many Catholics. To say that something is out of date is a criticism, and usually a rather severe criticism. When Pope John equivalently invited the members of the Church to point out what was out of date, it was clear at once that many thought that much was out of date; and they were happy to have a papal license to say what they thought. Within a few years such a vast amount of criticism of the institutional Church has been published that I can do no more than point out what appear to me to be the major criticisms. Others might well choose other points of emphasis. Whatever be the points selected for discussion, the important fact is that the illusion that all Catholics were perfectly contented with the institutional Church has been shattered; and it will not be rebuilt.

It is a common criticism to say that the Church is conservative or even reactionary; but this criticism does not mean much unless it is made more specific. Conservatism taken by itself is neither a virtue nor a vice; the word "reactionary" is used to signify an undesirably rigid conservatism, but this too needs specification in concrete cases. If one must choose between slowness to change and volatility, clearly the better posture for any society is slowness to change; the other extreme is instability. But actually we are not dealing with extremes, and a reasonable discussion of the problem demands that we avoid extreme positions or charging each other with extreme positions. Yet the very criticisms of which we have just spoken illustrate this point. The criticisms reveal a lag between the institutional Church and the thoughts and feelings of many of its members; when change occurs after such a lag, it comes too rapidly for assimilation and causes pain.

The Church is indeed too slow to change; but why is it slow? It is too simple to attribute exaggerated conservatism to mere indolence. The institutional Church displays a manifest tendency to absolutize the existing structures. Both official and theological publications often show a naive attempt to identify the existing structures with New Testament structures. To use an obvious example, these writings may appeal to the commission which Jesus gave Peter to teach with authority, a commission which has been transmitted to the Roman Pontiff. It is an exegetical fact that the New Testament nowhere quotes Jesus as giving a commission to Peter to teach with authority, nor does it indicate anywhere that this commission, if given, is transmitted to the Roman Pontiff. The appeal assumes that what is, has been from the beginning. Exaggerated conservatism is the result of failure to recognize the historical contingency of the concrete institutional Church; and by historical contingency I mean what I have just said, that what is has not been from the beginning. The structures of the concrete institutional Church are the result both of the institution of the Church by Jesus and of historical development; but the two forces at work must be distinguished. It would seem to follow that what originated in historical contingency remains subject to historical contingency, and never reaches a form in which it becomes immutable. Some critics speak of the idolatry of institutions. Idolatry may be too strong a word, but one who attributes divine attributes to a creature is very close to idolatry—at least material idolatry, if one will pardon the expression.

The same absolute view of the concrete institutions lies behind the appeal to tradition. Tradition, when it is examined, shows historical contingency; not infrequently the tradition is no more than a continuation of a particular response to a particular problem, not always made with profound thought. Since the Church once responded to heresy by burning heretics, the Church had to wait for the Second Vatican Council for a clear statement of religious liberty, a statement which was recognized as the only Christian response once it was made. Traditions are raised above examination when they are identified with the beliefs and ways of an institutional structure which has reached perfection. One need only examine what the structure has done to see what it should do now. The dogmatic claim of infallibility is really very moderate when it is compared to the claims implicit in appeals to traditions. The institutional Church is perhaps the only society of men which succeeds in correcting its mistakes without ever confessing that it has made them.

It is very commonly alleged that the Church is over-centralized on all levels—Rome and the dioceses, the bishop and the diocesans, the clergy and the laity. In each instance the authority is conceived as absolute in the sense that it is not restrained by any principle within the area over which the authority is exercised. Thus when collegiality was first mentioned on the theological scene, many responded that collegiality is foreign to the whole theory and history of ecclesiastical authority. No one could say this who has read the New Testament, but not all Catholics have read the New Testament. The theory permits the authority to reserve all decisions to himself. The practice does not permit this impossible type of authority, but the authority is free to reserve to himself all the decisions which he can manage. The administration of the modern Church shows a creeping authoritarianism. This type of authority cannot be exercised without a bureaucratic structure; and the bureaucratic structure of the Church has shown no signs of shrinking. Bureaucracy acts by establishing policy in more and more detail, aiming at the ideal of a policy decision for every conceivable case. It strengthens its control by demanding review of an ever greater number of decisions and by reserving approval to central headquarters for more and more decisions. To manage an enterprise of this type requires a large number of people, most of whom are engaged in purely secretarial work.

In any other type of social enterprise this would be called over-management. It is one of the novelties of the new criticism that it is now called over-management in the Church too. In other enterprises over-management is called mismanagement; the world of politics and business often recognizes that over-management destroys responsibility and initiative together with personal interest and personal engagement, and overworks its staff with tasks which prevent them from getting anything done. Over-management has everything to do with the common criticism that Church authority manages, but does not lead, and never inspires. It suggests either a real hunger for power or a total lack of confidence in any one who is not in the actual operations of management. The real work of the Church lies in the "field," not in curial and chancery offices. Yet in the modern Church a career in management usually means that the candidate for management will have little or no experience in the field. Were charismatic leadership manifest, it would substitute for experience; but charismatic leadership is perhaps that quality which is in shortest supply. When the Church encounters a genuine and urgent crisis, such as war and revolution, it has in most of the modern world remained inarticulate. The bureaucracy has developed no routine for war and revolution comparable to its routine for petitions for nullity. It produces no leaders because a bureaucracy is designed precisely to make leadership not only unnecessary but dangerous.

The overmanagement of the Church is seen at the extreme in the relations of clergy and laity. In most modern European languages "the Church" in popular speech has come to be synonymous with the hierarchy and the clergy. "The Church says" means that the hierarchy and the clergy say. The actions of the Church mean the actions of the hierarchy and the clergy. A career in the Church means a career in the clergy. The service of the Church is rendered by the professional religious persons, clergy and religious. Certainly the hierarchy and the clergy can speak for the Church and act for the Church in a peculiar way, and criticisms of the existing situation are not intended to destroy this representative character of the clergy. But the implication of the word "Church" in such uses as those mentioned draws an unwarranted distinction between the Church and the laity; and this cannot be the implication of a distinction between clergy and laity. The laity are often—one might say usually—considered to be the passive members of the Church, the members who are spoken to and to whom things are done. The "activity" of the laity emphasized as if it were the only genuine and important activity open to them is contribution to the expenses of Church operations.

The passivity of the laity is clearly seen in countries and regions in which there is a tradition of clerical domination. The tradition may be rooted in more than one cause. It may come from the cultural and educational deprivation of the laity, or from the support of the clergy by strong political governments, or inversely, from the identification of the clergy with classes which are oppressed by strong political governments. The clergy may assert leadership because no one else is capable of asserting it. When clerical leadership, whatever be the conditions in which it is rooted, is invested with the sanctity of Church office, it can elicit a docility which is nearly perfect. The laity then look to the clergy for leadership and for decision in almost all questions, public as well as private, political as well as moral, intellectual as well as theological.

In spite of numerous efforts to organize "lay activity" in some specific and concrete form, lay activity has generally remained too vague to be implemented. As soon as a program of lay activity is proposed, clerics either attempt to direct it or the laity involved turn to the clergy for direction. The excellent documents of the Second Vatican Council on the secular as the area of lay activity still await some practical execution. It is not surprising that laymen who have read these documents are restless when the hierarchy and the clergy reassert the passive position of the laity. One sees little encouragement of lay initiative, and a cool reception towards new lay organizations founded precisely for a closer involvement of the laity in the activities of the Church. When an exhortation to lay activity is followed almost without delay by an affirmation of the traditional monarchical government of the episcopacy, the laity are inclined to doubt the sincerity of the exhortation. The Church is to a large extent deprived of the resources of the laity for the execution of its mission, not only because lay leadership rarely appears but even more because so many ecclesiastics cannot think of the laity in any terms except passive.

The structure is criticized both for its pomp and display and for what the pomp and display signify. Ecclesiastical pomp is the application of the symbols of royalty to high office in the Church. In the modern world it is recognized that the absolute power which the pomp symbolizes is also outdated. There are, of course, still absolute governments in the world; but modern Western governments attempt to hide the absolutism behind a facade of democratic symbols. The Church is candidly absolutist in its claims of power; it is the power of God, above human criticism and discussion. It accepts no response except total obedience; and it allows no limits to the use of its power except those limits which it imposes upon itself. There is no appeal from this power, and no legitimate way of removing oneself from its jurisdiction. The absolute power is responsible to no one except God; no subject has a claim or a right which it can urge, nor can any one sit in judgment on its actions. It is justified as paternal authority, in spite of the fact that paternal authority is by definition exercised upon the immature.

If such claims were made by a modern political government, they would be rejected everywhere in the Western world. It is an obvious response that the Church is not a political government; but there are a few other considerations. The first consideration is that this type of absolute government is rejected because it is regarded in the Western world as inconsonant with the dignity and the freedom of the individual person. The Church has the task of showing that absolute claims for Church authority are not inconsonant with the dignity of the individual person. Frankly, it has not made the effort; it simply reasserts its absolute power. That the Christian is subject to God does not mean that his obedience due to God can be given to human beings. A second consideration is that the Church must allow itself to be measured by the standards of the New Testament. The New Testament offers no support for an absolute Church government. A third consideration is that while the Church is not a political society, it has taken on some of the features and some of the procedures of the political society. These features have no direct connection with the mission of the Church, and they can be judged by the standards of political structures and political action.

As long as the Church chooses to appear absolute, it does not speak with clarity and conviction to many of its members in the Western world, that part of the world which once was Christendom. No doubt many Catholics find a security in the absolute Church government which they would not find in something else; the Church seems to them to manifest a stability which will outlast the mutable world of politics. But others of her members see not stability but rigidity and an unwillingness to deal with the members of the Church as adult human beings. They see an inconsistency between their position in the political, business and professional worlds and their position in the Church. The Church itself does nothing to reconcile the two positions. Analogies are drawn between the absolute government of the Church and the absolute governments of fascism and communism. Unfair and misleading as these analogies may be, they are drawn, and the absolute government of the Church furnishes the occasion for them.

We have observed that the Church has taken on some of the features and the procedures of political government; this is another area of criticism. The methods by which ecclesiastical authority executes its policies and decisions are not always purely ecclesiastical. Critics recognize that the line which they wish to draw here is thin; but they are not content with the theory of absolutism which leaves it entirely to the hierarchy to determine when its processes are truly ecclesiastical. The entire theory of "spiritual" penalties, as incorporated in Canon Law, has been questioned. The spiritual penalties of excommunication, suspension, interdict and other similar censures either separate a person from the Catholic communion or reduce his status within that communion. Up to early modern times the "spiritual" penalties were inflicted with the prospect of death, fines or imprisonment; and they were inflicted with knowledge of these possibilities. In the modern world these additional civil sanctions are recognized as political means of executing ecclesiastical decisions, and in the modern world they are rejected. But there are other kinds of pressure which the Church is sometimes able to exert. Economic and social pressure, while they do less damage than the death penalty or imprisonment, can do serious damage. The treatment of recalcitrant members, especially if they are priests, is not always marked by broad compassion and forgiveness; it is not only a matter of excluding the member from the Catholic community, but of pursuing him vindictively with actions against his reputation and his livelihood. It is particularly offensive when these actions are carried on surreptitiously.

Where the Church disposes of wealth and political influence, it can and does employ these as persuasions or threats. These are evidently secular and political means of accomplishing one's will. However holy may be the purpose of the Church, it is not ecclesiastical when it employs these means. Churchmen have dealt with civil governments on the basis of compromise. One hesitates to resurrect the ghost of *The Deputy,* and any conclusions drawn without the documents are rash. But the Church has here been suspected of a compromise, and the suspicion rests, among other things, on the fact that such compromises are not unknown in the history of the Church. Two obvious facts are that there was no Catholic statement about the genocide of European Jews and that the Catholic Church was tolerated in National Socialist Germany. If the Church has the evidence to dispel the suspicion, it owes it to itself to make this evidence public. By its very existence the Church is a moral power; and it is difficult for this moral power not to have political effects. It is important that the effects be determined by the Church and not by governments.

Criticisms of the wealth of the Church are heard more frequently. The criticism is hardly new in the history of the Church, but it takes a different direction; the remarks are made less about the accumulation of wealth and its use for merely personal gain, and more about the uses of the wealth for Churchly rather than for social goods. The use of wealth for magnificent churches is hardly possible in the modern climate of opinion. The erection of institutions for the upper and middle classes rather than for the poor is likewise criticized, not always fairly, for the record of the Church in this area seems to be better than many think. Attacks on the absolutism are made more frequently concerning the spending of money than about anything else. Church authorities do not think they are accountable for their funds to the Church at large; there is a growing feeling that they are accountable, and the feeling is expressed by the group which contributes the funds. These criticisms, I have said, bear less frequently on the use of funds for personal gain; but it is noticed that a career in the Church promises and often delivers wealth and power, precisely the things which a career in business and politics promises.

In the last few years a growing number of both clergy and laity have shown an identity crisis; they are uncertain both about the mission of the Church and their place in the mission. This may not be the fault of the institutional structure; but many of them have said that the institutional Church has not given them an identity. The statement must be examined to see what degree of truth there is in it; it does not seem antecedently probable that we have in such instance a purely personal breakdown. If one says simply that these are personal failures, he may be unfair to the individuals concerned and willfully blind to his own responsibility. It is the mission of the Church to show its members what Christianity means. If some of the members say that the Church has failed in this part of its mission, their witness cannot be dismissed as mere prejudice. Any one who is acquainted with a few of these cases knows that the fault is not all on one side.

The number of such cases has reached the point where some speak of a crisis of vocations. If such a crisis exists, it is a serious problem for the Church. No one pursues a religious or clerical vocation and remains in it except by his own free choice. If this vocation ceases to attract a sufficient number of candidates, the Church must ask why it does not attract them. Some of the criticisms already mentioned may be alleged among the reasons. If the criticisms are invalid, this should be shown; to ignore them is to abandon any effort to reach those who are professional religious persons or who might become such. The most alarming feature of the crisis is a general refusal either to admit that it exists or to search into its causes. Ultimately this appears to be a refusal to accept modifications in the existing structures and practices.

In reviewing these criticisms, our purpose has been simply to set them forth, not to defend them or to analyze them or to refute them. The scope of this presentation does not permit such treatment. Merely to set forth the criticisms could be an unfair presentation; these criticisms do not reveal the reality of the Church. The important fact is that they are widely uttered and widely accepted. Certainly some types of criticism are exaggerated; but an exaggerated criticism may fasten on a valid point. The fundamental question is whether criticism is possible, and whether it can serve the Church. Many of the members of the Church are now convinced that criticism is necessary and useful. They point out these and other areas in which the Church needs to change; the changes suggested may be of doubtful value in some instances, but the critics are convinced that the Church will do better to risk a doubtful change than to adhere to institutional features and practices which are proved to be out of date at best, harmful to the mission of the Church at worst.

It should be assumed that criticism of the institutional Church will continue; it should also be assumed that it arises from concern for the good of the Church. The Church here does not mean the abstract structure nor the concrete structure, meaning the hierarchy and the clergy, but the whole assembly of the people of God. It should not be assumed that criticism is an attack on the hierarchical institution as such nor on its individual members as persons. It is meant to be an attempt to point out areas in which the institutional Church is imperfectly fulfilling its mission. It should be accompanied by an offer to assist the institutional Church wherever it is possible. Those who believe that change is necessary should be willing to work within their ability for the changes in which they believe. The criticism should initiate friendly discussion of the problem without allowing the problem to be prejudiced by either party to the discussion. Should the Church prove able to engage in such discussions, it would do much to neutralize many of the criticisms which have been uttered. There are signs that such discussion is possible.

POSSIBILITIES

CRITICISM is usually expected to be constructive, a term which is not always carefully used. But I take it that constructive criticism means at least an effort to suggest some way in which the thing criticized can be improved. It could happen that one would have no suggestion for the improvement of a particularly unhappy diocese or parish except that the incumbent bishop or pastor be relieved of his office. Constructive criticism would not seem to demand that the critics present a replacement. If criticism has to be so silenced until the critic could present a clearly superior program, there would be very little criticism of anything. Drivers who are daily annoyed by congested and dangerous traffic may present their criticisms of the condition; they will say that it is up to the traffic engineers to find ways to relieve the congestion and the danger. Critics of inequitable and extortionate tax laws demand that legislators and tax attorneys revise the laws. One need not be a traffic engineer to recognize congested and dangerous traffic, nor need one be a tax attorney to recognize inequitable and extortionate taxation. Nor need one be a prelate to recognize defects in the institutional Church; and one may ask that prelates, who are presumably expert in institutional Church management, take measures to correct the situations which are criticized. So many people said so long that liturgical worship was meaningless to them that reform was finally instituted, a reform which was actually several centuries late. The criticisms were as valid in the sixteenth century as they were in the twentieth. The critic of the institutional Church may conclude that criticism is rarely weighed on its own merits; it receives attention only when it is voiced by so many people that it can no longer be ignored.

This may help to explain the acid tone of some criticisms of the institutional Church.

The criticisms reviewed previously are presented as samples of conditions which the critics would liken to traffic conditions or inequitable taxes or archaic liturgy. They believe that these conditions are recognized, but that it is neither within their power nor their duty to propose concrete practical measures of dealing with the situations. Most of the critics accept the institutional Church as a permanent reality with which they are ready to live. They have no desire to destroy the institutional Church and reduce Catholicism to a formless horde of believers, nor simply to sever their connection, even privately, with the institutional Church. They believe that the institutional Church must reform itself; and there is nothing un-Catholic about this conviction.

These remarks are not made simply as a disclaimer of responsibility for constructive practical suggestions. In fact a number of practical suggestions have been made in recent years. Not many suggestions which have come from outside the official structure have been accepted; it is not clear that they have even been known or considered. But if the presentation made here is not to be one-sided, the constructive suggestions should also be reviewed. When we review them, we shall find that a few constructive suggestions offer some promise of meeting most of the criticisms.

The first change that may be suggested is a change of attitude rather than a change of practice; and no obvious practical measures occur which can bring about this change of attitude. Attitudes are formed by long habits of thought and action, and they are not altered except by a long educational process. Yet it is evident that the institutional Church must realize that it is now, as it has always been, in a process of evolution. Knowledge of the history of the Church shows how flexible the Church has been; the pose of monolithic rigidity is not a true image of its historic reality. We have spoken of the idolization of the structure; but this idol is not easy to smash. The Second Vatican Council has opened the way to flexibility in the structure; many are impatient because so many of the hierarchy seem not to have realized what the Council did, or seem to have rejected the acts of the Council. Others in the Church can do nothing except to lose no opportunity to create and foster an attitude sympathetic to change. This means that agitation, as some call it, must continue.

Since the Church is in constant evolution, evolution will continue whether it is desired or not. The Church can choose between guided and controlled evolution, or evolution which is left to chance. Many of the historical changes in the Church were the result of chance in the sense they they were forced upon the Church by the events of history. Such changes were made too late, and the character of the change was too often determined by the unhealthy conditions which the delay of change had brought about. The Church can lead history rather than be led by it; at least it is able to exercise more decision about the direction its own history will take. It should not take a French Revolution to revise the relations between the Church and the lower classes. If evolution is not controlled, upheaval seems to be the sure result. Refusal to adapt and to modify is an invitation to disaster.

In all fairness to the institutional Church, it must be noticed that idolization of the structure is not limited to the officers of the institutional Church. The attitude is shared by many of the faithful. They have formed this attitude because of the religious instruction they have received, and in this instruction the institutional Church has played the major part. The faithful reflect the image of the Church which their prelates have projected. "The open Church" must be proclaimed to every one in the Church; and it is not easy to convince the faithful that they have cherished a false image of the Church. To touch their minds requires more than usual skill and prudence; for one must retain their sympathy while he seeks to change their thinking.

The idolization of the Church takes another form which must be corrected by another change in attitude. Like the first change suggested, this change also cannot be achieved rapidly. The attitude which I mean is difficult to define, but I try to summarize it by saying that the Church is seen as a thing rather than as persons, a super-thing indeed, a kind of half-divine reality which can be distinguished from its members. This description seems to fit idolatry. The processes of the institutional Church do not always exhibit a primary interest in persons as persons; and it is not proper to speak of persons as "souls" as if they did not attain full reality until they become disembodied spirits. It is doubtful that the officers of the institutional Church deliberately intended to be inhuman; and it is a practical suggestion that they be reminded whenever they exhibit inhumanity with noble intentions. When the institutional processes and the routine of bureaucracy cross the purposes and the welfare of the individual person, as they often must in an imperfect world, the character of the institution is shown by its attitude in such difficult cases. It can cut corners either in favor of the person or in favor of the impersonal reality of the institution or the processes. The institutional Church is widely thought to have a habitual bias in favor of the impersonal. Doctrine is more important than believers in the institution; and this in spite of the fact that the Church has never existed without the impediment of a vast amount of erroneous beliefs shared both by the pastors and by the sheep. There is a well known canonical principle which can be rendered, "In a doubtful case the presumption is in favor of the validity of the marriage." In this principle the marriage has become an impersonal juridical reality; the presumption is explicitly against the persons who are involved in the case.

In very recent years the inhumanity of the institutional Church towards those who are on its lowest levels has become public knowledge. Priests and religious are sometimes denied basic human and civil liberties. They can recover these liberties only by departing from the institutional Church; many of them do not wish to do this. No one can be assured of a happy and contented life; but no one should be deprived of the possibility because some one else has planned it that way. There are manifest efforts to retain the professional religious people in subjection as far as it is possible; and one sees again that the thing is preferred to the person. Such a campaign to sustain total subjection will not produce just what the institutional Church needs, a personal and enthusiastic dedication on the lower levels of operation. Such dedication can be expected when those who are engaged in the works of the institutional Church are treated as persons, and not before.

Again it appears that agitation must continue; the agitation concerning this problem will consist in the assertion of personal dignity and its defense, whether for oneself or for another. One may indeed appeal to the gospel precept to deny oneself; but the gospel does not impose this on subjects any more than it does on prelates. The precept must be taken in a context in which the officers are told explicitly that they are at the bottom level of the Church. This saying of Jesus has not been honored in the Church since the apostolic age. Jesus asserted himself against the authorities of his own Jewish religious community; and it is strange that this has never been proposed by those who speak of the imitation of Christ. When religious authorities act corruptly, one must ask oneself if it is necessary to do something to resist the corruption. Attacks on the dignity of the human person by institutional officers are corruption in the Church.

Respect for persons can be better assured by some structural modifications which have been suggested by many. Our scope does not permit discussion of these modifications in detail, but they can be summed up in two words: decentralization and democratization. Both of these steps are urgent unless the institutional Church is to go deeper in trouble than it has already gone. Decentralization means the reversal of the structure which has been criticized: fewer decisions are made by Rome for the whole Church, fewer decisions are made by the bishop for the diocese, fewer decisions are made for the laity by the clergy. Decentralization does not imply, as many seem to fear, that the centers of authority lose their authority; it means that the authority is exercised in some other way than detailed and rigid directions. One can think of objectives stated with clarity and definition but with very loose statements about the way the objectives are to be achieved. It is difficult to understand why a bishop, who presumably is engaged with weighty matters worthy of episcopal attention, should waste his time and the time of others by deciding whether the Eucharist may be celebrated in a private home. If his clergy and laity cannot be trusted to do this without his permission and supervision, it is hard to think of an area in which they can be trusted. There is simply no reason why matrimonial cases should ever be referred to Rome; nothing has happened to prove that the Roman courts and canonical attorneys are superior to the courts and attorneys of the dioceses. In this instance the process of centralization does deny the right to a reasonably quick solution of one's case; justice deferred is justice denied.

Decentralization is simply a polite word for freedom of action, and this is the real objective. It must be insisted upon that genuine personal responsibility is directly proportioned to the freedom of decision which a person possesses. Initiative stands in the same proportion; that centralization stifles initiative is so obvious that it does not deserve comment. A centralized bureaucracy is incapable of initiative, and it does not permit others to exercise it. The experiment of the worker priests in France had much promise as well as many problems; it was simply no business of Rome to decide how a local problem should be solved, and the Roman action is an excellent example of the abuse of centralized authority. Decentralization cannot be postponed until the subordinates prove themselves worthy of trust, because centralization never permits them to do anything which would prove this. One trusts persons by trusting them, not by testing them as if they might be counterfeit.

Decentralization is more difficult than many seem to realize. The existing structures of the institutional Church are organized for centralization and for nothing else; quite possibly they would collapse with decentralization, and some would say that this would be a good thing. But it would not be the controlled evolution of which we have spoken. The institutional Church must embark deliberately on a course of separating itself from various areas of control and decision. The reorganization of the Roman Curia instituted by Paul VI seems to be a new denomination of offices rather than a reorganization of offices. What is sought is a repeal of Parkinson's Law by a sharp reduction in the persons employed in the ecclesiastical bureaucracy. Nothing else will show a serious intention to decentralize. Offices should not be given new titles or consolidated in other departments, but simply annihilated where possible, have less authority where they must be retained. The Congregation of the Faith, which still looks like the Holy Office under another name, is a medieval institution which met a medieval need in ways for which the Church is still apologizing. If the bishop is an authentic teacher in his diocese, the need for a super-inquisitorial office in Rome is not immediately apparent. For most of its history the Church got along without it. Now that its historical character is fairly well demonstrated, it seems very likely that the Church would get along well without it now.

Decentralization means the end of the kind of moral imperialism which the clergy and the hierarchy have so long exercised, or tried to exercise. The teaching and preaching Church has given so much attention to specific directions for specific moral cases that it may occasionally have neglected some of the weighty things of the law—like justice, mercy, and faith. One sometimes has to conclude that the reason why so many Catholics do not love their neighbor is that the commandment has not been proclaimed to them as clearly and specifically as the prohibition of contraception. There should be no room for moral imperialism here either; but it seems a safe Christian practice to proclaim the commandment of love. Paul and the gospels were quite specific about it. The problem is really more than moral imperialism: it is also the selection of topics where moral imperialism operated. But behind the selection is the principle, implicit rather than explicit, that nothing is morally important or unimportant unless the clergy declare it so. They can declare something unimportant by giving it little or no attention. Forming one's conscience means to ask the priest what to do, and to feel free to ignore what he does not mention with emphasis. A general view of the Catholic conscience in this day and year seems to suggest that the result of moral imperialism is confusion of conscience.

The second of the two words in which we summarize the suggestions for structural changes is democratization. Collegiality is the more common term in modern discussions; but democratization introduces some emphases which should be considered. Democratization refers both to the status symbols of pomp and to the processes of government. It is doubtful that the Church could take any single step which would more quickly and surely restore its image than the abandonment of all symbols of rank and prestige. Symbols are important, and the abandonment of these symbols would not only foster confidence in the laity, it would affect the thinking and sentiments of those who now bear the symbols. Such titles as holiness, excellency, eminence, and others should be dropped for the personal name. Respect can be shown without using the titles of nobility. With the titles go the archaic and expensive garb which designates the prelate; there is no reason why this finery should be retained even in liturgical use. The prelate should dress as simply as any one with the title of father; the priest is not really a father, and the title is unbecoming. Clerical dress can elicit both undeserved contempt and undeserved privilege and respect; it sets the cleric apart as a sacred person, a person who deserves more than the usual respect and honor. If the pomp were renounced, the hierarchy and the clergy would be compelled to depend on their inner personal resources; and this demand ought to be made. The abandonment of pomp would signify community and accessibility, and would witness to the belief that the Church is one. Is it necessary to wait until all concerned reach an agreement before pomp is renounced? Any one in the Church who wishes to renounce the degree of pomp which is his should be free to do so; and I suspect that many would follow quickly, although they might hesitate to be the first to be unconventional.

Possibly the democratization of the symbolism of power is necessary before the democratization of power itself becomes a real possibility. The abandonment of pomp is calculated to destroy the image of power as it has been known; and unless this image is destroyed, it is scarcely realistic to think of democratizing the processes. By democratizing the processes I do not imply that the Church should become a democratic government in the usual sense of the term, although I have never seen a convincing argument that a democratic government is alien to the constitution of the Church. But I do mean a sharing of decisions in the sense that each person concerned in a decision has a share proportionate to his involvement in its execution. No blueprint exists for such shared decisions, and it is impossible to write one which would be practical. A world-wide Church cannot find a blueprint which would be equally suitable everywhere. But once the principle of the shared decision were accepted, it should not be difficult for each region and each level of Church government to find practical ways of realizing the principle. Some ways have been suggested and instituted already; but the limited success of these efforts illustrates a remark made earlier, that the structures of the institutional Church are organized for absolute centralization and do not suit anything else.

The synod of bishops, instituted since the Second Vatican Council, was a sincere effort to decentralize the relations of Rome and the bishops. Most observers thought that the first session of the synod was a blank. This is no reason for discouragement; the bishops did not know what they were to do, and it was not entirely their fault. It is clear that up to this time the synod has meant nothing for decentralizing the vast bureaucracy of the Roman Curia, nor has the Curia made any perceptible move towards decentralization. The synod of bishops has been given no responsibility, nor has it asserted any responsibility. Unless it assumes decisions which hitherto have been reserved to the Papacy, meaning the Pope and the Roman Curia, it will be no more meaningful than the Russian Parliament. If it awaits responsibility as a gift, it seems doubtful that any now living except those who are children will see the synod exercise any responsibility. Yet there are hopeful recent signs that many bishops are aware that they share a collegial responsibility for the whole Church, and this awareness will find more expression. The major obstacle, it must be said candidly, is the number of bishops who feel no such responsibility.

Diocesan senates of priests and lay councils in the dioceses and the parishes are efforts to widen the base of decision on these levels. These organizations so far run the scale from great promise to almost utter failures; and the major cause in each instance seems to be the attitude of the bishop, which itself shows that democratization has not advanced very far. It does seem clear that organizations on the diocesan and parochial level show a deeper awareness of responsibility and a greater desire for shared decisions than the synod of bishops has shown, and they have moved more rapidly towards democratization.

Any idea of democratization must include elections. The Pope is the only elected officer of the institutional Church, but the electorate could hardly be narrower. It is limited to the candidates for the office, and the candidates have all been selected by the officer for whom they elect a replacement; they represent no one but themselves. Election was the first way in which the Church chose bishops, and a return to the original practice should be seriously considered. Election would remove certain problems which now exist, and the problems which it would create might, upon examination, turn out to be good risks. It is difficult to believe that the body of clergy and laity in any diocese cannot recognize the qualities desirable in a bishop; if they cannot, they are spiritually so ill that the system of Roman appointment is not enough to cure them. Certainly the determination of the franchise is a problem; but once the principle of election is accepted, this becomes a problem of detail which can be solved by practice and experience. The electorate for the Papacy should certainly be broadened far beyond the College of Cardinals; how far, again, is a problem of detail. No change in anything is possible if problems of detail are declared insoluble before the problems are studied.

Synods, senates, boards and councils do not exhaust the possibilities of democratization, and they should not be thought to exhaust them. Democratization is a program to involve each member of the Church more responsibly in the mission of the Church. The engagement is not equal for all. It is not to be expected that any member of the Church will have the same responsibility as the Pope in the whole Church and the bishop in the diocese. Hence no one will have a power of decision equal to that of these officers. It does not follow that others have no power of decision where they are responsible, but something close to this often happens. Democratization, apart from new structures, means that the superior officer must deal more closely with those whom he governs while at the same time giving them more freedom of decision than they normally have now. Bishops have been heard to say that this type of personal government would impose an intolerable burden on their time and energies. This is not immediately clear. On the hypothesis that subordinates would have more freedom of decision and operation, it is quite possible that the burdens of the bishop would be lightened by consulting each one involved in decision. The number of decisions which the bishop must make would be sharply reduced from the number which now come before him: and consultation would issue in decisions which with reasonable assurance could be expected to be satisfactory to those who have the responsibility for their execution. Consultation is another instance of a possibility which should not be rejected because of problems in detail which have not been studied. A clear defect of absolutism and centralization is that bishops are sometimes unaware of the thoughts and feelings of those whom they govern, and they are sometimes disagreeably surprised. One would think that some expenditure of time in acquiring this information would be well worthwhile. It would not be worthwhile in an absolutely centralized structure, because in such a structure what the subjects think and feel is of no importance to any one except themselves. It can be said with certainty that this attitude cannot be sustained in the contemporary Church.

Authority and power are not the same thing. Authority can be powerless, and power without authority can be irresponsible. No one seriously intends to weaken authority in the Church through decentralization and democratization. Those who suggest these changes honestly believe that they will strengthen authority. If there be those who fear freedom, which they cannot distinguish from license or anarchy, or who do not trust any one else to be responsible besides themselves, let them reflect that authority loses power when it does not have the full and willing cooperation of those whom it governs. With those who simply like power because it is good to have power no discourse is possible. Such are few in the Church, we hope. The power of the hierarchy, as distinguished from its authority, resides purely and simply in the persons who submit to its decisions. This submission cannot be coerced in the modern Church; and when it was possible to exercise coercion, the power of the Church and its government were weak because the consent of the governed was weak. The strength of the execution is not the strength of the governing officer, but the personal strength of all those who make his decision their own. Democratization insures this as well as anything can. Whether the Church is to become stronger or weaker in the decades to come may depend more than anything else on whether it decides to decentralize and democratize its institutional structure.

BIBLIOGRAPHY

Bedoyere, Michael de la, (ed.) *Objections to Roman Catholicism*. Philadelphia: Lippincott, 1965.
Callahan, Daniel. *Honesty in the Church*. New York: Scribners, 1965.
Congar, M.J. *Power and Poverty in the Church*. Baltimore: Helicon, 1964.
Dulles, Avery R. *The Dimensions of the Church*. Westminster: Newman, 1967.
Küng, Hans. *The Church*. New York: Sheed & Ward, 1967.
McKenzie, John L. *Authority in the Church*. New York: Sheed & Ward, 1966.
Todd, John M., (ed.) *Problems in Authority*. Baltimore: Helicon, 1962.

Biographical Notes

CONTRIBUTORS

*Baltazar, Eulalio R., Instr., Univ. of Dayton, 1962-1964, Asst. Professor, 1964-1967, Assoc. Professor, 1967-, Vis. Professor, St. Bernard's Sem. (N.Y.) 1968-, Vis. Professor, Villanova Univ., Summer, 1968, Vis. Professor, Federal City Coll. (Washington, D.C.), 1969-70.

*Burghardt, Walter J. Professor, Woodstock Coll. (Md.),†† 1946-, managing ed., *Theological Studies,* 1946-, co-ed., *Ancient Christian Writers,* 1958-, Cath. Theol. Sc. Am. (Cardinal Spellman Award, 62), President, North American Academy of Ecumenists, member of the International Papal Theological Commission.

*Dulles, Avery, Assoc. Professor, Woodstock Coll. (Md.),†† 1960-, mem. Archdiocesan Comm. Christian Unity, Baltimore, 1962-, Assoc. ed. *Concilium,* 1963-, mem. bd. dir., Georgetown Univ., 1966-1968, consultor, Papal Secretariat for Dialogue with Non-Believers, 1966-, mem. Cath. Comm. Intellectual and Cultural Affairs, 1967-, bd. trustees, Fordham Univ., 1969-, adv. council, U.S. Cath. Conf., 1969-.

*Fontinell, Eugene, Instr., Iona Coll., 1951-1954, Asst. Professor, Coll. of New Rochelle, 1954-1958, Assoc. Professor and Chmn., 1958-1961, Asst. Professor, Queens Coll. (N.Y.), 1961-1966, Assoc. Professor and Chmn., 1966-.

Häring, Bernard, four yrs. military chaplain in World War II mostly on the Russian front, Professor, Gars, Germany, 1947-1950, Professor, Academia Alfonsiana, Rome, 1950-1957, Professor, Alphonsianum Institute, Rome, 1957-, Vis. Professor, Yale Univ., Vis. Professor, Union Theological Sem., New York, 1968.

*Maly, Eugene H., Instr. Athenaeum of Ohio, 1950-1955, Asst. Professor, 1955-1959, Assoc. Professor, 1959-1960, Professor, 1960-, ed. *Bible Today,* 1962-, Cath. Bibl. Asn. Am. (pres. 1962-1963).

*McKenzie, John L., Mem. Faculty, West Baden Coll., 1942-54, Professor, Loyola Univ. (Ill.), 1954-1965, Vis. Professor, Univ. of Chicago, 1965-1966, Professor, Univ. of Notre Dame, 1966-, Cath. Bibl., Asn. Am. (secy. 1947, pres. 1963-1964), Soc. Bibl. Lit. (pres. 1965-1966), Rsch. Prof., De Paul Univ., 1970.

*Noonan, John T., Jr., Assoc. Professor, Univ. of Notre Dame, 1961-

1963, Professor, 1964-1966, Professor, Univ. of Calif. Berkeley, 1967-, mem. spec. staff, Nat. Security Council, 1954-1955, Chmn., Brookline Redevelopment Authority, Mass., 1958-1960, ed. *Natural Law Forum*, 1961-, Guggenheim Fellow, 1965-1966.

*Papin, Joseph, Docent, Univ. of Nijmegen, Holland, 1946-1947, Professor, St. Andrew's Abbey & St. Procopius Coll., 1947-1950, Professor, & Acting Chmn., De Paul Univ., 1950-1953, Prof., Univ. of Notre Dame, 1953-1963, Pres., Academic Middle European Federal Club, 1950-54, Vis. Professor, Loyola Univ. 1951-, Rsch., Rome, Cairo, Jerusalem, 1958, Pres. Intern. Mariological Congress, multilingual session, Lourdes, 1958, Vis. Professor, Valparaiso Univ., 1962, Rosemont Coll., 1964, Professor & Director, Graduate Studies, Villanova Univ., 1963-.

*Pelikan, Jaroslav, member of faculty of Philosophy & History, Valparaiso Univ., 1946-1949, Professor, Concordia Sem., 1949-1953, Professor, Univ. of Chicago, 1953-1962, Vis. Professor, Univ. of Notre Dame, 1959, Titus Street Professor, Yale Univ., 1962-.

*Stendahl, Krister, Stud. pastor, University Upsala, 1948-1950, Instr., 1951-1954, Docent, 1959, Asst. Professor, Harvard Divinity School, 1954-1956, Assoc. Professor, 1956-1958, Morrison Professor, 1958-1963, Frothingham Professor, 1963-1968, Dean & John Lord O'Brian Professor, Divinity, 1968-.

EDITOR
Joseph Papin

ASSOCIATE EDITORS

†Cleary, James J., Instr., Villanova Univ., 1956-1960, Asst. Professor, 1960-1969, Assoc. Professor, 1969-, Catalog Editor, 1960-, Acting Chmn., 1962-1963, Asst. to the Vice President for Academic Affairs, 1969-.

†Eigo, Francis A., Instr., Villanova Univ., 1966-1968, Asst. Professor, 1968- .

ASSISTANT EDITORS

McCartney, James, Instr., Catholic Univ. of America, 1970-.

†O'Rourke, John F., Instr., Villanova Univ., 1962-1966, Asst. Professor, 1966-1969, Acting Chmn., 1965-1969.

†Reino, Joseph C., Teaching Fellow, Univ. of Pennsylvania, 1945-1951, Instr., Penn State Center, Swarthmore, 1951-1956, Asst. Professor, La Salle College, 1956-1959, Asst. Professor, Villanova University, 1960-1965, Assoc. Professor, 1966-.

* Biographical information taken from the *Directory of American Scholars*, 1969.
† Biographical information taken from the *Villanova University Bulletin*.
†† Now in New York, N.Y.

Index of Names

Aaron
92
Abbott, Walter M.
11
Abel
84, 104, 115
Abelard
84, 104
Abraham (Abram)
28, 62, 63, 84, 86, 92, 115, 118, 135, 164, 192, 203
Adam
91, 97, 118
Agar
135
Ahern, Barnabas
V
Albright, W. F.
165, 166, 177, 183, 184
Alexander III
220
Alexander VI
262
Alexander of Hales
221
Alfrink, Bernard
V
Alszeghy, Zoltan
238, 240
Altizer, Thomas J. J.
41
Alfonso de' Ligouri
222
Ambrose
98, 100, 112, 216, 220, 221
Anselm
114
Apollinaris
113
Aristides
189, 190, 205
Aristobulus
98

Aristotle
104, 105, 106, 107, 111, 137, 226, 227, 228, 242, 243, 244, 247, 251, 252
Armenti, Joseph
14
Arnobius
99, 114
Artemon
107
Athanasius
84, 113, 120
Athenagoras
95, 112, 119
Attwater, Donald
11
Audet, J. P.
163
Augustine
VIII, 7, 54, 60, 84, 88, 89, 94, 98, 102, 103, 104, 112, 114, 115, 116, 118, 121, 122, 123, 124, 216, 221, 245

Baillie, John
52
Ballard, E.
132
Baltazar, Eulalio R.
V, 10, 11, 13, 40, 41, 223, 279
Bar-Cochba
191, 196, 197
Baron, Salo Wittmayer
196, 206
Barnabas
83, 85, 102
Barnhurst, William J.
13
Barth, Karl
11, 40, 52, 224
Baum, Gregory
41

281

Baumgartner, H. M.
  150
Baur, F. C.
  83
Bea, Augustin
  47, 51
Becker, Johannes
  222
Bedoyere, Michael de la
  278
Ben-Chorin, Schalom
  199, 207
Ben-Gurion, David
  207
Benedict XIV
  213, 220, 221
Benjamin
  204
Benoit, Pierre
  44
Berdyaev, Nicholas
  10, 11
Berger, Peter L.
  41
Bergson, Henri
  30
Bieler, Ludwig
  221
Billuart, Charles
  221
Blake, Eugene Carson
  V
Blau, Joseph
  41
Blewett, John
  41
Bloch, Ernest
  168, 169, 183
Blondel, Maurice
  59, 80
Boccard, E. de
  206
Boethius
  105
Bonhoeffer, Dietrich
  11, 152, 153, 182
Boniface VIII
  148, 255
Bonwetsch, Nathanael
  117

Bouillard, Henri
  2, 21, 40
Bouyer, Louis
  228
Boyle, Denis A.
  14
Braaten, Carl
  52, 53
Bradley, Joseph M.
  13
Brady, Elizabeth M.
  14
Brandon, S. G. F.
  183
Braunsberger, O.
  220
Bröker, Werner
  240
Bromiley, G. W.
  11
Brown, Raymond
  44
Bruderle, Charles P.
  V
Brunner, Emil
  52
Buber, Martin
  11, 90, 157, 177, 179, 183, 189, 207
Buchanan, Neil
  11
Buckley, John M.
  13
Bultmann, Rudolf
  11, 50, 52, 170, 224
Burgh, W. G.
  150
Burghardt, Walter J.
  V, 10, 13, 186, 207, 279
Burt, Donald X.
  V, 13
Busch, Thomas W.
  13

Cain
  104, 190
Cajetan
  220
Callahan, Daniel
  278

INDEX OF NAMES

Camus, Albert
  33, 34, 41, 42
Canisius, Peter
  220
Carey, John J.
  42
Casey, Thomas M.
  13
Celsus
  83, 95, 99, 117, 122, 195, 206
Cerinthus
  91
Chadwick, Henry
  206, 221
Chardin, Pierre Teilhard de
  3, 4, 9, 30, 40, 41, 49, 139, 225, 229, 230, 232, 241, 242, 244, 245, 248, 249, 250, 251, 252
Charles the Great
  137
Chenu, M.-D.
  11
Childs, Brevard
  167, 169, 170, 183
Chouraqui, André
  202, 203, 206
Cicero
  105, 121
Cleary, James J.
  V, 14, 180
Clement of Alexandria
  92, 98, 99, 100, 108, 109, 111, 114, 116, 119, 121, 122, 138, 192, 215, 221
Cobb, J. B., Jr.
  79
Cohen, Morris Raphael
  16, 40, 42
Congar, Yves M. J.
  10, 11, 44, 278
Constantine
  103, 104, 122, 137
Coreth, Emerich
  40
Cornelius
  132, 194
Corte, Nicholas
  244
Cotter, A. C.
  252

Cox, Harvey
  10, 153, 154, 182
Crabtree, Arthur B.
  13
Crowe, F.
  228
Cullmann, Oscar
  228, 229, 231
Cummings, Raymond L.
  13
Curran, Charles E.
  V
Cyprian
  85, 92, 102, 115, 120, 194, 206
Cyril
  90, 113, 120

D'Arcy, M. C.
  11
Daley, Edward L.
  9
Daniel
  206
Daniélou, Jean
  11, 62, 80, 88, 204, 206
Dante
  122
David
  118, 123, 160
Davis, Charles
  257, 262
Deborah
  181
Deissler, A.
  184
Delitzsch, Franz
  179
Democritus
  111
Denzinger, H.
  222
Dewart, Leslie
  42, 49, 81, 182, 247
Dewey, John
  16, 18, 19, 24, 25, 26, 27, 28, 29, 31, 35, 38, 40, 41, 42
Didache
  92
Didymus, Arius
  89, 111, 113

Diekmann, Godfrey
  V
Dionysius
  122
Doms, Herbert
  218, 222
Donceel, J.
  251, 252
Dostoevsky
  13
Doyle, John P.
  14
Driscoll, John M.
  V, 1, 9
Dru, Alexander
  11
Duddington, Natalie
  10
Duhr, Bernhard
  221
Dulles, Avery
  11, 13, 52, 253, 278, 279
Dulton, John E. L.
  221
Duns Scotus
  8

Ebert, Herman
  253
Ebion (Hebrew word for "poor")
  91
Eckbert
  221
Eigo, Francis A.
  V, 14, 280
Eli
  92
Eliade, Mircea
  167, 169, 183, 184
Engels, Friedrich
  241
Ennis, Arthur J.
  V, 13
Erasmus
  3
Esau
  190
Euclid
  107

Eusebius
  88, 90, 94, 98, 103, 104, 116, 122, 221
Eutyches
  106
Eve
  97

Falk, Heinrich
  253
Falls, Thomas B.
  205
Farrell, William E.
  13
Feuerbach, Ludwig
  38
Fichter, Joseph
  V
Filson, F. V.
  252
Finance, J. de
  238
Flahiff, George
  V
Flew, Antony
  42
Flick, M.
  238
Flora
  118
Fontinell, Eugene
  V, 13, 15, 42, 279
Francis of Assisi
  147
Francoeur, Robert
  239
Frank, S. L.
  10, 11
Frankfort, H.
  184
Friedberg, E.
  220
Fromm, Erich
  132, 139, 183
Fuchs, Joseph
  218, 222
Funk, F. X.
  205, 206

Gallen, Lawrence
  13

INDEX OF NAMES

Garaudy, Roger
42, 241
Garnett, A. Campbell
150
Gibbon, Edward
104
Gilbert, Arthur
186, 188, 189, 205
Gilbert, Stuart
41
Gildea, Joseph J.
V, 9
Glen-Doepel, William
10
Gogarten, Friedrick
151
Gottschalk
84
Gratian
216, 220, 221
Green-Armytage, A. H. N.
11
Greene, M.
227
Gregory I
123
Gregory IX
212
Gregory of Nazianzus
114
Gregory of Nyssa
111, 113, 123, 220
Gury, Jean
217, 221, 222
Gustafson, James
V

Hague, René
11
Hamilton, William
41
Hannah
181
Hargrove, K. T.
182
Häring, Bernard
V, 10, 11, 125, 150, 218, 222, 279
Harnack, Adolph
11, 81, 107, 117

Hartshorne, Charles
30
Harvey, Van A.
53, 56
Hedley, Robert
13
Hegel, Georg
128, 144, 227
Hegesippus
82, 90
Heinitz, Kenneth
168, 183
Hense, O.
221
Heraclitus
111
Herford, R. Travers
206
Hermas
82
Herod
87
Hesiod
94, 97
Hick, John
42
Hilary
114
Hippolytus
92, 107, 115, 190, 192, 194, 205, 206
Homer
94, 97, 99, 108
Hostiensis
220
Hughes, John E.
13
Hughes, Philip E.
11
Hulsbosch, A.
238, 239, 251
Hürth, Francis
218
Huxley, Julian
138

Ice, Jackson Lee
42
Ignatius
86

Innocent III
  147
Irenaeus
  82, 85, 86, 90, 91, 101, 115, 116, 118, 120, 190, 192, 205
Isaac
  135
Isaiah
  87, 92, 120

Jacob
  92, 115, 158
James
  82, 83, 132, 206
James, Henry
  40, 42
James, William
  17, 18, 19, 24, 26, 28, 29, 35, 36, 39, 40, 41, 42
Jaspers, Karl
  11
Jeremiah
  98
Jerome
  88, 90, 121, 216
Jeshu Hanotzri
  195
Job
  166
Johann, Robert
  42, 224, 242
John
  63, 76, 93, 148
John XXIII
  55, 134, 263
John Chrysostom
  89, 92, 221
John of Damascus
  114
Josephus
  88, 98, 122
Joshua
  171
Julian
  83, 94, 95
Jung, Carl
  236
Justin Martyr
  84, 85, 88, 90, 92, 94, 97, 98, 99, 102, 115, 118, 120, 190, 191, 194, 196, 205, 206
Justinian
  104

Katsh, Abraham I.
  V, 10
Kennedy, Grace
  14
Kerrigan, Linda
  14
Kleist, James A.
  205
Klekotka, John A.
  14
Kraus, H.-J.
  176, 179, 184, 185
Krol, John
  9
Küng, Hans
  11. 201, 204, 207, 278

Lactantius
  94, 120, 122
Latourelle, René
  11, 123
Lawrence, J.
  182
Lazor, Bernard A.
  V, 13
Leclerq, H.
  220
Leitch, J. W.
  252
Lindner, Dominic
  222
Lomastro, James H.
  14
Lombard, Peter
  216, 221, 222
Lonergan, Bernard J.
  V, 9, 10, 11, 40
Lubac, Henri de
  11, 154, 182
Luckman, Thomas
  41
Luke
  82, 86
Luther, Martin
  3, 115

INDEX OF NAMES

Macbeth
29
MacIntyre, Alasdair
42, 150
Macquarrie, John
155, 182
Maffei, Scipio
213, 221
Maimonides
90
Major, John
217, 222
Maly, Eugene H.
V, 152, 279
Marc, André
40
Marcion
83, 90, 114, 117, 119
Marcus Aurelius
6
Maritain, Jacques
241, 242
Markham, James J.
13
Marx, Karl
9, 128, 168, 241
Mascall, Eric L.
154, 182
Massimini, Anthony
13
Matthew
86, 91
Mayr, E.
227
McCabe, H.
182
McCarthy, Dennis J.
162, 183
McCartney, James J.
V, 14, 280
McDermott, John J.
40, 42
McFadden, Charles
13
McKenzie, John L.
44, 162, 254, 278, 279
Melanchthon, Philip
112
Metz, Johannes B.
10, 11, 177

Michalson, Carl
42
Migne, J. P.
220
Miller, John H.
206
Minucius Felix
98
Miriam
181
Molina, Luis de
8, 220
Moltmann, Jürgen
172, 177, 235
Monihan, Terrence
13
Montague, G.
185
Mooney, Christopher
10
Moran, Gabriel
201, 207
Morgan, Anthony
14
Moses
62, 63, 82, 85, 86, 91, 97, 98, 99,
118, 119, 120, 121, 136, 177, 256
Muck, Otto
40, 42
Munck, Johannes
48
Murphy, Roland E.
V, 10
Murray, John Courtney
11, 13, 177, 184

Navarrus
220
Nestorius
81, 106
Nicetas
194
Niebuhr, H. Richard
11, 52, 53, 56, 62, 74, 79, 80
Noah
63, 118
Nogar, Raymond
13, 227
Noonan, John T., Jr.
148, 208, 220, 221, 222, 279

North, Robert
  12, 238, 239
Novak, Michael
  42
Novatian
  120

O'Brien, Justin
  41
O'Neill, Luke
  42
O'Reilly, Sister Mary George
  V
O'Rourke, John F.
  V, 14, 280
Ogden, Schubert
  42
Organon
  105
Origen
  86, 87, 88, 91, 93, 94, 96, 97, 98, 102, 103, 109, 110, 111 112, 114, 115, 117, 118, 119, 190, 192, 195, 205, 206, 216, 221
Osborn, E. F.
  100
Otto, Rudolf
  135
Otto the Great
  137

Panikkar, R.
  80
Pannenberg, Wolfhart
  53, 79, 80
Papin, Joseph
  V, 1, 9, 10, 12, 40, 253, 280
Paul
  46, 48, 63, 64, 65, 66, 68, 74, 79, 83, 91, 121, 133, 137, 199, 200, 202, 204, 216, 249, 250, 256, 275
Paul VI
  8, 9, 238, 240, 274
Pearson, Birger
  51
Pelikan, Jaroslav
  10, 13, 81, 280
Pettazzoni, R.
  171

Peter
  83, 132, 133, 256, 263
Philo
  86, 88, 98, 119
Phineas
  206
Pickar, Charles H.
  9, 14
Pierce, Charles Sanders
  18, 26
Pilate, Pontius
  87, 99, 190, 191, 206
Pire, Fr.
  6, 9
Pius V
  213, 220
Pius XII
  55, 218, 222, 238, 253
Plato
  24, 98, 99, 100, 105, 109, 110, 226, 227, 228
Pliny
  94
Pohle, Joseph
  253
Polanyi, Michael
  60, 61, 62, 80
Polycarp
  193, 194, 205, 206
Porphyry
  96
Praxeas
  113, 114
Ptolemy
  118
Pythagoras
  98

Qoheleth
  172
Quadratus
  94
Quinn, C.
  252

Radbertus
  106
Rahner, Karl
  9, 10, 12, 40, 60, 61, 64, 67, 68,

78, 80, 230, 238, 244, 245, 248, 252
Ramsey, Paul
10
Rand, E. K.
106
Randall, John Herman, Jr.
27, 30, 41, 42, 227
Ratramnus
106
Raymond of Peñafort
212
Regan, Daniel T.
13
Reino, Joseph C.
V, 280
Reiser, O. L.
227
Reynolds, Joseph J.
14
Richards, Robert L.
155, 183
Richardson, Alan
53, 56
Ringgren, H.
176, 184
Ritschl, Albrecht
52
Robinson, J. M.
79
Robinson, John A. T.
18, 40, 41, 42, 153, 154, 182
Rongione, Louis A.
14
Ruane, Eugene J.
13
Rufas, Musonius
221
Rufinus
120
Russell, Robert P.
V

Sabatier, Auguste
67
Sagnard, François M. M.
221
Samuel
172

Sanchez, Thomas
217, 222
Sarah
135, 181
Sartre, Jean Paul
204
Saul
160
Scanlon, Michael J.
V
Schaff, Adam
155
Schaub, Franz
220
Schillebeeckx, E.
11
Schleiermacher, Friedrich
90
Schlick, M.
150
Schmaus, Michael
12
Schmidt, Joanne M.
14
Schnackenburg, Rudolf
44
Schneider H. W.
151
Schoenherr, Walter
13, 14
Schónmetzer, Adolf
222
Schoonenberg, Peter
V, 10, 238, 239, 251, 252
Schottroff, Willy
176, 184
Seneca
97
Sheed, Rosemary
11
Sherman, James J.
9
Shylock
196
Simon
90
Simon, Marcel
206
Simpson, G. G.
227

Sixtus V.
  213, 220
Smith, Eric E.
  253
Smith, Joseph P.
  205
Smulders, Piet
  238, 239, 252
Socrates
  94, 97, 109, 121
Soloviev (Solovyev, Solovyov), Vladimir
  10, 12, 13, 14
Solus, Joseph
  14
Sophocles
  180
Soto, Domingo de
  220
Sozomenus
  116
Speiser, E. A.
  162, 164, 183
Spinoza
  89
Stalker, D. M. G.
  252
Stanford, Edward V.
  9
Stanley, David
  44, 249
Stendahl, Krister
  V, 4, 10, 13, 44, 198, 206, 280
Stephen
  206
Suarez, Francis
  8
Symmachus
  100

Tanenbaum, Marc
  197, 198, 206
Tatian
  96, 99, 112
Tavard, George H.
  12
Tertullian
  83, 86, 92, 94, 97, 98, 99, 100, 101, 102, 110, 111, 113, 114, 115, 116, 117, 119, 120, 194, 206, 249

Thayer, H. S.
  43
Theodore of Mopsuestia
  89, 113, 114, 120
Theodosius II
  104
Theodotus
  107
Theophilus
  95, 98, 100, 122
Thill, Carmelita
  14
Thomas Aquinas
  7, 8, 54, 90, 102, 112, 114, 128, 220, 222, 227, 241
Thomas of Celano
  123
Tillich, Paul
  12, 52, 70
Tirrell, Charles D.
  13
Todd, John M.
  278
Torrance, T. F.
  11
Totaro, Robert C.
  13
Trajan
  94
Trapé, Augustine
  9
Trypho
  85, 87, 118, 205

Urban III
  220

Vaganay, Léon
  205
Valensin, Auguste
  80
Valentinus
  118
van Buren, Paul M.
  154
van der Voort, A.
  165, 183
van Onna, Ben
  251

INDEX OF NAMES

Van Roey, Ernest Joseph
 220
Vergil
 101, 121, 122
Versfeld, M.
 251, 252
Von Allmen, J. J.
 252
von Engelhardt, Moritz
 102
von Hefele, Karl Joseph
 220
von Hildebrand, Dietrich
 217
von Rad, Gerhard
 160, 161, 162, 163, 172, 181, 182, 183, 184, 252

Wagler, R.
 151
Weigel, Gustave
 12, 13
Weiser, A.
 185
Welsh, Robert J.
 V, 1, 9
Werner, Martin
 119
Wetter, Gustav A.
 10

White, Andrew
 222
Whitehead, Alfred North
 30, 40, 43
Wilde, Robert
 205
William of Auxerre
 212
Williams, Gardner
 151
Wimmer, Joseph
 13
Wright, Chauncey
 17, 18
Wright, G. Ernest
 45

Yahweh
 87, 135, 158, 159, 160, 161, 165, 171, 173, 176, 177, 178, 183, 184, 199, 202, 203, 204

Zachary
 56
Zakkai, Johanan ben
 196
Zammit, P.
 220
Zech, Franz X.
 220
Zimmerli, W.
 173, 184